THE CHURCH AT PRAYER

THE CHURCH AT PRAYER

An Introduction to the Liturgy

New Edition

Edited by Aimé Georges Martimort
with the Collaboration of R. Cabié, I. H. Dalmais
J. Evenou, P. M. Gy, P. Jounel, A. Nocent, and D. Sicard

Volume I

PRINCIPLES OF THE LITURGY

by

Irénée Henri Dalmais, Pierre Marie Gy,
Pierre Jounel, and Aimé Georges Martimort

Translated by Matthew J. O'Connell

THE LITURGICAL PRESS
Collegeville, Minnesota

Cover design by Donald A. Molloy

THE CHURCH AT PRAYER—VOLUME I: PRINCIPLES OF THE LITURGY is the autho-
rized English translation of *L'Eglise en Prière: Principes de la liturgie*, published by Desclée,
Paris-Tournai, 1983.

Nihil obstat: Rev. Robert C. Harren, J.C.L., *Censor deputatus.*

Imprimatur: ✛ George H. Speltz, D.D., Bishop of St. Cloud, March 17, 1987.

Excerpts from the English translation of *The Roman Missal* © 1973, 1985, International
Committee on English in the Liturgy, Inc. (ICEL); excerpts from the English translation of
The Liturgy of the Hours © 1974, ICEL; excerpts from the English translation of General
Norms for the Liturgical Year and the Calendar (1969), the General Instruction of the Liturgy
of the Hours (1974), and the General Instruction of the Roman Missal (1975) from *Documents on the Liturgy 1963-1979: Curial, Papal, and Conciliar Texts* © 1982, ICEL. All rights
reserved.

Excerpts of prayers translated from the old Latin Roman Missal (Canon) are from *The
Maryknoll Missal* edited by the Maryknoll Fathers (New York: Kenedy, 1964). All rights
reserved.

Library of Congress Cataloging-in-Publication Data

Dalmais, Irénée Henri, 1914–
   Principles of the liturgy.

   (The Church at prayer ; v. 1)
   Translation of Principes de la liturgie.
   Includes bibliographies and index.
   1. Catholic Church—Liturgy. I. Gy, Pierre.
II. Jounel, Pierre. III. Title. IV. Series:
Eglise en prière. English ; v. 1.
BX1970.E313 1986 vol. 1   264'.02 s   87-3889
[BX1970]   [264'.02]
ISBN 0-8146-1363-2

Contents

Contributors to Volume I

Irénée Henri Dalmais, O.P., *Professor of the Institut Supérieur de Liturgie in Paris*

Pierre Marie Gy, O.P., *Director of the Institut Supérieur de Liturgie in Paris, Consultor of the Congregation for Divine Worship*

Pierre Jounel, *Honorary Professor in the Institut Catholique of Paris, Consultor of the Congregation for Divine Worship*

Aimé Georges Martimort, *Honorary Dean of the Faculty of Theology in Toulouse, Consultor of the Congregation for Divine Worship*

Preface

The third French edition of the present work was published in 1965, less than two years after the promulgation of the Constitution on the Liturgy of Vatican II. It was clear, of course, that this solemn document was but the starting point of a work of restoration and reform that could be carried out only gradually.

Now, twenty years after the Constitution *Sacrosanctum Concilium*, the reform of the liturgy is virtually complete. A task of immense scope, unparalleled in the history of the Church, brought bishops and liturgists together from all over the world, first in the Council for the Implementation of the Constitution on the Sacred Liturgy (1964–69) and then in the Congregation for Divine Worship (1969–75). The problems that the contemporary world and its culture (or, rather, its varied cultures) raise for the prayer of the Church were pointed out with great clarity by the Council, which also enunciated the principles to be followed in solving them. The application of these principles, however, led to a revision of perspectives and to decisions that we could not have clearly anticipated in 1965.

The new liturgical books take, in fact, a new approach to the act of celebrating: they always begin with instructions or introductions that are quite different in character from the rubrics of old, since they include doctrinal and spiritual guidelines, the pastoral aspect, and possible ways of adapting the rites in question.

This bold new approach would not have been possible without the work done, especially in the twentieth century, by the historians of liturgy and the theologians. The first French edition of *The Church at Prayer* was an attempt at a summary assessment of all that labor. But far from putting an end to research, the liturgical reform gave it a new stimulus because it raised new problems or called for a more profound and scholarly grasp of the tradition. Moreover, it was no longer isolated pioneers, as in the days of Duchesne and Batiffol, Baumstark and Andrieu, who ventured into this field. On the contrary: teams now meet periodically, as at the Semaines de Saint-Serge, and students are trained at liturgical institutes (the Liturgical Institutes of Paris and of San Anselmo in Rome have celebrated the twentieth anniversary of their foundation).

Scholars have been devoting their efforts especially to the prehistory of the Christian liturgy and to its beginnings and its relation to Jewish prayer. In addition, the comparative method initially developed by Baumstark has given a splendid impulse to the study of the Eastern and Western liturgies. It is no longer possible to reconstruct the history of the Roman liturgy without locating it in this broader framework. That same larger perspective is indispensable especially for answering doctrinal questions about the sacraments and for resolving the sensitive problem of adaptation to local Churches, as well as for inspiring the creative responses that adaptation calls for. The controversies to which the liturgical reform has given rise in various places are to be explained by an ignorance of the tradition and of the diversity it allows.

For all these reasons it has not been possible simply to correct and reprint *The Church at Prayer*. An entirely new edition is called for that will, on the one hand, highlight the spiritual and pastoral directions taken in the liturgical reform with which the name of Pope Paul VI will be permanently linked, and that will, on the other, set forth more fully than in earlier editions what we know of the varied expressions the Church has given to its prayer according to historical and geographical circumstances.

In keeping with the procedure adopted earlier for *L'Introduction à la Bible*, we shall publish separately each of the four parts of this new edition of *The Church at Prayer*. Practical considerations made us begin with Volume IV: *The Liturgy and Time*. Here, now, is Volume I: *Principles of the Liturgy*.* Fathers Dalmais and Gy have done new and more broadly based versions of the two chapters that were originally the work of the lamented Dom Bernard Botte. Monsignor Jounel has revised his previous contribution and, in addition, has provided (in Section II, Chapter IV) a study of the dedication of churches in the light of the new rite, which itself owes a good deal to him.

Finally, let me remind the reader of the limits of this work; they are the same as those mentioned in 1961 in the very first French edition. Readers will not find here a complete exposition that includes the entire content of the instructions and introductions to the new liturgical books, any more than they would have found in earlier editions a complete course in rubrics. For that kind of information they must turn to the practical instruction that is given to students in institutions of priestly formation.

---

*Part I—an earlier and shorter version of the present volume I—of the original *L'Eglise en prière* (third edition) was translated into English as *Introduction to the Liturgy*, English edition by A. Flannery and V. Ryan (New York: Desclée, 1968). Part II (= volume II of the present series) was translated as *The Eucharist*, English edition by A. Flannery and V. Ryan (New York: Herder and Herder, 1973).

In addition, the contributors always suppose that their readers have at hand at least the main liturgical texts now in use. We urge them to be constantly rereading these texts and, even more, to discover the meaning of the rites by participating in them. It is by meditating on the texts, those now in use and those of the past, and by participating as fervently as possible in the liturgical celebration, that we will be able to enter with understanding into the mysteries of the praying Church, in which Christ himself is present and active.

Aimé Georges Martimort

Abbreviations

Gen	Genesis	Dan	Daniel
Exod	Exodus	Ezra	Ezra
Lev	Leviticus	Neh	Nehemiah
Num	Numbers	1–2 Chr	1–2 Chronicles
Deut	Deuteronomy	Bar	Baruch
Josh	Joshua	Jdt	Judith
Judg	Judges	1–2 Mac	1–2 Maccabees
1–2 Sam	1 and 2 Samuel	Sir	Sirach
1–2 Kgs	1 and 2 Kings	Tob	Tobit
Isa	Isaiah	Wis	Wisdom
Jer	Jeremiah	Matt	Matthew
Ezek	Ezekiel	Mark	Mark
Hos	Hosea	Luke	Luke
Joel	Joel	John	John
Amos	Amos	Acts	Acts of the Apostles
Obad	Obadiah	Rom	Romans
Jonah	Jonah	1–2 Cor	1–2 Corinthians
Mic	Micah	Gal	Galatians
Nah	Nahum	Eph	Ephesians
Hab	Habakkuk	Phil	Philippians
Zeph	Zephaniah	Col	Colossians
Hag	Haggai	1–2 Thess	1–2 Thessalonians
Zech	Zechariah	1–2 Tim	1–2 Timothy
Mal	Malachi	Titus	Titus
Ps (Pss)	Psalm(s)	Phlm	Philemon
Job	Job	Heb	Hebrews
Prov	Proverbs	Jas	James
Ruth	Ruth	1–2 Pet	1–2 Peter
Cant	Canticle of Canticles	1–3 John	1–3 John
Eccl	Ecclesiastes	Jude	Jude
Lam	Lamentations	Rev	Revelation
Esth	Esther		

WORKS MOST FREQUENTLY CITED

AAS	*Acta Apostolicae Sedis* (Rome, then Vatican City, 1909ff.)
Acta sanctorum	*Acta sanctorum collecta . . . a Sociis Bollandianis* (3rd ed.; Paris: Palme, 1863ff., then Brussels: Bollandistes).
ALW	*Archiv für Liturgiewissenschaft* (Regensburg: F. Pustet, 1950ff.).
Andrieu, *OR*	M. Andrieu, *Les Ordines Romani du haut moyen âge* (5 vols. Spicilegium Sacrum Lovaniense 11, 23, 24, 28, 29; Louvain: Spicilegium, 1931ff.). A sixth volume is in preparation.
Andrieu, *PR*	M. Andrieu, *Le Pontifical Romain au moyen âge* (4 vols. ST 86, 87, 88, 99; Vatican City, 1938–41).
Brightman	F. E. Brightman, *Liturgies Eastern and Western* I. *Eastern Liturgies* (Oxford: Clarendon Press, 1896). Only Volume I was published.
CCL	Corpus Christianorum collectum a monachis O.S.B. abbatiae S. Petri in Steenbrugge, Series Latina (Turnhout: Brepols, 1954ff.).
CECSL	Consilium ad exsequendam Constitutionem de sacra liturgia (Council for the Implementation of the Constitution on the Sacred Liturgy).
CSCO	Corpus Scriptorum Christianorum Orientalium editum consilio Universitatis Catholicae Americae et Universitatis Catholicae Lovaniensis (Louvain, 1903ff.).
CSEL	Corpus scriptorum ecclesiasticorum Latinorum editum consilio et impensis Academiae litterarum . . . Vindobonensis (Vienna: Tempsky, 1866ff.).
DACL	*Dictionnaire d'archéologie chrétienne et de liturgie*, edited by F. Cabrol, H. Leclercq [and H. Marrou] (Paris: Letouzey et Ané, 1907–53).
DBS	*Dictionnaire de la Bible: Supplément* (Paris, 1928ff.).
Denz	H. Denzinger, *Ritus orientalium . . . in administrandis sacramentis . . .* (2 vols. Würzburg: Stahel, 1863; repr., Graz: Akademische Druck, 1961).
DOL	*Documents on the Liturgy 1963–1979. Conciliar, Papal, and Curial Texts.* Edited by the International Commission on English in the Liturgy (Collegeville: The Liturgical Press, 1982).
DS	*Enchiridion symbolorum, definitionum et declarationum de rebus fidei et morum*, edited by H. Denzinger. 32nd ed. by A. Schönmetzer (Barcelona: Herder, 1963).
EDIL	*Enchiridion documentorum instaurationis liturgicae* I. *1963–1973* (Turin: Marietti, 1976).
EL	*Ephemerides liturgicae* (Rome: Edizioni liturgiche, 1887ff.). For years with two series the references are to the series *Analecta ascetico-historicae*, without this being expressly stated.

Fabre-Duchesne	P. Fabre and L. Duchesne, *Le Liber censuum de l'Eglise romaine* (3 vols. Paris: E. de Boccard, 1910–52).
GCS	Die griechischen christlichen Schriftsteller der ersten Jahrhunderte, edited by the German Academy of Sciences in Berlin (Berlin: Akademie Verlag, 1897ff.).
Ge	Old Gelasian Sacramentary = Ms. Reginen. Lat. 316 in the Vatican Library, ed. L. K. Mohlberg, P. Siffrin, and L. Eizenhöfer, *Liber sacramentorum Romanae aeclesiae ordinis anni circuli* (REDMF 4; Rome: Herder, 1960).
Gell	Sacramentaire de Gellone, Paris, Bibl. Nat., ms. lat. 12048, ed. A. Dumas (CCL 159; Turnhout: Brepols, 1981).
GILH	*General Instruction of the Liturgy of the Hours,* trans. in *DOL.*
GIRM	*General Instruction of the Roman Missal,* trans. in *DOL.*
GNLYC	*General Norms for the Liturgical Year and the Calendar,* trans. in *DOL.*
GR	Gregorian Sacramentary, ed. J. Deshusses (Spicilegium Friburgense 16; Freiburg: Universitätsverlag, 1971, 1979²).
Hänggi-Pahl	A. Hänggi and I. Pahl, *Prex eucharistica. Textus e variis liturgiis antiquioribus selecti* (Spicilegium Friburgense 12; Freiburg: Universitätsverlag, 1968).
HBS	Henry Bradshaw Society for Editing Rare Liturgical Texts. London, 1891ff.
JLW	*Jahrbuch für Liturgiewissenschaft,* ed. O. Casel (Münster: Aschendorff, 1921–41).
JTS	*Journal of Theological Studies* (London: Macmillan, and then Oxford: Clarendon Press, 1900ff.).
Le	The sacramentary formerly known as the Leonine Sacramentary. Manuscript of Verona, Bibl. Capitolare, LXXXV [80]. — Ed. L. C. Mohlberg, L. Eizenhöfer, and P. Siffrin, *Sacramentarium Veronense* (REDMF 1; Rome: Herder, 1955–56).
LH	*The Liturgy of the Hours* (4 vols.; New York: Catholic Book Publishing Co., 1975ff.). Latin: *Liturgia Horarum* (Rome, 1971).
LMD	*La Maison-Dieu. Revue de pastorale liturgique* (Paris: Cerf, 1945ff.).
LO	Lex orandi (Paris: Cerf, 1944–70).
LP	L. Duchesne, *Le Liber pontificalis. Texte, introduction, et commentaire.* 2nd ed. by C. Vogel (3 vols.; Paris: E. de Boccard, 1955–57).
LQF	Liturgiegeschichtliche (later: Liturgiewissenschaftliche) Quellen und Forschungen (Münster: Aschendorff, 1919ff.).
LXX	The Septuagint. — Ed. A. Rahlfs, *Septuaginta id est Vetus Testamentum graece iuxta LXX interpretes* (3rd ed., 2 vols. Stuttgart: Württembergische Bibelanstalt, 1935).
Mansi	J. D. Mansi, *Sacrorum conciliorum nova et amplissima collectio* (31 vols.; Florence-Venice, 1757–98. Reprint and

	continuation, vols. 1–53; Paris, Leipzig, and Arnheim, 1901–27).
Martène	E. Martène, *De antiquis Ecclesiae ritibus*. (References to the various editions are given in A. G. Martimort, *La documentation liturgique de dom Edmond Martène* [ST 279; Vatican City, 1978]).
MGH	Monumenta Germaniae historica (Hannover: Hahn, and Berlin: Weidmann, 1826ff.).
MR	*Missale Romanum*, 2nd typical ed., March 27, 1975.
MTZ	*Münchener theologische Zeitschrift* (Munich, 1950ff.).
OC	*Oriens christianus. Halbjahrshefte für die Kunde des christlichen Orients* (Wiesbaden, 1901ff.).
OCA	Orientalia christiana analecta (Rome: Pontificio Istituto Orientale, 1923ff.) (1923–34: Orientalia christiana; 1935ff.: Orientalia christiana analecta).
OCP	*Orientalia christiana periodica* (Rome: Pontificio Istituto Orientale, 1935ff.).
OR I, etc.	*Ordo Romanus*. Unless the contrary is indicated, the number accompanying this abbreviation is the one assigned in Andrieu, *OR*.
OR Mab	*Ordo Romanus* according to the numbering in J. Mabillon, *Musaei Italici* II (Paris, 1969) = PL 78:851-1372.
OS	*L'Orient syrien* (Paris, 1956–67).
PG	J. P. Migne, Patrologiae cursus completus, Series graeca (Paris-Montrouge, 1857–66). 161 volumes.
PL	J. P. Migne, Patrologiae cursus completus, Series latina (Paris-Montrouge, 1844–64). 221 volumes.
PLS	A. Hamann, *Supplementum Patrologiae Latinae* (Turnhout: Brepols, 1958–74). 5 volumes.
PO	Patrologia orientalis. First editors: R. Graffin and F. Nau (Paris: Firmin-Didot, then Turnhout: Brepols, 1903ff.).
POC	*Proche-Orient chrétien* (Jerusalem: Ste. Anne, 1951ff.).
PR	Pontificale Romanum (Roman Pontifical).
PRG	C. Vogel and R. Elze, *Le pontifical romano-germanique du Xe siecle* (ST 226, 227, 269; Vatican City, 1963–72). 3 volumes.
QL	*Questions liturgiques et paroissiales*, then simply *Questions liturgiques* (Louvain: Abbaye du Mont Cësar, 1910ff.).
RAC	*Reallexikon für Antike und Christentum*, ed. T. Klauser (Stuttgart: Hiersemann, 1950ff.).
RBén	*Revue bénédictine* (Abbaye de Maredsous, 1884ff.).
RechSR	*Recherches de science religieuse* (Paris, 1910ff.).
REDMF	Rerum ecclesiasticarum documenta, Series maior: Fontes (Rome: Herder, 1955ff.).
Renaudot	E. Renaudot, *Liturgiarum orientalium collectio* (Paris, 1716. More accurate 2nd ed.: Frankfurt: E. Baer, 1847, in 2 volumes).

RevSR	*Revue des sciences religieuses* (Strasbourg: Palais Universitaire, 1921ff.).
RHE	*Revue d'histoire ecclésiastique* (Louvain, 1900ff.).
ROC	*Revue de l'Orient chrétien* (Paris: Leroux, then Paris: Picard, 1896ff.).
RR	Rituale Romanum (Roman Ritual).
RTAM	*Revue de théologie ancienne et médiévale* (Louvain: Abbaye du Mont César, 1929ff.).
Sacramentary	*The Sacramentary*, revised according to the second typical edition of the *Missale Romanum*, March 27, 1975 (Collegeville: The Liturgical Press, 1985).
SC	Sources chrétiennes. Collection ed. by H. de Lubac and J. Daniélou (later: C. Mondésert) (Paris: Cerf, 1942ff.).
SCDW	Sacred Congregation for Divine Worship (May 8, 1969, to July 11, 1975, and from April 5, 1984).
SCR	Sacred Congregation of Rites. When this abbreviation is followed by a number, the reference is to *Decreta authentica Congregationis sacrorum rituum* (Rome, 1898–1927). 7 volumes or, more accurately, 5 volumes and 2 of appendixes.
SCSDW	Sacred Congregation for the Sacraments and Divine Worship (from July 11, 1975, to April 5, 1984).
SE	*Sacris erudiri. Jaarboek voor Godsdienstwetenschappen* (Steenbrugge: St.-Pietersabdij, 1948ff.).
ST	Studi e testi (Rome, then Vatican City, 1900ff.).
TA	Texte und Arbeiten, published by the Archabbey of Beuron, 1917ff. (Unless there is an indication to the contrary, the references are to the first section of this series.)
TS	Texts and Studies. Contributions to Biblical and Patristic Literature (Cambridge: Cambridge University Press, 1882ff.).
TU	Texte und Untersuchungen zur Geschichte der altchristlichen Literatur (Leipzig, then Berlin: Akademie Verlag, 1882ff.).
VSC	Vatican Council II, Constitution *Sacrosanctum Concilium* on the Sacred Liturgy. Latin text: *AAS* 56 (1964) 97–138. The translation of this document is that found in *DOL* (above).
ZKT	*Zeitschrift für katholische Theologie* (Innsbruck, 1877ff.).

Introduction

BASIC GENERAL BIBLIOGRAPHY

a) Comprehensive works:

Dictionnaire d'archéologie chrétienne et de liturgie, ed. F. Cabrol, H. Leclercq [and H. Marrou]. (15 vols., each in two parts; Paris: Letouzey et Ané, 1907–53.) At times, readers can still find what they want, especially when the articles are signed H. I. Marrou, L. Petit, or A. Wilmart.

Righetti, M., *Manuale di storia liturgica* (4 vols.; Milan: Ancora, 1945; 2nd ed., 1950–59; 3rd ed., 1964–69). Spanish trans.: *Historia de la liturgia* (2 vols.; Biblioteca de autores cristianos 132 and 144; Madrid: Editorial Católica, 1955–56).

Paquier, R., *Traité de liturgique* (Neuchâtel: Delachaux et Niestlé, 1954). Reflects the liturgical work of the Reformed school of Neuchâtel.

Leitourgia. Handbuch des evangelischen Gottesdienstes, ed. K. Müller and W. Blankenburg (5 vols.; Kassel: Stauda, 1952–70). The work largely transcends the viewpoint of Lutheranism, especially vol. 5 on *Der Taufgottesdienst*, which contains G. Kretschmar's brilliant history of baptism.

Anàmnesis. Introduzione storico-teologica alla liturgia, by the Professors of the Pontificio Istituto Liturgico di Sant'Anselmo, Rome, under the direction of S. Marsili (Turin: Marietti, 1974ff.). Three of the five planned volumes have appeared.

Meyer, H. B., *et al.*, *Gottesdienst der Kirche. Handbuch der Liturgiewissenschaft*, announced for publication by Pustet, Regensburg, beginning in 1983.

b) Most important periodicals:

Archiv für Liturgiewissenschaft (Regensburg: Pustet, 1950ff.). Successor to *Jahrbuch für Liturgiewissenschaft* (see below).

Ecclesia orans (Rome: Sant'Anselmo, 1984 ff.).

Ephemerides liturgicae (Rome: Edizioni liturgiche, 1887ff.). This journal won recognition especially from 1927 on by reason of its series, *Analecta ascetico-historica* (1927–47). The series entitled *Ius et praxis* ceased publication after 1947.

Jahrbuch für Liturgiewissenschaft, ed. O. Casel (15 vols.; Münster: Aschendorff, 1921–41). *Register* (1 vol.), ed. A. Häussling (1982).

La Maison-Dieu. Revue de pastorale liturgique (Paris: Cerf, 1945ff.).

Notitiae. Commentarii ad nuntia et studia de re liturgica, published by the [Consilium; Sacred Congregation for Divine Worship, Sacred Congregation for the Discipline of the Sacraments and Divine Worship, and, again, Sacred Congregation for Divine Worship] (Vatican City, 1965ff.).

Oriens christianus. Halbjahrshefte für die Kunde des christichen Ostens (1901ff.).

Orientalia christiana periodica (Rome: Pontificio Istituto Orientale, 1935ff.).

Orient syrien (Paris, 1956–67).

[The preceding three periodicals do not deal exclusively with the liturgy, but in them are to be found most of the important studies by historians of the Eastern liturgies.]

Questions liturgiques (1910–14), then *Questions liturgiques et paroissiales* (1919–69), and then *Questions liturgiques* once again (1970ff.) (Louvain: Abbaye du Mont César, 1910ff.).

Rivista liturgica (Abbazia di Finalpia and Turin-Leumann: ElleDiCi, 1914ff.). This periodical merits a place in the present list chiefly because of its *Bollettino bibliografico*, which has occupied the final issue of each year since 1970.

Sacris erudiri. Jaarboek voor Godsdienstwetenschappen (Steenbrugge: Sint Pietersabdij, 1948ff.). Despite the subtitle, not all articles are in Flemish; on the other hand, the content has, over the years, become less and less restricted to the liturgy.

c) Collections of texts:

Assemani, J. A., *Codex liturgicus Ecclesiae universae* (13 vols.; Rome: Bizzarini, 1749–66; reprinted: Paris-Leipzig: Welter, 1902.

Henry Bradshaw Society for Editing Rare Liturgical Texts (London, 1891ff.). In principle, a volume each year.

Brightman, F. E., *Liturgies Eastern and Western 1. Eastern Liturgies* (Oxford: Clarendon, 1896). Only vol. 1 appeared.

Denzinger, H., *Ritus orientalium...in administrandis sacramentis* (2 vols.; Würzburg: Stahel, 1863; reprinted: Graz: Akademische Druck, 1961).

Hänggi, A., and Pahl, I., *Prex eucharistica. Textus e variis liturgiis antiquioribus selecti* (Spicilegium Friburgense 12; Freiburg, Schw.: Universitätsverlag, 1968).

Kaczinski, R., *Enchiridion documentorum instaurationis liturgicae I (1963–73)* (Turin: Marietti, 1976).

Liturgiegeschichtliche [then *Liturgiewissenschaftliche*] *Quellen und Forschungen*, founded by L. C. Mohlberg (Münster: Aschendorff, 1919ff.).

Lodi, E., *Enchiridion euchologicum fontium liturgicorum* (Rome: Edizioni liturgiche, 1979). One vol. plus a mimeographed booklet, *Clavis methodologica cum commentariis selectis* (Bologna, 1979).

Mabillon, J., *De liturgia Gallicana libri III* (Paris: Martin et Boudot, 1685) (= PL 72).

_____, *Musaeum Italicum* (2 vols.; Paris: apud vid. E. Martin [etc.], 1687–89; 2nd, unchanged ed.: Montalant, 1724) (= PL 78).

Martène, E., *De antiquis Ecclesiae ritibus; De antiquis monachorum ritibus.* On the various editions see A. G. Martimort, *La documentation liturgique de Dom Edmond Martène* (ST 279; Vatican City, 1978).

Renaudot, E., *Liturgiarum orientalium collectio* (2 vols.; Paris: J. B. Avignard; 2nd ed.: Frankfurt: Baer, 1847).

Rerum ecclesiasticarum documenta, Series maior: Fontes (Rome: Herder, 1955ff.).

Texte und Arbeiten, published by the Erzabtei Beuron (Beuron: Beuroner Kunstverlag, 1917ff.).

Textus patristici et liturgici, quos edidit Institutum Liturgicum Ratisbonense (Regensburg: F. Pustet, 1964ff.). The series contains chiefly the work of K. Gamber.

Tomasi [Thomasii, Tommasi], G. M., *Opera omnia*, ed. A. F. Vezzosi (7 vols.; Rome: Typ. Palladis, 1747–54).

d) Principal lists of liturgical books:

Gamber, K., *Codices liturgici latini antiquiores* (2nd ed. in 2 vols.; Spicilegii Friburgensis Subsidia 1; Freiburg, Schw.: Universitätsverlag, 1968).

Weale, W. H., *Bibliographia liturgica. Catalogus missalium ritus Latini ab anno M.CCCC.LXXIV. impressorum*, re-edited by H. Bohatta (London: B. Quaritch, 1928).

Bohatta, H., *Liturgische Bibliographie des XV. Jahrhunderts mit Ausnahme der Missale und Livres d'Heures* (Vienna: Gilhofer & Rauschburg, 1911).

_____, *Bibliographie der Breviere 1501-1850* (Leipzig: Hiersemann, 1937; reprinted: Stuttgart: Hiersemann, 1963). The list of incunabula breviaries had appeared in the *Gesamtkatalog der Wiegendrucke* 3 (Leipzig, 1932), 2-94.

Leroquais, V., *Les sacramentaires et missels manuscrits des bibliothèques publiques de France* (3 vols. of text, 1 of plates; Mâcon: Protat, 1924).

_____, *Les breviaires manuscrits des bibliothèques publiques de France* (5 vols. of text, 1 of plates; Mâcon: Protat, 1934).

_____, *Les pontificaux manuscrits des bibliothèques publiques de France* (3 vols. of text, 1 of plates; Mâcon: Protat, 1937).

_____, *Les psautiers manuscrits des bibliothèques publiques de France* (2 vols. of text, 1 of plates; Mâcon: Protat, 1940-41).

Grégoire, R., "Repertorium liturgicum Italicum," *Studi medievali* (Spoleto) 9 (1968) 465-92. Lists only the Latin liturgical mss. written in Italy from the seventh to the twelfth century.

Salmon, P., *Les manuscrits liturgiques latins de la Bibliothèque Vaticane* (5 vols.: ST 251, 253, 260, 267, 270; Vatican City, 1968-72).

Janini, J., *Manuscritos litúrgicos de las bibliotecas de España* (2 vols.; Facultad de Teología del Norte de España 38; Burgos: Ed. Aldecoa, 1977, 1980).

e) Collections of liturgical studies:

Bibliotheca "Ephemerides liturgicae" (Rome: Edizioni liturgiche, 1932ff.). The series has had two sections: *Sectio historica,* which started in 1932, ended in 1974, and contains 38 volumes; and *Sectio "Subsidia,"* which began in 1974.

Conférences Saint-Serge. Semaines d'études liturgiques. Semaines VIII, IX, X, XII, XIII (1961-63, 1965-66) were published as LO 35, 39, 40, and 46-48; Semaine XVII (1970) was published in *EL* 94 (1980); Semaines XVI (1969) and XXI (1973) ff. were published in the Bibliotheca "Ephemerides liturgicae," Subsidia.

Cours et Conférences [de la Semaine liturgique de Maredsous; then:] des Semaines liturgiques (14 vols.; Maredsous; then: Louvain: Mont César, 1912-37). The conferences of the 1938 week were published in *QL* 24 (1939); those of 1939 could not be published.

Lex orandi. [Collection du Centre de pastorale liturgique; then] Collection de recherches du Centre National de pastorale liturgique. (48 vols.; Paris: Cerf, 1944-70).

Liturgica (3 vols.; Montserrat, 1956-66). These volumes appeared in the collection Scripta et documenta 3, 10, 17.

Studia Anselmiana: Analecta liturgica (Rome: Editrice Anselmiana, 1979ff.).

f) Writers who have contributed in major ways to the advancement of the history and theology of the liturgy in the nineteenth and twentieth centuries:

Andrieu, M., *Les "Ordines Romani" du haut moyen âge* (5 vols.: Spicilegium Lovaniense 11, 23, 24, 28, 29; Louvain, 1931ff.). A sixth volume of indexes is in preparation.

_____, *Le Pontifical romain au moyen âge* (4 vols.: ST 86, 87, 88, 89; Vatican City, 1938-41).

Batiffol, P., *Histoire du bréviaire romain* (Paris: Picard, 1893; 3rd revised ed., 1911); ET: *History of the Roman Breviary,* trans. A. M. Y. Baylay (New York: Longmans, Green, 1912).

_____, *Leçons sur la messe* (Paris: Gabalda, 1918; 8th ed., 1941).

_____, *Etudes de liturgie et d'archéologie chrétienne* (Paris: Gabalda et Picard, 1919).

Baumstark, A. See the list of his writings in *EL* 63 (1949) 187–207.

Beauduin, L., *La piété de l'Eglise* (Louvain: Mont César, 1914).

_____, *Mélanges liturgiques recueillis parmi les oeuvres de Dom Lambert Beauduin* (Louvain: Mont César, 1954).

Bishop, E., *Liturgica historica* (Oxford: Clarendon, 1918). A collection of his articles.

Botte, B. See the list of his publications drawn up by F. Petit in *Mélanges liturgiques offerts au R.P. Dom Bernard Botte* (Louvain: Mont César, 1972), xix–xxxii, and completed by the same in *QL* 61 (1980) 88–92.

Bouyer, L. In addition to numerous articles, especially those published in *LMD*, the following books are particularly notable: *Le mystère pascal* (LO 6; Paris: Cerf, 1945); ET: *The Paschal Mystery*, trans. Sr. M. Benoit (Chicago: Regnery, 1950). *La vie de la liturgie: Une critique constructive du mouvement liturgique* (LO 20; Paris: Cerf, 1956); ET: *Liturgical Piety* (Notre Dame, Ind.: University of Notre Dame Press, 1955. British title: *Life and Liturgy*). *Le rite et l'homme: Sacralité naturelle et liturgie* (LO 32; Paris: Cerf, 1962); ET: *Rite and Man: Natural Sacredness and Christian Liturgy*, trans. M. J. Costelloe (Notre Dame, Ind.: University of Notre Dame Press, 1963). *Eucharistie: Théologie et spiritualité de la prière eucharistique* (Paris: Desclée, 1966, 1967[2]); ET: *Eucharist. Theology and Spirituality of the Eucharistic Prayer*, trans. C. U. Quinn (Notre Dame, Ind.: University of Notre Dame Press, 1968.

Callewaert, C., *Liturgicae institutiones* (3 vols.; Bruges: Beyaert, 1919–44). The various volumes were revised during the same years.

_____, *Sacris erudiri. Fragmenta liturgica . . . ne pereant* (Steenbrugge: Sint Pietersabdij, 1940).

Capelle, B., *Travaux liturgiques de doctrine et d'histoire* (3 vols.; Louvain: Mont César, 1955–67).

Casel, O. See the list of his publications drawn up by O. Santagada in *ALW* 10 (1967) 7–77.

Dix, G., *The Shape of the Liturgy* (Westminster: Dacre Press, 1945).

Dölger, F. See the list of his publications in T. Klauser, *Franz Joseph Dölger, Leben und Werk* (Münster: Aschendorff, 1956).

Duchesne, L., *Les origines du culte chrétien, étude sur la liturgie avant Charlemagne* (Paris: Thorin, 1189; Paris: E. de Boccard, 1920[5]); ET: *Christian Worship: Its Origin and Evolution*, trans. M. L. McClure (London: SPCK, 1903).

Grea, A., *La sainte liturgie* (Paris: Bonne Press, 1909).

Guardini, R. *Vom Geist der Liturgie* (Ecclesia orans 1; Freiburg: Herder, 1918); ET: *The Spirit of the Liturgy*, trans. A. Lane (London: Sheed & Ward, 1930).

_____, *Von heiligen Zeichen* (Rothenfels, 1922–23, 1927[2]); ET: *Sacred Signs*, trans. G. C. H. Pollen (London: Sheed & Ward, 1930).

Guéranger, P., *Institutions liturgiques* (3 vols.; Le Mans: Fleuriot; then Paris: Lanier [etc.], 1840–51. 2nd ed. in 4 vols.: Paris: Palme, 1878–85).

_____, *L'année liturgique*. Publication began in 1841; many editions, with the number of volumes varying according to the edition. ET: *The Liturgical Year*, vols. 1–11 trans. L. Shepherd; vols. 12–15, trans. Benedictines of Stanbrook (Westminster, Md.: Newman, 1948–50).

_____, *Mélanges de liturgie, d'histoire et de théologie* (Solesmes, 1887).

Hanssens, J. M., *Institutiones liturgicae de ritibus orientalibus* (Rome: Pontificia Università Gregoriana, 1930–32). Only volumes II and III with an Appendix appeared.

_____, *La liturgie d'Hippolyte* I (OCA 155; Rome: Pontificio Istituto Orientale, 1959); II (Rome: Pontifica Universita Gregoriana, 1970).

_____, (ed.), *Amalarii opera liturgica omnia* (3 vols.: ST 138–40; Vatican City, 1948–50).

Jungmann, J. A. See the list of his publications in B. Fischer and H. B. Meyer, *J. A. Jungmann, ein Leben für Liturgie und Kerygma* (Innsbruck: Tyrolia-Verlag, 1975), 156–233.

Klauser, T., *Gesammelte Arbeiten zur Liturgiegeschichte, Kirchengeschichte und christlichen Archäologie*, ed. E. Dassmann (Münster: Aschendorff, 1974).

Lefebvre, G., *Liturgia, ses principes fondamentaux* (Lophem lez Bruges: Abbaye Saint-André, 1920, 1922²); ET: *Catholic Liturgy: Its Fundamental Principles*, trans. by a Benedictine of Stanbrook (New York: Benziger, 1924). The author is known especially for his *Missel quotidien*, first published in 1920, with countless reprintings thereafter.

Leroquais, V. The introductions to his various lists of liturgical books (section *d*, above) are an important contribution to the history of rites.

Lietzmann, H., *Messe und Herrenmahl, eine Studie zur Geschichte der Liturgie* (Arbeiten zur Kirchengeschichte 8; Berlin: de Gruyter, 1926, 1955³); ET: *Mass and Lord's Supper*, trans. D. H. G. Reeves, with Introduction and Supplementary Essay by R. D. Richardson (Leiden: Brill, 1953–79).

Mohlberg, L. C. See the list of his publications in *Miscellanea liturgica in honorem L. C. Mohlberg* 1 (Bibliotheca EL 22; Rome: Edizioni liturgiche, 1948), xv–xxxix, with supplement in *EL* 78 (1964) 59–62.

Vagaggini, C., *Il senso teologico della liturgia. Saggio di liturgia pastorale generale* (Rome: Ed. Paoline, 1957, 1965⁴); ET: *Theological Dimensions of the Liturgy*, trans. L. J. Doyle and W. A. Jurgens (Collegeville: The Liturgical Press, 1976).

Vogel, C., *Introduction aux sources de l'histoire du culte chrétien au moyen âge* (Spoleto: Centro italiano di studi sull'alto medioevo, 1966; reprinted: Turin: Bottega d'Erasmo, 1975).

Wilmart, A. See the list of his publications in J. Bignami-Odier, L. Brou, and A. Vernet, *Bibliographie sommaire des travaux du père A. Wilmart* (Sussidi eruditi 5; Rome, 1953).

Definitions and Method

A. G. Martimort

§1. Definitions

I. THE WORD "LITURGY"

BIBLIOGRAPHY

> P. Oppenheim, "Name und Inhalt der Liturgie bei den Alten," *Theologische Quartal-schrift* 113 (1932) 35–53.
> E. Raitz von Frentz, "Der Weg des Wortes 'Liturgie' in der Geschichte," *EL* 55 (1941) 74–80.
> H. Strahmann, "Leitourgeō," *Theological Dictionary of the New Testament* 4 (German original, 1942), 215–31.
> A. Romeo, "Il termine *leitourgia* nella grecità biblica," in *Miscellanea liturgica in honorem L. C. Mohlberg* 2 (Rome: Edizioni liturgiche, 1949), 467–519.
> S. Daniel, *Recherches sur le vocabulaire du culte dans le Septante* (Etudes et com-mentaires 61; Paris: Klincksieck, 1966), 56–117.
> S. Marsili, "Liturgia," in *Anàmnesis* 1 (Turin: Marietti, 1974), 33–45.

The word "liturgy," which is now standard and has been canonized by the magisterium, is nonetheless relatively modern in the West. It hardly occurs before the twentieth century in the official documents of the Church.[1] It was popularized in the nineteenth century by many books and articles addressed to the general public.

---

1. The expression *libri liturgici*, which quickly became standard, occurs as early as 1832 in SCR 2692; in 1897 *liturgia ambrosiana* occurs in SCR 3948, and in 1898 "de usu

Latin writers of the Middle Ages used the titles *De divinis officiis* or *De ecclesiasticis officiis*[2] for their treatises on the liturgy; from the sixteenth century on, other titles were preferred: *De ritibus Ecclesiae* or *De sacris ritibus*.[3]

The Latin adjective *liturgicus* and noun *liturgia* were probably first used by Georg Cassander in 1588, with reference to Byzantine practice,[4] but they soon acquired an established place in the language of ecclesiastical scholarship.[5] On the other hand, it was only in the eighteenth century that they acquired their present meaning as referring to the entire cultic activity of the Church; in Bona and Mabillon, as in the first scholars to use the words, they still referred only to the Mass.[6]

This early limitation reflects the usage of the Greek Church in which, at least in the Middle Ages and later, the noun *leitourgia* and related terms (*leitourgos, leitourgikos*) referred solely to the Eucharistic celebration.[7] The ecclesiastical writers of antiquity[8], following the New Testament, had also used *leitourgia* primarily for the cultic service of God, but they had not excluded broader meanings, such as spiritual sacrifice or charitable

---

linguae slavicae in sacra liturgia," in SCR 3999. The 1917 Code of Canon Law definitively accepts *liturgia* in can. 447, §1, 4°; 1257; etc. See the definition given of liturgy by Pius XI in the Encyclical *Divini cultus* (December 20, 1928), no. 1; see *Official Catholic Teachings: Worship and Liturgy*, ed. J. J. Megivern (Wilmington, N.C.: McGrath, 1978), no. 138 [henceforth: Megivern, with margin number], or in A. Bugnini, *Documenta pontificia ad instaurationem liturgicam pertinentia* (Rome: Edizioni liturgiche, 1953), 60.

2. *De ecclesiasticis officiis* is the title of treatises by Isidore of Seville (PL 83:737–826), John of Avranches (ed. R. Delamare [Paris: Picard, 1928]), Pseudo-Alcuin (PL 101:1173–1286), Rupert of Deutz (CCL, Continuatio medievalis, 7), of the *Summa* of John Beleth (CCL, Continuatio medievalis, 41–41A), and, as late as 1568, of Melchior Hittorp's *De catholicae Ecclesiae divinis officiis ac ministeriis* (Cologne: apud G. Calenium, 1588). — The treatise of Amalarius on the subject is entitled *Liber officialis* (ed. J. M. Hanssens, ST 139), that of Prepositinus, *Tractatus de officiis* (ed. J. A. Corbett [Notre Dame, Ind.: University of Notre Dame Press, 1969]). William Durandus chose as his title *Rationale divinorum officiorum*.

3. Sixtus V established the *Congregatio sacrorum rituum* in 1588; as late as 1700 E. Martène gave his great collection the title *De antiquis Ecclesiae ritibus*.

4. G. Cassander, *Liturgica de ritu et ordine dominicae coenae quam celebrationem Graeci liturgiam, Latini missam appellarunt* (Cologne, 1558); see C. de Sainctes, *Liturgiae sive missae sanctorum Patrum Jacobi*, etc. (Antwerp, 1562).

5. James of Joigny, known as Pamelius, *Liturgica Latinorum* (2 vols.; Cologne: apud G. Calenium, 1571).

6. J. Card. Bona, *Rerum liturgicarum libri duo* (Rome, 1671); J. Mabillon, *De liturgia Gallicana libri tres* (Paris: Martin et Boudot, 1685). — See Benedict XIV, Brief *Quam ardenti studio* (March 25, 1752) at the beginning of the Roman Pontifical: "viris . . . de rerum liturgicarum peritissimis."

7. See J. M. Hanssens, *Institutiones liturgicae de ritibus orientalibus* 2 (Rome: Pontificia Università Gregoriana, 1930), 21–41.

8. *Ibid.*, 62; A. Romeo, "Il termine *leitourgia* nella grecità biblica," in *Miscellanea liturgica in honorem L. C. Mohlberg* 2 (Rome: Edizioni liturgiche, 1949), 513–17.

works.[9] The Septuagint, on the other hand, seems to have reserved *leitour-gein* and its derivatives for the activity of the Levites.[10]

On this point, then, Christian usage did not depend on the language of the Septuagint. Nor did it reflect the religious vocabulary of Hellenism, for although in the documents of late antiquity *leitourgein* and *leitourgia* did occasionally have a cultic meaning, they usually referred specifically to "public service," that is, a function—whether political, technical, or religious—that was exercised in the interests of the people as a whole.[11]

II. DEFINITION OF THE LITURGY

BIBLIOGRAPHY

H. Schmidt, *Introductio in liturgiam occidentalem* (Rome: Herder, 1960), 47–87 (especially 48–60).

S. Marsili, "Verso una teologia della liturgia," in *Anàmnesis* 1 (Turin: Marietti, 1974), 47–84; "La teologia del culto nel Vaticano II," *ibid.*, 85–105; "La liturgia culto della Chiesa," *ibid.*, 107–36 (each of these chapters is preceded by an extensive bibliography).

1. *First attempts at a definition (1909–47)*

From the beginning of the liturgical movement (1909) down to Vatican Council II, most authors tried to give a definition of liturgy that would briefly summarize its nature and essential characteristics. The task was especially difficult because the liturgy is a living thing, simultaneously rich in content and yet one; it can be understood only through participation and cannot easily be reduced to concepts. For this reason none of the definitions proposed seemed satisfactory.

In fact, some of the definitions given, even by persons of renown, were simply wrong. In his Encyclical *Mediator Dei* (November 20, 1947) Pius XII expressly rejected two such definitions:[12]

---

9. In the New Testament, *leitourgia* means the performance of Jewish cult in Lk 1:23; Heb 9–10; and the work of Christ that was prefigured by Jewish cult, in Heb 8:2-6. The word is used perhaps once for Christian public worship in Acts 13:2. It refers to noncultic service in Rom 13:6; 15:16, 27; 2 Cor 9:12; Phil 2:17, 25, 30; etc.

10. In the LXX *leitourgia* regularly means cultic service: Exod 28–39 (13 times); Num 4:8, 18, and *passim*; 2 Chron 31:2; Ezek 40–46 (16 times); etc. A noncultic meaning is much less frequent: Josh 1:1 (ms. *A*); 1 Kgs 1:15, 19, 21; 2 Chron 22:8. — The Latins translated *leitourgia* as *ministerium*: Augustine, *Enarr. in ps.* 135, 3 (CCL 40:1959; PL 37:1757), or as *officium* (e.g., Lk 1:23 Vg.), or, finally, as *munus*: see O. Casel, "Leitourgia munus," *OC*, 3rd series, 7 (1932) 289ff.; H. Frank, *JLW* 13 (1933) 181–85.

11. J. Oehler, "Leiturgie," in Pauly-Wissowa-Kroll, *Realencyklopädie der klassischen Altertumswissenschaft* 12/2 (Stuttgart: Metzler, 1925), 1871–79.

12. No. 12; *AAS* 39 (1947) 532; trans. Megivern 204.

It is an error, consequently, and a mistake to think of the sacred liturgy as merely the outward or visible part of divine worship or as an ornamental ceremonial.[13] No less erroneous is the notion that it consists solely in a list of laws and prescriptions according to which the ecclesiastical hierarchy orders the sacred rites to be performed.[14]

In an Instruction of September 3, 1958, the Sacred Congregation of Rites made a clear distinction between "liturgical actions" and "pious exercises" (*pia exercitia*); the Council subsequently adopted it. It is no longer possible, therefore, to confuse the two as had happened when authors went to the other extreme and eliminated from the definition of liturgy any mention of the conditions that the Church sets for it.[15]

Finally, confusion has too often been caused by using the same word "liturgy" for the action of the Church at prayer and the science of liturgy.

In the Encyclical *Mediator Dei*, Pius XII did not simply reject definitions that turned the liturgy into something wholly external and secondary. He also emphasized the supernatural reality contained in the liturgy and urged theologians to follow the pioneers of the liturgical movement[16] and base their understanding of the liturgy on the priesthood of Christ and on a correct idea of the Church as mystical body of Christ: "The liturgy is nothing more nor less than the exercise of this priestly function [of Christ]."[17]

---

13. The words "as merely the outward . . . ornamental ceremonial" (Latin: "utpote divinis cultus partem . . . externam solummodo ac sensibus objectam, vel quasi decorum quemdam caerimoniarum apparatum") reproduce the definition which J. Navatel gave in his article, "L'apostolat liturgique et la piété personelle," *Etudes* 137 (1913) 452, and which P. Oppenheim, *Notiones liturgiae fundamentales* (Turin: Marietti, 1941), 7, translated into Latin as: "Partem mere sensibilem caeremonialem et decorativam cultus catholici." — Critique of Navatel's article: L. Beauduin, "Une mise au point nécessaire," *QL* 4 (1913) 83–104.

14. This second definition, which still describes the liturgy from the outside, is for practical purposes that of C. Callewaert, *De sacra liturgia universim* (1919; Bruges: Beyaert, 1944⁴, p. 6): "cultus publicus ab Ecclesia quoad exercitium ordinatus, seu ordinatio ecclesiastica exercitii cultus publici." — J. M. Hanssens' article, "La définition de la liturgie," *Gregorianum* 7 (1927) 204–28, was directed especially against such a definition of the liturgy.

15. This is what J. A. Jungmann tried to do in his "Was ist Liturgie?" *ZKT* 53 (1931) 83–102; but see *idem*, "Liturgie und pia exercitia," *Liturgisches Jahrbuch* 9 (1959), 79–86. — Without emphasizing it, *VSC* 13 supposes the distinction as fully established; see n. 28, p. 14.

16. V. Thalhofer and L. Eisenhöfer, *Handbuch der katholischen Liturgik* (Freiburg: Herder, 1912²), 1:6–15; L. Beauduin, "Essai de manuel fondamental de liturgie," *QL* 3 (1912) 58–62; 5 (1920) 85–90, 217–28; G. Lefebvre, *Catholic Liturgy: Its Fundamental Principles*, trans. by a Benedictine of Stanbrook (New York: Benziger, 1924), 2–6; T. Michels, "Die Liturgie im Lichte der katholischen Gemeinschaftsidee," *JLW* 1 (1921) 109–16; etc.

17. Encyclical *Mediator Dei*, no. 22; *AAS* 39 (1947) 529 (Megivern 201); see no. 3: "In obedience, therefore, to her Founder's behest, the Church prolongs the priestly mission of Jesus Christ mainly by means of the sacred liturgy" (Megivern 182); Latin: "Ecclesia, igitur,

2. *Definition of Vatican Council II (1963)*

In its Constitution *Sacrosanctum Concilium* on the Sacred Liturgy (promulgated December 4, 1963), Vatican II begins its explanation of "General Principles for the Reform and Promotion of the Sacred Liturgy" with a section on the "Nature of the Liturgy and Its Importance in the Church's Life." The teaching deliberately avoids scholarly formulations and uses the language and categories of the Bible and the Fathers; the following passage may nonetheless be read as a definition of the liturgy:

> Rightly, then, the liturgy is considered as an exercise of the priestly office of Jesus Christ. In the liturgy, by means of signs perceptible to the senses, human sanctification is signified and brought about in ways proper to each of these signs; in the liturgy the whole public worship is performed by the Mystical Body of Jesus Christ, that is, by the Head and his members.[18]

There is here an easily recognizable echo of *Mediator Dei*,[19] but the Council adds several important points to what the Encyclical had said:

a) The liturgy, which is comprised essentially of the sacraments, is in its entirety a sacred sign, as is the Church itself.[20] The visible element of the liturgy is an efficacious sign of a supernatural reality. The efficacy varies depending on whether the signs are sacramental or nonsacramental, but it is analogous in the two cases, since it is due to the presence of Christ and the action of the Holy Spirit. The liturgy is therefore a *sacramentum* or "mystery," in the sense that the Fathers give to these two terms.[21]

b) In liturgical action not only does the Church's prayer of adoration and petition arise to God, but the graces of redemption also descend upon the Church and its members. This twofold movement, which is implicitly asserted as soon as the liturgy is linked to the priesthood of Christ, had not been made sufficiently clear in some older definitions of the liturgy.[22]

---

accepto a conditore suo mandato fideliter obtemperans, sacerdotale Iesu Christi munus imprimis per sacram liturgiam pergit" (*AAS*, p. 522). — See p. 249ff.

18. *VSC* 7 (*DOL* 1 no. 7); see also 26.

19. *Mediator Dei*, no. 20; *AAS* 39 (1947) 528–29.

20. *VSC* 2 and 5; see the Dogmatic Constitution *Lumen gentium* 1, 9; the theme of the Church as a sacrament occurs in many texts of Vatican II.

21. In addition to the text cited above see *VSC* 33, 59, 60. — It is not possible to accept the view proposed by M. Righetti in his *Manuale di storia liturgica* 1 (Milan: Ancora, 1950²), 6, according to which the material and sensible element is "integral but secondary." The learned author completely revised his treatment in the 3rd edition (1964).

22. The Council returns to this point in a number of passages: *VSC* 2, 5, 6, 10, 33, 59, 102. The two aspects had already been emphasized in *Mediator Dei* 20–22, 27, etc. — See p. 245ff.

c) The precise place and nature of the liturgy emerge very clearly when it is located within the economy of salvation. The liturgy is then seen to make real, under mysterious signs, what the Old Testament had foreshadowed in figures, what Christ accomplished in his Pasch as he "passed" from among human beings to the Father, and what will be manifested fully in the heavenly liturgy. This is why the Council emphasizes these various perspectives at such length in the opening pages of the Constitution.[23]

d) The liturgy belongs to the Christian people, whose baptism authorizes them to take an active part in it under the direction and presidency of the ministerial priesthood.[24]

These essential characteristics of the liturgy will be developed in greater detail in the course of this volume. The reader can already see, however, in what sense and with what reservations it is possible to apply to the Christian liturgy the categories of worship (or cult), external worship, public worship, and others, which have been standard in the writings of liturgists and the documents of the magisterium, including those of the Council itself. These ideas were established and carefully distinguished on the basis of rational concepts, but are of themselves quite inept for expressing the supernatural riches of the Church's prayer, since while the latter indeed satisfies the needs of the human heart, it also outstrips the heart's expectations in astonishing ways.

III. LITURGICAL "ACTIONS"

In place of older terms such as "rites," "ceremonies," and "functions," Vatican II speaks of "liturgical actions"[25] when referring to each of the units that make up the liturgy: the celebration of a sacrament, Vespers, the dedication of a church, and so on. The word "action," which was

---

23. *VSC* 5–8. — See A. Bugnini, "La liturgia è l'esercizio del sacerdozio di Gesù Cristo per mezzo della Chiesa," *Asprenas* 9 (1959) 4. — See pp. 259–63.

24. *VSC* 26: "Actiones liturgicae non sunt actiones privatae, sed celebrationes Ecclesiae, quae est 'unitatis sacramentum,' scilicet plebs sancta sub episcopis adunata et ordinata. Quare ad universum Corpus Ecclesiae pertinent illudque manifestant et afficiunt; singula vero membra ipsius diverso modo, pro diversitate ordinum, munerum et actualis participationis, attingunt." *DOL* 1 no. 26 (and elsewhere) translates *actiones* as "services." — See pp. 96–97.

25. *VSC* 7, 26, 48, 112. — But the same term had already been used by Pius XI, Encyclical *Divini cultus* (December 20, 1928): *AAS* 21 (1929) 33: "quasi actio sacra praecellenter" (Megivern 138: "the eminently sacred action") and especially by the SCR, Instruction of September 3, 1958, nos. 1 and 12 (Megivern 646 and 662, with "services" for *actiones*).

familiar to the early Church and advocated by the liturgical movement,[26] highlights several points: that the liturgy brings into intense play all the activities of those who are present; that it has an objective and real result, independent of the edification that the participants feel (they are "accomplishing" something); that it has a movement, a rhythm, a dynamic unity proper to it, despite the fact that a student can also go on and analyze separately the different agents, the successive phases, the words and gestures, the visible elements and the invisible realities. The liturgy exists only at the time when it is being celebrated; that is why it is unintelligible to those who do not participate in it, while on the contrary its reality is perceived to the extent that those present are involved in it.

The Eucharist is the supreme action: "Do this in remembrance of me." It is a sacrifice, that is, the highest possible activity of human life.

IV. "POPULAR DEVOTIONS OF THE CHRISTIAN PEOPLE"

BIBLIOGRAPHY

B. Capelle, "Liturgique et non liturgique," *QL* 15 (1930) 3–15 (= *Travaux liturgiques* 1 [Louvain: Mont César, 1955], 44–53).
M. Righetti, *Manuale di storia liturgica* 1 (Milan: Ancora, 1964[3]), 16–20.
C. Koser, "Liturgical Piety and Popular Devotion," in W. Baraúna (ed.), *The Liturgy of Vatican II*, Eng. ed. by J. Lang (2 vols.; Chicago: Franciscan Herald Press, 1966), 1:221-62.
S. Marsili, "Liturgia e non-liturgia," in *Anàmnesis* 1 (Turin: Marietti, 1974), 137–56.
A. Caprioli, "Preghiera cristiana e liturgia," in *Mysterium. Miscellanea . . . Salvatore Marsili* (Turin-Leumann: ElleDiCi, 1981), 457–83.

The problem of the relationship between the liturgy and devotions arose from the very beginning of the liturgical movement, often in a polemical context. The devotions in question had often been more popular than the liturgy, for they were more congenial to the faithful, being in the vernacular and having a greater appeal to their sensibilities. A number of these devotions had in fact originally been intended as replacements for the liturgy, for example, the "Little Offices" in the Books of Hours or the rosary. Some of them, however, were likely to make their practitioners forget the liturgical year, especially Lent and the Easter season, since they were in competition with these. This explains the insistence of the pioneers in the liturgical movement on the primacy of the liturgy and the priority the faithful should give to it.

---

26. G. Dix, *The Shape of the Liturgy* (Westminster: Dacre Press, 1945[2]), 2, 12–13; P. Bayart, *Les divins offices* (Paris: Bloud et Gay, 1948), 52; I. H. Dalmais, "La liturgie, acte de l'Eglise," *LMD* no. 19 (1949) 8–11.

The Apostolic See made these principles its own, especially in its reform of Holy Week in 1955: "The faithful are to be taught the incomparable value of the liturgy, which at all times, but especially during these days, is by its nature far superior to other kinds of devotional practices, excellent though these are."[27] Following the lead of *Mediator Dei*, Vatican II was careful to approve "popular devotions of the Christian people . . . provided they accord with the laws and norms of the Church," but the Council also went on to say that "these devotions should be so fashioned that they harmonize with the liturgical seasons, accord with the sacred liturgy, are in some way derived from it, and lead the people to it, since, in fact, the liturgy by its nature far surpasses any of them."[28] Under these conditions, "popular devotions" (*pia exercitia*) are not only legitimate but praiseworthy and sometimes necessary. Their pastoral importance is emphasized in the popular traditions of the Christian countries; they can help bring to the liturgy those who are too far removed from it; and they provide collective expression for groups or forms of piety that cannot be acknowledged by the liturgy.

But where precisely does the difference between "liturgical action" and "popular devotion" lie? The line of separation is somewhat fluid, since certain devotions have been readily accepted into the liturgy[29] or have even become feasts and found a place in the Calendar—although they have had to be removed later on, when the liturgy was reformed.[30] Moreover, the distinction has sometimes been explained according to criteria that are unacceptable: the liturgy does not derive its value from its literary qualities nor exclusively from its historical past. Nor is the distinction to be explained solely by the fiat of ecclesiastical authority; it is true, of course, that people will recognize as liturgical the actions contained as such in the books officially promulgated by the competent authorities; on the other hand "popular devotions" do not become liturgical[31] if the bishop orders them or presides at them or even if they are called for by the Apostolic See.[32] The authentic distinguishing characteristic of the liturgy is to be sought in its structure and its content, which express and actualize the economy of salvation, for this alone makes it possible for the liturgy to bring the entire Christian people together in oneness of mind and heart.

---

27. SCR, *Instructio de Ordine hebdomadae sanctae instaurato rite peragendo*, 23: *AAS* 47 (1955) 847.

28. *VSC* 13 (*DOL* 1 no. 13).

29. For example, the greeting of the Blessed Virgin at the end of Compline or the renewal of baptismal promises during the Easter Vigil.

30. See *The Church at Prayer* IV, 126–27.

31. As J. A. Jungmann thought at one time; see no. 15, p. 10.

32. *VSC* 13.

§2. The Science of Liturgy

BIBLIOGRAPHY

On the method of liturgical science:

R. Guardini, "Über die systematische Methode in der Liturgiewissenschaft," *JLW* 1 (1921) 97–108.

F. Brovelli, *Per uno studio delle liturgia* (Venegono [no publisher named], 1976). Excerpt from a thesis presented to the faculty of theology in Milan.

A. Häussling, "Liturgiewissenschaft zwei Jahrzehnte nach Konzilsbeginn," *ALW* 24 (1982) 1–18.

H. W. Gartner and M. B. Merz, "Prolegomena für eine integrative Methode in der Liturgiewissenschaft," *ALW* 24 (1982) 165–89.

The aim of liturgical science is to provide a more profound and organic understanding of the liturgy. It was precisely this understanding that paved the way for the reform required by Vatican II. At the present time, the goal of this science is to help cope with the problems raised for the liturgy by ecumenism and by the need of adapting itself to different cultures.

Like all the sacred sciences, the science of liturgy presupposes faith, since this alone makes it possible to perceive the supernatural realities contained under the liturgical signs and, more generally, to understand fully the language of the liturgy, based as this is on revelation. But even faith is not enough; since the liturgy is an action, as we have just seen, it is intelligible only to those who really participate in it, and in the measure of their participation. Before being an object of study, the liturgy is an expression of life, and a liturgical science that is not grounded in that life will fail of its object; it may be able to analyze external details more or less correctly, but it will not grasp their true meaning. A description of the night office of Byzantine monks, or even a reading of its texts, will not give knowledge of it "from within"; active participation alone can give this kind of knowledge.

On the other hand, the understanding of liturgy that comes from experience of it in faith must be developed by means of scientific disciplines: history first, and then theology. The sciences of the human person can also provide a measure of light, and this too must not be neglected.

I. THE IMPORTANCE OF LITURGICAL HISTORY

BIBLIOGRAPHY

F. Cabrol, *Introduction aux études liturgiques* (Paris: Bloud, 1907).

P. de Puniet, "La méthode en matière de liturgie," in *Cours et conférences des Semaines liturgiques* 2 (1913 [1914]) 41–77.

L. C. Mohlberg, *Ziele und Aufgaben der liturgiegeschichtlichen Forschung* (LQF 1; Münster: Aschendorff, 1919).

A. Baumstark, *Vom geschichtlichen Werden der Liturgie* (Ecclesia orans 10; Freiburg: Herder, 1923).

L. C. Mohlberg, *Nochmals Ziele und Aufgaben für das Studium des christlichen Kultes* (Rome: Herder, 1957).

Scientific liturgical history, which was a seventeenth-century creation, showed the clergy and faithful the value and riches of the liturgy, its importance in the Church's tradition, the precise meaning of rites and prayers, the distinction between the essential and the secondary, and the unity and variety of the euchological heritage. The origin of rites sheds light on their true meaning, helps to determine their greater or lesser importance, and brings an understanding of how they either transcend or are dependent on cultures. The medieval liturgists lacked this fund of knowledge and were therefore satisfied to give rites an allegorical interpretation that was wholly external and arbitrary. But the work of historians had a further important result: it helped the Church recognize the need for a liturgical reform, and it provided the data necessary for it.

Historians cannot be satisfied to explain the external and material progression of rites; they must attempt also to understand the inner attitude with which these rites were practiced and lived by the clergy and faithful at each period.

The variety of liturgies in the Church inspired A. Baumstark to apply the comparative method that had brought so much light to other fields, for example, language. Rites common to several liturgies can sometimes be explained by borrowing; sometimes, however, they are to be explained by a common origin, and in this case it becomes possible to reconstruct the form the rites had in a time prior to known documents. The comparative method also plays a very important part in determining how widespread an ecclesial phenomenon is and how to evaluate its theological significance.[33]

Also to be emphasized here is the important role of the science of language, or philology, in the study of liturgy. Prayers and rubrics are texts that date from widely separated periods; within the same language (Latin, for example) words and expressions have divergent meanings depending on period and region and on the groups using them. When a text is translated from another language, knowledge of the original is also necessary

---

33. A. Baumstark, *Liturgie comparée* (Chevetogne, 1940[2]); 3rd ed., revised by B. Botte (Chevetogne, 1953); ET: *Comparative Liturgy*, trans. F. L. Cross (Westminster, Md.: Newman, 1958). — The first edition had originally appeared as articles in *Irénikon* 11 (1934) 5-34, 129-46, 293-327, 358-94, 481-520; 12 (1935) 34-53.

in order to solve difficulties and understand the full meaning of the text.[34] More generally, liturgical texts must be subjected to the same kind of literary analysis that is done on literary and philosophical masterpieces in the universities.

A final point: in addition to their study of written documents (liturgical books, records of ecclesiastical proceedings) and descriptions or didactic treatises, historians of the liturgy profit greatly from the study of the ancient places of worship and cult furnishings that archaeologists have brought to light, and from a knowledge of artistic documents, that is, ancient depictions of the liturgy in mosaics, frescoes, murals, sculptures, engravings, miniatures, and so on. Archaeological discoveries have frequently led to renewed interest in liturgical history; on the other hand, it has perhaps been sometimes forgotten that archaeology can be only an auxiliary science for historians of liturgy.[35]

II. THEOLOGICAL REFLECTION ON HISTORICAL DATA

The results gained by historians must then become an object of theological study; this aspect was perhaps somewhat neglected by the scholars who had to fight to give history the place it deserves, but it has recovered its full importance in our questioning age. What is the significance of the facts that have been observed? When do we have an unimpeachable tradition, and when a simple abnormality? Should the evolution that has been traced be regarded as progress or regression? What is the value, in terms of supernatural realities, of the signs that have been analyzed? Answers to such questions require a broad knowledge of theology and, in particular, an exact understanding of the *loci theologici* and of the nature of the Church and the sacraments (this understanding has now been facilitated by the teaching of Vatican II).[36] Also needed is a keen sense of pastoral responsibilities. This is why the bishops and the Apostolic See have ultimate authority in settling controversies; one of the best-known interventions of this kind is the Constitution *Sacramentum ordinis* of Pius XII in 1947.[37]

---

34. The works especially of B. Botte and C. Mohrmann have shown how greatly the liturgist needs scientific philology; several of these works will be mentioned at different points in the present volume.

35. There are as yet no recent works summarizing the contributions of archaeology and iconography, but the reader may profitably consult a few articles on specific subjects, in particular L. de Bruyne, "L'initiation chrétienne et ses reflets dans l'art paléochrétien," *RevSR* 36 (1962) 27–86.

36. See Section III, Chapter III, p. 273ff.

37. This Constitution will be discussed in *The Church at Prayer* III.

III. CONTRIBUTION OF THE HUMAN SCIENCES

BIBLIOGRAPHY

L. Bouyer, *Rite and Man: Natural Sacredness and Christian Liturgy*, trans. M. J. Costelloe (Notre Dame, Ind.: University of Notre Dame Press, 1963).

La Maison-Dieu no. 91 (1967) 67–179; 93 (1968) 103–45: *Liturgie et sciences humaines* (Colloque international de Louvain, June 1967).

H. Auf der Maur, "Das Verhältnis einer zukünftigen Liturgie zur Religionswissenschaft," *ALW* 10 (1968) 327–43.

F. A. Isambert, "Fête," *Encyclopaedia universalis* 6 (1970) 1046–51.

La Maison-Dieu no. 106 (1971) 79–116: *Célébration* (articles by A. Guillermou, F. A. Isambert, J. Y. Hameline).

F. A. Isambert, "Réforme liturgique et analyses sociologiques," *LMD* no. 128 (1976) 76–110.

A. Vergote, "Eclipse ou renouveau du sens du sacré dans l'actuelle liturgie," *ibid.*, 111–15.

F. Isambert, "Magie, religion, symbole . . .," *LMD* no. 133 (1978) 147–56.

_____, *Rite et efficacité symbolique, essai d'anthropologie sociologique* (Rites et symboles 8; Paris: Cerf, 1979).

Both the theological study of the liturgy and its pastoral application can profit by the sure results of the sciences established in our era for the study of the human person: anthropology, religious psychology, sociology, linguistics, comparative history of religions. The laws at work in assemblies, feasts, and communication help solve certain problems connected with the liturgical assembly, while at the same time showing the originality of the latter; in addition, since liturgy is made up of signs, the chief of which are the sacraments, semiology can shed new light on it. In another area, the effort of Dom Odo Casel to integrate the history of the liturgy into the religious and cultural setting of antiquity has demonstrated its fruitfulness as well as its limitations;[38] the history of cultures can help scholars see how the liturgy fits into cultures as well as how it transcends them.[39]

---

38. See p. 266ff.

39. B. Neunheuser, *Storia della liturgia attraverso le epoche culturali* (Bibliotheca EL, Subsidia 11; Rome: Edizioni liturgiche, 1978); E. Cattaneo, *Il culto cristiano in Occidente* (Bibliotheca EL, Subsidia 13; Rome: Edizioni liturgiche, 1978).

HISTORY OF THE LITURGY

LITURGICAL RITES AND FAMILIES

Introduction

GENERAL BIBLIOGRAPHY

L. Duchesne, *Christian Worship: Its Origin and Evolution*, trans. M. L. McClure (New York: Benziger, 1903), 1–45.
A. Baumstark, *Comparative Liturgy*, rev. by B. Botte, trans. F. L. Cross (Westminster, Md.: Newman, 1958).
M. Righetti, *Manuale di storia liturgica* 1 (Milan: Ancora, 1864³) 101–85.
Anàmnesis 2. *La liturgia, panorama storico generale* (Turin: Marietti, 1978) (by S. Marsili, J. Pinell, A. M. Triacca, T. Federici, A. Nocent, B. Neunheuser).

The ritual expressions that found a place in the practice of the various Christian communities were gradually reduced to unity under the prevailing influence of a few centers. The latter were for the most part the major ecclesiastical sees that in the course of time acquired jurisdiction over Churches of lesser importance and became known as patriarchates in the Romano-Byzantine Empire or, outside the frontiers of the empire, as catholicates.

Other liturgically influential centers had a spiritual rather than a jurisdictional status; for example, the major monastic centers or, in the West, the religious Orders.

The breakup of geographical alignments as a result of doctrinal divergences offset these centralizing tendencies and thus promoted the survival of local usages; this was the case especially in the East.

Finally, the spread of printing greatly contributed to the standardization of liturgical usages during the past four centuries. But apart from the discipline gradually established in the Catholic Church of the Latin rite after the Council of Trent,[1] this standardization of liturgical usages was primarily a matter of customary law.

By and large, two main liturgical groups are easily recognizable. One is the West with its Latin tradition, where in the course of the second

---

1. See pp. 72–76, 118–19.

millennium the Roman liturgy was adopted almost unanimously, though with allowance for some variants, adaptations, and additions. The other is the Eastern group, which, however, has continued to manifest a far greater degree of variation. Nonetheless the Byzantine liturgy ultimately prevailed over wide areas of the East, for it was adopted by all the Churches of the Orthodox Communion, that is, the Churches that profess the faith formulated by the Council of Chalcedon and completed by the Second and Third Councils of Constantinople.

Unlike the Latin West until Vatican II, the Christian East has always accepted a plurality of liturgical languages.[2]

---

2. See pp. 161–64.

Chapter I

The Liturgy in the First Four Centuries

I. H. Dalmais

During this period the Christian liturgy seems to have been for the most part improvised on the basis of some schemata taken primarily from Jewish usage and adapted to the new situation that was created by the teachings of Jesus, especially regarding baptism and the commemorative paschal meal. In the course of the latter, the traditional Jewish "blessings" (*berakoth*) were transformed into a *eucharistia*, as can already be seen in the *Didache*, which dates from around the turn of the first century.[1] About the year 150 St. Justin provides a brief description of these rites.[2] Book VII of the *Apostolic Constitutions* (*ca.* 380) contains a revised version of the *Didache* and in addition has preserved for us echoes of an ancient Christianized Jewish prayer book.[3]

Book VIII of the *Apostolic Constitutions* is to a great extent a revised version of an ancient document that has also been transmitted in canonical collections of Egyptian origin and especially in a Latin translation that is, unfortunately, fragmentary. The research work of R. H. Connolly (1916), Gregory Dix (1937), and Bernard Botte (1963) has made possible a fairly reliable reconstruction of the original document, as well as its identification with the *Apostolic Tradition* (*Apostolikē Paradosis*). This docu-

---

1. *Didache* 9–10; ed. W. Rordorf and A. Tuilier, SC 248:174-83 (Paris: Cerf, 1978); see *The Church at Prayer* II, pp. 13 and 23–24.

2. St. Justin, *Apologia I* 61 and 65–67, ed. L. Pautigny (Textes et documents 1; Paris: Picard, 1904), 126–31, 139–45; see *The Church at Prayer* II, pp. 14–17.

3. *Constitutiones Apostolorum* VII, 33–49, ed. F. X. Funk, *Didascalia et Constitutiones Apostolorum* 1 (Paderborn: Schöningh, 1905), 424–59; see L. Bouyer, *Eucharist. Theology and Spirituality of the Eucharistic Prayer*, trans. C. U. Quinn (Notre Dame, Ind.: University of Notre Dame Press, 1958), 119–35.

ment is mentioned on the base of a statue discovered near the Agro Verano in 1551 and regarded as representing Hippolytus of Rome. If these hypotheses are valid, the document dates from the first third of the third century.[4] In any case, the text played a fundamental role and had great influence, especially in the East. It seems to reflect a liturgical tradition that is primarily Antiochene. If the dating is correct, it would be contemporary with another (Syrian) canonical document, *The Teaching (Didascalia) of the Apostles*, a revised version of which provides the framework for the first six books of the *Apostolic Constitutions*.[5]

These various documents are our main source of information about the liturgy of the first three centuries. Some supplementary information can be gleaned from the writings of the Fathers, especially those of Tertullian[6] and St. Cyprian,[7] from the Acts of the martyrs and, above all, from inscriptions.[8] For the eastern Syro-Mesopotamian area, finally, we have a few texts that are difficult to date and put in context, in particular the *Odes of Solomon*, which probably date from the first half of the second century,[9] and the descriptions and formularies of baptism and the Eucharist that have made their way into the *Acts of Thomas*, which were probably compiled in the third century.[10]

---

4. B. Botte (ed.), *La Tradition Apostolique de Saint Hippolyte: Essai de reconstitution* (LQF 39; Münster: Aschendorff, 1963), with a complete critical apparatus and the essential bibliography; a less technical edition by B. Botte, SC 11bis (Paris: Cerf, 1968). — Edition of the Latin translation (Verona palimpsest, Bibli. Capit., ms. LV): E. Tidner, *Didascaliae Apostolorum, Canonum ecclesiasticorum, Traditionis apostolicae versiones latinae* (TU 75: Berlin: Akademie Verlag, 1963). — See J. M. Hanssens, *La liturgie d'Hippolyte* 1 (OCA 155; Rome: Pontificio Istituto Orientale, 1959); 2 (Rome: Pontificia Università Gregoriana, 1970).

5. *Didascalia Apostolorum*, ed. Funk (n. 3, above); trans. of the Syriac version and the Verona Latin fragments by R. H. Connolly, *Didascalia Apostolorum* (Oxford: Clarendon, 1929); French trans. by F. Nau, *La Didascalie des Douze Apôtres* Paris: Lethielleux, 1912²).

6. See E. Dekkers, *Tertullianus en de geschiedenis der liturgie* (Brussels: De Kinkhoren, 1947).

7. See V. Saxer, *Vie liturgique et quotidienne à Carthage vers le milieu du IIIᵉ siècle: Le témoignage de saint Cyprien et de ses contemporains d'Afrique* (Studi di antichità cristiana 29; Vatican City, 1969).

8. Although largely outdated on many points, the compilation of F. Cabrol and H. Leclercq, *Reliquiae liturgicae vetustissimae* (2 vols.; Monumenta Ecclesiae liturgica 1-2; Paris: Firmin-Didot, 1902-13), provides a collection of documents for which there is no substitute.

9. *The Odes of Solomon*, ed. and trans. J. H. Charlesworth (Oxford: Clarendon Press, 1973); French trans. by J. Guirau and A. G. Hamman, *Les Odes de Salomon* (Coll. Quand vous priez; Paris: Desclée De Bouwer, 1981). New English trans. by J. H. Charlesworth in *The Old Testament Pseudepigrapha*, ed. J. H. Charlesworth, 2 (Garden City, N.Y.: Doubleday, 1985), 725-71.

10. Syriac text of the *Acts of Thomas* translated in W. Wright, *Apocryphal Acts of the Apostles* 1 (London, 1871), 171-333; Greek text translated in R. A. Lipsius and M. Bon-

Sources of information become much more abundant from the mid-fourth century on. Chief among these sources are the sets of catechetical discourses to the newly baptized on the "mysteries" of Christian initiation, or the "mystagogical catecheses," as they are called. The most detailed and the richest in teaching are those that have been transmitted under the name of St. Cyril, bishop of Jerusalem from 350 to 386, but that in their present form date perhaps only from the time of his successor, John II (386–416).[11] A like importance must be assigned to the last four catecheses of Theodore of Mopsuestia, which were discovered, in a Syriac translation, in 1932;[12] they were probably delivered in about 390. Almost contemporary are a number of catechetical addresses that John Chrysostom gave at Antioch.[13] In the West, two treatises of St. Ambrose, *De sacramentis* and *De mysteriis*, have the same kind of interest; these too had their origin in baptismal catecheses.[14] There is also a good deal of information to be gleaned from the sermons of the Fathers.[15]

Finally, some surviving liturgical formularies may go back to this same period. This is very likely the case with the collection published under the title *Prayer Book (Euchologion) of Serapion*,[16] because the name Serapion occurs at the head of two of the prayers. The Alexandrian origin

net, *Acta Apostolorum apocrypha* 2 (Leipzig: Mendelsohn, 1903), 99–288. Trans. R. McL. Wilson in *New Testament Apocrypha*, ed. E. Hennecke and W. Schneemelcher, 2 (Philadelphia: Westminster, 1965), 425–531.

11. *Catecheses mystagogiques*, ed. A. Piedagnel and trans. P. Paris (SC 126; Paris: Cerf 1966).—Bibliography on these catecheses in C. Renoux, "Hierosolymitana," *ALW* 23 (1981) 149–60.

12. *Homélies catéchétiques*, ed. and trans. R. Devreesse and R. Tonneau (ST 145; Vatican City, 1949).

13. John Chrysostom, *Huit catéchèses baptismales inédites*, ed. A. Wenger (SC 50; Paris: Cerf 1957); to these must be added the catecheses published in A. Papadoupoulos-Kerameus, *Varia Graeca sacra* (Saint Petersburg, 1909), 154–83. — See P. Rentinck, *La cura pastorale in Antiochia nel secolo IV* (Analecta Gregoriana 178; Rome: Pontificia Università Gregoriana, 1970).

14. Ambrose of Milan, *Des sacrements, Des mystères*, new edition by B. Botte (SC 25bis; Paris: Cerf, 1961).

15. For the evidence in the sermons of St. John Chrysostom see F. van de Paverd, *Zur Geschichte der Messliturgie in Antiocheia und Konstantinopel gegen Ende des vierten Jahrhunderts. Analyse der Quellen des Johannes Chrysostomos* (OCA 187; Rome: Pontificio Istituto Orientale, 1970). — For St. Augustine: W. Rötzer, *Des heiligen Augustinus Schriften als liturgiegeschichtliche Quelle* (Munich: Hueber, 1930). — For St. Ambrose: V. Monachino, *S. Ambrogio e la cura pastorale a Milano nel secolo IV* (Milan: Centro de documentazione e studi religiosi, 1973). — For Chromatius of Aquileia: J. Lemarie, "La liturgie d'Aquilée au temps de Chromace," in: *Chromace d'Aquilée, Sermons* 1 (SC 154; Paris: Cerf, 1969), 82–108.

16. Ed. F. E. Brightman, "The Sacramentary of Serapion of Thmuis," *JTS* 1 (1899–1900) 88–113, 247–77; F. X. Funk, *Didascalia et Constitutiones Apostolorum* 2 (Paderborn: Schöningh, 1905), 158–95.

of the collection is certain, but the attribution to Serapion, bishop of Thmuis and friend of St. Athanasius, continues to be disputed, as does the precise nature of the collection itself.[17] The surviving recensions and adaptations of the *Apostolic Tradition*[18], as well as the compilation of the *Apostolic Constitutions* belong to this same period.

---

17. B. Capelle, "L'anaphore de Sérapion," *Le Muséon* 59 (1946) 425–43; B. Botte, "L'Eucologe de Sérapion est-il authentique?" *OC* 48 (1964) 50–56.

18. The main recensions and adaptations are these: the *Canons d'Hippolyte*, ed. R. G. Coquin (PO 31/2); — the Egyptian *Sinodos*, Sahidic text ed. by W. Till and J. Leipoldt, *Der koptische Text der Kirchenordnung Hippolyts* (TU 58; Berlin, 1954), Ethiopic text ed. by H. Duensing, *Der aethiopische Text der Kirchenordnung des Hippolyt* (Göttingen: Vandenhoeck & Ruprecht, 1946), and Arabic text ed. by J. and A. Perier, *Les 127 canons des Apôtres* (PO 8/4); — the *Epitome* of Book VIII of the *Constitutiones Apostolorum*, ed. Funk 2:72–96; — and the *Testamentum Domini nostri Iesu Christi*, ed. by I. Rahmani (Mainz: Kirchheim, 1899; reprinted: Hildesheim: Olms, 1968).

Chapter II

The Eastern Liturgical Families

I. H. Dalmais

GENERAL BIBLIOGRAPHY

a) Most important collections of texts:

E. Renaudot, *Liturgiarum Orientalium collectio* (2 vols.; Paris, 1916; 2nd, more accurate ed.: Frankfurt: Baer, 1847).

J. L. Assemani, *Codex liturgicus Ecclesiae universae* (13 vols.; Rome: Bizzarini, 1749–66; reprinted: Paris-Leipzig: Welter, 1902).

H. Denzinger, *Ritus Orientalium . . . in administrandis sacramentis* (2 vols.; Würzburg: Stahel, 1863; reprinted: Graz: Akademische Druck, 1961).

F. E. Brightman, *Liturgies Eastern and Western* 1. *Eastern Liturgies* (Oxford: Clarendon, 1896). Only vol. 1 was published.

b) Bibliographies

J. M. Sauget, *Bibliographie des liturgies orientales 1900–1960* (Rome: Pontificio Istituto Orientale, 1962).

S. Janeras, *Bibliografia sulle liturgie orientali 1961–1967* (Rome: Pontificium Institutum Liturgicum Anselmianum, 1969).

Archiv für Liturgiewissenschaft, Literaturberichte: 11 (1969) 327–44 (O. Heiming); 19 (1978) 193–219 (H. Brakmann and W. Cramer); 24 (1982) 377–410 (H. Brakmann).

c) Manuals and general works

J. M. Hanssens, *Institutiones liturgicae de ritibus orientalibus* (Rome: Pontificia Università Gregoriana, 1930–31). Only vols. 2 and 3, on the Mass, were published (with an Appendix in a separate fascicle).

A. Raes, *Introductio in liturgiam orientalem* (Rome: Pontificio Istituto Orientale, 1947).

A. King, *The Rites of Eastern Christendom* (2 vols.; Rome: Catholic Book Agency, 1947–48).

A. Baumstark, *Comparative Liturgy*, rev. B. Botte, trans. F. L. Cross (Westminster, Md.: Newman, 1958).

Handbuch der Ostkirchenkunde (Düsseldorf: Patmos, 1971).

I. H. Dalmais, *Liturgies d'Orient* (Rites et symboles 10; Paris: Cerf, 1980).

From at least the fifth century our information is extensive enough to show the existence of the major liturgical families. Since the Church had adapted its own organization to the administrative framework of the empire, the great cultural and political centers exerted a growing influence. In the eastern half of the empire—which acquired complete autonomy beginning in 395 and became the Byzantine Empire—these centers were initially the two great cosmopolitan, yet profoundly Hellenized cities of Alexandria and Antioch. The Jewish communities in these cities had long been large and influential, and this fact could not fail to affect the Christian Churches.

Constantinople, which became the capital of this eastern empire and called itself the "New Rome," had no clearly defined Christian tradition of its own and would take over a great deal from Antioch, especially in matters liturgical. Despite the brevity of his tenure as bishop there (397?–404) St. John Chrysostom would leave an indelible mark on this Church.

The tenacious rivalry between the sees of Constantinople and Alexandria may have helped to preserve and perhaps even develop important peculiarities that justify recognition of an Alexandrian liturgical family, as distinct from another that bore the marks of Antiochene influence. In their subsequent development, however, the difference between the two would be much reduced.

The liturgy peculiar to Jerusalem, which became a great pilgrimage center in the course of the fourth century, would have a more or less profound influence on the various liturgies of both East and West.

These various observations already suggest the care that must be taken in any classification of the Eastern liturgies which have continued in use down to our day or about which we at least have fairly detailed information. It can be said that, as in the case of the Western Church, their structure and even a large part of their formularies were already in place by the sixth–seventh century, the period from which the earliest surviving manuscripts date.

§1. Syrian Group

The same basic structures (especially those of the Eucharistic anaphora and the baptismal rite) as well as some common formularies show that all the liturgies placed under this heading are indeed akin to one another. But it is also necessary to recognize from the outset the specific character of, on the one hand, the liturgical traditions that originated in Syria proper, with its prevailing Antiochene influence, and, on the other, of traditions preserved in the eastern regions of the empire, and especially in Upper

Mesopotamia (Chaldea), where Semitic cultures had been far more successful in resisting Hellenization.

I. EASTERN SYRIAN (SYRO-MESOPOTAMIAN) TYPE

a) *The Assyro-Chaldean Rite*

BIBLIOGRAPHY

> G. P. Badger, *The Nestorians and Their Rituals* (2 vols.; London: Masters, 1852; reprinted: Plymouth, Michigan: Gregg, 1969).
>
> E. Tisserant, "Nestorienne (Eglise)," *Dictionnaire de théologie catholique* 11 (Paris: Letouzey, 1931) 157–223.
>
> W. de Vries, *Sakramententheologie bei den Nestorianern* (OCA 133; Rome: Pontificio Istituto Orientale, 1947).

This is the most archaic of all the forms of Christian liturgy, that is, the one that has to the greatest extent retained characteristics derived from its Semitic roots. The first centers in which this liturgy was celebrated are distinguishable as early as the end of the second century at Nisibis and Edessa (Urfa), whose Aramaic dialect, known as Syriac, was to become the common cultural and liturgical language of Christian communities throughout Asia. These communities would develop primarily, from the third to the seventh century, in the Persian Empire of the Sassanids, with their Mazdean religion, and then in the Caliphate of Baghdad; they would live, in other words, as minority, sometimes persecuted, often semiclandestine groups. Tradition assigns a liturgical reorganization to Catholicos-Patriarch Isho'yab III in the aftermath of the Arab conquest (*ca.* 650).[1]

Unfortunately, the only liturgical manuscripts that have come down to us are, with a few exceptions, very late (fourteenth–fifteenth centuries). But the surviving commentaries and liturgico-canonical responses show how very conservative this liturgy was.[2] The Eucharistic Anaphora of the Apostles Addai and Mari may go back in its essential lines to the third

---

1. A. Baumstark, *Geschichte der syrischen Literatur* (Bonn: Marcus & Weber, 1922; reprinted: Berlin: de Gruyter, 1968), 197–98.

2. The earliest commentary, that of Gabriel Qatraya bar Lipah (*ca.* 620), is in great part still unpublished. See S. H. Jammo, "Gabriel Qatraya et son commentaire sur la liturgie chaldéenne," *OCP* 32 (1966) 39–56; *idem, La structure de la messe chaldéenne du debut jusqu'à l'anaphore. Etude historique* (OCA 207; Rome: Pontificio Istituto Orientale, 1979), 29–48. The most important commentary is still the anonymous *Explanation of the Offices,* by "Pseudo-George of Arbela," ed. with Latin trans. by R. H. Connolly (CSCO 64 and 72 [Syriac], 71 and 76 [translation]).

century; it is very close in form to the Jewish *berakoth* for blessings at table.[3]

Except for baptism (in which every trace of a catechumenate has been eliminated) and ordinations, the liturgy of the sacraments is still in an embryonic stage, as is the structure of the liturgical year. The latter is based roughly on a "weeks of weeks" pattern and, especially in the case of the Sanctoral, is reduced to a few commemorations on Fridays.

The Office includes, in addition to the psalms, a very large number of hymns; the great poet here was St. Ephraem.[4]

The retention by the "Persian School" of the most rigorist traditions of Antioch, its refusal to enter into the various Christological discussions by accepting expressions regarded as innovative, and above all its determination (with an eye on the power of the easily offended Sassanids) to separate itself clearly from any seeming affection for Byzantium: all these factors surely contributed to intensify the conservatism of a Church that under Bar Sauma (484)[5] would make its own the teachings of Nestorius. Its two anaphoras in the Antiochene style, which have come down under the names of Theodore of Mopsuestia, interpreter *par excellence* of the Scriptures, and of Nestorius, have been adapted from a Greek text.[6] In this they differ from the ancient Aramaic Anaphora of the Apostles and are evidence of a desire to remain rooted in the Antiochene tradition, far removed though this is from the general climate and very structure of the Assyro-Chaldean liturgy.

This rite seems to have acquired its definitive form[7] chiefly in the great

---

3. Critical ed. with Latin trans. by W. F. Macomber, "The Oldest Known Text of the Anaphora of the Apostles Addai and Mari," *OCP* 32 (1966) 335-70. See *The Church at Prayer* II, pp. 29-34.

4. The poetical works of St. Ephraem have been given a critical edition with a German trans. by E. Beck in CSCO, where they occupy over twenty volumes. Beck also wrote numerous articles on these works; for a list see F. Graffin's Introduction to the edition of the *Hymnes sur le paradis* (SC 137), 11-12.

5. On Bar Sauma: A. Vööbus, *Les Messaliens et la réforme de Barsauma de Nisibe dans l'Eglise Perse* (Pinneberg, 1947).

6. F. E. Brightman, "The Anaphora of Theodore," *JTS* 31 (1930) 160-64; A. Baumstark, "Die Chrysostomos Liturgie und die syrische Liturgie des Nestorios," in *Chrysostomika. Studi e ricerche intorno a san Giovanni Crisostomo* (Rome: Pustet, 1908), 771-857.

7. For the history of the Chaldean liturgical books: C. Mousses, *Les livres liturgiques de l'Eglise chaldéenne* (Beirut, 1955). The missal was published at Mosul in 1901; French trans. by F. Y. Alichoran, *Missel chaldéen* (published by the author, 1982). P. Bedjan compiled a breviary in three volumes (Paris, 1917, and Rome, 1936); English trans. of the ferial office by A. J. Maclean, *East Syrian Daily Offices* (London: Rivington & Percival, 1894). The pontifical was established on the basis of fifteenth century manuscripts (Rome, 1957); Latin trans. by I. Vosté, *Pontificale iuxta ritum Syrorum orientalium id est Chaldaeorum* (4 facs.; Vatican City, 1937-38).

Monastery of the Pure Virgin (*At Tahira*), or Upper Monastery (*Deir al A'la*) as it is known, north of Mosul.[8]

b) *Expansion Across Asia*

BIBLIOGRAPHY

L. W. Brown, *The Indian Christians of St. Thomas. An Account of the Ancient Syrian Church of Malabar* (Cambridge: Cambridge University Press, 1956).

E. Card. Tisserant, *Eastern Christianity in India. A History of the Syro-Malabar Church from the Earliest Time to the Present Day*, adapted from the French by E. R. Hambye (London: Longmans, 1957).

The Malabar Church. Symposium in Honor of Rev. J. Placid Podipara, ed. J. Vellian (OCA 186; Rome: Pontificio Istituto Orientale, 1970).

The Assyro-Chaldean liturgy was carried across Asia along the Silk Route and was adapted in various ways as it went. Some bits of information and a very few fragments give a glimpse of what it looked like initially in China in the seventh to the ninth century. It seems, however, that when the "Nestorian" Church was introduced into the Middle Empire a second time during the Mongol period (13th–14th c.), it maintained a strict fidelity to the Assyro-Chaldean rite.[9]

Until the end of the sixteenth century, the same was probably true of the Christians of South India, who acquired their bishops from the Catholicos of Baghdad, at least from the time of Catholicos Timothy I (781–823) on. But in consequence of the Synod of Diamper (1599), the liturgy was almost completely Latinized,[10] except that the language used remained Syriac and the Mass retained the structure of the *Qorbana* (oblation) of the Chaldean rite. In 1934 Pius XI decreed the restoration of the ancient rite, except for a few adaptations, and, beginning in 1960, the Chaldean liturgical books were adapted and translated into Malayalam, the language of the state of Kerala. The problem of adjustments is still unsettled because, since 1971, new missionary exarchates have been established and entrusted to the Syro-Malabar Church.

II. WESTERN SYRIAN TYPE

This type descended from the Antiochene liturgy and has developed a wide variety of forms. The four rites presently in use can be divided

---

8. A. Rücker, "Das 'obere Kloster' bei Mossul und seine Bedeutung für die Geschichte der ostsyrischen Liturgie," *OC*, ser. III, 7 (1932) 181–87.

9. J. Dauvillier, "Les provinces chaldéennes de l'extérieur au moyen âge," in *Mélanges F. Cavallera* (Toulouse: Institut Catholique, 1948), 260–316.

10. J. Thaliath, *The Synod of Diamper* (OCA 152; Rome: Pontificio Istituto Orientale, 1958).

into two groups. The first comprises the rites in which Syriac is used and which claim a direct Antiochene origin: the Syrian rite (long called the "Jacobite" rite) and the Maronite rite. The second group comprises rites that have been influenced by other traditions: the Byzantine rite and the Armenian rite.

a) *The Syro-Antiochene ("Jacobite") Rite*

At Antioch and at least in other urban centers, the liturgy was for a long time celebrated in Greek. After the break with Constantinople and the establishment of a local Church, known as the "Jacobite" Church after its principal founder, Jacob or James bar Addai (6th c.),[11] Syriac gradually became the liturgical language, especially as a result of the translations of James of Edessa († 708).[12] In addition, the rite was gradually enriched with elements of Aramaic origin, especially the poetic compositions attributed to St. Ephraem[13] or to James of Sarug.[14]

The rite acquired its classic form in the second half of the twelfth century, in the time of Patriarch Michael the Great (1166–99), to whom the composition of the Pontifical is attributed.[15] In this work of reorganization, which was doubtless influenced by the presence of Latin sees in the Frankish principalities of Syria, the patriarch's main collaborator was the great theologian and liturgist Dionysius bar Salibi († 1171), the author of an extensive commentary on the rites of his Church[16] and to whom is attributed the standardization of the penitential rites. In the following two centuries the Syrian liturgy was enriched—and encumbered—with expansions, chiefly ceremonial, that displayed a craving for allegory. In addition, while Syriac remained the official liturgical language, the local Arabic language was increasingly used for the readings and for some prayers and songs.

The Syrian rite is characterized by numerous liturgical gestures and poetic texts. There are many rites of incensation, which seem indeed to

---

11. On James bar Addai or Burde'ana see A. Baumstark, *Geschichte der syrischen Literatur* (n. 1, p. 29), 174–75; I. Ortiz de Urbina, *Patrologia syriaca* (Rome: Pontificio Istituto Orientale, 1958) 153–54.

12. On James of Edessa: Baumstark 248–56; Ortiz de Urbina 166–71.

13. On St. Ephraem see n. 4, p. 30.

14. On James of Sarug: Baumstark 148–58; Ortiz de Urbina 97–101.

15. Published in 2 vols.; Charfé, 1950–52. Latin trans. by I. Vosté, *Pontificale iuxta ritum Ecclesiae Syrorum occidentalium id est Antiochiae* (4 fasc.; Vatican City, 1941–44).

16. Dionysius bar Salibi, *Expositio liturgiae*, ed. H. Labourt (CSCO 13; 1903) and trans. H. Labourt (CSCO 14; 1904). Other commentaries: R. H. Connolly and H. W. Codrington, *Two Commentaries on the Jacobite Liturgy by George Bishop of the Arab Tribes and Moses bar Kepha* (London: Williams & Norgate, 1913; reprinted: Plymouth, Michigan: Gregg, 1969).

have been the source of the form of prayer peculiar to this tradition, namely, the *Sedro* (well-ordered discourse), which comprises a doxology (*Prooemium*), a homily (the *Sedro* proper), and a prayer accompanying an offering of incense (*Etro*). In the ritual of ordination, which comes after the anaphora, the bishop first extends his hands over the sacred species and then extends them, wrapped in his cope, over the heads of the ordinands.

In addition to the specifically Antiochene Anaphora of the Apostles (of which the Byzantine Anaphora of St. John Chrysostom seems to be an adaptation[17]), the Syrian liturgy has taken as a prototype the Anaphora of St. James of Jerusalem.[18] Down to the fourteenth century many other anaphoras were modeled on these two; eighteen of them are still in use.[19] The Office of the Hours follows a weekly scheme called the *Shlimo* (simple).[20] Its chief characteristic is an extensive hymnography, which has resulted in an almost complete disappearance of the Psalter; the properly euchological part of the office consists essentially of *sēdrē* and of litanic formularies (*korozutē*) which, depending on their meter, are called the "Petitions" respectively of St. Ephraem or St. James (of Sarug) or Mar Balai.

b) *The Maronite Rite*

BIBLIOGRAPHY

P. Dib, *Etudes sur la liturgie maronite* (Paris: Lethielleux, 1919).

M. Hayek, *Liturgie maronite, histoire et textes eucharistiques* (Paris: Mame, 1964).

P. E. Gemayel, *Avant-messe maronite, histoire et structure* (OCA 174; Rome: Pontificio Istituto Orientale, 1965).

J. Tabet, *L'office divin maronite, étude du Lilyo et du Safro* (Kaslik, Lebanon, 1972).

---

17. Critical edition and Latin trans. by A. Raes, in *Anaphorae syriacae* I, fasc. 2 (Rome: Pontificio Istituto Orientale, 1940), 205–27; H. Engberding, "Die syrische Anaphora der zwölf Apostel und ihre Paralleltexte," *OC*, ser. III, 12 (1937) 213–47; A. Raes, "L'authenticité de la liturgie byzantine de saint Jean Chrysostome," *OCP* 24 (1958) 5–16.

18. Edition of the Greek text by B. C. Mercier (PO 26/2; 1946), with a French translation; of the Syriac text by A. Rücker, *Die syrische Jakobosanaphora* (LQF 4; Münster: Aschendorff, 1923), with a German translation; see A. Tarby, *La prière eucharistique de l'Eglise de Jérusalem* (Théologie historique 7; Paris: Beauchesne, 1972).

19. Forty anaphoras were translated into Latin by E. Renaudot in his *Liturgiarum orientalium collectio* 2. A collection of critical editions has been in progress for some years: *Anaphorae syriacae quotquot in codicibus adhuc repertae sunt, cura P. Instituti studiorum orientalium editae et latine versae* (Rome, 1939ff.) (volumes 1 and 2 have appeared; fasc. 1 of volume 3 appeared in 1981).

20. Msgr. David compiled an extensive collection, the *Fankit* (Mosul, 1886–96), for the liturgical seasons and feasts; a less extensive collection in 3 vols. was published at Kottayam in 1963 for the use of the Syrian Orthodox Church of South India.

A. Mouhanna, *Les rites de l'initiation dans l'Eglise maronite* (XRICTIANICMOC 1; Rome: Pontificio Istituto Orientale, 1978).

This branch of the Western Syrian rite is closely related to the Syro-Antiochene rite, from which it has been derived. It originated in the communities that had settled around monasteries in the Orontes valley of Central Syria, and in particular around the monastery that grew up at the tomb of Mar Maron, an ascetic who lived at the beginning of the fifth century. These communities accepted the doctrine of Chalcedon, but resisted Byzantinization; in the course of the sixth century they formed an autonomous Church and most of them were obliged to migrate, chiefly to the upper valleys of Mount Lebanon, where their patriarch made his residence, but also to Cyprus and the region of Aleppo. During the period of the Frankish principalities, the Maronites professed their firm attachment to the Catholic faith, and their union with the See of Rome was officially confirmed in 1215. The union subsequently led, especially from the sixteenth century on, to a reorganization on the Latin model, which was approved in 1736 at the Council of Mount Lebanon,[21] and to a regrettable Latinization of the external forms and ritual of the liturgy.

Because of its monastic and rural origins and because of the role that the monks (organized from the end of the seventeenth century on, in three Orders of the Western type) continued to play in it, the Maronite liturgy is characterized chiefly by its popular traits and by the pietism of many of the compositions peculiar to it, especially hymns and versified *sēdrē*, the oldest of which may go back to the eleventh century. For several centuries now, Arabic has acquired a large place in this rite and is in the process of becoming the dominant liturgical language. In addition, certain elements that may be very old indicate a kinship with the Assyro-Chaldean liturgy. This is true especially of the Anaphora of St. Peter (the *Sharar*), which is peculiar to the Maronite rite but is also fairly close to the Chaldean Anaphora of the Apostles.[22] It fell into disuse after the seventeenth century and was often replaced by an Anaphora "of the Holy Roman Church," which was modeled on the Roman Canon; at the present time the *Sharar* has recovered its place among the twelve anaphoras of the Maronite Missal.

The history of this rite is unfortunately difficult to reconstruct because

21. J. D. Mansi, *Sacrorum conciliorum nova et amplissima collectio*, continuata curantibus J. B. Martin and L. Petit, 38 (Paris, Leipzig and Arnheim: Welter, 1907), 141–49. On the council and its trials and tribulations see P. Dib, "Maronite (Eglise)," *Dictionnaire de théologie catholique* 10 (1927) 79–86.

22. Critical ed. and Latin trans. by J. M. Sauget, in *Anaphorae syriacae* II, fasc. 3 (1973) 275–327; French trans. in M. Hayek, *Liturgie maronite, histoire et textes eucharistiques* (Paris: Mame, 1964), 295–318. See *The Church at Prayer* II, pp. 29–34.

of an almost complete lack of documents from before the fifteenth century. When the great patriarch Stephen Duwaihi (1670–1704), called "Edenensis" (after Edhen, the village of his birth), attempted to restore the Maronite liturgy to its proper form, he ran into opposition from the Latinizing element at the Maronite College in Rome, from the Franciscans, and then from the Jesuits. Only in 1942 was an almost completely Latinized ritual replaced by one redacted in the spirit of Duwaihi. There is still no official edition of the Pontifical. In regard to the Missal and the Liturgy of the Hours an important work of restoration has been in progress since Vatican II, but the controlling perspective is primarily pastoral, and thus far there have been no truly scientific investigations of the documents or truly scientific comparative studies.

c) *The Byzantine Rite*

BIBLIOGRAPHY

H. J. Schulz, *The Byzantine Liturgy. The Development of Its Symbolic Form*, trans. M. J. O'Connell (New York: Pueblo, 1986).

M. Arranz, "Les grandes étapes de la liturgie byzantine . . . , essai d'aperçu historique," in *Liturgie de l'Eglise particulière et liturgie de l'Eglise universelle (Conférences Saint-Serge 22, 1975)* (Bibliotheca EL, Subsidia 7; Rome: Edizioni liturgiche, 1976), 43–72.

This rite is complex and can legitimately be called ecumenical; it is in many respects by far the most widespread and representative of all the liturgies of the Christian East. It came into existence between the sixth and ninth century in the privileged setting of Santa Sophia, the "Great Church" of Constantinople, and in the great monasteries of the imperial city. It acquired its definitive form during the Paleologue Restoration (1261–1453), chiefly in the monasteries of Mount Athos. The "hesychastic" spiritual renewal that took place on Mount Athos during that period exerted an influence far beyond the narrow boundaries of the late Byzantine Empire, into the Slavic world that had progressively adopted the Byzantine rite, in Slavonic, ever since the last third of the eighth century. At that time the Bulgarians had accepted Christianity and the Byzantine rite; a century later they transmitted the rite to the Russians, and then to the Serbs, who formed an autonomous Church in the thirteenth century.

The Patriarchate of Jerusalem and those parts of the old patriarchates of Alexandria and Jerusalem that remained faithful to the doctrine of Chalcedon and the liturgical usages of the empire (whence their name "Melkites," that is, "Emperor's men") adopted the Byzantine rite, with minimal variations, before the twelfth century; the liturgical language was Syriac in the beginning but Arabic from the fifteenth–sixteenth centuries on. In the form established by the Greek editions of the sixteenth century, which served as the model for revising the Slavonic versions, the Byzantine rite became the liturgy of all the Orthodox Churches and, apart from a few Latinisms, especially among the Ukrainian Ruthenians, of those sections of the Eastern Churches that reestablished union with Rome.

The form the Constantinopolitan liturgy had before the tenth century can be reconstructed with more or less certainty with the help of several sources: the commentary on the Eucharistic liturgy that is attributed to Patriarch Germanus (715-30)[23] and is the nucleus of the medieval *Historia ecclesiastica;*[24] some *Typika,* or service books, of the tenth and eleventh centuries;[25] and the later disquisitions of Symeon († 1429), archbishop of Thessalonica, a city that had showed greater fidelity than the capital to the ancient usages.[26] For after the iconoclasm crisis (726-843) and the migration to Constantinople of many Syro-Palestinian monks, especially to the monastery of St. John the Precursor (known as Studios), which was a center of resistance to imperial policies, a good many monastic customs were introduced and the service book (*Typikon*) of the Palestinian Laura of St. Sabas was adopted; the result was a profound orientalization of the old rite of Constantinople.

This new outlook controlled the reorganization of the books used in the celebration of the Liturgy of the Hours: the *Paraklitiki,* for daily use, with its cycle of eight weeks that corresponded, rather arbitrarily, to the eight tones used in psalmody (the organization of this book was attributed to St. John Damascene); the *Triodion* for Lent and the *Pentekostarion* for the Easter season, which followed the tradition of Studios. In these offices hymnody played a predominant role, as in the Syro-Palestinian tradition: *troparia* (stanzas), either singly or grouped in Canons that were related to the scriptural Odes of the morning office.[27]

In the Eucharistic liturgy, now called the "Divine Liturgy," the originally Antiochene anaphora that goes under the name of St. John Chrysostom was used more and more frequently, while the much longer

23. N. Borgia, *Il commentario liturgico di San Germano . . . e la versione latina di Anastasio Bibliotecario* (Grottaferrata: Abbazia San Nilo, 1912).

24. R. Bornert, *Les commentaires byzantins de la Divine Liturgie du VIIe au XVe siècle* (Archives de l'Orient chrétien 9; Paris: Institut français d'études byzantines, 1966), 125-80.

25. J. Mateos, *Le Typikon de la Grande Eglise, ms. Sainte-Croix n° 40, Xe siècle* (OCA 165-66; Rome: Pontificio Istituto Orientale, 1962-63). Other important *Typika* that have been published in part or in whole: A. Dmitrievskij, *Opisanie liturgitseskich rukopisej I. Typika* (Kiev, 1895; reprinted: Hildesheim: Olms, 1965); M. Arranz, *Le Typikon du Monastère du Saint-Sauveur à Messine* (OCA 185; Rome: Pontificio Istituto Orientale, 1969).

26. PG 155:175-750; see Bornert (n. 24), 245-70.

27. See N. Egender's introductions in *La prière des Eglises de rite byzantin I. La prière des Heures. Horologion* (Chevetogne, 1975), and III. *Dimanche, Office selon les huit tons, Octoêchos* (Chevetogne, 1972); M. Arranz, "Office, II en Orient," *Dictionnaire de spiritualité* 11 (Paris: Beauchesne, 1982) 707-20; *The Church at Prayer* IV, 238-39.

Cappadocian anaphora of St. Basil was reserved for the Sundays of Lent and some major vigils.[28] More importantly, the ceremonial used in the celebration was continually expanded with elements derived from the ceremonial of the imperial palaces. These expansions affected chiefly the rites of preparation (*Prothesis*) and entrance as well as the Offertory procession, known as the "Great Entrance," which gradually became the most intensely emotional moment in the entire celebration.[29] The theological emphasis was placed on the invocation (*epiclesis*) of the Holy Spirit, who transforms the bread and wine and manifests the presence of the Body and Blood of Christ.[30]

The "mystery" aspect of the celebration was underscored by the introduction of the iconostasis that separates the sanctuary from the nave. The iconoclasm crisis and some later developments in hesychastic monastic spirituality favored this introduction; thus the symbolic character assigned to sensible realities, turning these into reflections and images (icons) of a suprasensible order that the liturgy shows forth "in mystery," led to a view of the Eucharistic celebration as the "descent of heaven to earth" and as an anticipation of the parousia. St. John Chrysostom had sketched out and prepared the way for this "mystery" conception of the liturgy in the Antiochene tradition; it would find its full flowering first in the normative form the Byzantine rite acquired during the Paleologue era in the *Rule* (*Diataxis*) of Patriarch Philotheos Kokkinos (1350-54), who had received his training in an Athos monastery,[31] and later on in Muscovite Russia.[32]

The ritual of the sacraments was less affected by the evolution just described; on the other hand, it was made cumbersome by the multiplication of prayers and especially of litanies (*ectenies*). Disagreements with

---

28. Text of the liturgy of St. John Chrysostom in Brightman 309-44 (old Greek text) and 355-99 (modern Greek text) or in Hänggi-Pahl 223-39. See A. Jacob, "La tradition manuscrite de la liturgie de saint Jean Chrysostome (VIIIe-XIIe s.)," in *Eucharisties d'Orient et d'Occident* 2 (LO 47; Paris: Cerf, 1970), 109-38; G. Wagner, *Der Ursprung der Chrysostomosliturgie* (LQF 59; Münster: Aschendorff, 1973). Text of the Greek liturgy of St. Basil in Brightman 309-44 (old text) and 400-11 (modern text) or in Hänggi-Pahl 230-43. See B. Capelle, "Les liturgies 'basiliennes' et saint Basile," an appendix in J. Doresse and E. Lanne, *Un témoin archaïque de la liturgie copte de saint Basile* (Bibliothèque du Muséon 47; Louvain, 1960).

29. R. F. Taft, *The Great Entrance* (OCA 200; Rome: Pontificio Istituto Orientale, 1975, 1978²).

30. See *The Church at Prayer* II, pp. 146-47.

31. Bornert (n. 24) 227-29. Nicholas Cabasilas, *Explication de la Divine Liturgie* (SC 4bis; Paris: Cerf, 1967²); *A Commentary on the Divine Liturgy*, trans. J. M. Hussey and P. A. McNulty (London: SPCK, 1960); and see Bornert 215-44.

32. A. Petrovski, "Histoire de la rédaction slave de la liturgie de saint Jean Chrysostome," in *Chrysostomika* (n. 6) 859-928.

the Latins and a concern to avoid Latinizing influences probably contributed to this conservatism. A comparison of the Byzantine rite with others, especially the Syrian and the Armenian, shows that in many instances the former has kept more of the ancient sobriety. This is especially true of the ritual for ordinations.[33]

In the Slavic world, the Union of Brest-Litovsk (1595) led to numerous Latinizing changes in the liturgy among the Ruthenians of Galicia and the Ukraine, who had accepted union with Rome. This was especially true of the external setting and ceremonial of the celebration and of devotional expansions of the festal calendar. In the Orthodox Church, the reform effected by Nikon, the Russian patriarch (1652–66), in order to make the books of his Church conform to those of the Patriarchate of Constantinople, brought in its train the schism (*raskol*) of the Old Believers (*Staroveries*), who down to our own time have kept the older Slavic usages and are thus often more faithful to the old Byzantine rite of the tenth to the twelfth centuries.[34]

d) *The Armenian Rite*

BIBLIOGRAPHY

F. C. Conybeare, *Rituale Armenorum* (Oxford: Clarendon Press, 1905).

P. Ferhat, A. Baumstark, and A. Rücker, "Denkmäler altarmenischer Liturgie," *OC*, ser. II, 1 (1911) 204–14; 3 (1913) 16–31; 7–8 (1918) 1–82; ser. III, 1 (1927) 149–57; 5 (1930) 56–79.

C. Renoux, "Liturgie arménienne et liturgie hiérosolymitaine," in *Liturgie de l'Eglise particulière et liturgie de l'Eglise universelle (Conférences Saint-Serge, 22ᵉ Semaine d'etudes liturgique)* (Bibliotheca EL, Subsidia 7; Rome: Edizioni liturgiche, 1976), 275–88.

Christianity was officially adopted as the national religion of Armenia at the beginning of the fourth century under the influence of St. Gregory the Illuminator (*Lussarovits*); the next century saw the creation of a national alphabet. The Kingdom of Armenia then organized its liturgy between 415 and 450, taking as its model the usages of Jerusalem. In fact,

---

33. The oldest known euchologion is in ms. Vatic. Barberini gr. 336; until the publication of the edition promised by A. Jacob, readers may use the description given by A. Strittmatter, "The 'Barberinum S. Marci' of Jacques Goar," *EL* 47 (1933) 329–67, who for published texts refers to various works but especially to J. Goar, *Euchologion sive Rituale Graecorum*, editions of 1647 and 1730 (the latter reprinted: Graz: Akademische Druck, 1960). Other euchologia are described or published in Dmitrievski (n. 25), II. *Euchologia* (Kiev, 1901; reprinted: Hildesheim: Olms, 1965); see A. Jacob, "Les euchologes du fonds Barberini grec de la Bibliothèque Vaticane," *Didaskalia* 4 (1974) 131–222.

34. C. Kucharek, *The Byzantine-Slav Liturgy of St. John Chrysostom* (Combermere, Ontario: Alleluia Press, 1971).

it is to the Armenian Lectionary compiled at that time and to the Georgian Canonarion of the seventh–ninth centuries that we owe our somewhat detailed knowledge of this ancient liturgy that is no longer used.[35] The books confirm the information supplied by the *Travel Journal* of Egeria, a pilgrim from the Pyrenees (381–84),[36] and by the contemporary catecheses that have come down under the name of St. Cyril.[37]

The work thus begun by Catholicos Sahak the Great (387–428)[38] subsequently underwent many transformations; at the present time, however, we know very little about this series of changes and therefore have difficulty in distinguishing what was primitive. Syrian influence seems to have played little part, but the same cannot be said of influence from the Byzantine Empire. There had always been a Hellenophile movement in Armenia, and it was especially strong between the seventh and the eleventh century, despite the fact that Armenia broke ecclesial communion with Byzantium soon after the Synod of Dwin (506), at which it rejected the Christology of Chalcedon and gave allegiance instead to the Council of Ephesus. After the Seljuk conquests of the eleventh century the little kingdom of Armenia, which reestablished itself in Cilicia in the course of two centuries, cultivated close ties with the Frankish principality of Antioch. At that period the liturgy took over numerous Latin usages, especially in the setting and ceremonial of the Eucharistic celebration. These aspects were accentuated during short periods of union with Rome, until finally the liturgy was almost completely Latinized among the Armenians of the Austro-Hungarian Empire and the region of Aleppo, who had kept or restored this union. The result is a complex liturgy that in its general character resembles the Byzantine liturgy but which is also clearly distinguished from the latter not only by Latinisms but also by original characteristics of its own.

The most noteworthy of these original traits is undoubtedly the Calendar, which is similar to that of the Assyro-Chaldeans and the Syrians; all three are based on groups of weeks of weeks (*hebdomades*), the feasts

---

35. A. Renoux has edited, translated, and commented on the Armenian lectionary, using especially the Armenian codex, Jerusalem 121: PO 35/1: *Introduction. Aux origines de la liturgie hiérosolymitaine, Lumières nouvelles,* and 36/2: *Edition comparée du texte et de deux autres manuscrits* (1969–71); the Georgian Canonarion has been published by M. Tarchnischvili, *Le Grand Lectionnaire de l'Eglise de Jérusalem* (CSCO 189 for text and 205 for Latin trans.; Louvain, 1959–60).

36. Egeria, *Journal de voyage (Itinéraire),* ed. P. Maraval (SC 296; Paris: Cerf, 1982); text alone in CCL 175, ed. A. Franceschini and R. Weber. ET: *Egeria's Travels,* trans. J. Wilkinson (London: SPCK, 1971).

37. See p. 25.

38. See A. Renoux, "Isaac le Grand," *Dictionnaire de spiritualité* 7 (Paris: Beauchesne, 1971) 2007–10.

of the Lord being celebrated on Sundays and those of the saints on set days of the week.

Another original trait is a rich repertory of hymns. The Armenian rite differs, however, from the Syrian and Byzantine rites in that here an ancient heritage, the origins and chronology of which are still uncertain, was enriched by compositions of such great medieval poets as St. Gregory of Narek (tenth century)[39] and Narses Shnorkhali ("the Kindly," 1102–73).

By and large, however, in the structure of its rites the Armenian liturgy still follows closely the traditions of Jerusalem and Constantinople. On the other hand, the setting of the celebration, the arrangement of the altar, and, above all, the liturgical vestments as well as some secondary rites (especially at ordinations) relate this liturgy to medieval Western usage.

§2. The Alexandrian Group

I. THE COPTIC RITE

BIBLIOGRAPHY

O. H. E. Burmester, *The Egyptian or Coptic Church. A Detailed Description of Her Liturgical Services* (Cairo: Société d'archéologie copte, 1967).

As noted earlier, the Alexandrian group is far from being a well-structured whole like the Syro-Antiochene group. At an early stage, probably about the middle of the seventh century, in the time of Coptic Patriarch Benjamin (626–55), the Alexandrian tradition was influenced by the Antiochene; the result was a reorganization of all liturgical structures according to the Syrian model and the elimination of all but a few traces of the original Alexandrian traditions. We have very little knowledge, in fact, of what these traditions were. Some elements of the baptismal ritual and, more important, the structure of the Eucharistic anaphora are almost our only means of discerning how much these liturgical traditions differed from the Antiochene type and how, on the contrary, they displayed undeniable analogies with the Roman liturgy. It was pointed out earlier[40] that the origin and nature of the collection known as the *Euchologion of Serapion* are too uncertain, and many of its formularies too different from what we know of elsewhere, to let it be taken as an authoritative witness to Alexandrian usage. The same must be said of the rituals for baptism

---

39. Gregory of Narek, *Le livre de Prières*, trans. I. Kechichian (SC 78; Paris: Cerf, 1961).
40. See pp. 25–26.

and the Eucharist which A. Baumstark unearthed in 1901 and which he thought went back to the sixth century.[41]

There are, however, enough witnesses to the Alexandrian Eucharistic anaphora to let us recognize its peculiarities and, in some degree, to follow its development down to its definitive recensions. These include the Greek text known as the Anaphora of St. Mark; it has been transmitted chiefly in manuscripts of Melkite origin, which show to a greater or lesser extent the influence of Jerusalem and Constantinople.[42] The Coptic recension, known as the Anaphora of St. Cyril, shows some slight divergences from the Greek recensions.[43] This anaphora has for practical purposes fallen into disuse, since it had come to be reserved for the Sundays of Lent. For a long time now, the text in most regular use has been the Anaphora of St. Basil, which is of Cappadocian origin;[44] it is more sober than the Byzantine recension and may represent an older recension. The Anaphora of St. Gregory [of Nazianzus] the Theologian, which is likewise of Cappadocian origin and is used on feasts of the Lord, is exceptionally rich in doctrine and has the peculiarity of being addressed not to the Father but to the Son.[45]

Apart from the anaphora, the Coptic liturgical celebration is distinguished above all by the room allotted to rites of reconciliation with their great absolutions: that "of the Son" at the beginning of the celebration, immediately before the presentation of the gifts, and that "of the Father" before communion.

In addition, every Eucharistic celebration must be preceded by a double service of praise, intercession, and reconciliation: the "Evening Incense" and the "Morning Incense," in which, as the names indicate, incensations play an important part.[46] These services, while related to the *sēdrē* of the Syrian liturgy, differ from the latter in their structure and their more direct reference back to the services of the Mosaic liturgy (Exod 30:7-9). It is therefore possible to see in them a form of daily office that has been introduced into the monastic formularies making up the "Annual Psalmody";

---

41. A. Baumstark, "Eine aegyptische Mess- und Taufliturgie vermutlich des VI. Jahrhunderts," *OC* 1 (1901) 1-45.

42. R. G. Coquin, "L'anaphore alexandrine de saint Marc," *Le Muséon* 82 (1969) 307-56; C. H. Roberts and B. Capelle, *An Early Euchologium, the Der-Balizeh Papyrus* (Bibliothèque du Muséon 23; Louvain, 1949).

43. Brightmann 144-88 (English trans.); Hänggi-Pahl 134-39 (Latin trans.).

44. J. Doresse and E. Lanne, *Un témoin archaïque de la liturgie copte de saint Basile*, with an Appendix, "Les liturgies 'basiliennes' et saint Basile," by B. Capelle (Bibliothèque du Muséon 47; Louvain, 1960).

45. E. Hammerschmidt, *Die koptische Gregoriosanaphora* (Berliner byzantinische Arbeiten 8; Berlin: Akademie Verlag, 1957).

46. J. Marquess of Bute, *The Coptic Morning Service for the Lord's Day* (London, 1908²).

this last is itself closely connected with the specifically monastic form of daily psalmody found in the Horologion, which contains, besides the Psalter, only readings from the gospel and some troparia and prayers.[47] The Coptic repertory of hymns is in any case rather limited; its most remarkable part is the *Theotokia*, which are doubtless of Syro-Mesopotamian origin[48] and have won a place in the morning office, especially during the time of preparation for Christmas (month of Koiak).[49]

II. THE ETHIOPIAN RITE

The Ethiopian rite in the form now known to us (that is, from the fifteenth century on) is closely modeled on the Coptic rite. It takes a very large number of its components from this rite but adds rites and formularies of various origins, including some that are native.

The close relations that existed from the outset between the young Church in the Kingdom of Axum and the Patriarchate of Alexandria, were strengthened in the course of time, especially after the "Solomonic Restoration" of 1271. But it must not be forgotten that the first evangelizers of the country, St. Frumentius (known in Ethiopia as Abba Salama) and his brother Edesius (*ca.* 330), were Syrians, as were, doubtless, the "nine Roman saints" of two centuries later; the latter were probably monks fleeing from Justinian's persecution of views regarded as "Monophysite."

It seems certain that *The Testament of Our Lord Jesus Christ* was translated into Ge'ez back in that early period; its euchology (known precisely as *Kidan*, "testament") forms even today the nucleus of the daily office in Ethiopia, and its Eucharistic Prayer became the Anaphora of the Lord, which is still used. It is doubtful, on the other hand, that the *Apostolic*

---

47. M. Brogi, *La santa salmodia annuale della Chiesa copta* (Studia orientalia christiana, Aegyptiaca; Cairo: Centro francescano di studi orientali cristiani, 1962); H. Quecke, *Untersuchungen zum koptischen Stundengebet* (Publications de l'Institut orientaliste de Louvain 3; Louvain, 1970); *The Horologion of the Egyptian Church. Coptic and Arabaic Text from a Mediaeval Manuscript*, trans. and annot. O. H. E. Burmester (Studia orientalia christiana, Aegyptiaca; Cairo: Centro francescano di studi orientali cristiani, 1973).

48. E. O'Leary de Lacy, *The Daily Office and the Theotokia of the Coptic Church* (London, 1911).

49. For the Coptic calendar of saints see M. de Fenoyl, *Le sanctoral copte* (Recherches publiées sous la direction de l'Institut de Lettres orientales de Beyrouth 15; Beirut: Impr. catholique, 1960). For the Pontifical: E. Lanne, *Le grand Euchologe du Monastère Blanc* (PO 28/2; 1958); *idem*, "Les ordinations dans le rite copte, leurs relations avec les Constitutions apostoliques et la Tradition d'Hippolyte," *OS* 5 (1960) 81–106 (the ritual of ordinations was published, with a mediocre commentary, by V. Ermoni in *Revue de l'Orient chrétien* 3 [1899] 31–38, 191–99, 282–91, 425–34; 4 [1899] 104–15, 416–27, 591–604; 5 [1900] 247–53). For the Ritual: R. M. Wooley, *Coptic Offices* (London: SPCK, 1930). For the lectionary: V. Zanetti, "Premières recherches sur les lectionaires coptes," *EL* 98 (1984) 3–34.

Tradition became known otherwise than through the Arabic translation of the Coptic *Sinodos*.[50] This would mean that only in the fourteenth century at the earliest could the Ethiopian liturgy have adapted the Eucharistic Prayer of Hippolytus and turned it into the Ethiopian Anaphora of the Apostles. Other anaphoras come from various other sources, either by way of Jerusalem or by way of Egypt, where the fragments published by Dom Emmanuel Lanne[51] show a number of them to have been in use. Some seem to be of Syrian origin; some are typically Ethiopian compositions and are at times surprising in their structure, style, and inspiration.[52] They thus have something in common with the abundant hymnography, so tolerant of improvisation, that is produced by the *dabtara*, or singers and scribes, who form a characteristic class in the Ethiopian Church.[53]

The Ritual, for its part, remains closely dependent on the Coptic Ritual,[54] probably because until the second third of the twentieth century there was no native episcopate. But the rites of Christian initiation and of penance have been extensively enriched with elements borrowed from the most varied traditions, including those of the Latin West and Armenia. This happened because Ethiopian monastic centers in Jerusalem played as important a cultural and liturgical role as the monastic centers of Upper Egypt.

---

50. G. Horner, *The Statutes of the Apostles or Canones ecclesiastici* (London: William & Norgate, 1904); see also n. 18, p. 26.

51. Lanne, *Le grand Euchologe* (n. 49), 273–79.

52. E. Hammerschmidt, *Studies in the Ethiopic Anaphoras* (Berliner byzantinische Arbeiten 25; Berlin: Akademie Verlag, 1961); S. Euringer, "Die beiden gewöhnlichen äthiopischen Gregoriusanaphoren," *Orientalia christiana* 30 (1933) 63–142; *idem*, "Die äthiopischen Anaphoren des hl. Evangelisten Johannes . . . und des hl. Jacobus von Sarug," *ibid.*, 33 (1934) 1–122; *idem*, "Die äthiopische Anaphora des hl. Basilius," *ibid.*, 36 (1934) 135–223.

53. A. Van Lantschoot, *Horologion aethiopicum iuxta recensionem Alexandrinam copticam* (Vatican Press, 1940); B. Velat, *Etudes sur le Me'eraf, commun de l'office divin éthiopien* (PO 33; 1966); *idem*, *Me'eraf, commun de l'office* (text: PO 34/1-2; 1966); *idem*, *Soma Deggua, Antiphonaire du Carême* (text and trans.: PO 32).

54. S. Grébaut, "L'ordre du baptême et de la confirmation dans l'Eglise éthiopienne," *Revue de l'Orient chrétien* 26 (1927-28) 105–89; M. Chaine, "Le Rituel éthiopien," *Bessarione* 29 (1913) 38–71, 249–83, 420–51; 30 (1914) 11–41.

History of the Liturgy in the West to the Council of Trent

P. M. Gy

BIBLIOGRAPHY FOR A SURVEY

B. Neunheuser, *Storia della liturgia attraverso le epoche culturali* (Bibliotheca EL, Subsidia 11; Rome: Edizioni liturgiche, 1977).

E. Cattaneo, *Il culto cristiano in Occidente. Note storiche* (Bibliotheca EL, Subsidia 13; Rome: Edizioni liturgiche, 1978).

H. A. J. Wegman, *Christian Liturgy in East and West. A Study Guide to Liturgical History*, trans. G. W. Lathrop (New York: Pueblo, 1985).

§1. From the Fifth to the Eighth Century

BIBLIOGRAPHY

C. Vogel, *Introduction aux sources de l'histoire du culte chrétien au moyen âge* (Spoleto: Centro italiano di Studi sull'alto medioevo, 1966³; reprinted, 1975).

K. Gamber, *Codices liturgici latini antiquiores* (2 vols.; Spicilegii Friburgensis subsidia 1; Freiburg, Switz.: Universitätsverlag, 1968²).

By the middle of the fourth century at the latest, the liturgies of the West were being celebrated in Latin rather than Greek. They would remain in Latin until the twentieth century, except for Greek elements that made an appearance on certain occasions and for the use of Glagolitic liturgical books (books translated from Latin into Slavonic) in some Slavic countries that followed the Latin rite.[1]

---

1. See the bibliography on this subject in *LMD* no. 53 (1958) 37–38.

During the period from the fourth to the eighth century, the Latin liturgies differed from region to region, and the liturgy of Rome did not yet have the predominance it would enjoy in later times when other local liturgies would become quasi-exceptions to the rule. The Fathers—St. Augustine and St. Gregory the Great, for example[2]—were aware of liturgical diversity and did not see it as detracting from the unity of faith. Moreover, at Rome itself and probably elsewhere as well, the liturgy displayed differences from church to church.[3]

In addition to regional diversity, which was accompanied by many liturgical exchanges among the regions and even with the East (Jerusalem by reason of pilgrimages, and Constantinople, especially because of Greek influences at work in the West), this period saw the composition of many liturgical texts, as well as what might be called nuanced degrees of ecclesiality in the various celebrations.

In the period before the fourth century, either the celebrating bishop or priest usually improvised the liturgical prayers in accordance with traditional patterns. For example, the Eucharistic Prayer and the prayers for ordination in the *Apostolic Tradition* are only models meant to help celebrants in their improvisations. From the fourth to the seventh century, however, compositions multiplied[4] and quickly formed a heritage that was passed on in the Church and gave form to its prayer. This was already the case in the time of St. Ambrose as regards the Eucharistic Prayer of Rome and Milan, even if it is difficult to say whether the text cited by Ambrose[5] is an earlier form of the Roman Eucharistic Prayer or simply a Milanese variant of the latter. By the beginning of the seventh century new compositions became much less frequent (at least for the prayers of the Mass), first at Rome and then, a little later, in Spain.

During this period forms of prayer are distinguished less as liturgical or nonliturgical than by degrees of ecclesiality, the highest degree being the prayer of the local Church when gathered together, especially for Sunday Mass and Christian initiation, or (but the degree of ecclesiality is al-

2. St. Augustine, *Ep.* 54 to Januarius (PL 32:199–203); St. Gregory the Great, *Ep.* I, 41 to Leander of Seville (MGH *Epistulae* I, 57). See P. Meyvaert, "Diversity within Unity, A Gregorian Theme," *Heythrop Journal* 4 (1963) 141–62.

3. A. Chavasse, *Le Sacramentaire Gélasien* (Paris-Tournai: Desclée, 1958), 77–86, 518–19.

4. St. Augustine criticizes the use of poorly composed prayers in his *De baptismo contra Donatistas* VI, 25 (ed. M. Petschenig in CSEL 51:323; PL 43:213–14); see his *De catechizandis rudibus* 9, 13. Various African councils require that the text of prayers be approved; *e.g.,* Council of Carthage (397), can. 23 (ed. C. Munier in CCL 149:333; 1974). See A. Bouley, *From Freedom to Formula. The Evolution of the Eucharistic Prayer from Oral Improvisation to Written Texts* (The Catholic University of America Studies in Christian Antiquity 21; Washington, D.C.: The Catholic University of America, 1981).

5. Ambrose, *De sacramentis* IV, 5, 21–27 (ed. B. Botte; SC 25bis:114–16).

ready less) for the two principal Hours of the Divine Office. More limited celebrations that involve only a group or a family or a monastery (marriages, funerals; the monastic office) are on a lower rung of the ladder of ecclesiality.

I. THE ROMAN RITE

BIBLIOGRAPHY

> *Sacramentarium Veronense*, ed. L. C. Mohlberg (REDMF 1; Rome: Herder, 1956).
> *Liber sacramentorum Romanae Aeclesiae ordinis anni circuli* (The Old Gelasian Sacramentary), ed. L. C. Mohlberg (REDMF 4; Rome: Herder, 1960).
> *Le Sacramentaire Grégorien*, ed. J. Deshusses (3 vols.; Spicilegium Friburgense 16, 24, 38; Fribourg: Editions universitaires, 1971–82).
> T. Klauser, *Das römische Capitulare evangeliorum* (LQF 28; Münster: Aschendorff, 1935).
> M. Andrieu, *Les Ordines Romani du haut moyen âge* (5 vols.; Spicilegium sacrum Lovaniense 11, 23, 24, 28, 29; Louvain, 1931–61).
> J. Deshusses and B. Darragon, *Concordances et tableaux pour l'étude des grands sacramentaires* (Spicilegii Friburgensis subsidia 9–14; Fribourg: Editions universitaires, 1982–83).

The fourth century saw the multiplication, first of indirect evidence regarding the Western liturgy, and then of texts for these liturgies. The Roman rite, which in the Carolingian period would become the liturgy of the greater part of the West, was at this time still the liturgy only of the city of Rome, but it already exerted an extensive influence in Italy and beyond, as can be seen from the catecheses of St. Ambrose in the *De sacramentis*[6] and from a number of papal letters, for example, those of Innocent I to Bishop Decentius of Gubbio (416)[7] or Vigilius to Profuturus of Braga.[8]

The chief sources for the Roman liturgy of this period are the sermons of St. Leo I (440–461) and the three sacramentaries usually known as the Leonine, the Gelasian, and the Gregorian. The sermons of St. Leo I show that the main seasons and feasts of the liturgical year were already in place, except for the season of Advent, which would make its appearance in Rome in the second half of the sixth century.[9]

Sacramentaries were the books that, down to the Carolingian period and even beyond, supplied bishops and priests with the prayers they

---

6. *De sacramentis* III, 1, 5 (SC 25bis:94).

7. Ed. R. Cabié (Louvain: Publications universitaires, 1973).

8. PL 84:829–32. See the study of J. O. Bragança, "A carta do Papa Vigilio ao Arcebispo Profuturo de Braga," *Bracara Augusta* 21 (1968).

9. See *The Church at Prayer* IV, 92.

needed for the Mass and other liturgical actions. Other books contained the readings for Mass or Office, and still others (the Gradual, the Antiphonary) the texts to be sung.

The book known as the Leonine Sacramentary (because it was thought to have had St. Leo for its author in whole or in part) or the Verona Sacramentary (after the library in which it was preserved) is not yet organized according to the course of the liturgical year. It is a collection (based perhaps on originally independent booklets) of liturgical formularies that are classified according to the days of the civil year; its first part, however, from January to April, is mutilated. With a greater or less degree of probability, historians have attributed various of its formularies to popes of the fifth century or the first half of the sixth, especially St. Leo, St. Gelasius I (492–96), and Vigilius (537–55).[10]

The Sacramentary known as the Gelasian (its actual title is *Liber sacramentorum Romanae Aeclesiae ordinis anni circuli*), or Old Gelasian (to distinguish it from a later group of Frankish Gelasians of the second half of the eighth century) has been preserved in a single manuscript (Vatican *Reginenis lat. 316*), which was copied in Frankish territory in about the middle of the eighth century. It begins with the vigil of Christmas and contains texts for the entire year; the Sanctoral is separated from the temporal. A. Chavasse hypothesizes that apart from a small number of Frankish interpolations, the book represents the liturgy of a presbyteral church of seventh-century Rome, but that it is possible to distinguish in it elements of the liturgy of pre-Gregorian, sixth-century Rome.[11] Other liturgists reject this hypothesis and consider the Sacramentary to have been composed in Frankish territory.[12]

The Gregorian Sacramentary is known from a copy sent by Pope Hadrian I to Charlemagne between 784 and 791. The title of the book attributes it to St. Gregory. A comparison of the Gregorian *Hadrianum* with two slightly different manuscripts preserved at Padua and Trent shows that the Sacramentary was compiled at Rome in about 630. It contains at least eighty prayers that can be attributed with certainty or high probability to St. Gregory the Great (590–604).[13]

---

10. The Mohlberg edition lists all the attributions previously proposed. Add to the list: Gélase Ier, *Lettre contre les Lupercales et dix-huit messes du Sacramentaire Léonien*, ed. G. Pomarès (SC 65; Paris: Cerf, 1959).

11. See n. 3, p. 46.

12. See above all C. Coebergh, "Le sacramentaire gélasien ancien. Une compilation de clercs romanisants du VIIe siècle," *ALW* 7 (1961) 45–88.

13. H. Ashworth, "The Liturgical Prayers of St. Gregory the Great," *Traditio* 15 (1959) 107–61; *idem*, "Further Parallels to the *Hadrianum* from St. Gregory the Great's Commentary on the First Book of Kings," *ibid.*, 16 (1960) 364–73.

The Roman Eucharistic Prayer was distinguished both from its Gallican and Spanish counterparts and from the Eastern anaphoras in that it was the only anaphora used (whereas the Eastern liturgies had a number of anaphoras at their disposal) and that it varied only in the Preface and in certain paragraphs used on particular days. In Gaul and Spain all parts of the Eucharistic Prayer could vary.

Almost all the prefaces and prayers of the Roman Mass were probably composed during the period that ran approximately from St. Leo to St. Gregory. Their style, characterized by terseness and a rhythm based on the *cursus*, is often so close to that of St. Leo that he must have either created it or strongly influenced it. Their content bears the mark of the Christology of St. Leo and of Chalcedon (major feasts) and the teaching of St. Augustine on grace (Sunday Masses of Ordinary Time). With St. Gregory the prayers take on a more interior and monastic cast. This shift in emphasis shows in, for example, the liturgy of Easter and of the preparation for Easter; the baptismal aspect of these liturgies had become less important since the sixth century when, pagans having probably disappeared completely, the practice of infant baptism became universal and the prebaptismal scrutinies, which had formerly taken place on the Sundays of Lent, were assigned instead to weekdays.[14]

Apart from the texts for the liturgy the sacramentaries contain only brief instructions on how the liturgy is to be celebrated. These instructions are fuller, both for the Mass and for the other parts of the liturgy, in the *Ordines Romani* that were widespread outside of Rome; M. Andrieu, principal editor of these documents, has attempted to distinguish in them the part that is purely Roman and the part that represents Frankish adaptation.

Analysis of later manuscripts other than the sacramentaries and *Ordines* has enabled scholars to determine what the readings and sung parts of the Mass were, at least from the seventh century on. Further information on the Roman liturgy comes from the letters of the popes as well as from the biographical notices of them in the *Liber pontificalis*[15] and from the *Liber diurnus* or book of formulas used by the papal chancery.[16]

In the early Roman liturgy the sung texts of Mass and Office were taken almost exclusively from the Bible, and the only hymns were the *Gloria in excelsis* and, probably, the *Te Deum*. In the eighth century, nonbiblical sung texts, in many instances translations from Greek, made their appearance, especially in the Divine Office; at times these texts were dramatic

---

14. A. Chavasse, "Le carême romain et les scrutins prébaptismaux avant le IXe siècle," *RechSR* 35 (1948) 325–81.

15. Ed. L. Duchesne, revised by C. Vogel (3 vols.: Paris: E. de Boccard, 1955–57).

16. Ed. H. Foerster (Berne: Francke, 1958).

in style (responses in the nocturns of Holy Week). In the seventh and eighth centuries the celebrations of saints' feasts ceased to be limited to the place of their burial, as in the past. This was also the period when many Greek monks resided in Rome and when the Roman liturgy took over from the Greeks the song at the fraction of the host (the *Agnus Dei*), the adoration of the cross, the litany of the saints, and the principal Marian feasts.[17]

Beginning in the time of St. Gregory, who had himself been a monk before becoming pope, monasteries multiplied around the principal Roman basilicas. The Divine Office celebrated there was more highly developed than that of the Benedictine Rule but was influenced by the latter at certain points; the Rule, however, was itself dependent on the earlier Roman Office, at least for Lauds and Vespers.[18]

At this period and even as late as the eleventh century, the type of singing used in the Roman liturgy was what the historians call "old Roman" to distinguish it from Gregorian chant, which seems to have been a Frankish adaptation of it.[19]

II. THE AMBROSIAN RITE

BIBLIOGRAPHY

Il Sacramentario di Ariberto, ed. A. Paredi in *Miscellanea Adriano Bernareggi* (Bergamo: Opera Barbarigo, 1958), 329–488.

Sacramentarium Bergomense, ed. A. Paredi (Monumenta Bergomensia 6; Bergamo, 1962).

Das ambrosianische Sakramentar D 3-3 aus dem mailändischen Metropolitankapitel, ed. J. Frei (LQF 56; Münster: Aschendorff, 1974).

Das ambrosianische Sakramentar von Biasca, ed. O. Heiming (LQF 51; Münster: Aschendorff, 1969).

Sacramentarium triplex, ed. O. Heiming (LQF 49; Münster: Aschendorff, 1968).

P. Borella, *Il rito ambrosiano* (Brescia: Morcelliana, 1964).

It is probable that in Northern Italy there was a great deal of liturgical variety before the Carolingian period, and even afterwards at Aquileia (whose metropolitans had the title of patriarch from the sixth century on), Ravenna,[20] and Milan. Of these various liturgies the only one that has

---

17. See *The Church at Prayer* IV, 134–36.

18. Apart from the hymnal, the liturgical books of the Benedictine Office were later adaptations of local Roman books to the Rule. There also exist some Monte Cassino *Ordines* of the eighth century, after the monastery, which the Lombards had destroyed in about 585, had been restored in 720. See K. Hallinger, *Initia consuetudinis benedictinae* (Corpus consuetudinum monasticarum 1; Siegburg: F. Schmitt, 1963), 93–175.

19. See p. 169.

20. For Aquileia see the bibliography in E. Cattaneo, *Il culto cristiano in Occidente. Note storiche* (Bibliotheca EL Subsidia 13; Rome: Edizioni liturgiche 1978), 173–75. For Ra-

remained in use down to our time is the Ambrosian, which is used in Milan (and was formerly used in neighboring Churches as well). At the end of the fourth century, St. Ambrose, who had succeeded Bishop Auxentius, an Arian from Cappadocia, declared that he followed the Roman liturgy but also retained a degree of freedom in regard to it.[21] For example, he took from the East the antiphonal singing of the psalms, and he himself composed a new kind of hymn; among those attributed to him four are certainly authentic, and a number of others are probably authentic.[22]

The Ambrosian liturgical documents that have survived are almost all Carolingian or post-Carolingian and show themselves heavily influenced by the Roman or Romano-Frankish sacramentaries. Only a part of their euchology (especially the prefaces) is properly Ambrosian. There are points showing contacts with the East (some sung texts) and with the Gallican liturgy, although these cannot be interpreted as signs that the Ambrosian liturgy originated in the East (as M. Duchesne thought) or that Milan belonged to the same liturgical family as Gaul.

The Ambrosian liturgy received the mark of St. Charles Borromeo in the sixteenth century and of several great scholars in the nineteenth and twentieth. The Missal and Breviary were revised after Vatican II.

III. THE RITE OF GAUL

BIBLIOGRAPHY

> *Missale Gallican Vetus*, ed. L. C. Mohlberg, L. Eisenhöfer, and P. Siffrin (REDMF 3; Rome: Herder, 1958).
>
> *Missale Gothicum*, ed. L. C. Mohlberg (REDMF 5; Rome: Herder, 1961).
>
> P. Salmon, *Le Lectionnaire de Luxeuil* (2 vols.; Collectanea biblica 7 and 9; Rome: Abbaye de St.-Jérôme, 1944–53).
>
> H. Beck, *The Pastoral Care of Souls in South-East France during the Sixth Century* (Analecta Gregoriana 51; Rome: Pontificia Università Gregoriana, 1950).
>
> E. Griffe, "Aux origines de la liturgie gallicane," *Bulletin de littérature ecclésiastique* 52 (1941) 17–43.

---

venna: A. Chavasse, "L'oeuvre littéraire de Maximilien de Ravenne," *EL* 74 (1960) 115–20; F. Sottocornola, *L'anno liturgico nei sermoni di San Pietro Crisologo. Ricerca storico-critica sulla liturgia di Ravenna antica* (Studia Ravennatensia 1; Cesena, 1973). For the other Churches of Italy see the extensive bibliography in Cattaneo 176–83. — The liturgy of Benevento has been the subject of important publications of R. J. Hesbert: *La tradition bénéventaine dans la tradition manuscrite* (Paléographie musicale 14; Tournai: Desclée, 1931); *Graduel de Bénévent* (Paléographie musicale 15; Berne: P. Lang, 1971); "Les dimanches de carême dans les manuscrits romano-bénéventains," *EL* 48 (1934) 198–222; B. Baroffio, "Liturgie im beneventanischen Raum," in *Geschichte der katholischen Kirchenmusik* 1 (Kassel, 1972), 204–8.

21. See n. 6, p. 47.

22. See P. Borella, *Il Rito ambrosiano* (Brescia: Morcelliana, 1964), 55–56. The basic study is still that of L. Biraghi, *Inni sinceri e carmi di S. Ambrogio* (Milan, 1840), but the question deserves to be examined anew.

We know little about the liturgy of Gaul prior to its replacement by the Roman liturgy in the second half of the eighth century. This liturgy was less fully developed than that of Rome or Spain, and the few documents that have survived are already replete with Roman contributions. Almost all of these documents come from the same region (Kingdom of Burgundy) and give us no knowledge of what this liturgy was like elsewhere. The sermons of St. Caesarius of Arles († 542), the writings of St. Gregory of Tours († 594), and the Merovingian Councils provide some scattered details; in addition, the *Explanation of the Gallican Liturgy* of Pseudo-Germanus of Paris, written about 600 (after the *Dialogues* of St. Gregory and before the *De ecclesiasticis officiis* of St. Isidore of Seville, and not after the latter, as Wilmart thought[23]), has a twofold value for us: it shows that the liturgy of Gaul was subject to strong Eastern (especially Syrian) influences,[24] and it is the first example in the West of an allegorical interpretation of the liturgy.

In Gaul, and in Spain as well, not only the Preface but the parts of the Eucharistic Prayer that preceded and followed the words of consecration could vary.[25] Generally speaking, from a literary point of view the prayers of this rite were more prolix than those of Rome; from a theological point of view, they reflected to a greater extent the reaction to Arianism.

IV. THE HISPANIC OR MOZARABIC RITE

BIBLIOGRAPHY

    Oracional visigótico, ed. J. Vives (Monumenta Hispaniae sacra, Serie liturgica 1; Barcelona, 1946).

    Liber ordinum, ed. M. Férotin (Monumenta Ecclesiae liturgica 5; Paris: Firmin-Didot, 1904).

    Liber mozarabicus sacramentorum, ed. M. Férotin (Monumenta Ecclesiae sacra 6; Paris: Firmin-Didot, 1912).

    Liber commicus, ed. J. Pérez de Urbel and A. González (2 vols.; Monumenta Hispaniae sacra, Serie liturgica 2-3; Madrid, 1950–55).

    Antifonario de la catedral de León, ed. L. Brou and J. Vives (2 vols.; Monumenta Hispaniae sacra, Serie liturgica 5; Barcelona-Madrid, 1953–59).

---

23. *Expositio antiquae liturgiae gallicanae*, ed. E. C. Ratcliff (HBS 98; 1971). On its temporal precedence over Isidore: A. Van der Mensbrugghe, "L'*Expositio missae gallicanae* est-elle de S. Germain de Paris?" *Messager de l'Exarchat du Patriarche russe en Europe occidentale* 8 (1959) 217–49; *idem*, "Pseudo-Germanus Reconsidered," in *Studia Patristica* 5 (TU 80; Berlin, 1962), 171–84. On its independence of St. Gregory the Great: A. Gaudel, "Le problème de l'authenticité des lettres attribuées à S. Germain de Paris," *RevSR* 7 (1927) 298–99.

24. J. Quasten, "Oriental Influence in the Gallican Liturgy," *Traditio* 1 (1943) 50–78.

25. J. Pinell, "Anámnesis y epíclesis en el antiguo rito galicano," *Didaskalia* 4 (1974) 3–130.

M. S. Gros, "Estado actual de los estudios sobre la liturgia hispanica," *Phase* 16 (1976) 227–41.

J. Pinell, "Liturgia hispánica," *Diccionario de historia eclesiástica de España* 2 (Madrid, 1972) 1303–20 (extensive bibliography).

_____, "La liturgia ispanica," in *Anàmnesis* 2 (Turin: Marietti, 1978), 70–78, 190–201.

_____, *Liber missarum de Toledo* 2 (Toledo: Instituto de estudios visigótico-mozárabes, 1983). See "Introductión: Los manuscritos visigóticos," XVII–XXV.

The Spanish rite (often called the Mozarabic rite), which in the beginning was not clearly distinct from the rite of Gaul, made its way north of the Pyrenees in the Visigothic period. The seventh century was the period of its greatest euchological creativity. The rite was eventually suppressed at the urging of Popes Alexander II and Gregory VII (1067–80), on the grounds that it was doctrinally shaky (adoptianism) and that it strayed from Roman liturgical unity. But after Toledo was recaptured from the Arabs (1085), the Christians of that city, known as Mozarabs, won the continuance of the rite in their parishes, and it is still followed in a chapel of the Cathedral of Toledo. Despite the desire shown by the Fourth Council of Toledo (633) for liturgical unity in the Visigothic kingdom, a degree of diversity among the provinces remained, and Dom J. Pinell has distinguished in the Spanish liturgical manuscripts two partially different traditions, one of which in his opinion was Toledan (tradition A) and the other, more archaic, perhaps originated in Seville (tradition B).[26]

In the Spanish rite, as in the Gallican, all parts of the Eucharistic Prayer were variable. Generally speaking, the presidential prayers (often addressed to Christ) are lengthier than at Rome and display a very mannered literary form.

The Divine Office of this rite maintained, more clearly than other rites, the distinction between the Hours *ad matutinum* and *ad vesperum*, which were meant for the ecclesial community (the cathedral Office), and monastic extensions of the Office. On the other hand, the festive Office showed an increasing predominance of antiphons over psalms, the latter being reduced to one or two verses. The color and tone proper to the principal liturgical seasons were heavily emphasized. In the Sanctoral, the feast of December 18 was the only Marian feast until the ninth century, and there were many feasts of Spanish martyrs.

The Spanish liturgical books contain some texts borrowed from the Roman sacramentaries. On the other hand, some Spanish prayers and hymns made their way into the Roman liturgy in the Carolingian period.

---

26. J. Pinell, "El problema de las dos tradiciones del antiguo rito hispánico," in *Liturgia y música mozárabes* (Instituto de estudios visigótico-mozárabes de san Eugenio, ser. D., n. 1; Toledo, 1979), 3–44.

The work of St. Isidore of Seville († 636) is important not only for our knowledge of the Spanish liturgy but also and above all for its influence on liturgical ideas until the end of the Middle Ages.[27]

§2. From the Carolingian Period to St. Gregory VII

BIBLIOGRAPHY

> *Liber sacramentorum Gellonensis*, ed. A. Dumas and J. Deshusses (2 vols.; CCL 159 and 159A; Turnhout: Brepols, 1981).
> *Le Sacramentaire grégorien*, ed. J. Deshusses (3 vols.; Spicilegium Friburgense 16, 24, 28; Fribourg: Editions universitaires, 1971–82).
> C. Vogel and R. Elze, *Le Pontifical romano-germanique du dixième siècle* (3 vols.; ST 226–27, 269; Vatican City, 1963–72).
> R.-J. Hesbert, *Corpus antiphonalium officii* (REDMF 7–12; Rome: Herder, 1963–79).
> T. Klauser, "Die liturgischen Austauschbeziehungen zwischen der römischen und der fränkisch-deutschen Kirche vom achten bis zum elften Jahrhundert," *Historisches Jahrbuch* 53 (1933) 169–89; reprinted in T. Klauser, *Gesammelte Arbeiten* (Münster: Aschendorff, 1974), 139–54.
> C. Vogel, "Les échanges liturgiques entre Rome et les pays francs jusqu'à l'époque de Charlemagne," *Settimana di studio del Centro italiano di studi sull'alto medioevo* 7 (Spoleto, 1960), 185–295.
> J. Deshusses, "Les sacramentaires, état actuel de la recherche," *ALW* 24 (1982) 19–46.

When Charlemagne decreed that the Roman liturgical books should replace those hitherto used in the Frankish kingdom, his action simply brought to term a movement already under way. This had begun with numerous borrowings by Gallican books from the Roman liturgy and had continued under Pepin the Short with the introduction of Roman chant at Metz (St. Chrodegang) and the composition in Frankish territory of the mid-eighth-century Gelasian Sacramentary, which combined the Old Gelasian, the Gregorian, and some Gallican prayers.[27a]

---

27. On the Spanish liturgy see also Ildefonsus of Toledo, *Liber de cognitione baptismi* (PL 96:111–72). — On the liturgy in Africa we have a good deal of information from St. Augustine (see W. Rötzer, *Des heiligen Augustinus Schriften als liturgiegeschichtliche Quelle* [Munich: Hueber, 1930]), but almost no texts except for a fifth century series of psalter collects (A. Wilmart and L. Brou, *The Psalter Collects* [HBS 83; 1949], 72–111). — See C. Mohrmann, *Etudes sur le latin des chrétiens* III (Rome: Edizioni di storia e letteratura, 1955), 245–63. For the liturgy of the Celtic Church we have a few documents, the most important being the Stowe Missal, ed. G. F. Warner (HBS 31; 1915). These documents seem to be made up of eclectic borrowings.

27a. See especially: the Sacramentary of Gellone, ed. A. Dumas and J. Deshusses, 1981 (CCL 169–169a); Sacramentary of Autun (Phillipps 1667), ed. O. Heiming, 1984 (CCL 169c); Sacramentary of Saint Gall, 2nd ed. L. C. Mohlberg, 1939 (LQF 1–2); Sacramentary of Rheinau, ed. A. Hänggi and A. Schönherr, 1970 (Spicilegium Friburgense 15); etc.; see A. Chavasse, *Le sacramentaire dans le groupe dit "Gélasien du VIIIᵉ siècle" . . .* , Steenbrugge, S. Petersabdij, 1984, 2 vols.

But the papal sacramentary that Hadrian sent to France was not completely representative of the Roman liturgy nor, on the other hand, did it suffice to meet the new devotional needs felt in the Frankish territories. It therefore received various supplements, the most important being authored by a Visigoth, St. Benedict of Aniane (and not by Alcuin, as used to be thought),[28] who drew upon the eighth-century Gelasian and occasionally upon Spanish sources as well. Benedict was also commissioned by Emperor Louis the Pious to reform monastic life on the basis of the Benedictine Rule. In addition to Benedict of Aniane, and before him, the Englishman Alcuin exerted a profound influence, especially by the new emphases that he introduced into the liturgy and spirituality (place given to penance; feast of All Saints; devotion to the Trinity, the cross, and the angels). Especially to be noted are the votive Masses and private prayers that he either composed or introduced from British sources.[29]

Once the empire had been unified liturgically by use of a single Romano-Frankish liturgy, the center of vitality for the Roman liturgy in the next few centuries was to be found no longer at Rome but wherever the imperial court of the Carolingians and later the Ottonians resided and in the great Frankish monasteries. The liturgical unity achieved was complete only where the Roman models were sufficiently fixed and unchanging. A more or less extensive regional or local diversity persisted in some parts of the liturgy, for example, in the readings for the Masses of the Sundays after Pentecost and in the order and even the selection of the responses at Matins.

The liturgical manuscripts surviving from the Carolingian period are much more numerous than those from the preceding age. The Carolingian period, on the other hand, saw the emergence of a new book, the Pontifical, which contained the portion of the Sacramentary that the bishop needed for services apart from Mass. The Sacramentary, for its part, developed slowly into the complete Missal, especially as private Masses became increasingly common in the monasteries. Alongside these complete books there probably existed, especially in small churches, many abridged books or partial booklets, most of which have disappeared.[30] In addition,

---

28. J. Deshusses, "Le 'Supplément' au Sacramentaire grégorien: Alcuin ou S. Benoît d'Aniane?" *ALW* 9 (1965) 48–71. See also *idem, Le Sacramentaire grégorien* I, 349–605 (edition of the Supplement) and III, 66–75 (answer to objections).

29. H. Barre and J. Deshusses, "A la recherche du missel d'Alcuin," *EL* 82 (1968) 1–44. The texts have been published in J. Deshusses, *Le Sacramentaire grégorien* II, and in A. Wilmart, *Precum libelli quattuor aevi karolini* (Rome: Edizioni liturgiche, 1940). See also H. B. Meyer, "Alkuin zwischen Antike und Mittelalter. Ein Kapitel frühmittelalterlicher Frömmigkeitsgeschichte," *ZKT* 81 (1959) 306–50, 405–54.

30. P. M. Gy, "Typologie et ecclésiologie des livres liturgiques médiévaux," *LMD* no. 121 (1975) 7–21.

the ninth century saw the appearance of the first traces of notation for liturgical singing; knowledge of this had previously been handed on through memorization.

The Carolingian Renaissance reestablished among the clergy a nucleus of men who knew Latin and were capable of composing liturgical formularies in this language. At the same time, however, it brought a definitive separation between Latin and the nascent Romance languages. Liturgical productions in Latin were numerous, especially in the great Frankish monasteries: hymns (still peculiar to the monastic Office), the first versified offices, sequences and tropes.[31] These last, which were a kind of sung commentary enclosing the text of the Introit and other parts of the Mass and Office, were not a form of popular paraliturgy but a development within the festal liturgy, most often in the large monasteries. The liturgy also tended by and large to have a theatric element, a characteristic that found expression especially in the appearance of liturgical drama.[32]

The Romano-German Pontifical was compiled from 950 to 963 in the monastery of St. Alban at Mainz, close by the imperial court of the Ottonians. This book brought together many specifically Carolingian liturgical contributions and was to influence all of the Western liturgies, including that of Rome. Meanwhile, the breakup of the Frankish Empire in the ninth century led to divergent liturgical developments in the eastern and western parts of the empire. In the western part the monastery of Cluny, founded in 909, propagated its liturgy in the monasteries dependent on it and thus gave rise to a type of liturgy that was less closely related than in the past to the life of the diocesan churches. On the other hand, the monastic additions to the Divine Office were much expanded compared to those in use in the time of Benedict of Aniane,[33] but Cluniac liturgical spirituality should not be judged by the criticisms of St. Bernard, which proceeded from a quite different conception of the liturgy.

Carolingian writings on the liturgy differ among themselves both in their genre and in their theological tendencies. The genres range from a straightforward explanation of the texts of Mass (thus most of the *Expositiones missae*[34]) to regular treatises that include a whole theology of the

---

31. Hymns: J. Szöverffy, *Die Annalen der lateinischen Hymnendichtung* (2 vols.; Berlin: E. Schmidt, 1964-65). — Versified Offices: R. Jonsson, *Historia. Etudes sur la genèse des offices versifiés* (Stockholm: Almqvist & Wiksell, 1968). — Tropes: *Corpus Troporum*, under the direction of R. Jonsson (5 vols. thus far; Stockholm: Almqvist & Wiksell, 1975ff.).

32. See *The Church at Prayer* III.

33. K. Hallinger, "Überlieferung und Steigerung im Mönchtum des 8. bis 12. Jahrhunderts," in *Eulogia (Mélanges Neunheuser)* (Studia Anselmiana 68; Rome: Herder, 1979), 125-87.

34. A. Häussling, "Messe (*Expositiones Missae*)," *Dictionnaire de spiritualité* 10 (Paris: Beauchesne, 1980) 1083-90.

liturgy, as, for example, the writings of Amalarius and Florus.[35] These two writers opposed one another, representing as they did two contrasting conceptions of the liturgy. For Florus, as for the Latin Fathers (especially St. Augustine) whose works he cites extensively, the *actio* of the Mass is a mystery in the sense that it contains the economy of salvation as a whole. For Amalarius, whose work seems closely allied to the Antiochene (Theodore of Mopsuestia) and Byzantine liturgical explanations, all the parts of the liturgy contain mysteries; that is, they represent (as liturgical plays would do later on) either biblical events or moral ideas. Amalarius' interpretation, which Florus managed to have condemned at the time, was to have great success in the following centuries and to inspire most liturgical writings down to the end of the Middle Ages.

§3. From the Gregorian Reform to the Council of Trent

BIBLIOGRAPHY

S. J. P. Van Dijk and J. Hazelden Walker, *The Ordinal of the Papal Court from Innocent III to Boniface VIII, and Related Documents* (Spicilegium Friburgense 22; Fribourg: Editions universitaires, 1975).

M. Andrieu, *Le Pontifical romain au moyen âge* (4 vols.; ST 86–88, 99; Vatican City, 1938–41).

M. Dykmans, *Le cérémonial papal de la fin du moyen âge à la Renaissance* (4 vols.; Bibliothèque de l'Institut historique belge de Rome 24–26; Brussels: L'Institut historique belge de Rome, 1977–85).

Beginning with St. Gregory VII (1073–85) and the reform of the Church for which he was chiefly responsible, the liturgical unity effected by Charlemagne was erected into an ecclesiological principle. The popes claimed responsibility henceforth for liturgical decisions in all the Churches. This development had several results: the suppression of the Spanish liturgy and then of the remaining vestiges of the Celtic liturgies; the recognition of the fully liturgical status of the Divine Office in its Roman and Benedictine forms; the reservation, effected by Alexander III and Innocent III,[36] of the right of canonization to the pope, the act of canonization being subsequently accompanied by an order (more or less

---

35. Amalarius, *Opera liturgica omnia*, ed. J. M. Hanssens (3 vols.; ST 138–40; Vatican City, 1948–50); P. Duc, *Etude sur l'"Expositio Missae" de Florus de Lyon suivie d'une édition critique du texte* (Belley: Chaduc, 1937); A. Kolping, "Amalar von Metz und Florus von Lyon, Zeugen eines Wandels im liturgischen Mysterienverständnis in der Karolingerzeit," *ZKT* 73 (1951) 424–64.

36. S. Kuttner, "La réservation papale du droit de canonisation," *Revue historique de Droit français et étranger*, 4e sér., 17 (1938) 172–428; E. Kemp, *Canonisation and Authority in the Western Church* (Oxford: Oxford University Press, 1948).

properly observed) to celebrate the feast and, beginning with the institution of Corpus Christi by Urban IV (1264), by the promulgation of the texts for the feast.

Innocent III and his successors gave new importance to the liturgy of the papal chapel, which had become independent of that celebrated in the Lateran Basilica.[37] The principal books of the papal liturgy were the Ordinal, which regulated both Office and Mass (1213-16), and the Pontifical of the Roman Curia, which was compiled under Innocent III and revised under Gregory IX or Innocent IV.[38] The liturgy of the Curia was to be adopted by the Friars Minor and imposed on the churches of Rome by Nicholas III, and was to spread to some Churches of Italy and Southern France (Avignon, 1337; etc.), but not as extensively as used to be thought.[39] The liturgy of the Curia would be regarded, at least from the fourteenth century on, as simply that of the Church in Rome. On the other hand, many bishops would adopt the Pontifical of the Curia. The latter would subsequently have a rival in the pontifical that William Durandus I, bishop of Mende, drew up for his Church (1292-95) and doubtless for wider use as well.

During the stay of the popes in Avignon and after their return to Rome, the ceremonies peculiar to them were set down in more or less detailed consuetudinaries.

The period of the Gregorian reform saw the multiplication of religious Orders of monks and canons regular whose liturgy was no longer closely connected with the liturgy of the cathedral churches, as it had been in the past, but instead was more or less strictly conformed to the liturgy of the mother community, as was already the case in the Order of Cluny. This was the case among, for example, the Carthusians, the Cistercians, and the Friars Preachers. These religious families had rather different spiritualities of the liturgy. Thus St. Peter Damian in his little book *Dominus vobiscum*[40] offered hermits a theology of the liturgy that was still close to that of the Fathers. Saint-Dénis (under Suger) and many cathedrals were using the theology of Pseudo-Dionysius to inspire a liturgy fairly close to that of Cluny. St. Bernard, meanwhile, was imposing on the Cistercian Order a liturgy that, contrary to that of Cluny, was characterized

---

37. On the earlier connection of the two Offices see L. Fischer, *Bernhardi Cardinalis et Lateranensis Ecclesiae Prioris Ordo officiorum Ecclesiae Lateranensis* (Historische Forschungen und Quellen, Heft 2-3; Munich: Datterer, 1916).

38. S. J. P. Van Dijk and J. Hazelden Walker, *The Ordinal of the Papal Court from Innocent III to Boniface VIII, and Related Documents* (Spicilegium Friburgense 22; Fribourg: Editions universitaires, 1975), XLI.

39. P. M. Gy, "L'unification liturgique de l'Occident et la liturgie de la Curie romaine," *Revue des sciences philosophiques et théologiques* 59 (1975) 601-12.

40. PL 145:231-52.

by the primacy (inspired by Origen) of interior devotion, austerity in external ceremonial, and a rejection of most additions to the Divine Office,[41] except for the Office of the Dead (which probably originated in the funeral service of Roman monasteries before Charlemagne) and the Little Office of the Blessed Virgin, which took form in the Gregorian period or a little before. Cistercian liturgical spirituality, to which that of the Carthusians was related, was to have a strong influence on the new religious Orders, especially the Friars Preachers. At the end of the Middle Ages, the *devotio moderna* movement further accentuated the tension between meditation and external ceremonial and erected it into a system.

From the end of the twelfth century and especially from the thirteenth century on, bishops saw to it, by means of synodal statutes and pastoral visits, that the liturgy was properly celebrated in the parishes; parish priests had to follow the cathedral liturgy as far as possible and to have a ritual (*manuale*) for the sacraments.[42] But the liturgy was looked upon as an activity of clerics for the benefit of the faithful rather than as an action in which the faithful participated; in addition, it was celebrated in Latin, except for the prayers of the prone (General Intercessions)[43] and the words of consent at marriages.[44] During Mass or Office, the faithful, and this included the lay brothers in religious communities, united themselves to the liturgy by a general awareness and by reciting Our Fathers in a low voice. In the thirteenth century devout laypersons and tertiaries who could read began to recite the Little Office of the Blessed Virgin, and the Book of Hours gradually replaced the Psalter as the fundamental book for Christian devotion. Books of the Hours would be very widely used, in manuscript and later in printed form, in the fifteenth century and the first half of the sixteenth.[45] On the other hand, again in the thirteenth century, many benefice holders began to absent themselves from the choral celebration of the Office. This led to the multiplication of portable breviaries that these persons could use in order to fulfill their obligation of reciting the Office privately.

Sacramental practices evolved especially in the second half of the medieval period. Daily celebration of Mass in monasteries became gen-

---

41. S. Hilpisch, "Chorgebet und Frömmigkeit im Spätmittelalter," in *Heilige Überlieferung (Festschrift Herwegen)* (Münster: Aschendorff, 1938), 263–84; C. Waddell, "The Early Cistercian Experience of Liturgy," *Cistercian Studies* 12 (1971) 72–115.

42. P. M. Gy, "Collectaire, rituel, processional," *Revue des sciences philosophiques et théologiques* 44 (1960) 441–69.

43. J.-B. Molin, "L'*Oratio communis fidelium* au moyen âge en Occident du Xe au XVe siècle," in *Miscellanea liturgica . . . Lercaro* II (Rome: Desclée, 1967), 313–468.

44. J.-B. Molin and P. Mutembe, *Le rituel du mariage en France du XIIe au XVIe siècle* (Théologie historique 26; Paris: Beauchesne, 1974).

45. A. Labarre, "Heures (Livres d')," *Dictionnaire de spiritualité* 7 (Paris: Beauchesne, 1969) 410–31.

eral in the eleventh and twelfth centuries, while the celebration of private Masses also increased, in order both to pray for the deceased and to satisfy the personal devotion of priests.[46] The faithful received Communion only rarely, however, despite a tendency to more frequent communion in the most fervent circles from the end of the twelfth century on.[47] At the same time that the Church was urging people to have their children baptized as soon as possible, it was ceasing to give these children Communion under the species of wine at the moment of their baptism, and Communion under two species disappeared despite violent reaction from the Hussites. On the other hand, at least from the twelfth century on, confession acquired a central importance in Christian piety, and Canon 21 of the Fourth Lateran Council (1215) prescribed that, beginning with the "age of discretion," all were obliged to confess annually and receive Communion during the Easter season; this rule was effectively implemented, although with some variation, in determining the age of discretion.[48]

Even though the faithful were receiving Communion only infrequently, pressure from them led to an extensive development of Eucharistic worship. This development included in particular the introduction of the elevation of the species at the consecration of the Mass (Paris, first years of the thirteenth century[49]) and the establishment of the feast of Corpus Christi, first at Liège in about 1246 and then at the Roman Curia in 1264. The Roman celebration resulted from a decree of Pope Urban IV, which was, however, not fully implemented in the West until the first quarter of the fourteenth century.[50]

In the eleventh and following centuries the cult of the Virgin Mary developed both in the liturgy and outside of it. This was the period that saw the composition not only of the Little Office of the Blessed Virgin but of the *Salve regina* (probably in Aquitaine[51]) and many other Marian texts, some of which, litanic in form, were influenced by the Byzantine

---

46. O. Nussbaum, *Kloster, Priestermönch und Privatmesse* (Theophaneia 14; Bonn: Hanstein, 1961); A. Häussling, *Mönchskonvent und Eucharistiefeier. Eine Studie über die Messe in der abendländischen Klosterliturgie des frühen Mittelalters und zur Geschichte der Messhäufigkeit* (LQF 58; Münster: Aschendorff, 1973).

47. P. Browe, *Die häufige Kommunion im Mittelalter* (Münster: Regensbergsche Verlag, 1938).

48. L. Andrieux, *La première Communion* (Paris: Beauchesne, 1911); F. Gillmann, "Die *anni discretionis* im Kanon *Omnis utriusque sexus,*" *Archiv für katholisches Kirchenrecht* 108 (1928) 556–617.

49. Statuts de Paris, 80, in *Les statuts synodaux français du XIIIe siècle* I. *Les statuts de Paris et le synodal de l'Ouest (XIIIe siècle),* ed. O. Pontal (Paris: Bibliothèque nationale, 1971), 82.

50. See *The Church at Prayer* IV, 103–4.

51. M. Mundo, "El origen de la Salve visto de España," *Anuario de estudios medievales,* 1967, 369–76.

Akathistos Hymn, which had been translated into Latin during the Carolingian period (at Saint-Dénis rather than in Upper Italy[52]). Among the newly adopted Marian feasts[53] the most important was the Conception of Mary, which spread from England and elicited both enthusiasm and opposition. The feast of the Compassion of the Virgin (like the sequence *Stabat mater*) gave expression to a more affective type of devotion that went hand in hand with devotion to the passion of Christ, both during Holy Week and in Eucharistic worship.

Writings on the liturgy became numerous during the final centuries of the Middle Ages. Although the influence of Amalarius in favor of an allegorizing interpretation remained dominant, notably in Pope Innocent III, whose great treatise *De missarum mysteriis* benefited from his subsequent prestige as pope, there was also a reaction against allegory in the persons of John of Beleth, a pre-Scholastic, whose *Summa de ecclesiasticis officiis*[54] was the preferred treatise on the liturgy in the thirteenth century, and of St. Albert the Great, who sharply criticized Innocent III. The *Rationale divinorum officiorum* of William Durandus of Mende, a canonist as well as a liturgist, was a vast compilation that won success by its copiousness rather than by any creative genius in its author.

During the half century prior to the reform decreed by the Council of Trent, the beginnings of the anti-Protestant reaction lent prestige to earlier forms of piety, while at the same time the humanists were criticizing various devotional abuses and trying to introduce neoclassical forms (the hymnal of Ferreri) and give the Scriptures a controlling role in the liturgy. The last-named tendency marks the breviary which Cardinal F. Quiñones prepared at the request of Clement VII and which was used from 1535 to 1558; it gave preference to individual or private recitation.[55] The development of printing made it possible, at least in small dioceses, to abandon earlier local liturgies; it also ensured the success of printed rituals such as the *Sacerdotale* of Alberto di Castello, a Dominican (Venice, 1523).[56]

52. G. G. Meersseman, *Der Hymnus Akathistos im Abendland* (2 vols.; Spicilegium Friburgenses 2–3; Freiburg, Switz.: Universitätsverlag, 1958–60).

53. See *The Church at Prayer* IV, 138–41.

54. Ed. H. Douteil (2 vols.; CCL, Contin. mediev. 41–41A; Turnhout: Brepols, 1976).

55. See *The Church at Prayer* IV, 211–12 and 254.

56. E. Cattaneo, "Il Rituale romano di Alberto Castellani," in *Miscellanea liturgica . . . Lercaro* II (Rome: Desclée, 1967), 629–47.

Chapter IV

From the Council of Trent to Vatican Council II

P. Jounel

From the viewpoint of Western liturgical development, the four centuries between the Council of Trent and Vatican Council II can be divided into three periods: at the beginning and the end, a half century of intense renewal (1563–1614 and 1903–62), separated by three centuries of a stability rendered immobile by rubricism.

§1. The Liturgical Reform Set in Motion by the Council of Trent (1563–1614)

The dogmatic teaching of the Council of Trent on the sacrifice of the Mass and on the other sacraments reveals its precise meaning only in light of the changes that the Reformation introduced into the faith of the Church. The same can be said of the revision of the liturgical books that the Council of Trent, before ending in 1563, commissioned the pope to carry out. The Reformers had attacked the Roman liturgy not only in its theology but in its celebration, and had introduced radical innovations into it. It is important, therefore, to have a general grasp of the Reformed liturgies if we are to understand the objectives, and limitations, of the return to the "original standard of the Fathers" (*pristina Patrum norma*), which St. Pius V adopted when he undertook a revision of the Roman Missal and Breviary.

I. THE LITURGIES OF THE REFORMERS (1523–1556)

BIBLIOGRAPHY

P. Le Brun, *Explication littérale, historique et dogmatique des prières et des cérémonies de la messe* (Paris: chez Delaulne, 1716), 4:1–187.

G. Dix, *The Shape of the Liturgy* (Westminster: Dacre Press, 1945²), 613–74: "The Reformation and the Anglican Liturgy."

B. Thompson, *Liturgies of the Western Church* (Cleveland & New York: World, 1961).

L. Bouyer, *Eucharist: Theology and Spirituality of the Eucharistic Prayer*, trans. C. U. Quinn (Notre Dame: University of Notre Dame Press, 1968), 380–442.

I. Pahl, *Coena Domini. Die Liturgie des Abendmahls seit der Reformation, 1. Texte des 16./17. Jahrhunderts* (Spicilegium Friburgense 29; Fribourg, 1983).

The Anglican Prayer Book has been edited many times; e.g., *The First and Second Prayer Book of Edward VI*, introduced by D. Harrison (London, 1910; reprinted, 1968).

In the final centuries of the Middle Ages the original meaning of the liturgy of the Mass and the other sacraments had become obscured, and its celebration was marked by superfluous rituals and even superstitious practices. A great many synods and provincial councils in the first half of the sixteenth century became aware of the harm being done and called openly for a revision of the liturgical books. The revision was continually put off, but meanwhile the various groups within the Protestant Reformation were busy adapting the books to their own confessions of faith. Oddly enough, even though they denied the sacrificial character of the Mass, they retained and expanded the most questionable contributions of medieval devotion and thereby departed even further from the teaching of the Fathers on the Eucharist as a meal and a memorial of the paschal mystery. The rites of the Order of Mass (the only sacrament to be discussed here) were altered to suit the pleasure of each Reformation leader.

In 1523 Luther published his *Formula Missae*, which eliminated the Roman Canon except for the first part of the Preface and the account of institution (*Per Christum Dominum nostrum. Qui pridie*). This was followed by the *Sanctus*, while the *Benedictus* accompanied the elevation of the chalice and the host. Two years later, the *Deutsche Messe* (1525) dropped the Preface as well.

Luther claimed still to believe in the Real Presence of Christ in the Eucharist. In Zürich, meanwhile, Zwingli was denying it utterly. He developed a liturgy of the Supper (1525) that kept the *Ordo Missae* down to the *Sanctus* inclusive without any major change. The *Sanctus* was followed by the *Pater*; then came the account of institution and Communion, which the faithful received while seated. Any and all singing was prohibited. The Lord's Supper was to be celebrated only four times a year. Zwingli's liturgy inspired in turn those of Calvin in Geneva (1542) and Knox in Scotland (1556).

The *Order* of the Lord's Supper that is contained in the Anglican *Prayer Book* (1549 and 1552) as edited by Cranmer was very much influenced by Calvin. A rubric in it offers practical reasons for the custom of receiving Communion while kneeling, and says specifically: "Lest yet the same kneeling might be thought or taken otherwise, we do declare that it is not meant thereby, that any adoration is done, or ought to be done . . . unto the sacramental bread and wine there bodily received. . . . For . . . they remain still in their very natural substances."[1] According to the *Order* of 1552 the service includes, near the beginning, a reading of the Ten Commandments, each followed by a prayer of the congregation. After this recitation of the commandments come two collects, the epistle, the gospel, the homily, and the collection, this last being accompanied by some sentences from Scripture. Then comes the general confession, followed by absolution and the "comfortable words." The account of the institution of the Eucharist is located within a prayer of entreaty. Communion is given immediately afterwards. When the communion has been completed, the Our Father is said; this is followed by a prayer of thanksgiving for the gift received and by the singing or recitation of the *Glory to God in the highest*. At the end the congregation is dismissed with a blessing. In addition to this *Order* for the Lord's Supper, the *Prayer Book* contained the liturgy for the other sacraments and for the Sundays and feasts of the year, together with a fine service of prayer for morning and evening: *Matins* and *Evensong*.

Despite the diversity in their Eucharistic formularies the Lutheran, Reformed, and Anglican liturgies have kept a close kinship with the Liturgy of the Word in the medieval missals. More importantly, they contain two innovations that the Catholic Church would not adopt until 1963: celebration in the vernacular languages and participation in the chalice.

II. THE LITURGICAL ACTIVITY OF THE COUNCIL OF TRENT

BIBLIOGRAPHY

A. Michel, "Les décrets du Concile de Trente," in Hefele-Leclercq, *Histoire des Conciles* 10/1 (Paris: Letouzey, 1938).

H. Schmidt, *Liturgie et langue vulgaire. Le problème du langue liturgique chez les premiers Réformateurs et au Concile de Trente* (Analecta Gregoriana 53; Rome: Pontificia Università Gregoriana, 1950).

A. Duval, "La formule *Ego vos in matrimonium coniungo* au Concile de Trente," *LMD* no. 99 (1969) 144–53.

---

1. *The First and Second Prayer Book of Edward VI*, ed. D. Harrison (London, 1910; reprinted, 1968), 393.

_____, "L'extrême-onction au Concile de Trente," *LMD* no. 101 (1970) 127-72.

H. Jedin, "Il Concilio di Trento e la riforma dei libri liturgici," in *idem, Chiesa della fede, Chiesa della storia* (Brescia: Morcelliana, 1972), 391-425. In German: *EL* 59 (1945) 5-38.

A. Duval, "Le Concile de Trente et le baptême des enfants," *LMD* no. 110 (1972) 16-24.

_____, "Le Concile de Trente et la confession," *LMD* no. 118 (1974) 131-80.

E. Cattaneo, *Il culto cristiano in Occidente* (Bibliotheca EL Subsidia 13; Rome: Edizioni liturgiche, 1978), 360-70.

The documents that the Council of Trent had collected on liturgical reform dealt primarily with the celebration of Mass and the Divine Office. A special commission had drawn up a list of *abusus missae*. The Council ordered the elimination of the most important abuses in its disciplinary decree *De observandis et evitandis in celebratione missae*.[2] As for the Office, the first point to be decided was whether a revision should follow the model provided by the breviary that Cardinal Quiñones had composed in 1535 or should, on the contrary, keep to the traditional form. But the solution of the basic problems raised by the Reformers depended essentially on the dogmatic decisions the Council would make on the sacrifice of the Mass and the efficacy of the seven sacraments, as well as on the Council's answer to the Reformers' questions about the use of the vernaculars in public worship and about Communion under two species.

In its twenty-second session (September 17, 1562) the Council solemnly defined the sacrificial value of the Mass as well as the legitimacy of the rites used in its celebration. In the process it called attention to both of the tables that are set in the Eucharistic assembly: the table of God's Word, which is distributed *"ne oves Christi esuriant"* (ch. 8: "lest Christ's sheep go hungry"), and the table of the Lord's Supper, which by its nature invites to communion the faithful *"in singulis missis adstantes"* (ch. 6: "who are present at each Mass").

When the question of the language of liturgical celebration arose, the Council refused to permit use of the vernacular: *"Etsi missa magnam contineat populi fidelis eruditionem, non tamen visum est patribus, ut vulgari passim lingua celebretur"* (ch. 8: "While the Mass contains a great deal of instruction for the faithful, the Fathers did not think it good to let all of its parts be celebrated in the vernacular"). Because there was not enough time left to discuss the question of the participation of the faithful in the chalice, the Council left the decision to the pope.[3] It also charged him with the revision of the Missal and the Breviary.[4]

---

2. A. Michel, *Les décrets du Concile de Trente*, in Hefele-Leclercq, *Histoire des Conciles* 10/1 (Paris: Letouzey, 1938), 456-60.

3. *Ibid.*, 465-66.

4. *Ibid.*, 630.

The rule that Latin alone could be used in the liturgy was to remain unchanged until the Second Vatican Council. Participation of the faithful in the chalice, on the other hand, was granted by Pope Pius IV as early as 1564 to Germany and various countries of Central Europe. His successors, however, opposed the permission, and it was revoked for Bavaria in 1570. Bohemia was the last country to have it withdrawn, in 1621.[5]

III. THE TRIDENTINE MISSAL AND BREVIARY (1568–1570)

The decisions of the Council were quickly implemented. The *Breviarium romanum ex decreto sacrosancti Concilii Tridentini restitutum, Pii V. Pont. Max iussu editum* (The Roman Breviary restored by decree of the Sacred Council of Trent and published by order of the Supreme Pontiff Pius V) appeared in 1568. It was followed in 1570 by the *Missale romanum*. In order to understand the end result intended by St. Pius V, as well as the method followed by the commission that prepared the new books, we need only read the bulls of promulgation printed at the beginning of the two volumes.

The plan of the Pope, who in this matter faithfully reflected the intentions of the Council, was not to compose new liturgical books but to make the prayer of the Church conform *"ad pristinam orandi regulam"* ("to the primitive rule of prayer"), to revise the Missal *"ad pristinam sanctorum Patrum normam"* ("in accordance with the original standard of the holy Fathers"), and to establish uniformity in the celebration of the rites, *"cum unum in Ecclesia Dei psallendi modum, unum missae celebrandae ritum esse maxime deceat"* ("since it is most fitting that there be only one way of reciting the psalms in the Church of God and only one rite in the celebration of Mass").

This desire for a return to tradition meant first of all that there should be no alteration in the *Ordo psallendi*, which went back to the fifth century. It was regarded as desirable, moreover, that the missals printed during the past hundred years be compared with the earlier liturgical manuscripts preserved in the Apostolic Library. The improvement in the Breviary was evident both in the removal of the obligation to say the offices that had been added (offices of the Blessed Virgin and of the dead; the Gradual and penitential psalms) and in the correction or elimination of the most absurd hagiographical legends. The Missal saw the removal of some votive Masses that were tainted by superstition, and only four

---

5. C. Constant, *La concession à l'Allemagne de la communion sous les deux espèces. Etude sur les débuts de la réforme catholique en Allemagne (1548–1621)* (2 vols.; Bibliothèque des Ecoles françaises de Rome et d'Athènes 128 and 128bis; Paris, 1923).

of the many medieval sequences were retained. The Calendar, too, was simplified. There was also a first effort to restore the proper celebration of Sunday and of the ferial office.

Uniformity in celebration required a codification of the rules for celebration. As a result, general rubrics were now printed for the first time at the beginning of each of the two books. The *Ritus servandus in celebratione missae* ("Rite to be followed in celebrating Mass"), which Johannes Burckard, the papal master of ceremonies, had composed at the beginning of the century, was also inserted at the front of the Missal.[6] The rubrics of St. Pius V, which amounted to modern *Ordines romani*, were to exercise a considerable influence as the Roman liturgy spread throughout the world. This spread of the Tridentine Missal and Breviary, which accompanied the introduction of the Church into the Americas and the missionary expansion in the countries of the Pacific, was greatly aided by constant improvements in printing. It was juridically ensured by the papal decision, since the two bulls of promulgation obliged all churches to adopt the revised Breviary and Missal, unless they were excused by their profession of a local liturgy that was two hundred or more years old.

IV. THE POST-TRIDENTINE LITURGICAL BOOKS (1584–1614)

BIBLIOGRAPHY

P. Borella, *San Carlo Borromeo e il Ceremoniale dei vescovi* (Varese: Tip. Varese, 1937). Latin in *EL* 51 (1937) 64–80.

B. Löwenberg, *Das Rituale des Kardinals Julius Antonius Sanctorius. Ein Beitrag zur Entstehungsgeschichte des Rituale Romanum* (Munich, 1937).

E. Cattaneo, *Il culto cristiano in Occidente. Note storiche* (Bibliotheca EL Subsidia 13; Rome: Edizioni liturgiche, 1978), 371–78.

A. Nocent, "Storia dei libri liturgici romani," in *Anàmnesis* II (Turin: Marietti, 1978), 176–84.

M. Dykmans, "Paris de Grassi," *EL* 96 (1982) 407–63; 99 (1985) 382–417; 100 (1986) 270–317.

The immediate success of the Tridentine Breviary and Missal encouraged the popes to extend the reform to other books. Thus when Sixtus V established the Roman Congregations in 1587, he made it one task of the Congregation of Rites to correct the liturgical books, beginning with the Pontifical, the Ritual, and the Ceremonial. If he omitted mention of

---

6. J. W. Legg, *Tracts on the Mass* (HBS 27; 1904), 119–74. — See the important article of A. Frutaz, "Contributo alla storia della riforma del Messale promulgato da san Pio V nel 1570," in *Problemi di vita religiosa in Italia nel Cinquecento* (Italia sacra 2; Padua: Ed. Antenore, 1960), 187–214.

the Martyrology, it was because this had just been revised by Baronius and promulgated by authority of Gregory XIII (1584).

The work of revision and correction was carried out according to the method and spirit of St. Pius V's commission for the Missal and Breviary. In each case, the commissions started with the books presently in use. The Pontifical of Agostino Patrizi (1485), which itself had been the direct heir to the Pontifical of William Durandus (thirteenth century), served as the basis for the text of the Roman Pontifical that Clement VIII promulgated in 1595. The Roman Ceremonial of the same Patrizi (1488) and the work by Paride Grassi, *De caeremoniis cardinalium et episcoporum in eorum diocesibus* (1587), furnished the substance of the new Ceremonial for bishops that the same pope promulgated in 1600. Finally, the Ritual that Paul V promulgated in 1614 was dependent chiefly on the huge Ritual that Cardinal Giulio Antonio Santori had compiled with great learning (1584). These various existing documents were carefully analyzed and compared with available manuscript sources; efforts were made to present the rubrics more clearly. As far as the Ritual was concerned, an attempt was made to simplify the rites that Santori had sought to restore, and pastoral directives were added, this last being a novelty. Whereas Clement VIII had "suppressed and abolished" all other existing pontificals and had made it obligatory for bishops to follow the new Ceremonial, Paul V was satisfied to urge all bishops to accept the Ritual of the Church of Rome.

§2. Three Centuries of Liturgical Stability (1614–1903)

BIBLIOGRAPHY

Decreta authentica Congregationis sacrorum rituum ex actis eiusdem collecta (5 vols.; Rome: Vatican Press, 1898–1901; with two Appendixes, 1912 and 1927).

B. Gavanti, *Thesaurus sacrorum rituum seu commentaria in rubricas* (Milan, 1628); reissued as two vols. in one, with commentaries, by G. Merati (Venice: Zerletti, 1769).

S. Bäumer and R. Biron, *Histoire du bréviaire* 2 (Paris: Letouzey, 1905), 221–419.

P. Batiffol, *History of the Roman Breviary*, trans. A. M. Y. Baylay (New York: Longmans, Green, 1912), 236–330 (especially on the projects of Benedict XIV).

On the French liturgies of the seventeenth and eighteenth centuries:

H. Leclercq, "Liturgies néo-gallicanes," *DACL* 9 (1930) 1636–1729.

G. Fontaine, "Présentation des missels diocésains français du XVIIe au XIXe siècles," *LMD* no. 141 (1980) 97–166.

F. Brovelli, "Per uno studio dei messali francesi del XVIIIe secolo. Saggio di analisi," *EL* 96 (1982) 279–406.

On liturgical life in Italy and its difficulties in the eighteenth century:

E. Cattaneo, *Il culto cristiano in Occidente. Note storiche* (Bibliotheca EL Subsidia 13; Rome: Edizioni liturgiche, 1978), 416–538.

On the return to the Roman liturgy in France and on the further development of the Roman liturgy:

P. Guéranger, *Institutions liturgiques* 2 (Le Mans: Fleuriot, 1841; reprinted: Paris: Palmé, 1880).

P. Favrel, *Cérémonial selon le rite romain par Joseph Baldeschi traduit de l'italien et considérablement augmenté* (Dijon: Douiller, 1847).

L. Le Vavasseur, *Cérémonial selon le rite romain d'après Joseph Baldeschi . . . et d'après l'abbé Favrel* (Paris: Lecoffre, 1857). Many reprintings and updatings by Joseph Haegy and then by Louis Stercky down to 1940.

P. Jounel, *Le renouveau du culte des saints dans la liturgie romaine* (Bibliotheca EL, Subsidia 36; Rome: Edizioni liturgiche, 1986).

T. Klauser could describe the three centuries from the establishment of the Congregation of Rites to the coming of Pius X as the "age of the rubricists." The result of this "period of stoppage" was that "the spiritual life moved away from its sources and liturgical expression."[7] The period was characterized chiefly by the development of liturgical juridicism and a disproportionate growth in the cult of the saints. None of the reform tendencies that manifested themselves during that time managed to achieve the results expected of them.

1. *Rubrical rigidity and proliferation of feasts*

From the seventeenth to the twentieth century juridicism and casuistry played an increasingly important part in cultic practice and teaching, as the manuals on liturgy published for the use of clerics bear witness. This conception of the liturgy was fed chiefly by the decrees and responses that the Congregation promulgated in great abundance throughout the period. An official collection of these documents would be published under Pope Leo XIII beginning in 1898.

Rubrical rigidity did not prevent a proliferation of the feasts of the Lord, the Blessed Virgin, and the saints. To the 182 feast days in the Calendar of 1568, an additional 118 were added between 1584 and 1903, with almost all of the new feasts taking precedence over Sunday. Between the Council of Trent and Vatican Council II a number of major feasts were introduced (Sacred Heart, Precious Blood, Christ the King, Solemnity of St. Joseph), while other, older feasts were given new formularies (Immaculate Conception, Assumption). While the expansion of the cult of the saints can be partially explained by the ceaseless flowering of Catholic sanctity,

---

7. T. Klauser, *A Short History of the Western Liturgy: An Account and Some Reflections*, trans. J. Halliburton (London: Oxford University Press, 1969); see 120f. [This new English translation is from a revised and much expanded fifth German edition, and the cited words do not occur as such. I translate them from the French, which refers to: T. Klauser, *Petite histoire de la liturgie occidentale*, trans. from the German by M. Zemb (Paris: Cerf, 1956), 86. — Tr.].

its main cause was undoubtedly the admitted desire to substitute festal offices for the offices of Sundays and weekdays, because the former were shorter.

2. *Attempts at reform*

Meanwhile, however, other currents of thought did not cease to appear in the Church. There were many who found the reforms of Pius V to be overly timid and thought it necessary to go further in revising the liturgical books and restoring the cycle of the Lord to its due place. As early as 1588 the Congregation of Rites launched an inquiry into the need of reforming the liturgical books.[8] In the seventeenth and eighteenth centuries the discovery and publication of the ancient sacramentaries and *Ordines* gave the public access to hitherto unknown treasures of ancient prayer. Scholars like St. Giuseppe Cardinal Tomasi wanted the entire Church to profit from their labors.[9] But the force of inertia prevailed. The only reform of the liturgical books that was carried to a successful term was accomplished without the consent of the Holy See. This was the reform of the local liturgies in the dioceses of France.

The Tridentine Missal and Breviary were accepted in the dioceses of France between 1580 and 1610.[10] More than half a century later, a number of bishops who realized the inadequacies of the Roman books decided that it would be permissible for them to go back to their older books while revising these in the spirit that had governed the reform promulgated by St. Pius V. The Paris Missal of François de Harlay (1685) introduced only timid innovations by comparison with the Roman Missal. Little by little, however, a sense of autonomy grew, and in the eighteenth century 90 of the 139 dioceses in the France of that period acquired a local liturgy for themselves. In fact, over fifty of them adopted the Paris Breviary and Missal that had been promulgated in 1736 and 1738 respectively by Archbishop Charles de Vintimille.[11]

It is an error to speak of these diocesan liturgies as "neo-Gallican," because all of them retained the Tridentine *Ordo Missae* in its entirety. One may find fault with them for replacing the Roman Antiphonary with new and strictly biblical compositions, but one cannot fail to appreciate their choice of readings and the quality of their prayers. The Masses of Monday and Friday in each week had readings proper to them. Each week,

---

8. H. Vinck, "Enquête faite en 1588 sur la nécessité d'une réforme des livres liturgiques," *QL* 56 (1975) 113–25.

9. I. Scicolone, *Il Cardinale Giuseppe Tomasi di Lampedusa e gli inizi della scienza liturgica* (Cultura cristiana di Sicilia 6; Palermo: Istituto superiore di scienze religiose, 1981).

10. P. Guéranger, *Institutions liturgiques* 1 (ed. of 1841), 460–69.

11. G. Fontaine, "Présentation des Missels diocésains français du XVIIe au XIXe siècle," *LMD* 141 (1980) 100–101.

too, the whole Psalter was actually read in the Office. The Calendar had been pruned, and the hagiographical readings relieved of legendary stories. The prayers were taken from the newly published sacramentaries or were inspired by material in these books. It is not surprising, therefore, that the Missal of Paul VI should have derived some of its best prayers from these French liturgies (for example, the prayers after communion on June 29 and November 1).[12] Everyone knows, of course, of the relentless fight that Dom Guéranger conducted, from 1841 on, against these liturgies that he accused of Protestantism and Gallicanism, and the decisive victory he won over them in less than twenty years.

Pope Benedict XIV, aware of the need for renewing the Roman liturgy in answer to the petitions of many, entrusted the task to a commission of experts (1741–47). He was not satisfied with the results, however, and refused to ratify them. This scholarly pope thought that he could himself accomplish the reform he wanted, but he died before being able to carry it out. Faced with the immobilism of Rome, a number of German bishops undertook to correct their breviaries after the model of the French breviaries.[13]

§3. Liturgical Reform from St. Pius X to the Second Vatican Council (1903–1962)

BIBLIOGRAPHY

a) On the official documents:

A. Bugnini, *Documenta pontificia ad instaurationem liturgicam spectantia* 1 (1903–1953) and 2 (1953–1959) (Bibliotheca EL, sectio practica, 6 and 9; Rome: Edizioni liturgiche, 1953 and 1959).
Codex rubricarum, promulgated by Pope John XXIII: *AAS* 52 (1961) 593–740.
Pontificale Romanum, editio typica emendata, with commentary by C. Braga (Bibliotheca EL, sectio historica, 27; Rome: Edizioni liturgiche, 1962).
H. Vinck, "Essai de réforme générale du bréviaire par Pie X," *RHE* 73 (1978) 69–74. Summary of a typewritten thesis on *Les réformes liturgiques de 1911 à 1914* (Institut Supérieur de Liturgie, Paris).
La Maison-Dieu published and commented on most of the liturgical documents issued by authority of Pope Pius XII and John XXIII: *LMD* no. 13 (1948) (Encyclical *Mediator Dei*); *LMD* 42 (1955) (the reform of the rubrics); *LMD* 45 (1956) (restoration of Holy Week); *LMD* no. 63bis (1960) (the new code of rubrics).

---

12. P. Jounel, "Les sources françaises du Missel de Paul VI," *QL* 52 (1971) 305–16. To the texts listed there add the collect for the Vigil Mass of August 14, which is taken from the Cluny Missal of 1733.
13. S. Bäumer and R. Biron, *Histoire du Bréviaire* 2 (Paris: Letouzey, 1905), 336–71.

b) On the liturgical movement:

T. Bogler *et al.*, *Liturgische Erneuerung in aller Welt. ein Sammelbericht* (Maria Laach, 1950).

B. Botte, *Le mouvement liturgique, témoignages et souvenirs* (Paris: Desclée, 1973).

F. Brovelli, *Per un studio de "L'Année Liturgique" di P. Guéranger* (Bibliotheca EL, Subsidia 22; Rome: Edizioni liturgiche, 1981).

A. Haquin, *Dom Lambert Beauduin et le renouveau liturgique* (Recherches et synthèses, section d'histoire 1; Gembloux: Duculot, 1970).

O. Rousseau, *The Progress of the Liturgy: An Historical Sketch from the Beginning of the Nineteenth Century to the Pontificate of Pius X*, trans. by Benedictines of Westminster Priory, Vancouver, B.C. (Westminster, Md.: Newman, 1951).

B. Neunheuser, "Il movimento liturgico, panorama storico e lineamenti teologici," in *Anàmnesis* I (Turin: Marietti, 1974), 11–30.

Many articles in *Questions liturgiques et paroissiales* (from 1911 on) and in *La Maison-Dieu* (from 1945 on).

The liturgical reform that Pope St. Pius X undertook in 1903 gave birth to a movement that developed chiefly in the Abbey of Mont César at Louvain. But the way had been prepared for the movement by the renewal of liturgical life that Dom Prosper Guéranger (1805–75) had promoted. When he founded the Abbey of Solesmes (1833) he immediately made it a center of intense liturgical life; his influence, however, quickly spread beyond the walls of his abbey. In addition to carrying on his fight for the restoration of the Roman liturgy in France, he educated many priests and faithful in liturgical prayer by means of his *Année liturgique* (*The Liturgical Year:* nine volumes from 1841 to 1866), which one of his monks later continued. The influence of Solesmes won Germany over via the foundation of the Abbey of Beuron, then Belgium via the Abbeys of Maredsous and Mont César, which were both daughters of Beuron. Solesmes' audience would expand even further when the French abbey undertook the restoration of Gregorian chant. It was this that attracted the attention and won the confidence of Cardinal Giuseppe Sarto, patriarch of Venice and subsequently Pope Pius X.[14]

I. THE REFORM OF ST. PIUS X (1903–1914) AND THE FIRST PHASE OF THE LITURGICAL MOVEMENT (1909–1939)

The Motu Proprio *Tra le sollecitudini* (1903) of St. Pius X began the liturgical reform of the twentieth century not only because in it he laid down laws for singing in church and for the restoration of Gregorian chant, but also and above all because he exhorted the faithful to take an active part in the celebration of the mysteries, since this celebration is "the

---

14. P. Combe, *Histoire de la restauration du chant grégorien d'après des documents inédits* (Solesmes: Abbaye de Solesmes, 1969), 181–83.

primary and indispensable source of the true Christian spirit." Congregational singing is only a first step in participation in the liturgical mystery. Participation becomes full only when the faithful share in the Lord's table. That is why Pius X decided to urge Christians to frequent and even daily communion, as indeed the Council of Trent had done in its time. But to ensure a response to the call the Pope established the necessary and sufficient conditions for frequent communion (1905). A few years later he would add that even children are called to receive Communion once they have reached the age of reason (1910).

Once the basic condition for a restoration of the liturgical life had been put in place, Pius X could take up the reform begun by Benedict XIV. In 1911 he revised the Roman *Ordo psallendi* so that the entire Psalter would actually be read every week, and in 1913 he published the first norms that would give Sundays priority over the feasts of the saints. In 1907 he had published the first official edition of the *Graduale romanum*; this was followed in 1912 by an official edition of the *Antiphonale* for the Hours of the day.

The exhortation of Pius X to liturgical participation elicited a broad response; this was especially true of his efforts in behalf of frequent communion and the communion of children. His call to active participation by the faithful in the celebration was heard with special clarity by Dom Lambert Beauduin (1873–1960), a monk of Mont César in Belgium, who was also to be a pioneer in ecumenism. In 1909 Dom Beauduin launched a liturgical movement that would reach far beyond Belgium. His aim was to reach the great masses of the faithful. To this end he published a small missal for the people. At the same time, however, priests had to be prepared to become liturgical educators of the faithful, and for this purpose he organized annual liturgical courses and conferences at Louvain, while his abbey published a journal, *Les Questions liturgiques*.

Shortly afterward, another Belgian abbey, Saint-André in Bruges, adopted the same objectives. The Missal of Dom Gaspar Lefebvre, which was published by Saint-André, contributed greatly to the participation of the faithful in Sunday Mass and sung Vespers. In France, soon after World War I, Fr. Paul Doncoeur, a Jesuit, began to introduce the young to the liturgy, especially by means of the dialogue Mass. At this same period Pierre Paris, a Sulpician, was training Christian university graduates as teachers. In Germany the liturgical movement[15] reflected the influence of two great theologians: Professor Romano Guardini (1885–1968) and Dom Odo Casel (1886–1948), a monk of Maria Laach. The former

---

15. See the preface by R. d'Harcourt to the French translation of R. Guardini, *L'esprit de la liturgie* (Paris: Plon, 1930), 3–94, for the main lines of what Dom I. Herwegen, Abbot of Maria-Laach, preferred to call "the liturgical effort" rather than "the liturgical movement."

expounded the spirit of the liturgy, the latter developed a theology of the mysteries.[16] Thanks to Pius Parsch (1884-1954), a Canon Regular of Klosterneuburg, the German movement took a more popular form in Austria, but one that was heeded in all the German-speaking countries.

II. THE SECOND PHASE OF THE LITURGICAL MOVEMENT (1940-1962) AND THE REFORMS OF PIUS XII AND JOHN XXIII

From 1903 to 1914 the reforms of Pius X had preceded and given rise to the liturgical movement; after World War II, however, the developments sponsored by the liturgico-pastoral movement were ratified by Pius XII as he made his own the project of Pius X and adapted it to new conditions. Before 1940 the aim had been to bring the existing liturgy within reach of the people and to promote Gregorian chant. After the war there was a clearer perception of the need for a radical reform of the rites and for a partial introduction of the vernacular into the celebration.

The German liturgical movement provided strong support for the faith-life of Catholics when religion had to withdraw into the churches due to pressure from National Socialism. During the war (1943) the Centre de Pastorale Liturgique was founded in Paris with the support of Dom Lambert Beauduin. It was intended to be at once theological, biblical, and pastoral.[17] Its periodical, *La Maison-Dieu* (1954ff.), its sessions for priests, and its congresses won it a key place in French pastoral activity of that period. Its advisers were theologians of high repute; it was attentive to the needs of the Christian people; it urged fidelity to canonical norms; and it prepared the way in France for the reforms of Vatican Council II. The liturgical movement soon won the approval and encouragement of Pius XII and received directives from him (1947). From that point on the movement experienced some growth in all countries; bishops began to foster and direct it. Missionaries concerned themselves with the liturgical life (especially the liturgical aspect of the adult catechumenate) and became sensitized to the problems that the Roman liturgy created for converts from paganism and in non-Western cultures.

In 1947, even before issuing his Encyclical *Mediator Dei* on the liturgy, Pius XII established within the Congregation of Rites a commission charged with preparing a general reform of the liturgy. He himself had already taken specific steps to mitigate the law of Eucharistic fast in order to facilitate the celebration of Mass and reception of Communion in the evening

---

16. A. Gozier, *Dom Casel* (Paris: Editions de Fleurus, 1968), with bibliography of Casel, 179-85.

17. P. Duployé, *Les origines du Centre de Pastorale Liturgique 1943-1949* (Mulhouse: Salvator, 1968).

in countries at war. These measures were extended to the universal Church in the Apostolic Constitution *Christus Dominus* of 1953: henceforth the drinking of plain water would never break the Eucharistic fast, while the fast from other foods was limited to the three hours before communion.

The first fruit of the reform that Pius XII had decided on was the authorization to celebrate the Easter Vigil during the holy night itself (1951). Four years later came the restoration of Holy Week (1955). Meanwhile, the growth of the movement for a return to the Bible had been making people more attentive to the Word of God and its use in the liturgy. But if all were to have access to the celebration at the table of the Word, the Word would have to be proclaimed in the vernaculars. Pius XII did not think the situation sufficiently advanced to justify a sweeping change, and he contented himself with limited authorizations to read the epistle and gospel in the vernacular after they had first been read in Latin. He practiced the same circumspection in opening the door to singing in the vernacular at solemn liturgies (1953). On the other hand, he had already allowed the publication of bilingual rituals, especially in German and in French (1947).

As a first step to breviary reform, Pius XII simplified the rubrics (1955) and had a code of rubrics prepared, which John XXIII promulgated in 1960. The new pope also published a simplified rite for the dedication of churches and altars (1961). But he had already decided to leave it to the council now in preparation to formulate "the more important principles" (*altiora principia*) of a general reform of the liturgy (see the Motu Proprio *Rubricarum instructum* of 1960).

§4. The Liturgical Reform of the Second Vatican Council

Vatican Council II began its work with a discussion of the schema or preliminary draft for a liturgical Constitution that had been drawn up by a preparatory commission of bishops and experts from around the world. The Fathers spent no fewer than fifteen general meetings (October 22 to November 13, 1962) in discussing the reform of the liturgy.[18] But they introduced so many amendments into the original text that they were unable to produce a new text by the end of the first session of the Council; only at the end of the second session (December 4, 1963) did Pope Paul VI, "together with the venerable Fathers" ("*una cum Patribus Concilii*"), promulgate the Constitution *Sacrosanctum Concilium*, which had been approved by a vote of 2147 to 4.

18. On the preparation of the Constitution on the Liturgy and on the debates at the Council see C. Braga, "La preparazione della Costituzione *Sacrosanctum Concilium*," in *Mens concordet voci* (*Mélanges A. G. Martimort*) (Paris: Desclée, 1983), 381–403.

I. THE CONCILIAR CONSTITUTION ON THE LITURGY

BIBLIOGRAPHY

Constitution *Sacrosanctum Concilium* on the Liturgy: *AAS* 56 (164) 97–134. Official text and French translation in *LMD* no. 76 (1963); full commentary in *LMD* no. 77 (1964). English translation in *DOL* 1 nos. 1–131.

Acta Synodalia Sacrosancti Concilii Oecumenici Vaticani II 1 (Vatican Polyglot Press). This volume (in four parts) contains the schema submitted to the Fathers, along with their corrections (*emendationes*) and amendments (*modi*), which were examined by the conciliar commission.

A. G. Martimort, "Quelques aspects doctrinaux de la Constitution *Sacrosanctum Concilium*," in *Teologia, liturgia, storia. Miscellanea in onore di Carlo Manziana* (Brescia: Morcelliana, 1977), 179–96.

I. Oñatibia, "La eclesiología en la *Sacrosanctum Concilium*," *Notitiae* 21 (1983) 648–60.

SCDW, *Costituzione liturgica "Sacrosanctum Concilium." Studi* (Bibliotheca EL, Subsidia 38; Rome: Edizioni liturgiche, 1986).

After an introduction, the Constitution *Sacrosanctum Concilium* begins by expounding "general principles for the reform and promotion of the sacred liturgy" (ch. I); it then sets down a number of concrete directives regarding the mystery of the Eucharist (ch. II), the other sacraments and sacramentals (ch. III), the Divine Office (ch. IV), the liturgical year (ch. V), sacred music (ch. VI), and sacred art (ch. VII). Each of the main chapters begins with a short summary of biblical theology. For it is in biblical theology that the entire renewal of the liturgy is grounded, and the people of God cannot be brought to participate in the liturgy except to the extent that the table of the Word has first been made attractive to them. As a result, the liturgical constitution provides, above all else, an ecclesiology.

Chapter I begins by explaining the nature of the liturgy and its importance in the life of the Church. The liturgy is the place where the work of salvation that was accomplished by Christ in his paschal mystery and is continued by the Church is applied (5–6). As a result, Christ is present in the liturgy in many ways: in the assembly of the baptized, in the person of the celebrant, in the proclamation of God's Word, and in the sacraments, especially the Eucharist. "Rightly, then, is the liturgy considered as an exercise of the priestly office of Jesus Christ . . . by the Mystical Body of Jesus Christ, that is, by the Head and his members" (7). It is therefore a participation in the heavenly liturgy and provides a foretaste of this (8). Although it is not the sole activity of the Church, it is "the summit toward which the activity of the Church is directed; at the same time it is the fount from which all the Church's power flows" (10). By its nature, therefore, the liturgy calls for a "full, conscious, and active participation" of all the faithful in its celebrations. All of the faithful, being by baptism members of the priestly and kingly people, have the "right and duty" to take the part that is properly theirs in each liturgy (14). It is precisely in order to make this liturgical participation of the faithful easier and more fruitful that the liturgy must be reformed (21).

The Constitution goes on to explain the norms that must be followed in the renewal of the rites, the first being that "regulation of the liturgy depends solely on the authority of the Church" and that apart from the pope and, depending on the regulations set down in law, the bishops, "no other person, not even if he is priest, may on his own add, remove, or change anything in the liturgy" (22). Throughout the work of reform care must be taken to combine tradition and progress (23), and it must be kept in mind that "Sacred Scripture is of the greatest importance in the celebration of the liturgy" (24). Further norms derive from the hierarchical and communal nature of the liturgy (26–32) and from its didactic and pastoral character (33–36). It is at this point that the document touches on the problem of language in the liturgy; it recognizes that while the use of Latin is to be retained, "the use of the mother tongue . . . frequently may be of great advantage to the people" (36). Finally, the liturgy must be adapted to "the genius and talents of the various races and peoples" (37). In this last area, more than elsewhere, there is an important role for episcopal conferences (39), whose competence will be defined in later documents of the Council. In mission countries more radical adaptation of the liturgy may be needed (40).

Chapter II sets down rules for the revision of the *Ordo Missae*, after having recalled that the Eucharistic sacrifice is a memorial of the death and resurrection of Christ, a paschal banquet (47–54). The Council provides that in certain circumstances Communion may be received under both species (55) and that Mass may be concelebrated (57). In Chapter III the Council states that the sacraments "not only presuppose faith, but by words and objects they also nourish, strengthen, and express it; that is why they are called 'sacraments of faith'" (59). With regard to baptism the Constitution prescribes that a special ritual is to be drawn up for infants and that the catechumenate for adults is to be restored (64–68). The anointing of the sick is "not a sacrament for those only who are at the point of death" but for those also who are "in danger of death from sickness or old age" (73).

The Divine Office (ch. IV) is described as "the very prayer that Christ himself, together with his Body, addresses to the Father" (84). All the faithful are therefore urged to take part in it, either with a priest, or among themselves, or even individually (100). Chapter V reminds us that in the liturgical year "the mysteries of redemption . . . are in some way made present in every age, so that the faithful may lay hold of them" (102). "By a tradition handed down from the apostles" the liturgical year has for its foundation the weekly celebration of the Lord's Day, the day on which Christ was established as Lord by his resurrection; Sunday is therefore "the first holyday of all" (106). In Chapters V and VI, on sacred music and sacred art, the chief point to be noted is that while the Church is very concerned to preserve the treasures of her musical and artistic tradition, especially Gregorian chant (116), she "approves of all forms of genuine art possessing the qualities required and admits them into divine worship" (112).

II. THE IMPLEMENTATION OF THE CONCILIAR CONSTITUTION

BIBLIOGRAPHY

Enchiridion documentorum instaurationis liturgicae I (1963–1973) (Turin, 1976) (= *EDIL*). This volume contains all the documents published by the Holy See in implementing the conciliar constitution; references are also given to the translations of these documents into the principal languages.

Documents on the Liturgy 1963–1979. Conciliar, Papal, and Curial Texts, ed. by the International Commission on English in the Liturgy (Collegeville: The Liturgical Press, 1982).

Notitiae, journal of Consilium and its successors, for the publication of all decrees of limited scope (starting in 1965).

P. Marini, "Elenco degli *Schemata* del *Consilium* e della Congregazione per il culto divino (marzo 1964—luglio 1975)," *Notitiae* 18 (1982) 453–772. This fascicle of *Notitiae* was also published as a separate book (Vatican City, 1982).

Liturgia opera divina e umana. Studi sulla riforma liturgica offerti a S. E. Mons. Annibale Bugnini (Bibliotheca EL, Subsidia 26; Rome: Edizioni liturgiche, 1982).

A. Bugnini, *La riforma liturgica (1948–1975)* (Bibliotheca EL, Subsidia 30; Rome: Edizioni liturgiche, 1983).

On January 29, 1964, Pope Paul VI established a commission whose task was to be the implementation of the liturgical constitution (*Consilium ad exsequendam Constitutionem de sacra Liturgia* or simply "Consilium").[19] It comprised about fifty cardinals and bishops and more than two hundred experts and thus had a wide international representation. The Pope appointed as its head Cardinal Giacomo Lercaro, archbishop of Bologna, with Fr. Annibale Bugnini as his secretary. The latter was to remain in charge of the reform until 1975, when Paul VI suppressed the Congregation for Divine Worship, which he had established in 1969 as successor to the Consilium.[20]

---

19. Motu Proprio *Sacram liturgiam* (January 25, 1964): *AAS* 56 (1964) 139–44 (= *EDIL* 178–90 = *DOL* 20 nos. 276–89).

20. Apostolic Constitution *Sacra Rituum Congregatio* (May 8, 1969): *AAS* 61 (1969) 297–305 (= *EDIL* 1761–73 = *DOL* 94 nos. 678–84); Apostolic Constitution *Constans nobis* (July 11, 1975): *AAS* 67 (1975) 418–20 (= *DOL* 101 nos. 702–8).

The Consilium had a well-defined task: to revise the liturgical books in accordance with the norms set down by the Council, to provide instructions that would educate priests and faithful in the spirit that was to animate the renewal of worship, and also to make the reform gradually become a reality. But while the experts were quite familiar with the liturgical tradition and the sources on which they might draw in order to enrich the Roman body of prayers, they could not have suspected in advance the extent of the change that the use of the vernaculars in the liturgy would bring about.[21] The Council had launched a movement that had to be taken into account. Pope Paul VI's sure insight had seen that this movement could not be reversed. Within a few years the entire celebration would be in the vernacular in many parts of the world, and this in monasteries no less than in parishes. As a result the Council's directive that Latin should continue to be used in the Office quickly became a dead letter. Episcopal conferences were authorized as early as 1971 to permit the use of the vernacular throughout the Office and the Mass.[22]

As a result of the introduction of the vernacular it became desirable to have a larger number of prayers and songs, especially for the celebration of the Eucharist, for living languages are not as comfortable as Latin is with the continued use of the same formulas. At the Council not a single Father had proposed or even envisaged the introduction of several Eucharistic Prayers into the Roman liturgy. Yet this had been done by 1968.[23] In its labors the Consilium tried to remain scrupulously faithful to the norm set down in the Constitution *Sacrosanctum Concilium* (23), that tradition and progress were to be brought into balance.

Within the space of a year the Consilium published two documents that profoundly modified the celebration of the Eucharist. The first was the Instruction *Inter oecumenici*,[24] which promulgated the first innova-

---

21. Almost 350 languages or dialects are presently used in the liturgy. They are listed and classified in "Le lingue nella liturgia dopo il Concilio Vaticano II," *Notitiae* 15 (1979) 385–520.

22. SCDW, Notification *Instructione de Constitutione* on the Roman Missal, the book of the Liturgy of the Hours, and the Calendar (June 14, 1971): *AAS* 63 (1971) 712–15 (= *EDIL* 2575–81 = *DOL* 216 nos. 1769–77).

23. SCR, Decree *Preces eucharistica* and Norms (May 23, 1968) (= *EDIL* 1032–43 = *DOL* 241 no. 1930 and 242 nos. 1931–41); Letter *La publication* of Cardinal B. Gut, President of Consilium, to the Presidents of the Episcopal Conferences and National Liturgical Commissions (June 2, 1968), and Guidelines *Au cours des derniers mois* to assist in catechesis (June 2, 1968), in *Notitiae* 4 (1968) 146–55 (= *EDIL* 1044–62 = *DOL* 243 nos. 1942–44 and 244 nos. 1945–63).

24. September 26, 1964: *AAS* 56 (1964) 877–900 (= *EDIL* 199–297 = *DOL* 23 nos. 293–391); *Ordo missae, Ritus servandus* (January 27, 1965) (see *DOL* 196 no. 1340). — See Consilium, *De oratione communi seu fidelium* (*pro manuscripto*, January 13, 1865; 2nd ed., April 17, 1966; Vatican Polyglot Press, 1966); not a typical edition (= *DOL* 239 nos. 1890–1928).

tions to be introduced into the liturgy and described the setting of the celebration: the presidential chair, the lectern (ambo), the altar, the nave. Within a short time this Instruction would change the arrangement of churches throughout the world. The second document, the *Ordo* for concelebration and communion under both species, appeared at the beginning of 1965.[25] Henceforth the presbytery could manifest its unity around the altar, and the faithful could partake of the cup of the Lord.

The year 1967 brought the publication of two liturgico-pastoral instructions on sacred music[26] and the mystery of the Eucharist.[27] Meanwhile, the development of the rites of Mass that had begun in 1964 entered a new stage.[28] The work of the various study groups was also not slow in producing results. The Missal and the Lectionary for Mass, the Liturgy of the Hours, as well as the various rites making up the Pontifical and the Ritual, all appeared within a period of five years. In 1968, after the new Eucharistic Prayers, there came the rite for the ordinations of deacon, priest, and bishop.[29] In 1969 the rite for marriage was published,[30] as were the Calendar,[31] the *Order of Mass*,[32] the rite for the baptism of infants,[33] the Lectionary for Mass,[34] and the rite for funerals.[35]

---

25. *Ritus servandus in concelebratione missae et Ritus communionis sub utraque specie* (Vatican Polyglot Press, 1965), promulgated by SCR, Decree *Ecclesiae semper* (March 7, 1965): *AAS* 57 (1965) 410-12 (= *EDIL* 387-92 = *DOL* 222 nos. 1788-93).

26. SCR, Instruction *Musicam sacram* (March 5, 1967): *AAS* 59 (1967) 300-20 (= *EDIL* 733-801 = *DOL* 508 nos. 4122-90).

27. SCR, Instruction *Eucharisticum mysterium* (May 25, 1967): *AAS* 59 (1967) 539-73 (= *EDIL* 899-965 = *DOL* 179 nos. 1230-96).

28. SCR, Instruction (second) *Tres abhinc annos* (May 4, 1967): *AAS* 59 (1967) 442-48 (= *EDIL* 808-37 = *DOL* 39 nos. 445-74).

29. Apostolic Constitution *Pontificalis Romani recognitio* (June 18, 1968): *AAS* 60 (1968) 369-73 (= *EDIL* 1080-88 = *DOL* 324 nos. 1606-12); *Pontificale Romanum ex decreto sacrosancti Concilii Vaticani secundi instauratum, auctoritate Pauli pp. VI promulgatum: De ordinatione diaconi, presbyteri et episcopi* (Vatican Polyglot Press, 1968), promulgated by SCR, Decree *Per Constitutionem Apostolicam* (August 15, 1968) (= *EDIL* 1181 = *DOL* 325 no. 2613). English translation (International Commission on English in the Liturgy) of the Rite for the Ordination of Deacons, Priests, and Bishops in *The Rites of the Catholic Church* 2 (New York: Pueblo, 1980), 25-108.

30. *Rituale Romanum . . . Ordo celebrandi matrimonium* (Vatican Polyglot Press, 1969), promulgated by SCR, Decree *Ordo celebrandi matrimonium* (March 19, 1969) (= *EDIL* 1268-1332 = *DOL* 348 no. 2968). English translation in *The Rites of the Catholic Church* 1 (New York: Pueblo, 1976), 531-70; revised translation of the Introduction to the Rite in *DOL* 349 nos. 2969-86.

31. *Calendarium Romanum* (Vatican Polyglot Press, 1969), promulgated by SCR, Decree *Anni liturgici ordinatione* (March 21, 1969) (= *EDIL* 1268-1332 = *DOL* 441 nos. 3758-66. *General Norms for the Liturgical Year and the Calendar* (March 21, 1969) (= *DOL* 442 nos. 3767-3826).

32. Apostolic Constitution *Missale Romanum* (April 3, 1969): *AAS* 61 (1969) 217-22 (= *EDIL* 1362-72 = *DOL* 202 nos. 1357-66). — *Missale Romanum . . . Ordo Missae* (Vatican Polyglot Press, 1969), promulgated by SCR, Decree *Ordine Missae* (April 6, 1969) (= (See next page for notes 33, 34, 35.)

The next year, 1970, brought the promulgation of the rite for religious profession,[36] the *Roman Missal*,[37] and the rites for the consecration of virgins,[38] the blessing of an abbot and an abbess,[39] and the blessing of the oils and the consecration of chrism.[40] The Apostolic Constitution that promulgated the Liturgy of the Hours was dated November 1, 1970, but

---

EDIL 1373–1736, with variants in successive editions of the *General Instruction of the Roman Missal:* November 18, 1969, March 26, 1970, December 23, 1972, December 7, 1974 = *DOL* 203 no. 1367 [Decree] and 208 nos. 1376–1731 [General Instruction, 4th ed. of March 27, 1975]).

33. *Rituale Romanum . . . Ordo baptismi parvulorum* (Vatican Polyglot Press, 1969), promulgated by SCDW, Decree *Ordinem baptismi parvulorum* (May 15, 1969): *AAS* 61 (1969) 548 (= *EDIL* 1174–1842 = *DOL* 292 no. 2248). See SCDW, Declaration *Cum necesse sit* on the second typical edition of the rite of baptism for children (August 29, 1973) (= *DOL* 293 no. 2249). Translation of the rite in *The Rites of the Catholic Church* 1 (n. 30, above), 183–283, but with new translation of the Introduction in *DOL* 295 nos. 2285–2315.

34. *Missale Romanum . . . Ordo lectionum missae* (Vatican Polyglot Press, 1969), promulgated by SSCW, Decree *Ordo lectionum* (May 25, 1969): *AAS* 61 (1969) 548–49 (= *EDIL* 1858–91 = *DOL* 231 no. 1842 [Decree] and 232 nos. 1843–69 [Introduction]). — *Editio typica altera* (Vatican Polyglot Press, 1981), promulgated by SCSDW, Decree of January 21, 1981 (includes additions and modifications).

35. *Rituale Romanum . . . Ordo exsequiarum* (Vatican Polyglot Press, 1969), promulgated by SCCW, Decree *Ritibus exsequiarum*, August 15, 1969 (= *EDIL* 1921–47 = *DOL* 415 no. 3372). Translation of the rite of funerals in *The Rites of the Catholic Church* 1 (n. 30, p. 81) 645–720, but with new translation of the Introduction in *DOL* 416 nos. 3373–97.

36. *Rituale Romanum . . . Ordo professionis religiosae* (Vatican Polyglot Press, 1970; corrected reprint, 1975), promulgated by SCDW, Decree *Professionis religiosae* (February 2, 1970: *AAS* 62 (1970) 553 (= *EDIL* 2029–49 = *DOL* 391 no. 3229). Introduction to the rite: *DOL* 392 nos. 3230–48.

37. *Missale Romanum ex decreto sacrosancti Concilii Vaticani II instauratum, auctoritate Pauli pp. VI promulgatum* (Vatican Polyglot Press, 1970), promulgated by SCDW, Decree *Celebrationes eucharisticae* (March 26, 1970): *AAS* 62 (1970) 554 (= *EDIL* 2060 = *DOL* no. 213 no. 1765) — *Editio typica altera* (Vatican Polyglot Press, 1975), promulgated by SCDW, Decree *Cum Missale Romanum* (March 27, 1975) (= *DOL* 207 nos. 1374–75).

38. *Pontificale Romanum . . . Ordo consecrationis virginum* (Vatican Polyglot Press, 1970), promulgated by SCDW, Decree *Consecrationis virginum* (May 31, 1970): *AAS* 62 (1970) 650 (= *EDIL* 2082–92 = *DOL* 394 no. 3352). The rite of consecration to a life of virginity is in *The Rites of the Catholic Church* 2 (n. 29, p. 81), 132–64, but with new translation of the Introduction in *DOL* 395 nos. 3253–62.

39. *Pontificale Romanum . . . Ordo benedictionis abbatis et abbatissae* (Vatican Polyglot Press, 1970), promulgated by SCDW, Decree *Abbatem et Abbatissam* (November 9, 1970): *AAS* 63 (1971) 710–11 (= *EDIL* 2215–30 = *DOL* 398 no. 3276). The rites for the blessing of an abbot and an abbess are in *The Rites of the Catholic Church* 2, 115–31, but with new translation of the Introductions in *DOL* 399 nos. 3277–91.

40. *Pontificale Romanum . . . Ordo benedicendi oleum catechumenorum et informorum et conficiendi chrisma* (Vatican Polyglot Press, 1971), promulgated by SCDW, Decree *Ritibus Hebdomadae sanctae* (December 3, 1970): *AAS* 63 (1971) 711 (= *EDIL* 2231–43 = *DOL* 458 no. 3860). The rites for blessing the oils and consecrating the chrism are in *The Rites of the Catholic Church* 1, 515–27, but with new translation of the Introduction in *DOL* 459 nos. 3861–72.

the *General Instruction of the Liturgy of the Hours* appeared only on February 2, 1971.[41] The rite of confirmation was also promulgated in 1971.[42] In 1972 the rite for the Christian initiation of adults was published,[43] as well as the new arrangement of the chants for Mass,[44] the rites for the installation of readers and acolytes[45] and the rites for the visiting and anointing of the sick.[46] In 1973 there appeared the rites having to do with worship of the Eucharist outside of Mass[47] and the rite of penance.[48] The

41. Apostolic Constitution *Laudis canticum* (November 1, 1970): *AAS* 63 (1971) 527–35 (= *EDIL* 2196–2214 = *DOL* 424 nos. 3415–29). — *Officium divinum ex decreto sacrosancti Concilii Vaticani II instauratum, auctoritate Pauli pp. VI promulgatum. Liturgia Horarum iuxta ritum Romanum* (Vatican Polyglot Press, 1971–72. 4 vols.), promulgated by SCDW, Decree *Horarum liturgia* (April 11, 1971): *AAS* 63 (1971) 712 (= *EDIL* 2538, 2254–2537 = *DOL* 427 no. 3715). The *General Instruction of the Liturgy of the Hours* was issued in a first, nontypical edition on February 2, 1971; the definitive edition at the head of the *LH* has some variants. Translation in *DOL* 426 nos. 3431–3714.

42. Apostolic Constitution *Divinae consortium naturae* (August 15, 1971): *AAS* 63 (1971) 657–64 (= *EDIL* 2591–2604 = *DOL* 303 nos. 2499–2508). — *Pontificale Romanum . . . Ordo confirmationis* (Vatican Polyglot Press, 1971), promulgated by SCDW, Decree *Peculiare Spiritus Sancti donum* (August 22, 1971): *AAS* 64 (1972) 77 (= *EDIL* 2602–21 = *DOL* 304 no. 2509). The rite is in *The Rites of the Catholic Church* 1, 287–334, but with new translation of the Introduction in *DOL* 305 nos. 2510–28.

43. *Rituale Romanum . . . Ordo initiationis christianae adultorum* (Vatican Polyglot Press, 1972; corrected reprint, 1974), promulgated by SCDW, Decree *Ordinis Baptismi adultorum* (January 6, 1972): *AAS* 64 (1972) 252 (= *EDIL* 2539–2800 = *DOL* 300 no. 2327). The rite is in *The Rites of the Catholic Church* 1, 13–181, but with new translation of the Introduction in *DOL* 301 nos. 2328–2488.

44. *Missale Romanum . . . Ordo cantus missae* (Vatican Polyglot Press, 1972), promulgated by SCDW, Decree *Thesaurum cantus gregoriani* (June 24, 1972): *AAS* 65 (1973) 274 (= *EDIL* 2832–59 = *DOL* 534 no. 4275 [Decree] and 535 nos. 4276–4302 [Introduction])— see the *Graduale*, ed. by the Abbey of Solesmes (1974); but this is not an official edition.

45. Motu Proprio *Ministeria quaedam* (August 15, 1972): *AAS* 64 (1972) 529–34 (= *EDIL* 2877–93 = *DOL* 340 nos. 2922–38). — *Pontificale Romanum . . . De institutione lectorum et acolythorum; De admissione inter candidatos ad diaconatum et presbyteratum; De sacro coelibatu amplectendo* (Vatican Polyglot Press, 1972), promulgated by SCDW, Decree *Ministeriorum disciplina* (December 3, 1972): *AAS* 65 (1973) 274–75 (= *EDIL* 2294 = *DOL* 341 no. 2939). The rites (except for the commitment to celibacy) are in *The Rites of the Catholic Church* 1, 723–56, but with new translation of the Introductions in *DOL* 342 nos. 2940–48.

46. *Rituale Romanum . . . Ordo unctionis infirmorum eorumque pastoralis cura* (Vatican Polyglot Press, 1972), promulgated by SCDW, Decree *Infirmis cum Ecclesia* (December 7, 1972): *AAS* 65 (1973) 275–76 (= *EDIL* 2925–66 = *DOL* 409 no. 3320). The rite for the anointing and pastoral care of the sick is in *The Rites of the Catholic Church* 1, 573–642, but with a new translation of the Introduction in *DOL* 410 nos. 3321–61.

47. *Rituale Romanum . . . De sacra communione et de cultu mysterii eucharistici extra missam* (Vatican Polyglot Press, 1973), promulgated by SCDW, Decree *Eucharistiae Sacramentum* (June 21, 1973): *AAS* 65 (1973) 610 (= *EDIL* 3060–3108 = *DOL* 265 nos. 2089–90). The text of "Holy Communion and Worship of the Eucharist Outside Mass" is in *The Rites of the Catholic Church* 1, 449–512, but with new translation of the Introduction in *DOL* 266 nos. 2091–2103.

48. *Rituale Romanum . . . Ordo paenitentiae* (Vatican Polyglot Press, 1974), promul-

rite for the dedication of a church and an altar appeared in 1977.[49] In 1984 the *Liber benedictionum* and the *Caeremoniale* for bishops were published.[49a] A Roman martyrology is still in the works. During those fruitful years many other documents were published, such as the Directory for Masses with children,[50] the Instruction on extraordinary ministers of communion,[51] and the Instruction for Masses with small groups.[52]

This series of documents, which began a new page in the history of the Roman liturgy, introduced radical changes into current law. The new measures were ratified in the Code of Canon Law of 1983.[53]

gated by SCDW, Decree *Reconciliationem inter Deum et hominem* (December 2, 1973): *AAS* 66 (1974) 172–73 (= *EDIL* 3170-3216 = *DOL* 367 nos. 3063–65). The rite of penance is in *The Rites of the Catholic Church* 1, 341–445, but with new translation of the Introduction in *DOL* 368 nos. 3066–3109.

49. *Pontificale Romanum . . . Ordo dedicationis ecclesiae et altaris* (Vatican Polyglot Press, 1977), promulgated by SCSDW, Decree *Dedicationis ecclesiae* (May 29, 1977): *Notitiae* 13 (1977) 364–65 (= *DOL* 546 no. 4360). The rite for the dedication of a church and an altar is in *The Rites of the Catholic Church* 2, 185–293, but with a new translation of the Introductions in *DOL* 547 nos. 4361–4445.

49a. *Rituale Romanum . . . De benedictionibus* (Vatican Polyglot Press, 1984); promulgated by the SCDW, Decree *Benedictionum celebrationes* (May 31, 1984)—Caeremoniale episcoporum (Vatican Polyglot Press, 1984), promulgated by the SCDW, Decree *Recognitis* (September 14, 1984).

50. SCDW, *Directorium de missis cum pueris* (November 1, 1973): *AAS* 66 (1974) 30–46 (*EDIL* 3115-60 = *DOL* 276 nos. 2134–88).

51. Sacred Congregation for the Discipline of the Sacraments, Instruction *Immensae caritatis* (January 29, 1973): *AAS* 65 (1973) 264–71 (= *EDIL* 2967-82 = *DOL* 264 nos. 2073–88).

52. SCDW, Instruction *Actio pastoralis* (May 15, 1969): *AAS* 61 (1969) 806–11 (= *EDIL* 1843-57 = *DOL* 275 nos. 2120–33).

53. The slight changes occasioned by the new Code of Canon Law are detailed in "Variationes in novas editiones librorum liturgicorum ad normam Codicis . . . introducendae," *Notitiae* 20 (1983) 540–55. English translation by the International Commission on English in the Liturgy, *Emendations in the Liturgical Books Following upon the New Code of Canon Law* (Washington, D.C.: ICEL Secretariat, 1984).

STRUCTURE AND LAWS
OF THE
LITURGICAL CELEBRATION

A. G. Martimort

Introduction

The liturgy is a set of institutions that can be described, studied, and compared with other institutions by jurists, sociologists, and historians. At the same time, however, it is also a "mystery" in the sense that God is present and gives himself therein; in other words, it is also a supernatural reality which can be grasped only by faith and on which reflection is possible only by using the method of theology. For the liturgy is an essential activity of the Church; but the Church as "the society structured with hierarchical organs and the mystical body of Christ, the visible society and the spiritual community, the earthly Church and the Church endowed with heavenly riches, are not to be thought of as two realities. On the contrary, they form one complex reality that comes together from a human and a divine element."[1]

For this reason it is necessary, in studying the liturgy as a whole, to move back and forth constantly from the one level to the other. This second section will analyze the structure and laws of the liturgical celebration: the assembly and the various functions exercised in it, the dialogue established therein between God and his people, the signs performed in it, and the felt tension between unity and diversity. The third section of the book will attempt to develop a theology of the liturgical celebration; then, and for this purpose, to show how it is a mystery of salvation; and, finally, to bring out its value as a *locus theologicus* in which the faith of the Church is expressed and taught.[2]

---

1. Vatican II, Dogmatic Constitution *Lumen gentium* 8 (Flannery 357); see *VSC* 2; Pius XII, Encyclical *Mystici Corporis* (June 29, 1943): *AAS* 35 (1943) 221. — See C. Vagaggini, *Theological Dimensions of the Liturgy*, trans. L. J. Doyle and W. A. Jurgens (Collegeville: The Liturgical Press, 1976).

2. See the words used by Pius XII in an audience granted to Dom Bernard Capelle, December 12, 1935, in *QL* 21 (1936) 4, 134, 139.

Chapter I

The Assembly

BIBLIOGRAPHY

H. Chirat, *L'assemblée chrétienne à l'âge apostolique* (LO 10; Paris: Cerf, 1949).
A. G. Martimort, "L'assemblée liturgique," *LMD* no. 20 (1949) 153-75.
_____, "L'assemblée liturgique, mystère du Christ," *LMD* no. 40 (1954) 5-29.
_____, "Dimanche, assemblée et paroisse," *LMD* no. 57 (1959) 55-84.
_____, "Précisions sur l'assemblée," *LMD* no. 60 (1959) 7-34.
P. Massi, *L'assemblea del Popolo di Dio 1. Nella storia della salvezza (Principi di teologia biblica); 2. Nella liturgia (Principi di partecipazione attiva alla messa)* (Ascoli Piceno: Centro catechistico diocesano, 1962-63).
T. Maertens, *L'assemblée chrétienne. De la théologie biblique à la pastorale du XXᵉ siècle* (Collection de pastorale liturgique 64; Lophem lez Bruges: Abbaye Saint-André, 1964).
Y. Congar, "L'*Ecclesia* ou communauté chrétienne, sujet intégral de l'action liturgique," in *La liturgie après Vatican II* (Unam sanctam 66; Paris: Cerf, 1967), 241-82.
G. Cingolani, *L'"Assemblea" e la sua partecipazione al sacrificio eucaristico, nello sviluppo teologico dell'ultimo ventennio* (Rome, 1970 [no publisher named]).
J. Gelineau, *Dans vos assemblées. Sens et pratique de la célébration liturgique* I (Paris: Desclee, 1971), 17-58.
Y. Congar, "Réflexions et recherches actuelles sur l'assemblée liturgique," *LMD* no. 115 (1973) 7-29.
S. Marsili, "La liturgia culto della Chiesa," in *Anàmnesis* 1 (Turin: Marietti, 1974), 107-36.
Roles in the Liturgical Assembly, trans. M. J. O'Connell (New York: Pueblo, 1981). Papers of the Twenty-third Liturgical Conference at the Saint-Serge Institute in Paris, June 28 to July 1, 1976.

For the historian the first and most basic element of liturgy is undoubtedly the assembly. The very names used for the assembly in Christian antiquity are already revealing. As early as the third century the techni-

89

cal Greek word was *synaxis*, and it has continued in use,[1] but previously
syneleusis and even *synagogē* had been used.[2] In Latin, Tertullian uses
coetus and *convocationes*;[3] *collecta* is also found.[4] *Processio* is later, but
Tertullian already gives the verb *procedere* the technical liturgical sense
of "assembling, gathering together."[5] In any case, the first Christians were
more conscious of the movement and change of place required for the
assembly, and they preferred to use verbs when speaking of it: *synagein,
synerchomai, athroizomai, coire, convenire, congregari*,[6] these verbs sometimes being further specified by the addition of *epi to auto, in unum*.[7] Finally, the noun *ekklēsia*, which had such specifically biblical overtones
that it was transliterated into Latin and not translated, was used in referring not only to the entire group of scattered Christians but also to their
periodic gatherings for the Word of God and the Eucharist.[8]

It is to be noted, moreover, that liturgical prayers are always[9] formulated in the plural, since the celebrant speaks in the name of all or carries
on a dialogue with the people (*ho laos*). The people are said to surround
the altar (*circumstantes*), the deacon addresses them in his admonitions
and proclamations; it is for them that the Word of God is read; the priest
of the Mass speaks of them as offering the Eucharistic sacrifice together
with him: *nos servi tui sed et plebs tua sancta*.

§1. The Importance of the Liturgical Assembly in the Tradition of the Church

From the very beginning of the Church's history, the fact that Chris-

1. See the texts assembled by J. M. Hanssens, *Institutiones liturgicae de ritibus orientalibus* 2 (Rome: Pontificia Università Gregoriana, 1930), 24–34.

2. St. Justin, *Apologia I* 67: "syneleusis"; James 2:2: "synagogē."

3. Tertullian, *Apologeticum* 39, 2 (CCL 1:150): "Coimus in coetum et congregatio-
nem"; *idem, Ad uxorem* II, 4, 2 (CCL 1:388): "convocationes."

4. St. Jerome, *Ep.* 108, 20; see especially the *Acts of the Martyrs of Abitena* in P. Franchi
de'Cavalieri, *Note agiografiche* 8 (ST 65; Vatican City, 1935), 49–71.

5. Tertullian, *Ad uxorem* II, 4, 1: "Si procedendum erit." — On *processio* see B. Botte,
"*Processionis aditus*," in *Miscellanea liturgica in honorem L. Cuniberti Mohlberg* I (Rome:
Edizioni liturgiche, 1948), 127–33.

6. I have collected a number of passages in *LMD* no. 57 (1969) 55–74.

7. On *epi to auto* in Acts see L. Cerfaux, "La première communauté à Jérusalem,"
Ephemerides theologicae Lovanienses 16 (1939) 5–31, reprinted in *Recueil Lucien Cerfaux*
2 (1954), 125–56 (see especially 143 and 152, n. 1). — The phrase occurs several times in
St. Ignatius of Antioch, *Ephes.* 5, 3 and 13, 1; *Philad.* 6, 2, and 10, 1; *Magnes.* 7, 1–2, in
Camelot (ed.), SC 10:74, 82, 100, 146, 150.

8. This is evidently the case in 1 Cor 11–14 and in the expression *oikos ekklēsias* or
domus ecclesiae.

9. Except for biblical formulas and some private prayers such as the "apologies" (*apolo-
giae*) of the celebrant at Mass; see *The Church at Prayer* II, pp. 158–62.

tians gather regularly for prayer was regarded as characteristic of their way of life by those who described it to pagans.[10] The Acts of the Apostles speak often and with noteworthy emphasis of the gathering of the community for prayer,[11] while St. Paul has both directives and rebukes for the assembly (1 Cor 11 and 14).[12] Once the fervor of the first generation had receded into the past, the emphasis had to be put on the need Christians have of coming to the assembly; from that point on, pastors were not satisfied to reproach those who deserted it,[13] but described the spiritual benefits gained by attendance and based the need of this attendance on the very economy of salvation and the will of the Lord.[14] The sermons of St. John Chrysostom provide what is probably the most extensively developed patristic catechesis of the assembly.[15] Ascetical and canonical treatises also attest to the obligation Christians have of gathering together: the *Didache*, the *Teaching of the Apostles*, the *Apostolic Constitutions*.[16] Although the idea of the liturgical assembly became rather obscured in the course of the Middle Ages, it nonetheless remained implicit in the formulation of the commandment of Sunday observance.[17] Its restoration to its rightful place was one of the objectives of the liturgical renewal that have been achieved in the teaching of Vatican II.[18]

The actual assembly of Christians renders visible the gathering of humankind that Christ has accomplished; the grace that effects this gathering is mysteriously at work in every liturgical celebration. Without itself

---

10. Pliny the Younger, *Ep. X*, 96, ed. M. Schuster (Leipzig: Teubner, 1933), 363; St. Justin, *Apologia I 67*, ed. L. Pautigny (Paris: Picard 1904), 143; Philip Bardesanes, *The Book of the Laws of the Land 46*, ed. F. Nau, *Patrologia Syriaca 2* (Paris: Didot, 1907), 606–7; Tertullian, *Apologeticum 39* (CCL 1:150). — On all the texts cited in this paragraph of the text see A. Martimort, "Dimanche, assemblée et paroisse," *LMD* no. 57 (1959) 55–67.

11. Cerfaux (n. 7), in *Recueil* 2:125-26; see the table *ibid.*, 72-73.

12. As does James 2:1-4.

13. Heb 10:25; St. Ignatius of Antioch, *Ephes.* 5, 3 (SC 10:72).

14. St. Ignatius of Antioch, *Magnes.* 7, 1 (SC 10:100); St. Cyprian, *De dominica oratione 8*, ed. Hartel (CSEL 3/1:272; St. Ambrose, *De officiis ministrorum* I, 29, 142 (PL 16:64–65).

15. St. John Chrysostom, *Homilies on the obscurity of the prophets* 2, 3–4 (PG 56:181–82); *Homilies against the Anomeans 3. On the incomprehensibility of God 6* (PG 48:725); *Homilies against the Anomeans 11*, 3–4 (PG 48:801–2); *Homilies on 1 Corinthians 27*, 1–3 (PG 61:223–28); *36, 6* (PG 61:315); *Homilies on 2 Corinthians 18*, 3 (PG 61:526–27); *Homilies on 2 Thessalonians 4*, 4 (PG 62:491); *Sermons on Genesis 6*, 1 (PG 54:605); *Sermons on Hannah 5*, 1 (PG 54:669); and so on. — See *LMD* no. 57 (1959) 62–63.

16. *Didache 14*, 1, ed. W. Rordorf and A. Tuilier (SC 248), 192–93; *Didascalia apostolorum 13*, ed. R. H. Connolly (Oxford: Clarendon Press, 1929), 124–29 (Funk 2:59–63); *Constitutiones apostolorum* II, 59–63 (Funk 1:171–81).

17. *LMD* no. 60 (1959) 10–11; *LMD* no. 57 (1959) 74–82.

18. *VSC* 6, 10, 26, 41, 42, 106; Dogmatic Constitution *Lumen gentium* 11, 26; Decree *Presbyterorum ordinis* 5–6.

being a sacrament, the assembly is a sign that the biblical tradition enables us to understand.

§2. The Assembly Is a Sacred Sign

BIBLIOGRAPHY

In addition to the works listed in the preceding bibliography:

K. L. Schmidt, "Ekklēsia," *Theological Dictionary of the New Testament* 2 (original = 1938) 501–36.

L. Bouyer, *Liturgical Piety* (Notre Dame, Ind.: University of Notre Dame Press, 1955), 23–37: "From the Jewish Qahal to the Christian Ecclesia."

P. Tena Garriga, *La palabra ekklēsia. Estudio histórico-teológico* (Colectanea San Paciano, ser. teol. 6; Barcelona: Ed. Casulleras, 1958).

I. THE ASSEMBLY OF GOD'S PEOPLE IN THE OLD TESTAMENT

The arrival of the Hebrews' caravan at the foot of Sinai marked the beginning of a new and decisive phase in their history. Until then, they had been an unorganized throng of refugees and not a people, even though they had witnessed the wonderful deeds of God in Egypt and at the Red Sea. Now the Lord gathered all the children of Israel at the foot of Sinai; they heard his voice, received the Law from him, and promised to obey it: "You shall be to me a kingdom of priests and a holy nation." The covenant was ratified in the blood of the animals that Moses offered in sacrifice; from then on, the Hebrews were a people, the people of God (Exod 19–24).

In the biblical tradition this originating event was known as *Qahal Yahweh* or "assembly of Yahweh," a term that the Septuagint translated as *ekklēsia Kuriou;* the day at Sinai had been "the day of the assembly."[19] The Greek word *ekklēsia* brings out the first characteristic of this assembly, namely, that it was *convoked* by God himself;[20] secondly, when the Israelites were gathered, God was present in the midst of his people (Exod 19:17-18); thirdly, he spoke his Word there (Deut 4:12-13); and, finally, the gathering ended with the covenant sacrifice.[21] These four elements are found, in principle, in subsequent assemblies.

---

19. Deut 4:10; 9:10; 18:16; see 23:1-8.

20. *Ekklēsia* was the word commonly used in Greek cities for the regularly held assemblies of all citizens; see Pauly-Wissowa, *Realencyclopädie der klassischen Altertumswissenschaft* 5/2 (Stuttgart: Metzler, 1905), 2163–67.

21. See J. Lécuyer, *Le sacrifice de la Nouvelle Alliance* (Le Puy: Mappus, 1962), 9–51.

Some of these later assemblies[22] deserve special mention: the dedication of the temple by Solomon (1 Kgs 8; 2 Chron 6-7), the great Passover that marked the cultic reform under Hezekiah (2 Chron 29-30), the renewal of the covenant in accordance with the book "found" in the temple under Josiah (2 Kgs 23). Finally, after the return from the Exile there was the eight-day-long assembly that signaled the beginning of Judaism (Neh 8-9). The convocation was no longer a direct act of God but was done in his name; his presence was nonetheless ensured through signs: the cloud, the ark, the temple, or even simply the book we call the Bible. The reading of the book became an increasingly solemn event, for it was truly God who spoke in it.

As organized in the postexilic period, the passage of time was marked for the Jews by the anniversaries of these great assemblies of the past. These memorial days were celebrated in Jerusalem by faithful who came from all over the world on pilgrimage. And so it continued until the day when the coming of the Holy Spirit on the apostles revealed a new assembly, that of Jesus, to the throng that had gathered for one of the ancient feasts.

II. THE CHURCH OF CHRIST, ASSEMBLY OF THE NEW PEOPLE OF GOD

The mystery of salvation in Christ manifests itself concretely in the formation of a new people of God,[23] a gathering into unity of the scattered children of God (John 11:52), an assembly that is the Church (Matt 16:18). This assembly is convoked by heralds whom Christ sends (Matt 28:18-20). Its unity goes deeper than that of the ancient assemblies, for it is a body, a new temple, the Bride of Christ. The new covenant is sealed by the blood of a sacrifice that is forever one and irreplaceable: the Blood of Christ that is shed for the forgiveness of sins.

This people, more than the people at Sinai, is "a kingly and priestly people."[24] When Christians are incorporated into the Church through baptism they receive a character that delegates them to offer worship to God; as men and women consecrated to be the dwellings of the Holy Spirit and form a holy priesthood, they become the true worshipers whom the Father seeks (John 4:23). They are henceforth to offer spiritual sacrifices and to

---

22. Recall the assemblies for the consecration of Aaron and his sons (Lev 8:3) and of the Levites (Num 8:9); the one on Mount Ebal under the direction of Joshua (Josh 8:30-35); the one convoked by Jehoshaphat to beg God's protection against Moab and Ammon (2 Chron 20:5-14).

23. Vatican II, Dogmatic Constitution *Lumen gentium*, 9-13.

24. Exod 19:6; Isa 61:6; 1 Pet 2:4-10; Rev 1:6; 5:9-10; 20:6; *VSC* 6; and especially *Lumen gentium* 10-11.

"declare the wonderful deeds of him who called you out of darkness into his marvelous light" (1 Pet 2:9). And in fact the Book of Acts (2:42 and 47) shows the first Christians devoting themselves to prayer and the praise of God immediately after Pentecost.

III. THE LITURGICAL ASSEMBLY MANIFESTS THE CHURCH

All this explains why the liturgical assembly is the most expressive manifestation of the Church, its true "epiphany," for it shows and reveals what the Church is.[25] The assembly is so much the sign of the Church that in St. Paul one and the same word, *ekklēsia*, is used for both, while in the Acts of the Apostles the Church of the first days is seen as in almost continual assembly for prayer. The Fathers apply to each local liturgical assembly what belongs properly to the Church in its entirety. Thus it is the Body of Christ, so much so that Christians who do not join the assembly diminish the Body of Christ.[26] Christians are urged to gather "as in a single temple of God."[27] The voice of the assembly is the voice of the Church, the spouse of Christ, and the Mass—the sacrifice offered in the assembly—is the memorial and presence of the sacrifice of the cross that makes the Church to be. Here is how the Second Vatican Council sums up this teaching:

> This Church of Christ is really present in all legitimately organized local groups of the faithful, which, insofar as they are united to their pastors, are also quite appropriately called Churches in the New Testament. For these are in fact, in their own localities, the new people called by God, in the power of the Holy Spirit and as the result of full conviction (cf. 1 Thess 1:5). In them the faithful are gathered together through the preaching of the Gospel of Christ, and the mystery of the Lord's Supper is celebrated "so that by means of the flesh and blood of the Lord the whole brotherhood of the Body may be welded together."[28] In each altar community, under the sacred ministry of the bishop, a manifest symbol is to be seen of

---

25. *VSC* 41. — This is certainly not the only visible expression of the Church; there are also general councils, pilgrimages to Rome, teaching by pastors apart from the assembly, the charitable works of the community, and especially the sending of missionaries among infidels. The liturgical assembly is nonetheless the most common, ordinary, and accessible manifestation of the Church.

26. *Didascalia apostolorum* 13, ed. Connolly 124–25; see St. John Chrysostom, *Homilies on 2 Corinthians* 18, 3. In the modern period it was the idea of the Mystical Body that provided the starting point for a theology of the liturgy; see L. Lahaise, "La liturgie est l'Eglise en prière," *Cours et conférences des Semaines liturgiques* 14 (1937) 57–62; B. Capelle, "Théologie pastorale des encycliques *Mystici Corporis* et *Mediator Dei*," *LMD* 47–48 (1956) 67–80.

27. St. Ignatius of Antioch, *Magnes.* 7, 2 (SC 10:100).

28. Spanish prayer *Ad orationem dominicam*, attributed to St. Julian (PL 96:759B).

that charity and "unity of the mystical body, without which there can be no salvation."[29] In these communities, though they may often be small and poor, or existing in the diaspora, Christ is present through whose power and influence the One, Holy, Catholic and Apostolic Church is constituted.[30]

But in order that the universality of the Church may appear more clearly, it is also necessary that there be larger gatherings: stational Masses of the bishop, pilgrimages, congresses, and so on. In any case, because the assembly is the expression of the Church itself, it must be simultaneously a gathering of brothers and sisters in oneness of mind and heart and an organic body with distinct functions, as will be pointed out further on.

The assembly is never as transparent a sign as it should be; reading of the sign requires the exercise of faith.

IV. IT IS GOD WHO CONVOKES HIS PEOPLE

It must never be forgotten that, however great the efforts of pastor and faithful to ensure the gathering, it is God who calls his people together. His initiative is prior and prevenient; the assembly is an unmerited gift of God to humankind. The sacrifice of Christ, already accomplished on Calvary and made present anew through the Mass, is what founded the Church and now unites human beings in the assembly of the baptized. In addition, the assembly is called together and presided over by the bishop or his priests, who have power to do this by the mission they have received through apostolic succession and by the priestly character that configures them to Christ the Head.

V. THE PRESENCE OF THE LORD IN THE ASSEMBLY

"Where two or three are gathered (*synēgmenoi*) in my name, there am I in the midst of them" (Matt 18:20). The Fathers, and St. John Chrysostom in particular, apply these words of Jesus to the liturgical assembly in order to bring out the fact that this assembly includes a presence of the Lord.[31] The presence of Christ is linked to the sign of the gathering of the baptized in one place in order to pray; that is why it is customary in the monastic liturgy for those present to turn toward one another as they pray. But

---

29. St. Thomas Aquinas, *Summa theologiae* III, 73, 3.

30. Dogmatic Constitution *Lumen gentium* 26 (Flannery 381); this passage is repeated in SCR, Instruction *Eucharisticum mysterium* (May 25, 1967) 7 (= *EDIL* 905 = *DOL* 179 no. 1236). — See G. Cingolani, *L'"Assemblea" e la sua partecipazione al sacrificio eucaristico, nello sviluppo teologico dell'ultimo ventennio* (Rome, 1970), 31–43.

31. St. John Chrysostom, *Sermons on Genesis* 6, 1; *Sermons on Hannah* 5, 1 (PG 54:L 605 and 669).

this presence of the Lord is not sacramental in the strict sense of the word. Those gathered are there to hear the Word of God, which entails a further presence of the Lord. They are also there for the sacraments, which are actions of Christ, and especially for the Eucharist, which makes the glorious humanity of Christ really present.[32]

VI. THE ASSEMBLY PREFIGURES HEAVEN

The assembly is an image that anticipates the Church of heaven as glimpsed in the darkness of faith. This is why, in the visions of the Apocalypse, St. John describes heaven as a liturgical assembly: he sees there the same gathering of the people of God; he hears there the same acclamations, the same canticles (the Canticle of Moses in particular). In the earthly liturgy, like the heavenly, those assembled contemplate the risen Lord, the Lamb who has been slain; they see the glory of the Father reflected in him; they acclaim him by the glorious title of *Kyrios*. Like the heavenly assembly and in union with it—"with the whole company of heaven, venerating the memory of the saints"—the earthly assembly occupies itself with praise of God. The presence of Christ is the pledge and anticipation of his blessed return; thus liturgical prayer gives intense expression to eschatological expectation.[33]

§3. The People of God in the Assembly

I. THE GATHERING OF ALL THE PEOPLE

The assembly is open to all who meet two conditions: they have accepted the faith of the Church and have not publicly denied it; and they have received baptism or at least are preparing themselves for it in the catechumenate. The Church can, however, exclude certain kinds of guilty persons from its assemblies and its worship by imposing the penalty of excommunication or interdict. Furthermore, in ancient practice that is still attested in some liturgies, catechumens and public penitents were dismissed before the Eucharistic celebration proper.

The assembly is thus not reserved to a spiritual or intellectual elite, but is meant to bring together a whole people with all its rough edges, slow-wittedness, mediocrity, and limitations. That is precisely how the

---

32. *VSC* 7; see 33. — All this will be developed below in Section III, pp. 249–50.

33. *VSC* 8 (*DOL* 1 no. 8). — See O. Rousseau, "Le prêtre et la louange divine," *LMD* 21 (1950) 7–21; P. Prigent, *Apocalypse et liturgie* (Cahiers théologiques 52; Neuchâtel: Delachaux et Niestlé, 1964).

communities of the early Church show themselves to us in the sermons of St. Augustine, St. John Chrysostom, or St. Caesarius of Arles. A pastoral effort must therefore be made to guide this people in prayer during the liturgical celebration.

The members of the assembly are all sinners who look for God's mercy; this is why common prayer includes a public admission of sinfulness[34] and an appeal for the Lord's mercy. The assembly is not a gathering of the perfect; its spiritual poverty may even be scandalous, inasmuch as it is this group of sinners that must enable others to recognize the holy Church.

In the very first days of the Church's existence, the liturgical assembly in Jerusalem brought together all who believed in Christ. But the Church was meant to spread throughout the world; as a result, liturgical assemblies came to include only a part of the faithful, in accordance with the human limits set on gatherings: the Church of a region, a city, a village or neighborhood parish.[35] This establishment of the assembly at the local level is absolutely necessary; on the other hand, neither the local Church nor the local liturgical assembly is coextensive with the city or other human communities.[36] Moreover, the assembly must not be closed in on itself or isolated: it prays for the absent;[37] it gives a joyful welcome to brothers and sisters from other Churches who bring to it evidence of the catholicity of Christ's Church;[38] it seeks constantly to incorporate new members through baptism. Finally, while a certain local diversity is inevitable and traditional,[39] it must enhance and not hide the profound unity in faith and prayer that belongs to the Church spread throughout the world; the faithful from all countries must be able to participate, at least in some small way, in the liturgy of the place where they happen to be.

II. A GATHERING OF BROTHERS AND SISTERS AMID DIVERSITY

One of the essential laws of the economy of salvation is that the new people of God must bring human beings together despite all that humanly

---

34. *Didache* 14 (SC 248:192) already suggests a kind of penitential ritual: "prosexhomologēsamenoi ta paraptōmata hymōn."

35. See N. Maurice-Denis Boulet, "Titres urbains et communauté dans la Rome chrétienne," *LMD* no. 36 (1953) 14–32; E. Griffe, "Les paroisses rurales de la Gaule," *ibid.*, 33–62. — See *VSC* 42.

36. A. Chavasse, "Du peuple de Dieu à l'Eglise du Christ," *LMD* no. 32 (1952) 50–52; A. G. Martimort, "L'assemblée liturgique, mystère du Christ," *LMD* no. 40 (1954) 19; *idem*, "Précisions sur l'assemblée," *LMD* no. 60 (1959) 32–33.

37. A. G. Martimort, "L'assemblée liturgique," *LMD* no. 20 (1949) 163–64.

38. H. Chirat, *L'assemblée chrétienne à l'âge apostolique* (LO 10; Paris: Cerf, 1949), 18–21.

39. *LMD* no. 60 (1959) 24 and 32; Chavasse (n. 36). — *VSC* 37–38, 54.

divides them. Christ reconciled Jews and pagans, destroying the barrier that separated them and removing hatred (Eph 2:14). The birth of the Church on Pentecost was the reversal of Babel, as people from every nation heard together the voice of the apostles (Acts 2:6-11). There is no longer circumcised and uncircumcised, Jew and Gentile, Greek and barbarian and Scythian; no longer stranger and guest, slave and free. Instead, all of the baptized are one in Christ who is the Lord of all and who is all in all; there is only one faith, one baptism, one bread that we break, one cup of the Blood of Christ, one Body.[40] The liturgical assembly must manifest both these different origins and this union of brothers and sisters; it cannot accept the segregation of races, languages, conditions, and ages. "The Church exists not to divide those who come together, but to bring together those who are divided; that is what 'assembly' (*synodos*) means."[41]

The assembly must therefore promote the unanimity of hearts of which the early Church remains the ideal and model[42] and to which unanimity in forms of prayer gives external expression.[43] Christians must do violence to themselves and exercise a constant asceticism[44] in order to be reconciled with their brothers and sisters before offering their gift (Matt 5:23) and in order to do away with the scandalous distinctions of which St. Paul (1 Cor 11:12) and St. James (2:1-4) were already forced to complain. On the other hand, the assembly brings with it a grace of fraternal charity and unity.

III. ACTIVE AND INTELLIGENT PARTICIPATION

The active participation of the people in the liturgy, after having been so intensely experienced by the Christians of antiquity and so insistently called for by the Fathers, vanished more or less completely from the Middle Ages on. The faithful became strangers at the liturgy; sometimes they were deprived even of a view of the altar by the walls and rood lofts that set off the choir, and were thus worse off than the "silent spectators" of whom

---

40. Rom 10:12; 1 Cor 12:13; Gal 3:28; Eph 2:19; Col 3:11. See Rev 5:9.

41. St. John Chrysostom, *Homilies on 1 Corinthians* 27, 3 (PG 61:228).

42. Acts 1:13-14; 2:42-47; 4:33-37; 5:12. — See Cerfaux (n. 7), in *Recueil* 2:129-30, 150-52.

43. St. Cyprian, *De dominica oratione* (CSEL 3/1:271-72).

44. On this point see the important remarks of Y. Congar, "Réflexions et recherches actuelles sur l'assemblée liturgique," *LMD* no. 115 (1973) 21-25, which he himself sums up (23) in "three propositions: a) the Eucharist by its nature is not dependent on unanimity; b) it implies in its acceptance of differences a will to reconciliation; c) we need an ethic of conflicts."

Pius XI was to complain.[45] In 1903 St. Pius X took the initiative and began a return to tradition by maintaining that active participation in the holy mysteries and in the public and solemn prayer of the Church is "the first and indispensable source of the true Christian spirit."[46] His call, which was repeated by Pius XI in 1928, stimulated the liturgical movement and occasioned many doctrinal studies[47] that had their first fruits in the teaching of Pius XII in the Encyclical *Mediator Dei* (1947).[48]

The Second Vatican Council took an important doctrinal step forward when it showed that the right and duty of the faithful to take an active part in the liturgy are based on the baptism they have received[49] and on the nature of the Church as a kingly and priestly people who share, according to their state, in the priesthood of Christ and form a body that has various functions but is made one by the Holy Spirit. They experience and manifest this oneness by listening together to the Word of God, uniting themselves to the prayer of the celebrant, taking part through dialogue, singing, and bodily actions and gestures, and, at Mass, by sharing in the offering and Eucharistic communion.[50]

Participation must be not only active but intelligent and devout or interior.[51] For the liturgical action is a sign through which faith is to come into contact with the divine mystery that is accomplished therein; the action requires, therefore, a religious attention. The minds and hearts of the faithful must be in tune with their voices when they sing or carry on a dialogue;[52] they must make their own the prayer of the celebrant as they

---

45. Apostolic Constitution *Divini cultus* (December 20, 1928), no. 9: *AAS* 21 (1929) 40, and in A. Bugnini, *Documenta pontificia ad instaurationem liturgicam spectantia* (Rome: Edizioni liturgiche, 1953), 65.

46. Motu Proprio *Tra le sollecitudini* (November 22, 1903) (Bugnini 12–13).

47. Especially at the Sixteenth Liturgical Week in Louvain (1933): *La participation active des fidèles au culte* (Cours et conférences des Semaines liturgiques 11; Louvain: Mont César, 1934), with papers by B. Capelle, B. Botte, P. Charlier, A. Robeyns, and others.

48. *AAS* 39 (1947) 521–600, especially 552–62, which are entitled "The participation of the faithful in the offering of the Eucharistic sacrifice."

49. *VSC* 14; see earlier, SCR, Instruction of September 3, 1958, no. 93b: *AAS* 50 (1958) 656; St. Thomas Aquinas, *Summa theologiae* III, 63, 6. — Many writers have stressed the point that the deeper ecclesiological vision of Vatican II has shed new light on the participation of the faithful in the liturgy; see Cingolani (n. 30, p. 95), 61–80, and the authors he cites.

50. *VSC* 30; *GIRM* 3, 14–15, 20, 62 (= *EDIL* 1398, 1409–10, 1415–16, 1457 = *DOL* 208 nos. 1393, 1404–5, 1410, 1452).

51. These characteristics of participation are mentioned on almost every page of the Constitution on the Liturgy: *VSC* 11 (scienter, actuose, fructuose); 14 (plenam, consciam atque actuosam); 19 (internam et externam); 21 (plena, actuosa, communitatis propria); 48 (per ritus et preces id bene intelligentes, sacram actionem conscie, pie et actuose participent); 50 (pia et actuosa).

52. St. Benedict, *Regula monachorum* 19: "Let us stand to sing the psalms in such a way that our minds are in harmony with our voices (sic stemus ad psallendum, ut mens

listen to it; they must listen to the Word of God with docility.[53] At certain moments the celebration will require them to recollect themselves in a sacred silence. The faithful must therefore be given an understanding of the rites and texts; to meet the need a variety of pastoral activities must come into play, in particular a catechesis of the rites and, possibly, the services of a commentator. But all this would have been insufficient if the Council, and then Paul VI, had not boldly decided to allow the liturgy to be celebrated in the language of the participants.[54]

The Council also decreed that the reform of the liturgical books should be such that the Christian people might more easily grasp the meaning of the rites and might participate in the celebration in a fuller and more communal way.[55] This directive has been followed faithfully in formulating the rubrics and especially by starting each new liturgical book with introductions (*Praenotanda* or *Institutiones*) that are conspicuously pastoral in character.[56]

It follows from all this that the Christian cult possesses an originality distinguishing it from the pagan cults of antiquity, so much so in fact that its celebration required an entirely different kind of building. The liturgical assembly is no longer a gathering of spectators such as might be found in a theater; in it there are no onlookers but only actors. It seeks and attains to a unanimity, both interior and expressed, that, far from alienating the freedom of each member, is the fruit of this freedom when it is moved by the Holy Spirit.

IV. A CELEBRATING PEOPLE

Using paradox, St. Jerome says: it is not the festivity that gives rise to the assembly but the assembly that creates the festivity: "to see one another is the source of greater joy."[57] And, speaking of Pentecost, St.

---

nostra concordet voci nostrae)"; trans. in *RB 1980: The Rule of St. Benedict*, ed. T. Fry et al. (Collegeville: The Liturgical Press, 1981), 216–17. See *VSC* 11.

53. *VSC* 33.

54. On catechesis see *VSC* 35, 3; SCDW, Circular Letter *Eucharistiae participationem* to presidents of the conferences of bishops (April 27, 1973), no. 19 (= *EDIL* 3055 = *DOL* 248 no. 1993). — The subject of liturgical languages will be taken up in Chapter III of this section, pp. 161–67.

55. *VSC* 21.

56. See B. Neunheuser, "The Relation of Priest and Faithful in the Liturgies of Pius V and Paul VI," in *Roles in the Liturgical Assembly*, trans. M. J. O'Connell (Liturgical Conference Saint Serge 23; New York: Pueblo, 1981), 207–19.

57. *Commentaria in Ep. ad Galatas* 2, 4 (PL 26:378): "Non quo celebrior sit dies illa qua convenimus, sed quo, quacumque die conveniendum sit, ex conspectu mutuo laetitia maior oriatur."

John Chrysostom explains further: "The fifty-day period is over but the festivity is not, for every assembly is a festivity. How prove this? By the words of Christ himself: 'Where two or three are gathered in my name, I am in their midst.' If Christ is in the midst of the assembled faithful, what further evidence is needed that there is a festivity?"[58]

As a matter of fact, the assembly gathers primarily to celebrate with joyous thanksgiving the events of the mystery of salvation. It may also be convoked, however, for penitential rites: litanies, Lenten stations, vigils; but these penitential rites are almost always a preparation for a feast day.

A feast extends beyond the assembly proper; the faithful gladly prolong it by prayer and extraliturgical ceremonies that can at times achieve a high level of expression and form part of a people's cultural heritage. Feasts have often inspired sacred games or plays; they bring rejoicing to cities and families. By their nature they call for leisure, suspension of work, and holiday. These accompanying phenomena, including those that are secular, are very important from a pastoral viewpoint, provided their connection with the liturgy is realized or reestablished.[59]

§4. The Various Functions in the Assembly

BIBLIOGRAPHY

LMD no. 61 (1960): "Les fonctions liturgiques d'après la Tradition."
LMD no. 115 (1973): "Les ministères dans l'assemblée chrétienne."
E. J. Lengeling, "Der liturgische Dienst des Bischofs," in A. Kuhne (ed.), *Die liturgische Dienste* (Paderborn, 1982), 11–29.

An assembly, then, is a gathering of a people as brothers and sisters and in oneness of mind and heart, and all of its members take an active part. At the same time, however, it brings into play a series of different functions. Not everything can be done by everyone. The decision that

---

58. *Sermons on Hannah* 5, 1 (PG 54:669).

59. There is a fine passage in Neh 8:9-17 on prolonging the liturgical feast. — On the abstention from work on days of assembly see H. Dumaine, "Dimanche," *DACL* 4 (1920) 943–56. — On the various ways of prolonging the liturgical feast see J. Leclercq, "Devotion privée, piété populaire et liturgie au moyen âge," in *Etudes de pastorale liturgique* (LO 1; Paris: Cerf, 1944), 149–83; O. Casel, "La notion de jour de fête," *LMD* no. 1 (1945) 23–36; M. H. Vicaire, "Célébration liturgique et joie de la cité," *LMD* no. 22 (1950) 129–45; M. Righetti, *Manuale di storia liturgica* 2 (Milan: Ancora, 1955²), 400–8; K. Young, *The Drama of the Medieval Church* (2 vols.; Oxford, 1933); O. Hardison, *Christian Rite and Christian Drama in the Middle Ages. Essays in the Origin and Early History of Modern Drama* (Baltimore: Johns Hopkins, 1965). — On the general idea of a feast, F. A. Isambert, "Note sur la fête comme célébration," *LMD* no. 106 (1971) 101–10; J. P. Manigne, "De la fête et de ceux qui la font," *LMD* no. 109 (1972) 147–51.

this be so is not one of simple human prudence and for the sake of good order and convenience. It is so in virtue of the instituting action of Christ and the nature of the Church. An assembly has a president, who is the celebrant; and between the latter and the people there are intermediaries who carry out ministerial services: "In liturgical celebrations each one, minister or layperson, who has an office to perform, should do all of, but only, those parts which pertain to that office by the nature of the rite and the principles of liturgy."[60]

This differentiation of functions turns the assembly into an organic body that is the expression and manifestation of the Mystical Body of Christ (1 Cor 12:12-30),[61] and the liturgy into a harmonious whole in which each member plays his or her proper role.[62]

I. THE CELEBRANT .

BIBLIOGRAPHY

> J. Lécuyer, "Le célébrant, approfondissement théologique de sa fonction," *LMD* no. 61 (1960) 5-29.

The celebrant, who is a bishop or a priest, "presides over the assembly in the person of Christ."[63] This formula of Vatican II sums up three traditional statements:

a) A liturgical action has a president who is in effective charge of the assembly and leads its prayer. In antiquity his role included the assignment of the various functions, the choice of the texts to be read or sung, and the giving of the signal for beginning and ending the chants.[64]

b) This president is the celebrant; in other words, it is he who prays, performs the sacred actions, and breaks both the bread of God's Word and the Eucharistic bread for the people. He is therefore by no means just someone who sees to good order.

---

60. *VSC* 28 (*DOL* 1 no. 28).

61. *VSC* 26 (*DOL* 1 no. 26): "Liturgical services [*actiones*] . . . involve the whole Body of the Church; they manifest it and have effects upon it; but they also concern the individual members of the Church in different ways, according to their different orders, offices, and actual participation." — See *GIRM* 58 (= *EDIL* 1453 = *DOL* 208 no. 1448).

62. See St. Clement of Rome, *Ep. ad Corinthios* 40-41, ed. A. Jaubert, SC 167 (Paris: Cerf, 1971), 166-71.

63. *VSC* 33; see the Dogmatic Constitution *Lumen gentium* 21; Decree *Presbyterorum ordinis* 2, 6, and 13.

64. The practice is easily discernible in the sermons of St. Augustine and as late as the eighth century in *OR* I (Andrieu, *OR* 2:67-108).

c) He is president and celebrant not by appointment of the assembly or because of his human qualities, but because by ordination he has the priestly character proper to bishop or presbyter. In virtue of this character, he plays the part of Christ (he acts *in persona Christi*); he is the sign that the community does not gather by simple spontaneous agreement but is called together by the Lord in order to receive his Word and his gifts.[65] It is by reason of his identification with Christ as head and mediator that the celebrant can represent the entire Church and interpret its mind; this is why the liturgy attributes the importance it does to the celebrant's prayer.[66] When he consecrates the Eucharist, Christ becomes present in it.[67]

It is not enough, however, for the celebrant to have received priestly ordination; he must also share, within the unity of the Church, in the mission inherited from the apostles. Thus the primary celebrant, the celebrant *par excellence*, is the local bishop, and no one can preside over a liturgical action except by his command or permission; we find St. Ignatius of Antioch already laying heavy emphasis on this point in his letters.[68] In fact, the bishop presides even if he is not the celebrant.[69] His chair is so located that he is the center and focal point of the entire assembly.[70]

> The bishop is to be looked upon as the high priest of his flock, the faithful's life in Christ in some way deriving from and depending on him.
> Therefore all should hold in great esteem the liturgical life of the diocese centered around the bishop, especially in his cathedral church; they must be convinced that the pre-eminent manifestation of the Church is present in the full, active participation of all God's holy people in these liturgical celebrations, especially in the same eucharist, in a single prayer, at one altar at which the bishop presides, surrounded by his college of priests and by his ministers.[71]

Presbyters, who are the bishop's fellow workers and receive their mission from him, preside over the assembly in his place and in union with him,[72] but they cannot perform certain rites that are reserved to him by divine or ecclesiastical law.

---

65. See Y. Congar, "Réflexions et recherches actuelles sur l'assemblée liturgique," *LMD* no. 115 (1973) 14.

66. On the prayer of the celebrant see pp. 156–61.

67. *VSC* 7.

68. St. Ignatius of Antioch, *Magnes.* 3–4 and 6 (SC 10:96–98); *Trall.* 2–3 (SC 10:112–13); *Rom.* 9 (SC 10:136–37); *Philad.* 4 (SC 10:142–45); *Smyrn.* 8–9 (SC 10:162–63).

69. *GIRM* 59 (= *EDIL* 1454 = *DOL* 208 no. 1449).

70. See below, Chapter IV, p. 204.

71. *VSC* 41 (*DOL* 1, no. 41). See also *VSC* 26; Dogmatic Constitution *Lumen gentium* 26 and 28; *GIRM* 59 (= *EDIL* 1454 = *DOL* 208 no. 1449). — E. J. Lengeling, "Der liturgische Dienst des Bischofs," in A. Kuhne (ed.), *Die liturgischen Dienste* (Paderborn, 1982), 11–29.

72. *VSC* 42; Dogmatic Constitution *Lumen gentium* 28; Decree *Presbyterorum ordinis* 2.

The oneness of the priesthood is given expression in concelebration, in which several bishops or priests celebrate and take a real part in the properly priestly actions under the presidency of one of their number; the concelebration of Mass, now happily restored and a familiar occurrence in the Latin Church, reaches its highest degree of meaningfulness when priests concelebrate with their bishop, especially at presbyteral ordinations and in the chrismal Mass.[73] Episcopal consecration is not to be conferred by less than three concelebrating bishops.[74] Among the Byzantines, Armenians, and Copts, anointing of the sick has traditionally involved the concelebratory action of several priests.[75]

The faithful are reminded of the celebrant's dignity by the vestments he wears, the place he occupies (at his chair or at the altar), the ministers who serve him, the procession that accompanies him, and the marks of respect given to him. At his arrival and departure the faithful are to stand; they are to stand also and especially when he raises his voice in prayer.

In the absence of any priest a deacon can preside and celebrate certain rites; this is true especially of solemn baptism, the Liturgy of the Hours, and funerals.[76] Finally, the Church has acknowledged in the past and still acknowledges today certain local circumstances in which the faithful cannot obtain a priest for the Sunday assembly; even in such cases of unavoidable necessity the connection with the priesthood and the celebration of the Eucharist must be made clear.[77]

II. MINISTERIAL SERVICE IN GENERAL

Among the ministers who perform a service in the liturgical assembly, some are ministers of God's Word and are entrusted with the proclamation of the readings; others are ministers of the celebrant whom they assist and serve; others, finally, are more directly at the service of the people whom they lead or over whom they exercise a vigilance.

Some of these functions are reserved strictly to those who have received sacred Orders. Others are exercised regularly but not exclusively by ministers—acolytes and readers—who receive an "institution" with a blessing proper to them.[78]

---

73. VSC 57; Decree *Presbyterorum ordinis* 7–8.

74. See *The Church at Prayer* III.

75. Again, see *The Church at Prayer* III.

76. Vatican II, Dogmatic Constitution *Lumen gentium* 29; Paul VI, Motu proprio *Sacrum diaconatus ordinem* (June 18, 1967) 22–23: AAS 59 (1967) 701–2 (= EDIL 966–67 = DOL 309 nos. 2533–46).

77. Paul VI, Address to the Bishops of Central France during their *Ad limina* Visit (March 26, 1977), in *Osservatore Romano*, March 27, 1977 or *Notitiae* 13 (1977) 151–52 (= DOL 449 no. 3842).

78. Paul VI, Motu Proprio *Ministeria quaedam* (August 15, 1972): AAS 64 (1972) 529–34 (= EDIL 2877–93 = DOL 340 nos. 2922–38).

Deacons are the Church's ministers *par excellence,* as their very name *diakonoi,* "servants," indicates.[79] They are primarily servants of the bishop, but they also serve priests in the liturgical celebration; in addition, especially in the Eastern tradition, they are assigned to lead the people in their participation by telling them, through proclamations, what attitudes, external and internal, to adopt, and by suggesting prayer intentions in the form of litanies. They come and go from celebrant to people, so that the Byzantine tradition has compared them to the angels who in Jacob's vision ascend and descend the ladder that reaches to heaven.[80] Deacons prepare the gifts for the Eucharist and help in distributing Communion; in particular, they have the function, in most of the rites, of presenting the chalice.[81] Finally, at a rather early date, deacons were assigned to certain readings in the assembly; at Rome, from the time of St. Gregory the Great on, the only reading reserved to them has been the gospel.[82]

III. MINISTERS OF READING

Since the reading of God's Word has a very extensive part to play in the liturgical assembly, there have from the very beginning been *readers* distinct from the celebrant, just as there had been in the synagogue. But this function very quickly gave rise to a permanent hierarchical ministry into which participants were initiated by a blessing of the bishop.[83] On

---

79. Vatican II, Dogmatic Constitution *Lumen gentium* 29; *GIRM* 61 (= *EDIL* 1456 = *DOL* 208 no. 1451).

80. On deacons generally: Hippolytus of Rome, *Traditio apostolica* 8 (ed. Botte, LQF 39, pp. 22–25); *Constitutiones Apostolorum* VIII, 10 (Funk 1:488f.), etc.; Niceta of Remesiana, *Opusc. de psalmodiae bono* 3 (PL 68:376); *De septem ordinibus ecclesiae* (ed. Kalff), p. 40; St. Isidore of Seville, *De eccles. officiis* II, 8 (PL 83:789); Yves of Chartres, *De excellentia eccles. ordinum* (PL 162:517). — The Eastern tradition has been studied in greater detail by S. Salaville and G. Nowack, *Le rôle du diacre dans la liturgie orientale* (Athens: Institut français d'études byzantins, 1962); M. Hayek, "Le ministère diaconal dans l'Eglise maronite," *OS* 9 (1964) 291–322; A. Kniazeff, "The Role of the Deacon in the Byzantine Liturgical Assembly," in *Roles in the Liturgical Assembly* (n. 56, p. 100), 167–80.

81. St. Ambrose, *De officiis* I, 204 (PL 16:84); see J. Brinktrine, "Mysterium fidei," *EL* 44 (1930) 493–500.

82. St. Gregory the Great, Synod of 595, in *Registrum* (ed. P. Ewald; MGH *Epist.*) 1:363. — See *Constitutiones Apostolorum* II, 57, 7 (Funk 1:161).

83. In the description of the liturgy that is given by St. Justin, *Apologia I* 67 (ed. Pautigny 142), *ho anaginōskōn* is already mentioned as distinct from the *proestōs* and the deacons. The function of reader is a permanent one in Hippolytus, *Traditio apostolica* 11: "The reader is instituted when the bishop gives him the book, for he does not receive a laying on of hands" (Botte, LQF 39, pp. 30–31). An ordination in the strict sense was practiced at Carthage in the time of St. Cyprian; see the latter's *Ep.* 29 (ed. Bayard, 1:70–71); *Ep.* 38 (1:95–96); *Ep.* 39 (1:97–100). For the history of this ordination or institution down to the new Rite of 1972, see *The Church at Prayer* III.

the other hand, readers in the narrow sense saw themselves gradually excluded from the proclamation of the more venerable texts, which were entrusted instead to those at a higher level in the hierarchy. In Roman practice, for example, the gospel is reserved to the deacon, as we just saw, or to the celebrant if there is no deacon. Where instituted readers are lacking, their ministry can be given to other laypersons.[84]

From the beginning the liturgical tradition has known and practiced the solo singing of psalms that are meant, like the other readings, to be heard for their own sake; the same minister who did the other readings also did this solo singing,[85] except in the Antioch region, where there were psalmists who had received a blessing distinct from that of the readers.[86] The *General Instruction of the Roman Missal* has endeavored to restore the position of the psalmist by making it distinct from that of the reader, but without providing an institution to the function: "The cantor of the psalm is to sing the psalm or other biblical song that comes between the readings. To fulfill their function correctly, these cantors should possess singing talent and an aptitude for correct pronunciation and diction."[87]

---

84. *GIRM* 66 (= *EDIL* 1461 = *DOL* 208 no. 1456). Despite 1 Cor 14:34, the Church has always allowed the readings to be done by women in monasteries of women, at least in the East. *GIRM* 70 (= *EDIL* 1465 = *DOL* 208 no. 1460) leaves it to the episcopal conferences to decide on this matter for assemblies of the faithful and to determine the conditions under which women may read. On the translators, *hermeneutai*, of antiquity in Palestine see below, Chapter III, p. 162.

85. This was the case with the reader of whom Victor of Vite speaks in his *De persecutione Vandalica* I, 13 (PL 58:197): the man was pierced through the throat by an arrow while singing the alleluia in the pulpit on Easter; he dropped his book and collapsed. The Roman deacons were also psalmists before the time of St. Gregory the Great, who took away from them the readings that required too much musical ability: Synod of 595 (see n. 82, p. 105).

86. The psalmists (*psaltoi, psaltōdoi*) or singers (*ōdoi*) appear in the *Constitutiones Apostolorum* II, 28, 5, III, 11, 1 and 3; VI, 17, 2; etc.; they are also found in the Canons of Laodicea, canons 15, 23, and 24. The tradition of psalmists and singers has been continued in the two Antiochene rites: The Pontifical of the Western Syrians blesses them with a formulary that is today not distinguished from that for tonsure, while the Maronites (Lebanese synod of 1736) clearly distinguish cantors as the first minor order. Among the Byzantines, traces of this "order" seem quite dubious, e.g., the euchologion in ms. Barberini 390; see J. Morin, *Commentarius de sacris ecclesiae ordinationibus* (Amsterdam, 1695²), 85–86; A. Michel, "Ordre," *Dictionnaire de théologie catholique* 11:1393. — Psalmists never existed in the West, contrary to the *Statuta ecclesiae antiqua* and the writers and liturgical books influenced by them; see B. Botte, "Le rituel d'ordination des *Statuta ecclesiae antiqua*," RTAM 11 (1939) 229, 237–40; see also Andrieu, *OR* 3:542.

87. *GIRM* 67 (*DOL* 208 no. 1457). See the *Ordo lectionum missae* (editio typica altera, 1981), no. 56. — In the past the Church made a distinction between widows and deaconesses, with the latter being established as a kind of *ordo* by a sacred blessing. The deaconesses had an apostolic and caritative role in the community and, in some countries, helped in the baptism of women; see A. G. Martimort, *Les diaconesses, essai historique* (Bibliotheca EL, Subsidia 24; Rome: Edizioni liturgiche, 1982).

IV. MINISTERS OF ALTAR AND CELEBRANT

The deacons are the chief ministers of the altar and the celebrant. Their role in the Mass is described in detail in the *General Instruction of the Roman Missal* (61 and 127-41) or, for celebrations at which the bishop presides, in the *Caeremoniale episcoporum*.

Traditionally, there have also been other ministers instituted for service at the altar and for helping the celebrant and deacon; these are the acolytes of the Latin liturgy and the subdeacons of the Eastern rites. They are concerned chiefly with the preparation of the altar, the sacred vessels, and the material for the Eucharist. In our own times, acolytes have regained the role they had in Roman antiquity as extraordinary ministers of the Eucharist.[88] When a liturgical celebration is of a more solemn kind, it is fitting that there be several acolytes, with one of them carrying the cross in the procession and the others the candlesticks with the lighted candles.[89] The role of the thurifer, who is in charge of the censer, and (except for the ministry of the Eucharist) the various functions of the acolytes when the latter are lacking, can be entrusted to males from among the faithful or to clerics or members of the choir.[90]

V. MINISTRIES FOR THE SERVICE OF THE PEOPLE

As we saw earlier, deacons serve not only the celebrant but the people as well; this service is more limited in the West, more extensive in the East.[91]

The Instruction issued by the Congregation of Rites on September 3, 1958, gave official recognition, under the name of "commentator," to a minister whose function had been rendered especially necessary by the fact that the people did not understand Latin, the language that used to be spoken exclusively in the liturgy.[92] The difficulty has since been eliminated; the *General Instruction of the Roman Missal* continues, nonetheless, to acknowledge some value in the office of commentator: "This

---

88. Paul VI, Motu Proprio *Ministeria quaedam* (August 15, 1972), VI: *AAS* 64 (1972) 532-33 (= *EDIL* 2886 = *DOL* 340 no. 2931); *GIRM* 65, 142-47 (= *EDIL* 1460, 1537-42 = *DOL* 208 nos. 1455, 1532-37).

89. *GIRM, ibid.*

90. *GIRM* 70 (= *EDIL* 1465 = *DOL* 208 no. 1460): "Laymen, even if they have not received institution as ministers, may perform all the functions below those reserved to deacons." — On the traditional exclusion of women and girls from this ministry see A. G. Martimort, "La question du service des femmes à l'autel," *Notitiae* 16 (1980) 8-16.

91. Details on the deaconal admonitions will be given below in Chapter III, p. 153.

92. SCR, Instruction on Sacred Music and Sacred Liturgy (September 3, 1958), 96; text in *Official Catholic Teachings: Worship and Liturgy*, ed. J. J. Megivern (Wilmington, N.C.: McGrath, 1978), 180-88.

minister provides explanations and commentaries with the purpose of introducing the faithful to the celebration and preparing them to understand it."[93] In this activity, however, the commentator is simply a substitute for the deacon.

In antiquity the need was felt for the services rendered by porters or doormen; their function was to welcome the faithful and show them to their places, to exclude those who had no right to take part in the liturgy, and to ensure good order in the assembly, especially when the time came for Eucharistic communion. This service was sometimes performed by deacons; Rome, however, for many centuries had clerics who received the minor Order of porter. These functions were subsequently entrusted to laypersons and have today been restored to a place of honor by liturgico-pastoral advances.[94]

VI. THE *SCHOLA CANTORUM* OR CHOIR

A liturgical celebration normally requires the services of a group of the faithful who have greater skill in the musical arts; their role is to train the congregation and to perform the music that accompanies an action, or songs that are too difficult for the people. In the Syrian East this group consisted of ascetics, known as the "sons" or "daughters of the covenant." In the Byzantine world it was known as the choir, *choros.* In medieval Rome it was called the *schola cantorum;* the origins of this group are far from clear, although recent historians have at least eliminated many legends.[95]

The growth of active participation of the faithful in the liturgy should not cause the important role of the *schola cantorum* even today to be forgotten. It is true that in periods of liturgical decadence singers and *schola* had a tendency to infringe upon the role of the people and that the hierarchy frequently had to warn against this abuse. In its proper place, however, the *schola cantorum* provides a real group-ministerial service.[96] It must be so positioned in the church that it is really a part of the assembly but without distracting the faithful.[97] In the recruitment and training of its

---

93. *GIRM* 68a (= *EDIL* 1463 = *DOL* 208 no. 1458). See *VSC* 35, 3.

94. *GIRM* 68b (= *ibid.*). — On the history of the office of porter see *The Church at Prayer* III.

95. On the Roman *schola cantorum* see M. Andrieu, "Les ordres mineurs dans l'ancien rite romain," *RevSR* 5 (1925) 233–39; E. Josi, "Lectores, schola cantorum, clerici" *EL* 44 (1930) 282–90.

96. *VSC* 29, 114; SCR, Instruction *Musicam sacram* (March 5, 1967), 19–23 (= *EDIL* 751–55 = *DOL* 508 nos. 4140–44); *GIRM* 63 (= *EDIL* 1458 = *DOL* 208 no. 1453).

97. *GIRM* 274 (= *EDIL* 1669 = *DOL* 208 no. 1664).

members there must be a concern not only for technical skill but for spiritual quality.[98]

VII. ORGANISTS AND MUSICIANS

When the liturgical celebration allows the playing of instruments in certain cases and under certain conditions,[99] the musicians are then servants of the liturgy in which they are directly participating, although theirs is not a true ministerial service. They must observe the laws of the liturgy and, to this end, acquire the necessary knowledge of them, and they must make the spiritual effort their external participation supposes.[100]

The organ—by which is meant the true or pipe organ—has been given its letters patent of nobility by Vatican II.[101] The role of organists is an especially sensitive and important one: they accompany the singing, often play solos, and must promote the continuity and harmonious movement of the celebration, especially by their improvisations. Consequently, they require a very special competence in both music and liturgy.[102]

§5. Liturgical Actions Without a Congregation

The emphasis that the liturgical movement and then the documents of the magisterium have put on the essentially communal character of the liturgy and on developing this aspect of the celebration has at times been misinterpreted as a rejection of any celebration that does not bring the people together in the manner described.

a) In fact, however, in addition to the assembly, which is the sign and source of unity and by which is meant "the shared celebration of the eucharist, especially on Sundays and holy days, around the bishop and within the assembly of the parish, whose pastor is the bishop's representative,"[103] there have traditionally been at all times more limited, optional gatherings on other days; their continuing value is emphasized in the 1969 In-

---

98. SCR, Instruction *Musicam sacram* 24–25 (= *EDIL* 756–57 = *DOL* 508 nos. 4145–46).

99. *VSC* 120; SCR, Instruction *Musicam sacram* 62–65 (= *EDIL* 794–97 = *DOL* 508 nos. 4183–86).

100. SCR, Instruction *Musicam sacram* 67 (= *EDIL* 799 = *DOL* 508 no. 4188).

101. *VSC* 120.

102. *VSC* 120; SCR, Instruction *Musicam sacram* 62, 67 (= *EDIL* 794, 799 = *DOL* 508 nos. 4183, 4188). — See A. Deprez, "La musique d'orgue et les organistes," *Cours et conférences des Semaines liturgiques 1912* (Maredsous, 1913), 188–207; J. Kreps, *Le rôle unificateur de l'organiste liturgique* (Louvain: Mont César, 1921).

103. This passage is from the introduction (= *EDIL* 1843 = *DOL* 275 no. 2120) of the Instruction cited in the next note.

struction of the Sacred Congregation for Divine Worship on "Masses with special groups."[104] Such groups are promoted

> not for the sake of creating *ecclesiolae* or privilege, but to serve the faithful's particular needs or to deepen the Christian life in accord with the requirements and capacities of the members of these groups. This brings the advantages that spring from a special spiritual or apostolic, common bond and from the desire to help one another toward spiritual growth.[105]

b) In addition, certain liturgical actions do not involve the participation of the people. The prayer of monks or nuns, for example, only gradually became a liturgical prayer. A monastery or chapter does not by its nature bring the faithful together in assembly (in fact, such assemblies are even excluded in the churches of Orders following the eremitical life), nor is it necessary that their Office have a member of the hierarchy as its president. Nonetheless, by mandate of the Church such an Office is celebrated in the name of the Christian people. That is why this service is now always an act of public worship paid to God in the name of the Church. The same is true of the Liturgy of the Hours that is performed without any choral celebration or even individually by a cleric, a monk or nun, or one of the faithful.[106]

On the other hand, while the solemn celebration of most of the sacraments has traditionally taken place in the assembly and while this practice is to be encouraged,[107] urgency, necessity, and various less pressing considerations of propriety can at times mean that the minister of the sacrament is alone with the recipient. This is even the normal case with the sacrament of penance, since individual confession and individual absolution remain the ordinary rule when the faithful are reconciled with God and the Church, unless individual confession is physically or morally impossible.[108] In all these cases, the communal character of the sacramental liturgy is ensured at least by the action of the minister, which is an action of the Church, especially if the minister has received sacred Orders.

---

104. SCDW, Instruction *Actio pastoralis* (May 15, 1969): *AAS* 61 (1969) 806–11 (= *EDIL* 1843–57 = *DOL* 275 nos. 2110–33).

105. *Ibid.* (= *EDIL* 1844 = *DOL* 275 no. 2121). — See R. Coffy, "La signification du phénomène 'groupes,'" *LMD* no. 100 (1969) 123–29.

106. See *The Church at Prayer* IV, 182–84.

107. *VSC* 27 (*DOL* 1, no. 27): "Whenever rites, according to their specific nature, make provision for communal celebration involving the presence and active participation of the faithful, it is to be stressed that this way of celebrating them is to be preferred, as far as possible, to a celebration that is individual and, so to speak, private."

108. *Rituale Romanum, ordo paenitentiae* (ed. typica, December 2, 1973), Praenotanda 31; see the Rite of Penance, 31, in *The Rites of the Catholic Church* 1 (New York: Pueblo, 1976), 355.

Even the celebration of Mass by a solitary priest is valid. Following the Council of Trent,[109] the magisterium has had to repeat on various occasions that such a Mass remains a public and social act, since the Church is already present in the person of the priest and since the fruits of the sacrifice are for the entire Church. Such a Mass is also legitimate if it is celebrated under the requisite conditions of time and place. One should not speak of a "private" Mass (the term that used to be habitual in describing it), nor has any one the right to scorn or neglect such Masses.[110]

One ought, then, never to lose sight, either in spiritual outlook or in pastoral action, of the great principle of which Vatican II reminds the Church:

> Liturgical services are not private functions, but are celebrations belonging to the Church, which is the "sacrament of unity," namely, the holy people united and ordered under their bishops.
>
> Therefore liturgical services involve the whole Body of the Church; they manifest it and have effects upon it; but they also concern the individual members of the Church in different ways, according to their different orders, offices, and actual participation.[111]

---

109. Council of Trent, Session 22, chapter 6 and canon 8 (DS 1747 and 1758).

110. *VSC* 27; SCR, Instruction *Eucharisticum mysterium* (May 25, 1967), 3rd and 44 (= *EDIL* 901 and 942 = *DOL* 179 nos. 1232 and 1273); *GIRM* 209–11 (= *EDIL* 1604–6 = *DOL* 208 nos. 1599–1601).

111. *VSC* 26 (*DOL* 1 no. 26).

Chapter II

From Local Assembly to Universal Church

Diversity and Unity in the Liturgy

GENERAL BIBLIOGRAPHY

H. de Lubac, *Les Eglises particulières dans l'Eglise universelle* (Collection Intelligence de la foi; Paris: Aubier, 1971) ET: *Particular Churches in the Universal Church,* in *The Motherhood of the Church and Particular Churches in the Universal Church,* trans. S. Englund (San Francisco: Ignatius Press, 1982).
Y. Congar, "Initiatives locales et normes universelles," *LMD* no. 112 (1972) 54–69.
P. Harnoncourt, *Gesamtkirchliche und teilkirchliche Liturgie* (Untersuchungen zur praktischen Theologie 3; Freiburg: Herder, 1974).
R. Civil, "La liturgia e le sue leggi," in *Anàmnesis* 1 (Turin: Marietti, 1974), 181–207.
Liturgie de l'Eglise particulière et liturgie de l'Eglise universelle. Conférences Saint-Serge XXIIe, 1975 (Bibliotheca EL, Subsidia 7; Rome: Edizioni liturgiche, 1976).
A. Pistoia, "Dal rapporto 'rito-assemblea' al rapporto 'liturgia-Chiesa,'" in *Mysterion. . . Miscellanea liturgica. . . Salvatore Marsili* (Quaderni di Rivista liturgica, new ser. 5; Turin-Leumann: ElleDiCi, 1981), 233–58.

If the assembly of the praying Christian people, especially at the Eucharist, is to be the authentic "epiphany" of the Church that was described in the preceding chapter, then the further point made there must be verified. That is, the assembly must always show itself as one with the *catholica* or Church that is spread throughout the world; more accurately, the assembly must show itself as the very presence of this universal Church in a particular place and as a symbol of that charity and unity of the Mystical Body without which salvation is impossible.[1] Consequently, just as

---

1. See the Dogmatic Constitution *Lumen gentium* 26, cited in the preceding chapter at n. 30, p. 95.

113

the violence done in bringing together people who are different is felt in the local assembly, so, too, the organization of the liturgy will show a tension between the two poles of local Church and universal Church. In different historical periods and situations there will be a shifting balance between two requirements: on the one hand, the local rootedness of the praying community, and on the other the unanimity of the Churches in letting the single voice of the Spouse of Christ make itself heard without distortion. This is why the liturgy has always obeyed certain laws, but these laws have taken very different forms depending on place and time.

§1. From the Beginning to the Council of Trent

I. INITIATIVE AND TRADITION (FIRST TO FOURTH CENTURY)

BIBLIOGRAPHY

L. Bouyer, "L'improvisation liturgique dans l'Eglise ancienne," *LMD* no. 111 (1972) 7–19.

E. Dekkers, "Créativité et orthodoxie dans la *Lex orandi*," *LMD* no. 111 (1972) 20–30.

E. J. Lengeling, "Ordnung und Freiheit in der Liturgie der frühen Kirche," in *Einheit und Vielfalt, Festgabe H. Aufderbeck* (Leipzig: St.-Benno, 1974) 52–74. See E. J. Lengeling, *Liturgie. Dialog zwischen Gott und Mensch* (Freiburg: Herder, 1981), 74–83.

A. Nocent, "Dall'improvisazione alla fissazione delle formule e dei riti," in *Anàmnesis* 2 (Turin: Marietti, 1978), 131–36.

L'Année canonique 23 (1979): "La tradition apostolique, régulatrice de la communauté ecclésiale aux premiers siècles" (articles by C. Perrot, S. Légasse, J. Schmitt, A. Jaubert, P. Grelot, W. Rordorf, J. Liébaert, S. Charalambidis, C. Mondésert, A. G. Martimort, C. Munier, M. Jourjon).

A. Bouley, *From Freedom to Formula: The Evolution of the Eucharistic Prayer from Oral Improvisation to Written Texts* (Studies in Christian Antiquity 21; Washington, D.C.: Catholic University of America Press, 1981).

Historians of the liturgy have stressed the well-documented fact that in the early centuries the celebrant's prayer was not prescribed for him by a written text but was left to his own initiative and even to his powers of improvisation. In 150 St. Justin bears witness that "he who presides raises prayers and eucharists to heaven as much as he can."[2] In his *Apostolic Tradition*, which dates from the beginning of the third century, Hippolytus of Rome provides the text of prayers for ordination and the celebration of the Eucharist, but he also tells the reader:

---

2. St. Justin, *Apologia I*, 67, 5, ed. L. Pautigny (Textes et documents 1; Paris: Picard, 1904), 142–43. But the phrase *hosē dynamis auto* may simply mean "as he is able."

Let the bishop give thanks in the way we indicated earlier. It is not at all necessary that he say the same words that we have used, as if he had to try to repeat them from memory in his thanksgiving to God; rather, let each one pray according to his ability. If one man is able to pray at some length and offer a solemn prayer, well and good. But if another offers a shorter and simpler prayer, let him not be prevented, provided his prayer be sound and orthodox.[3]

It is possible to read and interpret these and other[4] texts anachronistically, as if they left celebrants of the second and third centuries an unrestricted freedom to follow private inspiration in expressing both their personal sentiments and those of the assembly. As a matter of fact, in the exercise of their freedom they were obliged to meet three requirements. The first is the one mentioned by Hippolytus: "provided his prayer be sound and orthodox"; this demand was all the more urgent, since heresies were already a serious threat to the true faith and since, in controversies with heretics, the prayer of the liturgy was soon to be invoked—and rightly so—as the expression and witness of the Church's faith.

A further point is that while liturgical prayers may at times have been improvised, they also followed a well-defined plan and had to express themes made obligatory for the celebrant by the very celebration itself. In this respect, the prayer of Christian communities resembled that of the Jews, for it was only at a late date that Jewish prayer was standardized in a detailed way in written formulas; in the time of Christ it was still regarded as satisfactory if prayers were faithful to a basic framework and gave expression to traditional themes organized according to an unvarying pattern. As a result, "improvised prayers could be very organic and profoundly traditional despite the freedom being exercised."[5]

Finally, it must not be forgotten that the bishop was recognized as president of the liturgy and pledge of its authenticity in the ecclesial communities of the first centuries. St. Ignatius of Antioch states this forcefully at the beginning of the second century: "Only that Eucharist is to be regarded as legitimate which is celebrated under the presidency of the bishop or of the person whom the bishop has put in charge of it. Where the bishop is, there is the community, just as where Christ Jesus is, there is the Catholic Church."[6]

But through the bishop and the succession in which he stands there is present in the communities the tradition that originated in the apostles,

---

3. *Traditio apostolica* 9, ed. Botte (LQF 39), 28–29.

4. Collected in E. J. Lengeling, "Ordnung und Freiheit in der Liturgie der frühen Kirche," in *Einheit und Vielfalt. Festgabe H. Aufderbeck* (Leipzig: St.-Benno, 1974), 52–74.

5. L. Bouyer, "L'improvisation liturgique dans l'Eglise ancienne," *LMD* no. 111 (1972), 14.

6. St. Ignatius of Antioch, *Smyrn.* 8, 1–2 (SC 10:163).

that is, the deposit received from the Lord,[7] the unwritten law that is to be faithfully passed on. This tradition, this law, regulates the sacraments and especially the Eucharist (1 Cor 11:23). It is worth noting that the first ascetical or disciplinary treatises claimed to be records of the teaching (*Didache, Didascalia*) or tradition (*Paradosis*) of the apostles; sometimes they adopted the literary form of a "testament" or showed the apostles themselves discoursing to disciples.

On the other hand, the tradition received did not settle all points; each bishop, each Church, was able to give the liturgy a particular form and figure. The freedom was limited, however, and the sometimes bitter controversies that arose among the Churches on points of discipline, such as the date of Easter, called attention to the need of some unanimity. As early as the second century, in the decision pronounced by Pope Victor, the bishops of Rome began to assert their inherent and supreme right to lay down laws for the liturgy of the entire Church: everywhere on earth Christians were to celebrate the same mystery of the Lord on the same day.[8]

II. LOCAL CUSTOMS AND REGIONAL DECISIONS (FIFTH TO SEVENTH CENTURY)

BIBLIOGRAPHY

J. Gaudemet, *Les sources du droit de l'Eglise en occident du IIe au VIe siècle* (Initiations au christianisme ancien; Paris: Cerf and C.N.R.S., 1985).

The controversies of the fourth century raised far more serious issues, since they were concerned with faith in the Trinity and Christ and led to painful schisms. For this reason, in the period around 400 various African councils issued regulations that celebrants were not allowed to ignore, and thus put an end to free improvisation of liturgical prayers: henceforth celebrants were to use texts approved in council or at least written texts that had first been submitted to the judgment of several bishops.[9] St. Au-

---

7. M. Jourjon, "La tradition apostolique chez saint Irénée," *L'Année canonique* 23 (1979) 193–202.

8. A principle clearly formulated in the fifth century by St. Leo the Great; texts collected in M. B. de Soos, *Le mystère liturgique d'après saint Léon le Grand* (LQF 34; Münster: Aschendorff, 1958), 31–34.

9. Council of Hippo (393), can. 21 (repeated by the Council of Carthage, 397): "Let no one in praying replace the Father's name by the Son's or the Son's by the Father's, and prayer at the altar is always to be addressed to the Father; and anyone who copies down prayers for his use from some other source is not to say them unless he has first shown them to more learned brethren." Council of Carthage (407), can. 103 (repeated as canon 12 of the Council of Milevis in the *Hispana* collection): "At the altar all bishops are to use the prayers approved by the council." Council of Carthage (419) (canon 103 in the *Excerpta*): "It was also decreed that prayers approved by the council, whether prefaces, commenda-

gustine, meanwhile, was complaining that the faithful were laughing at the barbarisms of some celebrants and their defects in reading.[10]

The decisions of the African councils were not limited to the subject of improvisation. These councils, along with frequent episcopal assemblies in Asia and the East, also handed down decisions on many questions of divine worship. In most instances, they dealt with points of detail in sacramental practice and with the elimination of abuses. Frequently, however, they also approved or encouraged innovations in singing and prayer. As a result, some regions began to follow a common set of usages; in the West, for example, this was true of Southern Gaul. The kingdom of the Visigoths would subsequently carry centralization still further; thus the Fourth Council of Toledo (633) prescribed "that there be but a single *ordo* of prayer and psalmody throughout Spain and Gaul: a single *ordo* for the celebration of Mass and a single *ordo* for the morning and evening Offices, so that there may no longer be divergences in ecclesiastical usage among us who are united by the same faith and under the same rule."[11] In the East, the Church of Armenia benefited as early as the end of the fourth century from the organizational genius of Catholicos Sahak,[12] while later on, in the seventh century, the liturgy of the Eastern Syrians was reformed and brought into unity by Patriarch Ishô'yab III († 680).

Peaceful exchanges also took place between Churches as a result of the prestige enjoyed by certain great bishops such as Basil of Caesarea and John of Constantinople or by places of pilgrimage, such as Jerusalem. The extension to the universal Church of the feasts of Christmas, Epiphany, and Ascension took place very rapidly during the fourth century, without there having been any need of specific decisions to this effect.[13] In like manner, the symbols of faith came increasingly to be

---

tions, or impositions of hands, are to be used by all in celebrating, nor are others to be said that are in disagreement with the faith, but only those composed by men of greater prudence." Texts in C. Munier, *Concilia Africae a. 345–a. 525* (CCL 149), 39, 333, 365, 218.

10. St. Augustine, *De catechizandis rudibus* 9, 13, in *Oeuvres de saint Augustin* 11. *Le magistère chrétien*, ed. and trans. G. Combés and J. Farges (Paris: Desclée De Brouwer, 1949), 50–51. — See E. Dekkers, "La codification des prières liturgiques, le rôle de saint Augustin," in *Forma futuri. Studi in onore del card. M. Pellegrino* (Turin: Bottega d'Erasmo, 1975), 845–55.

11. Canon 2, in J. Vives, *Concilios visigóticos e hispano-romanos* (España cristiana, Textos 1; Barcelona-Madrid: Instituto Enrique Flórez, 1963), 188. The "Gaul" to which this canon refers was the province of Narbonne, which was part of the Visogothic Kingdom.

12. On Sahak (387–438) see J. Mécérian, *Histoire et institutions de l'Eglise arménienne* (Beirut: Imprimerie Catholique, 1965), 47–53, and A. Renoux, "Isaac le Grand," *Dictionnaire de spiritualité* 7 (1971) 2007–10. On the liturgical reform of Ishô'yab III see A. Baumstark, *Geschichte der syrischen Literatur* (Bonn: Marcus-Weber, 1922; reprinted, 1968), 197–201.

13. See *The Church at Prayer* IV, 78–82.

formulated in the same terms, until finally the Nicene-Constantinopolitan symbol was adopted by the entire Catholic world.

Meanwhile, however, the Christian mind held firmly to the principle that was eventually to be formulated by St. Gregory the Great: *"In una fide, nihil officit sanctae Ecclesiae consuetudo diversa"* ("As long as there is unity in faith, diversity in usage is not detrimental to Holy Church").[14] St. Augustine had already spoken kindly of the diversity found in the disciplinary and liturgical customs of his time, because it highlighted the agreement and unity that existed in essentials. In his view, Christians who traveled or emigrated were to follow local custom wherever they might be; St. Monica had learned this to her cost when she went from Africa to Milan.[15] Italy, being a link between East and West, showed a good deal of diversity; local Churches did not necessarily adopt Roman usage,[16] even when they professed to follow it.[17] Within Rome itself, in fact, several usages, connected but different, coexisted peacefully; in addition to the papal liturgy there were the liturgies of the basilicas, titles, and monasteries.[18]

III. UNITY AND DIVERSITY IN THE MEDIEVAL CHURCH (EIGHTH TO FIFTEENTH CENTURY)

By the end of the seventh century several Churches of the West began spontaneously to imitate or even adopt the liturgy of Rome, which was richer in formularies and showed a greater literary beauty. The same trend toward unity manifested itself in the Byzantine Empire, to the advantage of the usages of Constantinople and Jerusalem; the only Churches that kept their liturgical autonomy were those that had not had, or no longer had, any ties with the empire and that celebrated the rites in their own languages.

---

14. St. Gregory the Great, *Registrum epistolarum* I, 41, ed. P. Ewald (MGH *Epist.* 1:57).

15. St. Augustine, *Ep.* 54–55, *Ad inquisitiones Ianuarii,* ed. A. Goldbacher (CSEL 34/2:158–213); *Confessiones* VI, 2, 2, ed. P. de Labriolle 1 (Paris: Belles Lettres, 1933), 118–20.

16. Milan was not the only place to have an autonomous local liturgy; also and especially worthy of mention are Aquileia and Benevento; see E. Cattaneo, *Il culto cristiano in Occidente. Note storiche* (Bibliotheca EL, Subsidia 13; Rome: Edizioni liturgiche, 1978), 173–83 (with bibliography). — The letter of Innocent I to Decentius, bishop of Gubbio (416; ed. R. Cabié, Bibliothèque de la RHE 58; Louvain, 1973), attests to diversity even in the Church of one of the Pope's suffragans; in the Middle Ages the letter would be "an important trump card in establishing papal centralization" (Cabié, 35).

17. St. Ambrose, *De sacramentis* 3, 5 (SC 25bis:94): "We are not unaware that this custom is not observed by the Church of Rome, whose model and form we follow in all things" (the reference is to the washing of feet after baptism).

18. A. Chavasse, *Le Sacramentaire gélasien* (Tournai: Desclée, 1958), xxiv–xxvi; J. Deshusses, "Les sacramentaires, état actuel de la recherche," *ALW* 24 (1982) 19–46.

Charlemagne made the trend official policy in his realm; he wanted to bring uniformity into the celebration of the liturgy and at the same time to reform the clergy. In this great undertaking his helpers, Alcuin and Benedict of Aniane, compiled the necessary books with the aid of models brought from Rome. Sacramentaries, lectionaries, and homiliaries spread the Roman *consuetudo*, along with an appropriate style of singing, throughout the Western empire. As a result, traces of Gallic usage disappeared very rapidly, while the Benedictine *Ordo psallendi* also replaced all other monastic usages. One consequence of this change of rite was that clerics could no longer rely on custom and living tradition and had to learn the Roman usages from books. The *Ordines Romani* and didactic collections compiled for this purpose brought about a change of mentality, since it was henceforth a written text, often poorly edited and poorly understood, that would determine the celebration and, by way of the rubrics, introduce persistent anomalies lasting in some cases down to the twentieth century.

The Pontifical compiled at St. Alban's in Mainz in the mid-tenth century was likewise very quickly accepted by most Churches, even by Milan and Rome, because it was far superior to previous attempts at pontificals. Milan nonetheless preserved its liturgical originality, though not without struggles, but Spain lost its by order of St. Gregory VII.

The unification achieved still left room for great diversity. All the Churches added the feasts of their own or regional saints to the Roman Calendar; they formed their own collections of votive Masses; they introduced local variants into the Roman Canon, especially in the lists in the *Communicantes*, the *Nobis quoque*, and the *Libera nos*; at various places in the Mass prayers of the celebrant were added, with each Church organizing them into an *Ordo Missae* of its own. The alleluia verses were likewise so varied that it is possible to identify the places to which the various manuscripts belonged. In the Office there were, outside of Milan, only two arrangements of the Psalter, the Roman and the Benedictine, but the lectionary of the saints and especially the responsorial bore witness to great freedom. Creativity showed itself in the hymns, sequences, and tropes. At the same time, however, there was a tendency to codify local usages in consuetudinaries and ordinaries. Meanwhile, at the papal court in Rome and Avignon, the masters of ceremonies were keeping increasingly detailed and precise daybooks and ceremonials. Furthermore, while the rituals retained their individuality, the Pontifical was moving toward uniformity; after a period of success for the Romano-German Pontifical of the tenth century, the Pontifical of William Durandus was adopted everywhere at the end of the thirteenth.

§2. Tridentine Liturgical Law and the "Age of the Rubricists," 1563–1963

BIBLIOGRAPHY

D. Bouix, *Tractatus de jure liturgico* (Paris: Périsse, 1886⁴).

F. Cimetier, "La liturgie et le droit canonique," in R. Aigrain, *La liturgie* (Paris: Bloud et Gay, 1935), 29–58.

P. Oppenheim, *Tractatus de jure liturgico* (3 vols.; Institutiones systematico-historicae in sacram liturgiam 2–4; Turin: Marietti, 1939–40).

F. McManus, *The Congregation of Sacred Rites* (The Catholic University of America Canon Law Studies 352; Washington, D.C.: The Catholic University of America, 1954).

M. Noirot, "Liturgique (droit)," *Dictionnaire de droit canonique* 6 (Paris: Letouzey et Ané, 1957), 535–94.

First the humanists, then the Protestant critics of the sixteenth century brought to light all the abuses that the Late Middle Ages had allowed into divine worship. The Council of Trent could not itself effect the reform that everyone wanted; but it was in accordance with the Council's desire and in its spirit that Popes St. Pius V, Sixtus V, Clement VIII, and Paul V undertook to unify and standardize the liturgy, while gradually taking from local bishops the power they had hitherto exercised. The new discipline thus created would be accurately summed up in the 1917 Code of Canon Law: "The Apostolic See alone has authority to organize the liturgy and approve liturgical books."[19]

There was no desire to touch the Eastern liturgies. Moreover, even in the Latin world no attempt was made originally to achieve uniformity; St. Pius V's intention was only to abolish usages that could not pride themselves on being two hundred years old,[20] while Paul V never strictly imposed the Roman Ritual he promulgated in 1614.[21] Meanwhile, however, the Missal and the Breviary were each preceded by a lengthy introduction, called the *Rubricae generales*, which anticipated all possible cases of interference between the various Offices and their formularies and described the gestures of the Mass in minute detail; the *Caeremoniale epis-*

---

19. Pius XII recalled this principle in his 1947 Encyclical *Mediator Dei*, no. 58: "It follows from this that the Sovereign Pontiff alone enjoys the right to recognize and establish any practice touching the worship of God, to introduce and approve new rites, as also to modify those he judges to require modification. Bishops, for their part, have the right and duty carefully to watch over the exact observance of the prescriptions of the sacred canons regarding divine worship" (*AAS* 39 [1947] 544; trans. in J. J. Megivern [ed.], *Official Catholic Teachings: Worship and Liturgy* [Wilmington, N.C.: McGrath, 1978], no. 237).

20. Bull *Quod a nobis* (July 8, 1568); Bull *Quam primum* (July 19, 1570).

21. Constitution *Apostolicae Sedi* (June 17, 1614): "We urge that as sons of the Roman Church they use henceforth in sacred functions the Ritual established by the authority of the same Church, which is both mother and teacher."

coporum gave directions for each minister in each sacred function; the reforms of 1911–14 would add further details in the form of *Additiones et Variationes*.

The reorganization of the Roman Curia that Sixtus V decreed in the Bull *Immensa* of January 22, 1588, created a new congregation *Pro sacris ritibus et caerimoniis*, which was headed by a cardinal and had for its task to continue the reform and correction of the liturgical books, to see to the proper performance of the sacred rites, and to solve difficulties connected with them. This congregation would continue in existence until 1969.[22] It was consulted with increasing frequency, since it was asked from all sides to decide on details not made clear in the liturgical books. Not all of its responses were published; a good many were included in the collection edited by Luigi Gardellini at the beginning of the nineteenth century, while the Congregation itself later gathered together all those (over four thousand) that it thought retained their value and published them in seven volumes (1898 to 1927) with the title *Decreta authentica Congregationis sacrorum rituum ex actis eiusdem collecta*.[23]

Knowledge of the liturgy was thus turned into a juridical science with the rubricists as its specialists. The latter sought to present syntheses of all the written laws contained in the liturgical books and the responses of the Congregation; they also went beyond the law, since each took into account the opinions of his predecessors.[24] To give one example: it was chiefly from the moment when, at the instigation of Dom Guéranger, the dioceses of France returned to the Roman liturgy, that the influence of

---

22. Despite successive changes in the organization of the Congregation, its liturgical competence remained essentially unchanged, as can be seen from canon 253 of the 1917 Code: "§1. The Congregation of Sacred Rites has authority to oversee and regulate everything having to do directly with the sacred rites and ceremonies of the Latin Church, but not with what relates only broadly to the sacred rites, e.g., rights of precedence and other matters of that kind. . . . §2. Its function is therefore especially to see to it that the sacred rites and ceremonies are carefully observed in the celebration of Mass, the administration of the sacraments, the performances of divine offices, and, in short, everything having to do with the worship of the Latin Church; to grant timely dispensations, etc."

23. The first three volumes, which appeared in 1898–1900, bring together 4,051 documents dating from 1588 to 1900; the fourth volume, published in 1900, contains the Instruction of Clement XI on the Forty Hours, together with appended decrees and commentaries; the fifth (1901) contains a general index of subjects. The collection was promulgated by authority of Pope Leo XIII in a decree of February 10, 1898; all earlier decrees not included in these volumes were abrogated. Two Appendixes were subsequently published and were equally official: Volume VI (Appendix I) was published by the Vatican Press in 1912, and [Volume VII] Appendix II in 1927; these volumes contain the decrees numbered 4,052 to 4,404 (years 1900–1926).

24. One of the best known was B. Gavanti († 1638), *Thesaurus sacrorum rituum seu commentarii in rubricas* (Milan, 1628), republished with commentaries by G. M. Merati (2 vols. in 1; Venice: Zerlettio, 1769).

the rubricists prevailed through the works of Italians Giuseppe Baldeschi and Pio Martinucci[25] and Frenchmen Pierre Favrel (1797–1855) and Léon Le Vavasseur (1822–92).[26] Le Vavasseur's books in particular went through countless editions, being continued into the twentieth century by Joseph Haegy (1860–1931) and then Louis Stercky (1867–1941).

The rubricists had to acknowledge, of course, that custom had traditionally had a privileged place in the general law of the Church; they were loath to accept it, however, in the exercise of the liturgical life, or at least they gave the most restrictive interpretation of it.[27] The rites were therefore always to be performed in a strictly identical manner, whether the people were present and whether the ceremony was taking place in a country long Christian or in a mission land. The only exception to this uniformity was introduced through the publication by Benedict XIII, in 1725, of a simplified ceremonial for small churches.[28]

§3. Unity and Diversity in the Reformed Liturgy of Vatican II

BIBLIOGRAPHY

> P. M. Gy, "La responsabilité des évêques par rapport au droit liturgique," *LMD* no. 112 (1972) 9–24.
>
> A. Caprioli, "Linee di statuto teologico della liturgia," *Communio* [Italian ed.] no. 41 (1978) 35–44.
>
> R. Kevin Seasoltz, *New Liturgy, New Laws* (Collegeville: The Liturgical Press, 1980).
>
> A. Pistoia, "Dal rapporto 'rito-assemblea' al rapporto 'liturgia-Chiesa': Il problema dell'adattamento e della creatività . . .," in *Mysterion. Miscellanea liturgica . . . Salvatore Marsili* (Quaderni di Rivista liturgica, new. ser. 5; Turin-Leumann: ElleDiCi, 1981), 233–58.
>
> A. Caprioli, "Dove va la liturgia. Riflessioni storico-teologiche sul problema liturgico," in *Studi ambrosiani in onore di Mons. Pietro Borella* (Archivio ambrosiano 43; Milan: Nuove Edizioni del Duomo, 1982), 75–91.

25. G. Baldeschi, *Esposizione delle sacre cerimonie* (4 vols.; Rome, 1839); modern republication in 2 vols. (Bibliotheca EL, sectio practica 4; Rome: Edizioni liturgiche, 1937–52); P. Martinucci, *Manuale sacrorum caeremoniarum* (Rome: B. Morini, 1869–72).

26. P. Favrel, *Cérémonial selon le rit romain par Joseph Baldeschi, traduit de l'italien et considérablement augmenté* (Dijon: Douiller, 1847); L. Le Vavasseur, *Cérémonial selon le rit romain d'après Joseph Baldeschi . . . et d'après l'abbé Favrel* (Paris: Lecoffre, 1857). — See J. A. de Conny, *Les cérémonies de l'Eglise expliquées aux fidèles* (Moulins: C. Desrosiers, 1873).

27. As did the Code of 1917, since it explicitly condemned (and therefore judged unreasonable: can. 2) the failure of the celebrant of Mass to observe the rubrics of his rite or his addition of ceremonies or prayers of his own; see M. Noirot in *L'Année canonique* 1 (1952) 129–40.

28. The title of this simplified ceremonial was *Memoriale rituum pro aliquibus praestantioribus sacris functionibus persolvendis in minoribus ecclesiis.*

In 1962 the conciliar assembly of bishops from throughout the world made it strikingly clear that the Church is present on all continents and in all cultures. It made the fact far more obvious than had the missionary outlook of Popes Pius XI, Pius XII, and John XXIII, or even the gradual establishment of indigenous episcopates or the opening of the College of Cardinals to Asia and Africa. No longer did the world consist of Christendom, identified with the old European nations, on the one side, and mission territories, on the other; there were now local Churches everywhere, all having the same dignity, the same rights, and the same duties. This situation, which was henceforth inescapably clear to all, was to have a decisive influence on liturgical reform. The Council Fathers therefore required that the revision of the liturgical books should be carried out with the assistance of bishops and experts from the various regions of the world.[29] More than anything else, the Council introduced a radical change of perspective in regard both to the authority responsible for liturgical legislation and to the spirit in which the legislation was to be applied. The Council's intention, moreover, was to promote an adaptation of the liturgy to the various cultures, and it established the principles and procedures that would ensure the authenticity of the adaptation. The change from the Tridentine discipline was so great that, not surprisingly, it was followed by a good deal of trial and error and by various forms of resistance.

I. THE AUTHORITY RESPONSIBLE FOR THE LITURGY

The Council could not envisage returning to the kind of liturgical freedom that reigned before the Council of Trent; such a return would be especially out of place in the present age in which the unity of the world is being stressed and communal solidarities are becoming more inclusive. The Constitution *Sacrosanctum Concilium* stresses, therefore, the need of preserving "the substantial unity of the Roman Rite,"[30] even while it also states, in keeping with tradition, that it holds "all lawfully acknowledged rites to be of equal rank and dignity" and pledges itself "to preserve them in the future and to foster them in every way."[31] It is for this reason that the Council reasserts the principle that "regulation of the liturgy depends solely on the authority of the Church, that is, on the Apostolic See and, accordingly as the law determines, on the bishop."[32] It even adds: "No other person, not even if he is a priest, may on his own add, remove, or change anything in the liturgy."[33]

---

29. VSC 25.

30. VSC 38 (*DOL* 1 no. 38).

31. VSC 4 (*DOL* 1 no. 4).

32. VSC 22, 1 (*DOL* 1. no. 22).

33. VSC 22, 3 (*DOL* 1 no. 22).

But the Council does introduce two important changes into the post-Tridentine discipline. The first has to do with the role of the bishop: as we have already seen, the Council reminds us that the bishop "is to be looked on as the high priest of his flock," and it requires that "both in attitude and in practice the liturgical life of the parish and its relationship to the bishop . . . be fostered among that faithful and clergy."[34] This teaching is repeated and developed in other conciliar documents.[35] As in the old legislation, the bishop, by reason of his office, has the right and duty of seeing to it that in his diocese the liturgical laws are observed in all celebrations and that no abuses are introduced. Henceforth, however, it is not enough that he be vigilant; he must also develop a pastoral program, foster the liturgical movement (*"actionem pastoralem liturgicam fovendam"*),[36] and promote and regulate the participation of the faithful in the liturgy, the beauty that holy objects ought to have, and the development of liturgical music. In order to discharge these duties, the bishop is to have a liturgical commission and, as far as possible, a commission for sacred music and another for sacred art.[37]

The second change is that Vatican II has inserted, between the Apostolic See and the diocesan bishop, a new agency, the episcopal conference. It can be said that in this area the Constitution on the Liturgy paved the way for further decisions of the Council, since the Decree *Christus Dominus*, which gave episcopal conferences their definitive official status, would not be promulgated until October 28, 1965.[38] In the interim it had already proved necessary, for the sake of implementing *Sacrosanctum Concilium*, to organize these "competent territorial bodies of bishops lawfully established," as they are described in article 22, §2; this was one of the subjects taken up in the Motu Proprio *Sacram liturgiam* of January 25, 1964, and in the First Instruction published by the Consilium on September 26 of the same year.[39]

An important measure of responsibility for the liturgy is given to the episcopal conference, an institution that in some respects replaces the provincial and regional councils of antiquity. The most important area of a conference's liturgical responsibility is that of making provisions for the use of the modern languages in the liturgy; these provisions are true

---

34. *VSC* 41 and 42 (*DOL* 1, nos. 41 and 42).

35. Dogmatic Constitution *Lumen gentium* 26; Decree *Christus Dominus* 15.

36. *VSC* 43.

37. *VSC* 45–46.

38. Decree *Christus Dominus* 36–38; see the passing references in *Lumen gentium* 23 and 29.

39. Motu Proprio *Sacram liturgiam* (January 25, 1964), X: *AAS* 56 (1964) 143 (= *EDIL* 189 = *DOL* 20 no. 288); SCR, Instruction *Inter oecumenici* (September 26, 1964) 23–31: *AAS* 56 (1964) 882–84 (= *EDIL* 221–29 = *DOL* 23 nos. 315–23).

decisions (*statuere*) and not simply requests or proposals; but the decisions, like those of plenary and provincial councils, must be presented to the Apostolic See in order that they may be *"probata seu confirmata"* ("approved, that is, confirmed").[40] The conferences also have the responsibility of preparing local rituals, if these be needed, especially for marriage. The rubrics of the new liturgical books leave room for some adaptation to local circumstances, with the conferences once again having authority to decide in these areas.[41]

This ratification of the acts of episcopal conferences is now a major responsibility of the Apostolic See, along with the preparation and publication of liturgical books. The pope has entrusted the task to the organizations that have successively replaced the Congregation of Rites: the Congregation for Divine Worship, from 1969 to 1975; the Congregation for the Discipline of the Sacraments and Divine Worship, from 1975 to 1984; and the Congregation for Divine Worship again, from 1984 on.

II. THE NEW SPIRIT IN LITURGICAL LEGISLATION

BIBLIOGRAPHY

A. M. Triacca, "Adattamento liturgico: utopia, velleità o strumento della pastorale liturgica," *Notitiae* 15 (1979) 26–45.

Except for the Ritual, the rubrics in the liturgical books of the Tridentine reform simply gave a detailed description of how the rite was to be performed; they seemed almost to ignore the possible presence of the Christian people at the celebration. Vatican II, on the contrary, wanted a liturgico-pastoral theology to be included in the legislation. The rubrics, said the Council, must provide for the part to be played by the faithful;[42] the latter, moreover, have a right to a catechesis of the rites from their pastors, especially since the liturgy is by its nature a source of rich instruction for the people.[43] "It is . . . of the highest importance that the faithful should readily understand the sacramental signs."[44]

The Council does not simply require that a pedagogical effort be made. In addition it says—and this is something new—that "provisions shall also

---

40. *VSC* 36, 3 (*DOL* 1 no. 36). This formula emerged from the conciliar debates and must be interpreted in the light of these and, in particular, of the official commentary that Msgr. Calewaert, bishop of Ghent and presenter of the text, gave to the Fathers as he asked for their approval; see *Emendationes* IV, 14–15.

41. *VSC* 38, 63b, 77, 110, 119, 120, 128.

42. *VSC* 31.

43. *VSC* 14, 19, 33–36.

44. *VSC* 59 (*DOL* 1 no. 59).

be made, even in the revision of the liturgical books, for legitimate variations and adaptations to different groups, regions, and peoples" and that this principle "should be borne in mind when rites are drawn up and rubrics devised."[45] The diversification is to be determined by the authority of the episcopal conferences. "Within the limits set by the *editio typica* of the liturgical books" and "in accord with the fundamental norms laid down in this Constitution" the conferences have authority "to specify adaptations, especially in the case of the administration of the sacraments, the sacramentals, processions, liturgical language, sacred music, and the arts."[46]

The revisers of the liturgical books have faithfully obeyed the instructions of the Council. Both the Missal and the book for the Liturgy of the Hours begin with a lengthy *Institutio* or Instruction, while the various parts of the Pontifical and the Ritual are prefaced by *Praenotanda* or Introductions. All of these documents give a doctrinal explanation of the rites and each of their parts; they provide for several ways of carrying out the liturgical actions, depending on the circumstances and the character of the assembly. Sometimes, in fact, the Apostolic See has even judged it advisable to publish special Instructions in order better to respond to particular situations; such are, for example, the Instruction on Masses with special groups[47] and the Directory for Masses with children.[48] A choice of several formulas is frequently given for one and the same liturgical action; invitations and introductions to actions are almost always offered as suggestions, "using these or similar words." The rubrics often invoke the pastoral or spiritual judgment of the celebrant: *"pro opportunitate," "laudabiliter," "De more," "ad libitum,"* although these must not be interpreted as invitations to do whatever he wants.

Furthermore, the episcopal conferences are to foster creativity in certain areas; the liturgical books often explicitly grant this latitude to the conferences, but the latter must exercise their authority with regard to texts that are to originate in this manner, so as to ensure both their orthodoxy and their liturgical appropriateness. The scope of this concession is necessarily limited: creativity is to be exercised only in the nonbiblical songs and not in the presidential prayers; translation of the latter into the modern vernaculars will of course require adaptations at times, but these must have the express approval of the Apostolic See.[49]

---

45. *VSC* 38 (*DOL* 1 no. 38).

46. *VSC* 39 (*DOL* 1 no. 39); see 63b, 68, 67.

47. SCDW, Instruction *Actio pastoralis* (May 15, 1969): *AAS* 61 (1969) 806–11 (= *EDIL* 1843–57 = *DOL* 275 nos. 2120–33).

48. November 1, 1973: *AAS* 66 (1974) 30–46 (= *EDIL* 3115–69 = *DOL* 276 nos. 2134–88).

49. See the next chapter, pp. 165–67.

Some priests are confused by the flexibility of the new legislation and think that each celebrant can simply exercise his own creativity; they are following a mirage: the supposed primitive ideal of improvisation.[50]

III. ADAPTATION TO THE CULTURES OF THE YOUNG CHURCHES

BIBLIOGRAPHY

B. Botte, "Le problème de l'adaptation de la liturgie," *Revue du clergé africain* 18 (1963) 307–30.

A. G. Martimort, "Adaptation liturgique," *EL* 79 (1965) 3–16.

A. T. Sanon, "L'africanisation de la liturgie," *LMD* no. 123 (1975) 108–25 (with an extensive bibliography).

C. Braga, "Un problema fondamentale di pastorale liturgica: adattamento e incarnazione nelle varie culture," *EL* 89 (1975) 5–39.

A. Chupungco, *The Cosmic Elements of Christian Passover* (Studia Anselmiana 72, Analecta liturgica 3; Rome, 1977).

H. Vinck, "La liturgie renovée en Afrique," *QL* 58 (1977) 51–60.

I. Auf der Maur, "Liturgie in den Evangelisationsgebieten besonders in Afrika," *ALW* 22 (1980) 282–319, especially 298–308.

A. Chupungco, "A Historical Survey of Liturgical Adaptation," *Notitiae* 17 (1981) 28–43.

J. Aldazábal, "Las 'otras' liturgias se renuevan," *Phase* 21 (1981) 109–36.

A. Chupungco, *Cultural Adaptation of the Liturgy* (New York: Paulist, 1982).

The possible adaptations provided for in the liturgical books will be insufficient in many of the young Churches formerly known as "mission territories." The debates at the Council and the evidence gathered at congresses or in periodicals have shown the need for a more thoroughgoing adaptation, whether one considers the difficulties encountered in various regions or whether one is concerned to adapt the rites to the genius of each people and accept some elements of their culture into the liturgy. The early Church, it is said, embodied its worship in cultural forms that today differentiate the various liturgical families of East and West.

The Council states clearly the general principles governing adaptation:

> Even in the liturgy the Church has no wish to impose a rigid uniformity in matters that do not affect the faith or the good of the whole community; rather the Church respects and fosters the genius and talents of the various races and peoples. The Church considers with sympathy and, if possible,

---

50. M. Thurian, "Creatività e spontaneità nella liturgia," *Unitas* 29 (1974) 8–16; B. Botte, "La libre composition des prières liturgiques," *QL* 55 (1974) 211–15; P. De Clerck, "Improvisation et livres liturgiques, leçons d'une histoire," *Communautés et liturgie* 60 (1978) 109–26. See Sr. Marie du Saint Esprit, "La créativité liturgique à travers quelques revues," *LMD* no. 114 (1973) 97–109.

preserves intact the elements in these peoples' way of life that are not indissolubly bound up with superstition and error. Sometimes in fact the Church admits such elements into the liturgy itself, provided they are in keeping with the true and authentic spirit of the liturgy.[51]

The application of the principles is inevitably a sensitive matter. On the one hand, Christianity must avoid every form of syncretism, which would set Christian rites side by side with rites or customs that are too closely associated with the pagan religions. On the other hand, given the rapid evolution of the indigenous civilizations, the acceptance of various local usages into the liturgy may give the impression of indulging in folklore, if care is not exercised. Only the local authorities can properly assess these difficulties.

But there are still more serious problems, in the solving of which the local Churches must look to all the other Churches, since the problems involve the unity of the faith, the authenticity of God's Word, and the sacramental dispensation. Christianity is a history of salvation; the revealed message has been set down in writings that require not only that we engage in the philological labor of translation but also that we come to understand a particular ancient civilization, that of the Israelites. The liturgy is based on foundational events of which it is the memorial, so that its celebration today makes a once-and-for-all event come alive again. Thus the Eucharist is not an ordinary meal but the memorial of the Last Supper; in more general terms, the sacramental signs are biblical signs, as we shall see further on. They allow for a certain degree of "free play" (*Spielraum*), as Joseph Pascher has said,[52] but this is limited; there must be fidelity to the meaning of the rite as willed by Christ.

Finally, adaptation must avoid the danger of tribal compartmentalization, which would end in the dismemberment of the local Church and obscure the manifestation of its unity despite, and amid, diversity. For example, as we saw earlier, the Church of the first centuries realized the importance of celebrating Easter everywhere on the same day.

All this explains why Vatican II established a special procedure for dealing with these problems. Since "in some places and circumstances . . . an even more radical adaptation of the liturgy is needed and [since] this entails greater difficulties," the episcopal conferences must "carefully and prudently weigh what elements from the traditions and culture of individual peoples may be appropriately admitted into divine worship." Adaptations that the conferences judge useful or necessary will not be decreed

---

51. *VSC* 37 (*DOL* 1 no. 37).

52. J. Pascher, *Form und Formenwandel sakramentaler Feier* (Münster: Aschendorff, 1949), 31ff.; French translation: *L'évolution des rites sacramentels* (LO 13; Paris: Cerf, 1952), 27ff.

by them but will be proposed to the Apostolic See, which alone will decide whether they are to be approved. However, "to ensure that adaptations are made with all the circumspection they demand," the Apostolic See will authorize the conferences "to permit and to direct, as the case requires, the necessary preliminary experiments," but for a limited time and only in assemblies in which the experiments can be properly carried out.[53]

---

53. *VSC* 40.

Chapter III

The Dialogue Between God and His People

GENERAL BIBLIOGRAPHY

J. A. Jungmann, *Die liturgische Feier* (Regensburg: Pustet, 1939). English translation by a monk of St. John's Abbey, Collegeville: *Liturgical Worship* (New York: Pustet, 1941). — Jungmann published a fourth, revised edition of this work under the title *Wortgottesdienst im Lichte von Theologie und Geschichte* (Regensburg: Pustet, 1965); English translation by H. E. Winstone and R. Brennan: *The Liturgy of the Word* (Collegeville: The Liturgical Press, 1966).

La parole dans la liturgie. XIIIe Semaine liturgique de l'Institut Saint-Serge, 1966 (LO 48; Paris: Cerf, 1970). See especially the lectures of H. Cazelles, K. Hruby, B. Botte, and I. H. Dalmais.

Gestes et paroles dans les diverses familles liturgiques. XXIVe Semaine liturgique de l'Institut Saint-Serge, 1977 (Bibliotheca EL, Subsidia 14; Rome: Edizioni liturgiche, 1978).

The liturgical formularies of the Eastern and Western Churches, past and present, when studied in the books containing them, display a very wide variety in style and literary genre. Liturgists have endeavored to draw up complete lists of these forms, to determine their sources, and to bring to light the laws governing their composition. In so doing they have discovered the riches contained in liturgical prayer; they have made possible a more objective study of the liturgical texts; and they have focused attention on the importance and originality of certain genres, such as acclamations, litanies, and invitational exhortations.

If, however, we were to approach the texts only in this manner, we would risk forgetting that they are intended for use in the concrete, living prayer of the Church and that in its actual celebration the liturgy is truly a dialogue between God and his people, as Vatican II teaches: "In the liturgy God is speaking to his people and Christ is still proclaiming his Gospel. And the people are responding to God by both song and prayer."[1]

This short statement sums up the teaching of the tradition as recalled, at the beginning of the liturgical movement, by Dom Guéranger and Dom Gréa. Dom Gréa in particular described the Office as "an unbroken conversation between Bridegroom and Bride":

> In her praise the Bride, that is, the Church, speaks of her Beloved and revels in counting all his beauties; in the readings the Beloved speaks to her and delights her with the sound of his voice; finally, in prayer the Bride who has found the Bridegroom . . . and recognized his presence and heard his voice, speaks to him in her turn and tells him of her longings, her sorrow and her joys, her needs and her gratitude.[2]

J. A. Jungmann thought it possible to see a "ground-plan" being followed in all liturgical celebrations, especially those of Christian antiquity:

> Reading, song and prayer, and the latter in two-fold form, namely the prayer of the people and the prayer of the priest. This is the ground-plan. . . . It is to be noted that this is not an arbitrary or fortuitous arrangement; rather it is in character with the essential nature of the Christian plan of redemption. Our salvation, typified by the divine word which we receive in the reading, comes from God. It descends from heaven to earth and stirs within the hearts of the faithful the echo of song. Thereupon the prayers and petitions of the Christian community are gathered up and brought back to God on high by the priest. There is something dramatic about this arrangement; through it we actually come to realize what is meant in saying that the Liturgy is the public worship of the Church.[3]

As a matter of fact, this structure is not found in all liturgical actions; nor does it occur in the period of origins as exactly as Jungmann seemed to think.[4] We can nonetheless admit that it does show the structure of "the public worship of the Church."

---

1. *VSC* 33 (*DOL* 1 no. 33).

2. A. Gréa, *La sainte liturgie* (Paris: Bonne Press, 1909), 2. — See *VSC* 84 (*DOL* 1 no. 84): "When this admirable song of praise is rightly performed . . . then it is truly the voice of a bride addressing her bridegroom."

3. J. A. Jungmann, *Liturgical Worship* (New York: Pustet, 1941), 80.

4. In *The Liturgy of the Word* (Collegeville: The Liturgical Press, 1966), which is the fourth, revised edition of *Liturgical Worship*, Jungmann acknowledges (viii) that exceptions to his rule have been brought to light by R. Zerfass in his dissertation *Die Rolle der Lesungen im Gemeindeoffizium orientalischer Riten* (1962), which was revised and published as *Die Schriftlesung im Kathedraloffizium Jerusalems* (LQF 48; Münster: Aschendorff, 1968). I myself was forced to voice some reservations about the "echo of song" as I studied the psalm and alleluia of the Mass; see n. 44, p. 142.

§1. The Word of God in the Assembly

Like the "Qahal Yahweh" of the Old Testament, the liturgical assembly is called together in order first of all to hear God speak to it. "O that today you would hearken to his voice! Harden not your hearts, as . . . in the wilderness" (Ps 95:7-8). One of the most essential traits of Christian worship, as of synagogal worship before it,[5] is that there is no liturgical action unless in it the Word of God is proclaimed and, above all, the Sacred Scriptures are read. Vatican II therefore says: "Sacred Scripture is of the greatest importance in the celebration of the liturgy. For it is from Scripture that the readings are given and explained in the homily and that psalms are sung."[6]

I. THE READING OF THE BIBLE IN THE LITURGY

A. Baumstark, *Comparative Liturgy* (3rd ed.; Westminster, Md.: Newman, 1958), 111-29.

D. Barsotti, *Il mistero cristiano e la parola di Dio* (Florence: Libreria Editrice Fiorentina, 1954). French trans. by A. M. Roguet, *La parole de Dieu dans le mystère chrétien* (LO 27; Paris: Cerf, 1954).

A. Card. Bea, "Valeur pastorale de la parole de Dieu dans la liturgie," *LMD* nos. 47-48 (1956) 129-48.

The Liturgy and the Word of God (Papers of the Third National Congress of the Centre de pastorale liturgique, Strasbourg, 1958; Collegeville: The Liturgical Press, 1959).

I. H. Dalmais, "La Bible vivant dans l'Eglise, proclamation liturgique, prédication, et imaginaire biblique," *LMD* no. 126 (1976) 7-23.

1. *Important place of reading from the Bible in the liturgy*

The Christian liturgy inherited from the synagogue the practice of reading passages from the sacred books at every gathering for prayer (Luke 4:16-21; Acts 13:27), but it gave this reading a new meaning, for the risen Christ himself on the road to Emmaus had "interpreted to them in all the scriptures the things concerning himself" before letting his disciples recognize him at the breaking of the bread (Luke 24:27 and 31). In like manner, he had shown the assembled apostles that everything written about him in the law of Moses and in the prophets and the psalms had to be fulfilled (Luke 24:44). This is why the Church has never ceased to have its people listen to the texts of the Old Testament and has defended the

---

5. On the biblical readings in the synagogue assemblies see K. Hruby, "La place des lectures bibliques et de la prédication dans la liturgie synagogale ancienne," in *La parole dans la liturgie* (LO 48; Paris: Cerf, 1970), 23-64; C. Perrot, "La lecture de la Bible dans les synogogues au Ier siècle de notre ère," *LMD* no. 126 (1976) 24-41.

6. VSC 24 (*DOL* 1 no. 24). The rest of the passage will be cited at n. 32, p. 140.

latter against its detractors. But to its reading from the Old Testament it adds "the teaching of the apostles" to which the first Christians "devoted themselves" (Acts 2:42) and, above all, the words of Jesus himself as found in the gospels. By the time of St. Justin these readings were already regarded as a traditional and essential part of the Sunday assembly: "The memoirs of the apostles and the writings of the prophets are read for as long as time permits."[7] These readings may have become a daily practice as early as the third century, at least in some places,[8] and the development of the liturgy in the fourth century gave them an even more important role.

Reading from the Bible everywhere kept its obligatory place at Mass, wherein the Liturgy of the Word and the Liturgy of the Eucharist were seen as symmetrical,[9] both being essential to the celebration of the Christian Sunday.[10] The Eastern Syrians read the law and the prophets, the Apostle and the gospel, in that order; the Western Syrians have as many as six readings; the Latin Churches have not had more than three. Rome itself generally used to have only two.

Other gatherings were marked by a more prolonged meditation on the Scriptures. This was true especially of vigils that were organized after the model of the Easter Vigil; here six, ten, or even fifteen readings from the Old Testament preceded the celebration of the feast and of the sacraments. At times a shortened form of the vigil became part of the evening Office.[11]

The prayer of the Hours, which consists chiefly of the singing of the Psalms, does not everywhere include readings from the Bible. The Roman and Benedictine Offices, however, have readings, long or short, in all the Hours.[12]

The Second Vatican Council stated its will that "in sacred celebrations there is to be more reading from holy Scripture and it is to be more varied and apposite,"[13] especially in the Mass and the Office.[14] This intention

---

7. St. Justin, *Apologia I*, ed. L. Pautigny (Textes et documents 1; Paris: Picard, 1904), 142–43.

8. Hippolytus, *Traditio apostolica* 39 and 41 (ed. Botte; LQF 39, pp. 86–89), would suggest this.

9. VSC 56 (*DOL* 1 no. 56): "The two parts that, in a certain sense, go to make up the Mass, namely, the liturgy of the word and the liturgy of the eucharist, are so closely connected with each other that they form but one single act of worship."

10. VSC 6 and 106; see *The Church at Prayer* IV, 19–21.

11. This is the case with the Byzantine *megaloi hesperinoi* or Great Vespers (Christmas, Epiphany, Annunciation, and so on) and the Milanese Vespers on the vigils of Christmas, Epiphany, and Pentecost.

12. *The Church at Prayer* IV, 220–22.

13. VSC 35, 1 (*DOL* 1 no. 35).

14. VSC 51 (*DOL* 1 no. 51): "The treasures of the Bible are to be opened up more lavishly, so that a richer share in God's word may be provided for the faithful. In this way

was brought to fruition in the *Ordo lectionum missae* of 1959 (second edition, 1981) and, in part, in the *Liturgia Horarum* that appeared in 1971. The whole of the four gospels is now presented to the faithful at the Sunday assembly in a three-year cycle, and at weekday Masses in a two-year cycle. On Sundays a reading from the Old Testament has been added to the traditional reading from Paul, again in a three-year cycle. In weekday Masses readings are taken now from the Old Testament, now from the New, in a two-year cycle.[15] In the Office of Readings that is part of the Liturgy of the Hours the one-year cycle given in the 1971 edition can be replaced by a more extensive program of readings that extends over two years.[16]

The Council also wished that "Bible services . . . be encouraged, especially on the vigils of the more solemn feasts, on some weekdays in Advent and Lent, and on Sundays and holydays. They are particularly to be recommended in places where no priest is available."[17] These celebrations, which include readings, songs, a homily, a prayer of the faithful, and the recitation of the Our Father,[18] are also appropriate in gatherings with catechumens and in ecumenical celebrations. The sacraments and blessings are now administered within the setting of a celebration of the Word in cases in which Mass is not celebrated.

2. Significance of the reading of the Bible in the liturgy

BIBLIOGRAPHY

A. M. Roguet, "La présence active du Christ dans la parole de Dieu," *LMD* no. 82 (1965) 8–28.

P. Bony, "La parole de Dieu dans l'Ecriture et dans l'événement," *LMD* no. 99 (1969) 94–123.

A. M. Triacca, "Celebrazione liturgica e parola di Dio: Attualizzazione ecclesiale della parola," in G. Zevini (ed.), *Incontro con la Bibbia* (Studi di teologia pastorale 23; Rome: Libreria Ateneo Salesiano, 1978), 87–120.

The reading of the Scriptures in their entirety bears witness to the conviction that the history of salvation derives its unity from the mystery of Christ; that is, that for Christians the Old Testament reveals its true

---

a more representative portion of holy Scripture will be read to the people in the course of a prescribed number of years." *VSC* 92a (*DOL* 1 no. 92): "[In the divine Office] readings from sacred Scripture shall be arranged so that the riches of God's word may be easily accessible in more abundant measure."

15. See *The Church at Prayer* II, pp. 197–202.

16. *GILH* 143–58; see *The Church at Prayer* IV, 222.

17. *VSC* 35, 4 (*DOL* 1 no. 35).

18. SCR, Instruction *Inter oecumenici* (September 26, 1964), 37–39 (*EDIL* 235–37 = *DOL* 23 nos. 329–31).

meaning in the light of the paschal mystery of Christ's death and resurrection. In addition, when the texts of the Bible are read in the liturgy by a reader or minister of higher rank, they are regarded as words that the prophets, the Apostle, or the Lord himself is speaking today to the listening faithful. This view of the readings is attested in the prayers, acclamations, or songs that accompany the readings in the various rites, especially those of the Eastern Churches.[19] It also finds striking expression in the ceremonies that everywhere accompany the proclamation of the gospel, and in the respect with which the book itself is safeguarded and carried in procession. The Apostle is present in and through his words;[20] Christ, above all, "is present in his word, since it is he himself who speaks when the holy Scriptures are read in the Church."[21] Because of the reading, this or that saving event truly takes place today for our sake;[22] at the very least, the reading should be heard as new and unexpected in its content and should stir wonder and stimulate us to conversion.

3. *Laws governing the reading of the Bible in the liturgy*

BIBLIOGRAPHY

G. Kunze, *Die gottesdienstliche Schriftlesung* 1 (Göttingen: Vandenhoeck und Ruprecht, 1947). (Only volume 1 appeared.)

_____, "Die Lesungen," in K. Müller and W. Blankenburg (eds.), *Leitourgia. Handbuch des evangelischen Gottesdienstes* 2 (Kassel: Stauda, 1955), 87–180.

C. Vogel, *Introduction aux sources de l'histoire du culte chrétien au moyen âge* (Biblioteca Studi medievali 1; Spoleto: Centro italiano di studi sull'alto medioevo, 1966), 252–61.

---

19. The texts are assembled in I. H. Dalmais, "Rites et prières accompagnant les lectures dans la liturgie eucharistique," in *La parole dans la liturgie* (n. 5, p. 133), 107–21, and in the article of A. G. Martimort that is cited below, in n. 21.

20. O. Rousseau, "La présence de l'Apôtre dans la liturgie de la messe," *Vie spirituelle* 96 (1957) 479–84.

21. *VSC* 7 (*DOL* 1 no. 7). — On this text of the Council and on this presence of Christ see A. G. Martimort, "*Praesens adest in verbo suo . . .,*" in *Acta Congressus internationalis de theologia Concilii Vaticani II* (Vatican Polyglot Press, 1968), 300–15; A. Cuva, *La presenza di Cristo nella liturgia* (Rome: Edizioni liturgiche, 1973), 72–96. — See also *GIRM* 33.

22. A. M. Triacca, "Celebrazione liturgica e parola di Dio: Attualizzazione ecclesiale della parola," in G. Zevini (ed.), *Incontro con la Bibbia* (Studi di teologia pastorale 23; Rome: Libreria Ateneo Salesiano, 1978), 105: "The word of God announces the history of salvation, while the liturgical celebration celebrates the word and thereby makes real here and now the mystery of salvation that the word contains and transmits"; *ibid.*, 112: "The relation which the liturgical assembly enters into with the word of God is such that it draws the *hic et nunc* of the celebrating assembly into the saving *heri et in saecula.*" — See the Eucharistic texts of St. Leo the Great in M. B. de Soos, *Le mystère liturgique d'après saint Léon le Grand* (LQF 34; Münster: Aschendorff, 1958), 52ff.

In principle, all the books of the Bible can be read in the liturgy, and read in their entirety, so that liturgical usage is the clearest expression of the biblical canon followed by each local church. Whence the method of continuous reading (*lectio continua*) which the synagogue followed for the books of the Law and which the Christian liturgies of antiquity followed, within limits, for the whole of the Canon. This method meant that at each gathering the reading of a book of the Bible began at the point where it had left off at the preceding assembly. This practice seems to have been followed in the form of an annual cycle for the Old Testament in the night Office at St. Peter's in Rome and at the Lateran (seventh–eighth centuries).[23] At least in the modern period the Byzantine liturgy in its weekday Masses has practiced a continuous reading of the epistles and gospels in a one-year cycle. The liturgical reforms of Vatican II sought to realize this ideal of continuous reading by means of two- and three-year cycles of readings.

As a matter of fact, the ancient lectionaries and books of pericopes suggest that since the annual cycle did not permit a fully continuous reading, most churches opted for a discontinuous reading in which, however, the pericopes followed according to their order in the book (the Germans call this a *Bahnlesung*).

Furthermore, the reading, whether continuous or discontinuous, was everywhere organized in such a way that certain books of the Bible were reserved to certain periods of the year and gave these a special character. For example, in almost all the liturgies the reading of St. John's Gospel is a characteristic of the fifty-day period after Easter, as is the reading of the Acts of the Apostles and, sometimes, the Apocalypse; in the Roman liturgy Isaiah is read especially during Advent; in antiquity many churches used to begin the reading of the Pentateuch in Lent.[24]

Even where continuous reading is still practiced it yields at certain times to another method in which selected passages are read. This evidently happens, first of all, on the major feasts of the Lord and during Holy Week, so that the events are commemorated by the reading of the sacred accounts of them; the method of selected passages is also used at catechetical gatherings of candidates for baptism. From as early as the end of the fourth century, the selection of texts adapted to each particular circumstance was one of the characteristic traits of the Jerusalem liturgy that elicited the

---

23. *OR* XIV, which doubtless gives the practice at St. Peter's in the second half of the seventh century (Andrieu, *OR* 3:39–41); *OR* XIII A, which gives the practice at the Lateran in the first half of the eighth century (Andrieu *OR* 2:481–88).

24. A. Baumstark, *Comparative Liturgy*, 3rd ed. trans. F. L. Cross (Westminster, Md.: Newman, 1958), 119–28.

admiration of Egeria the pilgrim.[25] Passages from different books of the New Testament and especially from books of the Old and New Testaments are often set side by side with the result that each sheds light on the other, and the development of revelation through the various stages of the economy of salvation emerges more clearly. This was the method traditionally followed in the Roman Lectionary for Lent, and it is the method that has, by and large, guided the selection of Old Testament texts in the present Sunday Lectionary.

In principle, the text of a pericope is read in its entirety, without omissions or alterations, because the text is inspired. But exceptions to this rule have always been admitted, either to avoid an excessively long reading or to highlight parallels or to emphasize one or other particular point. In modern liturgical books these omissions are carefully indicated by giving precise verse references for what is read.

Finally, "centonization" was practiced in various forms; that is, extracts from different books were combined to form a single text (a "cento"). The practice is still found today in the responses, although these are, properly speaking, songs—not readings. In the case of the gospel, the procedure had for its purpose to eliminate doublets and harmonize the several gospels; thus various churches developed a *Diatessaron* for themselves, but these were open to serious criticisms and have nowhere continued in use.[26]

In the beginning, the reader read from a complete Bible, and the celebrant would let him know what the pericope was or at least (in continuous reading) where he was to stop. As usages became more hard and fast, manuscripts appeared in which the beginning and end of pericopes were indicated in the margins; then came lists of pericopes (*capitularia*); and finally books—lectionaries and evangeliaries—containing the biblical extracts in the order of their use in the liturgy.[27]

---

25. Egeria, *Itinerarium* 25, 8; 29, 5; 47, 5; ed. P. Maraval, SC 296 (Paris: Cerf, 1982), 252–53, 270–71, 314–17; trans. J. Wilkinson, *Egeria's Travels* (London: SPCK, 1971), 127, 129, 146.

26. A. S. Marmadji, *Diatessaron de Tatien*, Arabic text with French translation (Beirut: Imprimerie catholique, 1935); C. van Puyvelde, "Le Diatessaron de Tatien," DBS 6 (Paris: Letouzey, 1960) 855–70; Ephraem of Nisibis, *Commentaire de l'évangile concordant*, introd., trans. and notes by L. Leloir (SC 121; Paris: Cerf, 1966). — For the Western liturgies: P. Salmon, *Le Lectionnaire de Luxeuil* (Collectanea biblica Latina 7; Rome: Abbaye de Saint-Jérome, 1944), lxx–lxxiii.

27. For the Latin liturgies there is a good list by B. Botte in E. Dekkers, *Clavis Patrum Latinorum* (Steenbrugge: St.-Pieters-Abdij, 1961²), nos. 1947–94.

II. THE COMMENTARY ON THE BIBLICAL READING

Reading of the sacred text is followed, at least in important liturgical actions, by a commentary of the celebrant in the form of a homily. The homily applies what has just been read to the concrete circumstances of the moment and the needs of those who are present. It is a pastoral act because it consists in breaking the bread of the Word; it is a truly liturgical act because it continues the effective action of the readings and forms a single whole with these. If the celebrant cannot himself deliver the homily, another priest or a deacon may do it, but care must then be taken not to weaken the connection of this preaching with the liturgical action.

The homily was inherited from the synagogue (Luke 4:20-21; Acts 13:15; etc.) and is attested as early as St. Justin.[28] It was practiced in all the Churches of antiquity at the Sunday assembly or even more often, sometimes daily, and was the source of most of the patristic commentaries on the Bible that have come down to us.[29]

If it was not possible to have the living words of the celebrant, some churches and especially the monasteries contented themselves at times with reading the writings of the Fathers, even while the latter were still alive, as in the case of the commentaries of St. Gregory the Great. The custom of reading the Fathers developed chiefly at the night Office, which is our present-day Office of Readings.[30]

Vatican II emphasizes the importance of the homily. The liturgical books in their turn constantly refer to its nature and role not only in the Mass but in the Office under certain circumstances and in the celebration of the sacraments, in which a catechesis of the rites is based on passages of the Bible.[31]

---

28. St. Justin, *Apologia I*, 67, ed. Pautigny (n. 7, p. 134), 142-43: "When the reader has finished, the president gives an address to warn us and exhort us to imitation of these splendid teachings."

29. A. Olivar, "La duración de la predicación antigua," in *Liturgica* 3 (Scripta et documenta 17; Monserrat: Abadía de Monserrat, 1966), 143-84; *idem*, "Preparación e improvisación en la predicación patrística," in *Kyriakon. Festschrift Johannes Quasten* (Münster: Aschendorff, 1970), 2:736-67; *idem*, "Quelques remarques historiques sur la prédication comme acte liturgique dans l'Eglise ancienne," in *Mélanges liturgiques offerts au R. P. Dom Bernard Botte* (Louvain: Mont César, 1972), 429-43.

30. St. Benedict, *Regula 9*; St. Gregory the Great, *Registrum epistolarum* XII, 6, ed. P. Ewald (MGH *Epist.*) 2:252; St. Caesarius of Arles, *Admonitio* or *Serm.* 1, 15 (CCL 103:11). — On the homiliaries for the Office see *The Church at Prayer* IV, 223-24.

31. *VSC* 24, 35, 52; *GIRM* 9, 41-42, 97 (EDIL 1404, 1436-37, 1492 = DOL 208 nos. 1384, 1431-32, 1487); SCR, Instruction *Liturgicae instaurationes* (September 5, 1970), 2 (EDIL 2175 = DOL 52 no. 513); *Ordo lectionum missae* (ed. typica altera, 1981, nos. 24-26).

III. INFLUENCE OF THE BIBLE ON THE LITURGY IN ITS ENTIRETY

BIBLIOGRAPHY

> J. Daniélou, *The Bible and the Liturgy* (Notre Dame: University of Notre Dame Press, 1956).
> _____, "The Sacraments and the History of Salvation," in *The Liturgy and the Word of God* (Collegeville: The Liturgical Press, 1959), 21–32.
> I. H. Dalmais, "La Bible vivant dans l'Eglise, proclamation liturgique, prédication et imaginaire biblique," *LMD* no. 126 (1976) 7–23.

The Bible is not only read and commented on; it also makes its influence felt on the liturgy in its entirety, as Vatican II insists:

> The prayers, collects, and liturgical songs are scriptural in their inspiration; it is from the Scriptures that actions and signs derive their meaning. Thus to achieve the reform, progress, and adaptation of the liturgy, it is essential to promote that warm and living love for Scripture to which the venerable tradition of both Eastern and Western rites gives testimony.[32]

In fact, as we shall see below, the Scriptures often provide the response of the assembly to the reading it has heard. The celebrant's prayer derives its style and inspiration from the Bible, even when it is not simply a meditation on the readings that have preceded it.[33] The signs used in the liturgy are primarily biblical signs.[34] Understanding of the sacraments is communicated by recalling biblical types in catechesis and in the major consecratory prayers.[35] The Bible and the liturgy show the same attitude of human beings to God, the same vision of the world and interpretation of history, so much so that there can be no liturgical life without an introduction to the Bible, while the liturgy in turn provides the Bible with a living commentary that enables it to manifest its full meaning. Periods in which this sense of the Bible has been lost have not produced lasting liturgical creations but have gone astray into artificial allegory or accommodative interpretations that, when they persist, prove rather embarrassing to us today.

---

32. *VSC* 24 (*DOL* 1 no. 34). — See the Dogmatic Constitution *Dei Verbum* 15–16.

33. This is still true of the collects of the Easter Vigil in the Roman liturgy, but it was a much more constant practice in the ancient liturgies, where each reading and even, and above all, each psalm was followed by a period of silence, which the celebrant brought to a close with a collect. On the psalter collects see *The Church at Prayer* IV, 204–5.

34. See Chapter IV, p. 173ff.

35. In addition to the works of J. Daniélou see the excellent synthesis of C. Rocchetta, *I sacramenti della fede. Saggio di teologia biblica sui sacramenti quali "meraviglia della salvezza" nel tempo della Chiesa* (Nuovi saggi teologici 19; Bologna: Edizioni Dehoniane, 1982).

IV. NONBIBLICAL READINGS IN THE LITURGY

BIBLIOGRAPHY

> H. Urner, *Die ausserbiblische Lesung im christlichen Gottesdienst* (Göttingen: Vandenhoeck und Reprecht, 1952).
> B. de Gaiffier, "La lecture des Actes des martyrs dans la prière liturgique en Occident," *Analecta Bollandiana* 72 (1954) 134–66.

As we saw above, the sermons of the Fathers were accepted into the liturgy as commentaries on the sacred text in place of the celebrant's homily. The present-day Liturgy of the Hours has gone further in its Office of Readings and included the best pages from the spiritual writers of all periods; it has done so under carefully defined conditions and with an eye always on the nature of the liturgy.[36]

Some Churches of antiquity occasionally used biblical apocrypha; these had been mistakenly regarded as authentic Scriptures and were quickly rejected once the error was realized.[37]

Two other kinds of writing have been accepted into the liturgy: letters of important bishops, and especially of the Bishop of Rome[38] (it is still the practice to read pastoral letters of the local bishop during the liturgy) and the Acts of the martyrs. The latter were read at Mass on the anniversary of the martyr in some Western Churches;[39] this preserved the Acts from the oblivion and falsification they suffered elsewhere. The Roman Church gives them room only in the Office of Readings. It would be "a serious abuse to substitute the word of a human being, however admirable, for the word of God."[40]

§2. The Response to God's Word

The people must respond to the Word of God that they have just heard. They do so in different ways: by silence, by acclamations, by songs. Some-

---

36. See *The Church at Prayer* IV, 222–25.

37. But some apocryphal texts were deliberately retained in sung texts when they were for practical purposes centos of authentic texts; see p. 146.

38. Thus the letter of St. Clement was read at Corinth from time immemorial, according to Bishop Dionysius, who also had read at the Sunday assembly a letter he had received from Pope St. Soter (third quarter of the second century); see Eusebius, *Historia ecclesiastica* IV, 23, 11, ed. G. Bardy I (SC 31), 205.

39. P. Salmon, *Lectionnaire de Luxeuil* (n. 26, p. 138), 181–83 (= PL 72:208). — B. de Gaiffier, "La lecture des Actes des martyrs dans la prière liturgique en Occident," *Analecta Bollandiana* 72 (1954) 134–66, has collected all the important documentation on the subject.

40. SCDW, Instruction *Inaestimabile donum* (April 3, 1980): *Notitiae* 16 (1980) 289. — See SCDW, Instruction *Liturgicae instaurationes* (September 5, 1970), no. 2a (= EDIL 2175 = DOL 52 no. 513a).

thing will be said further on of the general role of silence in the liturgy. It is enough here to note the desirability of providing for a short period of silence after the reading of God's Word and the homily, so that the people may meditate on what they have just heard and that it may be made as easy as possible for them "to receive into [their] hearts the full sound of the voice of the Holy Spirit."[41]

But the most popular and traditional way of receiving God's Word is by acclamations that correspond to the reading which has been proclaimed: *Deo gratias, Laus tibi Christe, Doxa soi Kyrie, doxa soi.*[42]

The Ambrosian liturgy has kept the practice of an *antiphona post evangelium*. Its origin is much debated: perhaps it accompanied the procession in which the Book of Gospels was returned to its place?[43] In any case, it is not a response of the people to the reading. None of the songs between the readings of the Latin Mass were originally responses;[44] they became responses only in the Middle Ages. On the other hand, in the Rule of St. Benedict each reading of the Office is already followed by a response or a verse.[45] Finally, in the Sunday Mass of the Roman rite the singing of the Creed is henceforth the response of the people to the Word of God that has been heard in the readings and the homily.[46]

§3. Song in the Liturgy

I. IMPORTANCE OF SONG IN THE LITURGY

BIBLIOGRAPHY

J. Quasten, *Musik und Gesang in der Kultur der heidnischen Antike und christlichen Frühzeit* (LQF 25; Münster: Aschendorff, 1930), 78–157.

---

41. *GILH* 202 (= *EDIL* 2455 = *DOL* 426 no. 3632); see *ibid.* 48 (= *EDIL* 2301); *GIRM* 23 = *EDIL* 1418 = *DOL* 426 no. 3478.

42. It was from Frankish usage that the rubrics of the Roman Mass took the responses "Deo gratias" and "Laus tibi Christe"; the Missal of Pius V prescribed these only for a read Mass. The Rule of St. Benedict has an "Amen" as acclamation after the proclamation of the Sunday gospel at the end of the nocturn.

43. P. Borella, *Il rito ambrosiano* (Biblioteca di scienze religiose III, 10; Brescia: Morcelliana, 1964), 159–61.

44. I discussed this question in my articles, "Origine et signification de l'alleluia de la messe romaine," in *Kyriakon. Festschrift Johannes Quasten* 2 (Münster: Aschendorff, 1970), 811–34, and "Fonction de la psalmodie dans la liturgie de la parole," in *Liturgie und Dichtung* 2 (Pietas liturgica 2; St. Ottilien: Eos Verlag, 1983), 837–56.

45. See *The Church at Prayer* IV, 215–19, 245.

46. *GIRM* 43 (= *EDIL* 1438 = *DOL* 208 no. 1433): "The symbol or profession of faith in the celebration of Mass serves as a way for the people to respond and to give their assent

T. Gerold, *Les Pères de l'Eglise et la musique* (Etudes d'histoire et de philosophie religieuse 25; Paris: Alcan, 1931).

J. Gelineau, *Voices and Instruments in Christian Worship. Principles, Laws, Applications*, trans. C. Howell (Collegeville: The Liturgical Press, 1964).

Le chant liturgique après Vatican II. Semaine d'études internationales, Fribourg (Switz.), August, 1965 (Kinnor 6; Paris: Fleurus, 1966), with contributions from J. Gelineau, H. Hucke, J. A. Jungmann, and others.

LMD no. 145 (1981): "Quel chant pour l'assemblée?" Issue includes the document *Universa laus* (1980) and a commentary by F. Rainoldi.

U. Bomm and W. Heckenbach, "Gregorianischer Gesang," *ALW* 23 (1981) 377-433 (a bibliography for 1976-78 with references to earlier years; but Part I is concerned more broadly with "Der christliche Kultgesang in der allgemeinen Musikgeschichte").

Christian antiquity had only to follow the advice of Paul the Apostle, who himself was continuing a biblical tradition, when it made song a normal expression of liturgical prayer: "Sing psalms and hymns and spiritual songs with thankfulness in your hearts to God" (Col 3:16); "Address one another in psalms and hymns and spiritual songs, singing and making melody to God with all your hearts" (Eph 5:19). In the Church of Corinth (Paul is again our source) there were even, perhaps, charismatic musical improvisations (1 Cor 14:26); in addition, the letters give us priceless remnants of liturgical songs used by the early community.[47]

In these passages song appears as a sign of joy, reminding us of what is said in James 5:13: "Is any [one among you] cheerful? Let him sing praise." In like manner, the heavenly Church, according to the Apocalypse, uses song to express its gratitude for redemption and its praise of the Lord (Rev 4:8, 11; 5:9-10; 14:3; 15:3-4; 19:1-8; etc.).[48]

Song is also regarded as a means of manifesting a unanimity of outlook, because by its rhythm and melody it produces such a fusion of voices that there seems to be but a single singer.[49] As a matter of fact, once there is question of more than a small group of people, song alone makes it possible for an assembly to express itself as one. The Fathers also emphasize the point that song makes words more forceful and intelligible and thus allows the participants to give a more intense assent to them and to

---

to the word of God heard in the readings and through the homily and for them to call to mind the truths of faith before they begin to celebrate the eucharist."

47. This is certainly the case in Eph 5:14 and 1 Tim 3:16, and perhaps in 1 Tim 6:15-16; Eph 1:4-14; Col 1:15-20.

48. A. Hamman, *La prière*. [1] *Le Nouveau Testament* (Tournai: Desclée, 1959), 351-71.

49. See Rom 15:6; St. Clement of Rome, *Letter to the Corinthians* 34, 7: "We too, being dutifully assembled with one accord, should, as with one voice, cry out to Him earnestly" (trans. J. A. Kleist, *The Epistles of St. Clement of Rome and St. Ignatius of Antioch* [Ancient Christian Writers 1; Westminster, Md.: Newman, 1946], 30); St. Ignatius of Antioch, *Ephes.* 4, 1-2; St. John Chrysostom, *Homilies on 1 Corinthians* 36, 6 (PG 61:315).
— See J. Quasten, *Musik und Gesang in den Kultur der heidnischen Antike und christlichen Frühzeit* (LQF 25; Münster: Aschendorff, 1930), 91-100.

meditate on them.[50] Music, finally, whether vocal or instrumental, can create a festive atmosphere and lend an air of triumph to certain manifestations; that is what it did at the great moments in Israel's liturgy.[51]

On the other hand, it is difficult to limit song and music to the strictly functional role that is properly theirs and not to let them escape from their place as servants. This fact accounts for the many hesitations of the hierarchy and the theologians toward this or that form of art. It also explains why the faithful may be tempted to be satisfied with aesthetic feeling and not move on to the text that the music is meant to make more attractive.[52]

II. BIBLICAL SONGS

1. *The privileged place of the psalms in the liturgy*

It seems that in the very early centuries the psalms were used in the liturgy only as readings and put on the same level as other passages of Scripture. But the period of persecutions saw the beginning of a movement to sing the psalms; this was then carried further by the Fathers of the late fourth century and by the monks. In about 210 we already find Tertullian describing the course of the Sunday assembly as follows: *"Prout Scripturae leguntur, aut psalmi canuntur, aut allocutiones proferuntur, aut petitiones delegantur."*[53]

---

50. For example, St. Augustine, *Confessions* IX, 6, 14, ed. P. de Labriolle, 2 (1926) 220; X, 33, 49–50 (pp. 276–78). — St. Pius X, Motu Proprio *Tra le sollecitudini* I, 1: "Since its [liturgical music] principal office is to clothe with befitting melody the liturgical text proposed for the understanding of the faithful, its proper end is to add greater efficacy to the text, in order that by means of it the faithful may be the more easily moved to devotion and better disposed to receive the fruits of grace associated with the celebration of the most holy mysteries" (text in A. Bugnini, *Documenta pontificia ad instaurationem liturgicam spectantia* 1 [Rome: Edizioni liturgiche, 1953], 14; translation in J. J. Megivern [ed.], *Official Catholic Teachings: Worship and Liturgy* [Wilmington, N.C.: McGrath, 1978], no. 30).

51. After the crossing of the Red Sea (Exod 15:1-20); at the entry of the Ark into Jerusalem (2 Sam 6:5); at the dedication of Solomon's temple (2 Chron 5:12). — All of these doctrinal perspectives are brought together in Pius XII's Encyclical *Musicae sacrae* (December 25, 1955), nos. 2-3 and 11-15: *AAS* 48 (1956) 6, 7, 11-13, and Bugnini, *op. cit.* (n. 50), 2 (1959) 28-29, 32-34. They are summarized in *VSC* 112-113.

52. There were already lively controversies over sacred music in the fourth and fifth centuries; see St. Augustine, *Confessions* X, 33, 49-50; St. Basil, *Letter* 207; Niceta of Remesiana, *De psalmodiae bono* (ed. C. H. Turner in *JTS* 24 [1923] 225-52). In the Middle Ages St. Thomas found himself somewhat at a loss in defending liturgical singing, in *Summa theologiae* II-II, 91, 2. — See. J. Jungmann, *Liturgical Worship* (n. 3, p. 132), 87-106.

53. Tertullian, *De anima* 9, 4 (CCL 2:792): "In the course of the service, she [a Montanist sister] finds the matter of her visions in the Scripture lessons, the psalms, the sermon, or the prayers" (trans. E. A. Quain in: Tertullian, *Apologetical Works* [New York: Fathers of the Church, Inc., 1950], 197).

The Psalter provided the essential content of the prayer of the Hours, whether of the people or of the monks. At Mass all the Churches provided that a minister (deacon, psalmist, or reader) should read or sing a psalm from the ambo; this psalm was part of the service of readings, and the people took part in the reading or singing through a refrain. Some vigil stations, especially vigils at the tombs of the martyrs, consisted in the singing of psalms.

In most of the Latin liturgies the psalms have also provided the chief accompaniment to the processions of the Mass: entrance songs, offertory songs, communion songs. They are sung at burials and in processions of thanksgiving. At the dedication of churches they accompany almost all of the gestures. The prayers of the psalms likewise have a major place in services for the sick and the dying.

The important place assigned to the psalms bears witness to the Church's conviction, so forcefully expressed by the Fathers and by St. Augustine in particular, that in the psalms the voice of Christ and his Mystical Body is heard; that they are the Lord's prayer to his Father and the prayer of God's people to their Lord.[54]

2. The biblical canticles

Other lyrical parts of the Bible have, like the psalms, been given a privileged place in the liturgical life of the Church. The Apocalypse already shows the predilection Christians have had for the Canticle of Moses (Rev 15:3). Antiquity gave special preference to eight Old Testament canticles, and these, together with the three transmitted in the Gospel of Luke, are to be found in the oldest collections.[55] Their traditional place was in the Easter Vigil and in morning prayer (Orthros or Lauds). Some of them were also given a place in the Mass (especially the Canticle of the Three Young Men[56]) and in the other Hours of the Office: the Canticle of Mary in Vespers, that of Zechariah in Lauds, and that of Simeon in Roman Compline, as canticles for the vigils of feasts.

---

54. For a detailed study of the liturgical interpretation of the psalms see *The Church at Prayer* IV, 190-206.

55. *Ibid.*, 207-11.

56. L. Brou, "Les 'bénédictions' ou Cantique des Trois Enfants dans l'ancienne messe espagnole," *Hispania sacra* 1 (1948) 21-33. Under the influence of Gallican and Spanish usages this same canticle became part of the Roman Masses for Ember Saturdays. The present Roman lectionary sometimes has a biblical canticle instead of a psalm after the first reading of the Mass.

3. *Other biblical songs*

BIBLIOGRAPHY

C. Marbach, *Carmina scripturarum* (Strasbourg: Le Roux, 1907).
P. Pietschmann, "Die nicht dem Psalter entnommenen Messgesangstücke auf ihre Textgestalt untersucht," *JLW* 12 (1932) 87–144.
P. Alfonzo, *I responsori biblici dell'ufficio romano* (Rome: Lateranum, 1936).

In addition to the psalms and canticles there are other songs taken from the Bible, the most important and universally used being the *Sanctus* (Isa 6:3). The same is true of most of the acclamations.[57] Special mention must be made, however, of the non-psalmic antiphons of the Mass, in particular some Roman offertory and communion antiphons, and above all of the responses accompanying the readings from Scripture in the ancient repertory of the Liturgy of the Hours. The choice of texts used in these responsories and the connections they suggest make them true masterpieces.

Some responses and antiphons are taken from the Prayer of Manasseh and from the third and fourth books of Esdras.[58] These apocrypha have had a lasting success because they are centos of inspired texts and express authentic biblical themes.

4. *The various kinds of psalmody*

As we saw earlier, the psalms were sometimes treated as simple readings to be heard in silence. Very soon, however, there came into existence the *responsorial psalmody* described by St. Augustine and St. Athanasius. Here a reader sang the song by himself, while the congregation used some words from it as a refrain or acclamation. This was, on the whole, the method used until 1969 for the *Benedictus es* in the Ember Day Masses and the one to which the Easterners have remained partially faithful.

The great bishops of the fourth century excogitated a more attractive type of psalmody that became known as antiphonal singing; the subject is, however, still too obscure for us to grasp the precise character of the innovation. In any case, the West has chiefly used still another method: singing in which two choirs alternate, while an antiphon almost always serves to begin and end the song.[59]

---

57. See pp. 150–52.

58. There is a list of these antiphons in C. Marbach, *Carmina scripturarum* (Strasbourg: Le Roux, 1907), 537–38; add to it the Improperia or Reproaches on Good Friday and a few other texts mentioned in M. Righetti, *Manuale di storia liturgica* 1 (Milan: Ancora, 1964³), 198; see also D. de Bruyne, "Fragments d'une apocalypse perdue," *RBén* 33 (1921) 97–109.

59. In certain circumstances the antiphons were repeated in the course of the psalm.
— Since L. Petit's article, "Antiphone dans la liturgie grecque," *DACL* 1 (1907) 2461–88,

A *response* is a form of psalmody in which the text is reduced to a few verses. Sometimes, in the Gregorian repertory, it has been given a very ornate melody (the Graduals; the responses for the nocturns); sometimes it has become a "short response" to be sung after an abbreviated reading (*capitulum* or "little chapter").

Are *verses* a final abridgment of responses? Their position after abbreviated readings suggests as much, but they have other uses as well; in particular, a group of verses has often served as a kind of litany, equivalent to the diaconal litanies that will be discussed a little further on.

III. NONBIBLICAL SONGS

BIBLIOGRAPHY

> G. del Ton, G. Schirò, and A. Raes, "Innografia," *Enciclopedia cattolica* 7 (Vatican City, 1951) 28–39 (presently the best survey).
> A. Baumstark, *Comparative Liturgy*, 3rd ed. trans. F. L. Cross (Westminster, Md.: Newman, 1958), 92–110 (on the liturgical poetry of antiquity).
> O. Heiming, *Syrische 'Eniâne und griechische Kanones* (LQF 26; Münster: Aschendorff, 1932).
> E. Wellesz, *A History of Byzantine Music and Hymnography* (Oxford: Oxford University Press, 1961²).
> M. Righetti, *Manuale di storia liturgica* 1:670–78 (on the compositions of the Latin Middle Ages).
> On the hymns of the Office in particular see *The Church at Prayer* IV, 211–15.

It seems that in the period before the biblical songs came to occupy the important place we have been reviewing, Christians were already singing new poetical compositions, fragments of which have come down to us in the letters of St. Paul. Such creations were not without their dangers, since heretics have always used them as tools of propaganda in the service of error; moreover, in periods of liturgical decline, such compositions prove to be very impoverished, thus detracting from the celebration of worship, and they tend to push their way in everywhere, to the point of displacing components of basic importance, such as the biblical psalms. These facts explain the periodic reaction against them: by the third century songs with Gnostic overtones had to be eliminated; in the fourth century, the Church had to protect itself against Arian songs; in the sixteenth it would have to reject the majority of medieval compositions. Rome was hostile to nonbiblical hymns until the twelfth century.

Abuses of this kind do not, however, justify banishing all nonbiblical compositions from the liturgy, as the French of the eighteenth century

---

these difficult problems connected with the original forms of psalmody have been given their only scientific treatment in A. Baumstark, *Nocturna laus* (LQF 32; Münster: Aschendorff, 1957), 124–43.

demanded in an excess of severity. On the contrary, the Church has always been open to hymnography: St. Ambrose decided to use the Arians' own weapons against them and to make the liturgy more appealing to the people. Magnificent masterpieces were created that deserve to remain a vital part of Christian prayer because of the spiritual riches they contain and their success as contemplations of the mysteries, even more than because of their literary beauty.

The earliest genre adopted was psalmody, that is, nonbiblical psalms, *psalmoi idiotikoi*, composed to resemble the psalms of the Bible. The best known are the Odes of Solomon[60] and, above all, the *Gloria in excelsis* and the *Te Deum*,[61] which we still sing.

In the East, hymn writing prospered from as early as the fourth century in Palestine and Syria; St. Ephraem is the best known of the poets of that age, but some compositions are also attributed to Severus of Antioch.[62] It was the Byzantine liturgy, however, that saw the finest productions in the form of *kontakia* and *canons*; the greatest names here are Romanus Melodus, Andrew of Crete, and St. John Damascene.[63] Troparies (a kind of antiphon) are another attractive element in the Greek liturgy, although they now occupy an almost excessive place. The *Akathistos Hymn* in honor of the Virgin is celebrated with special solemnity.[64]

In the West, the hymns of St. Ambrose, which St. Benedict adopted for the Office of his monks, served as a model for other compositions. It is chiefly in the Office that they are used, but some stanzas may replace texts from the psalms in processions and in sung parts of the Mass. To Sedulius and Prudentius, the masters of the classical period, we may add the names of some great Frankish poets.[65]

The Middle Ages inspired the splendid Marian antiphons that are still sung after Compline. That period also saw the development of genres that

60. *The Odes of Solomon*, ed. and trans. J. H. Charlesworth (Oxford; Clarendon Press, 1973). New English translation by Charlesworth in *idem* (ed.), *The Old Testament Apocrypha* 2 (Garden City, N.Y.: Doubleday, 1985), 725–71. See M. Pierce, "Themes in the *Odes of Solomon*," EL 98 (1984) 35–59.

61. On the *Gloria in excelsis* see B. Capelle, "Le texte du *Gloria in excelsis Deo*," RHE 44 (1949) 439–57 (= *Travaux liturgiques* 2:176–91). On the *Te Deum* see A. Baumstark, "*Te Deum* und eine Gruppe griechischen Abendhymnen," OC 34 (1937) 1–26.

62. On the hymns of St. Ephraem see *The Church at Prayer* IV, 213, and I. Ortiz de Urbina, *Patrologia syriaca* (Rome: Pontificio Istituto Orientale, 1958), 64–67. For the hymns of Severus of Antioch: PO 6:1–184, and 7:593–802 (Syriac text and English translation by E. W. Brooks).

63. See *The Church at Prayer* IV, 213–14.

64. *The Akathistos Hymn. Hymn of Praise to the Mother of God*, Greek text with English translation and introduction by G. G. Meersseman (Fribourg: University Press, 1958). See G. G. Meersseman, *Der Hymnos Akathistos im Abendland* (2 vols.; Spicilegium Friburgense 2–3; Freiburg, Schw.: Universitatsverlag, 1958–60).

65. Survey in P. Paris, *Les hymnes de la liturgie romaine* (Paris: Beauchesne, 1954).

do not fit as well into the liturgical actions, as, for example, sequences and tropes; the Tridentine reform retained very few of these, but historians are presently interested in them.[66]

Also to be mentioned are nonpoetic compositions that were allowed into the liturgy and remained there, especially the antiphons and responses drawn from the legends of the saints, and in particular those in the Offices of St. Lawrence, St. Agnes, and St. Martin.

The symbols or professions of faith fortunately became liturgical songs, even if at a relatively late date. In antiquity the symbols were "presented" to the candidates for baptism and then "given back" by them, but were used only in private prayer. But the symbol of Nicaea-Constantinople was introduced into the Mass liturgy, first in the East and then in the West, while another symbol, long attributed to St. Athanasius, was used in the form of psalmody in the Office.[67]

Finally, from the Middle Ages on, but more or less on the periphery of the liturgy, which was celebrated in Latin, there grew up a repertory of "songs" in the modern languages; these reflected the peculiar spirit of each country and, as such, were often of a very popular type. The documents of the Holy See in the pontificate of Pius XII emphasized the importance of these songs;[68] the new discipline initiated by Vatican II requires that a repertory of vernacular hymns in the proper sense of this word, that is, songs meeting the conditions required for being part of the liturgical action, be created and approved by the episcopal conferences.[69]

IV. DOXOLOGIES AND ACCLAMATIONS

Among the liturgical songs, mention must be made of two forms, the doxology and the acclamation. The texts of these are sometimes taken

---

66. For a survey see E. Costa, "Tropes et séquences dans le cadre de la vie liturgique au moyen âge," *EL* 92 (1978) 261–322, 440–71. For the texts of the sequences the principal publication is still that of G. Dreves, C. Blume, and H. Bannister, *Analecta hymnica medii aevi* (55 vols.; Leipzig: Reisland, 1888–1922), which is made more accessible by three volumes of indexes compiled by M. Lütolf (Bern: Francke Verlag, 1978). For the tropes there is a *Corpus troporum* being published by a team led by R. Jacobsson; five volumes have been published, 1975–86 (Acta Universitatis Stockholmiensis, Studia Stockholmiensia 21–22, 25–26, 32; Stockholm: Almqvist & Wiksel). — The most recent bibliography is in U. Bomm and W. Heckenbach, "Gregorianischer Gesang," *ALW* 23 (1981) 377–433, nos. 326–54.

67. See. M. Righetti (n. 58, p. 146), 225–35.

68. The essential study is that of H. Anglés, *La música de las Cantigas de santa María del Rey Alfonso el sabio* 3 (Barcelona: Biblioteca central, 1958). See also A. Gastoue, *Le cantique populaire en France, ses sources, son histoire* (Lyons: Ed. Janin, 1924); C. Rozier, "Hymns et cantiques en France du XIIIᵉ au XVIIᵉ siècle," *LMD* no. 92 (1967) 136–44.

69. SCR, Instruction *Musicam sacram* (March 5, 1967), nos. 47–61 (= *EDIL* 779–93 = *DOL* 508 nos. 4168–82); *GIRM* 26, 50, 56 (= *EDIL* 1421, 1445, 1451 = *DOL* 208 nos. 1416, 1440, 1446); *GILH* 178 (= *EDIL* 2431 = *DOL* 426 no. 3608).

from the Bible, sometimes freely composed, and they give the celebration a very characteristic tone.

1. *Doxologies*

BIBLIOGRAPHY

A. Stuiber, "Doxologie," *RAC* 4 (1958) 210–26.
B. Botte, *"In unitate Spiritus sancti,"* in B. Botte and C. Mohrmann, *L'ordinaire de la messe. Texte critique, traduction et études* (Etudes liturgiques 2; Paris: Cerf, 1953), 133–39.
M. Righetti, *Manuale di storia liturgica* 1 (Milan: Ancora, 1964³), 235–45.

The frequent occurrence of doxologies is indicative of the extent to which the liturgy is worship of the Blessed Trinity. Doxologies in Jewish prayer had been simple exclamations of praise and adoration of God, for example at the end of each book of the Psalter; in the New Testament letters and the Book of Revelation they are more fully developed and have become clearly Trinitarian.[70] They were very quickly taken over for use as conclusions of the great Christian prayers; by the fourth century the *Gloria Patri*[71] was already a congregational song, while its spread was aided by the fact that the text became a statement of Nicene orthodoxy against the Arians; it would soon become the final verse in all fully developed psalmody.[72] Other doxologies are full-blown hymns, for example, the *Te decet laus*, which is today limited to the monastic night Office of feasts, but which is of great antiquity.[73] The *Gloria in excelsis* and the *Te Deum* were also regarded as doxologies. Finally, it became customary to end almost all hymns with a stanza of praise to the Blessed Trinity.

2. *Acclamations*

BIBLIOGRAPHY

T. Klauser, "Akklamation," *RAC* 1 (1950) 216–23.
M. Righetti, *Manuale di storia liturgica* 1 (Milan: Ancora, 1964³), 208–16.
A. Kniazeff, "Des acclamations dans la liturgie byzantine," in *Gestes et paroles dans les diverses familles liturgiques*, XXIVᵉ Semaine liturgique de l'Institut Saint-Serge, 1977 (Bibliotheca EL, Subsidia 14; Rome: Edizioni liturgiche, 1978), 135–52.

---

70. Rom 9:5; 11:36; 16:25-27 (at least in most mss.); Gal 1:5; Eph 3:20-21; Phil 4:20; 1 Tim 1:17; 6:16; 2 Tim 4:18; Heb 13:21; 1 Pet 4:11; 2 Pet 3:18; Jude 25; Rev 1:6; 5:13; 7:12.

71. On the history and variants of the formula see J. Gaillard in *Catholicisme* 5 (1967) 59–61.

72. St. Benedict, *Regula monachorum* 9, 11, 13, 43, etc.

73. It is to be found in Greek in the *Constitutiones Apostolorum* VII, 98, 3 (Funk 1:456–58).

Acclamations attest to the popular and almost spontaneous style of the liturgical celebration; they are short formulas—and therefore easy to sing from memory and with one voice—that either express, as the case may be, acceptance of God's Word, faith, or agreement with a prayer, or else becomes cries of triumph as the Lord passes by under the signs of the gospel and the Eucharist. The most important of all acclamations, if we may judge by the persistence with which the Fathers describe it and comment on it, is *"Amen,"* a word that passed, untranslated, from the Jewish liturgy into the New Testament[74] and the Christian liturgy. In the early centuries, this acclamation typically expressed the active participation of the faithful in the Mass, where it served to proclaim faith in the Eucharist and to ratify prayers and the wishes that were voiced.[75]

"Alleluia" is another acclamation from the Bible, where it serves as a refrain in some psalms and, according to the Apocalypse, is sung in heaven.[76] Its usage in the liturgy became the object of some odd regulations[77] that differed from church to church and even set congregations bitterly at odds with one another. Also to be mentioned are *"Kyrie eleison,"* which was a response of the people to the deaconal litanies, or else a prayer repeated over and over; *"Deo gratias"; "Gloria tibi Domine"; "Doxa soi Kyrie"; "Hagios ho Theos";* and the Gallican *"Laus tibi Christe."*[78] Still other acclamations were responses to greetings from the celebrant or to invitations to prayer, thus creating a dialogue: *"Et cum*

---

74. Deut 27:15-26 (after the reading of each curse "all the people shall say 'Amen' "); 1 Chron 16:36 JB ("And let all the people say, 'Amen!' Alleluia!"); Neh 8:6; Ps 41:14; 72:19; 89:53; 106:48; 1 Cor 14:16; 2 Cor 1:20; Rev 3:14; 5:14; 7:12; 19:4.

75. St. Justin, *Apologia I* 65 and 67 (the manuscript tradition for the second passage is less certain); St. Dionysius of Alexandria, cited by Eusebius, *Historia ecclesiastica* VII, 9, ed. Bardy (SC 41) 2:175; St. Ambrose, *De sacramentis* 5, 25; St. Augustine, *Serm.* 272, 334, and 362 (PL 38:1247, 1469, 1632); etc. — I. Cecchetti, *L'Amen nella Scrittura e nella liturgia* (Vatican City: Vatican Press, 1942); G. M. Behler, "L'Amen," *Vie spirituelle* 112 (1965) 545–62, trans. from *Bibel und Liturgie* 37 (1964) 348–56; J. Diaz Castañeda, *El Amen de la misa, su valor catequístico y pastoral* (Barcelona: Herder, 1965); T. Ballarini, "II Cor 1, 19ss., Teologia dell'Amen," in *Miscellanea liturgica . . . Card. Lercaro* 1 (Rome: Desclée, 1965), 231–66.

76. Pss 104–106, 110–117, 134–135, 145–150; Rev 9:1-6. — St. Augustine comments on the word Alleluia in many sermons, e.g., 254, 256, and 362. — The monastic rules prescribed that on certain days or in certain Hours the Alleluia should be sung throughout the psalms.

77. For example, in St. Benedict, *Regula monachorum* 15. — Alleluia often serves as an acclamation during the procession for the gospel or for the offertory in the various Mass liturgies. On the Alleluia see H. Engberding, "Alleluia," *RAC* 1 (1950), 293–99; A. Rose, "L'usage et la signification de l'alleluia en Orient et en Occident," in *Gestes et paroles dans les diverse familles liturgiques* (Bibliotheca EL, Subsidia 14; Rome: Edizioni liturgiche, 1978), 205–34.

78. The Spanish liturgy had a special type of acclamation for use in certain cases: the *clamor*; see L. Brou, "Le psallendum de la messe . . .," *EL* 61 (1947) 45–54.

spiritu tuo," "Habemus ad Dominum," "Dignum et justum est"; some of these were inherited from the synagogue. The Fathers emphasized these acclamations too and commented on them.[79]

§4. The Prayer of the People

BIBLIOGRAPHY

J. A. Jungmann, *Liturgical Worship* (New York: Pustet, 1941), 107–24.

At times, then, the liturgical songs we have been describing have for their purpose to create an atmosphere of festivity or recollection; usually, however, they are essentially a prayer: a prayer of the people and more specifically a prayer of praise. This prayer has the appearance of being spontaneous. At certain points in the celebration, however, and especially after the readings and songs, there are periods of more intense prayer; the people are invited to it by exhortations and they give expression to it in different ways, after which the celebrant usually says a priestly prayer that summarizes and concludes the prayer of the faithful. At this point, the prayer, without ceasing to be contemplative praise, is above all one of intense petition; this form, too, obeys the instructions of the Apostle Paul (Phil 4:6; 1 Tim 2:1-2) and is found even in the earliest descriptions of the liturgical assembly.[80]

I. THE INVITATION TO PRAYER: THE EXHORTATIONS TO THE PEOPLE

In the Western liturgies it has often been the celebrant himself who urges the people to pray. In ancient Roman practice, which is maintained in the Missal of 1970, each of the solemn prayers of Good Friday is preceded by an introduction that the priest says: *"Oremus, fratres dilectis-*

---

79. St. John Chrysostom, *In 2 Cor. homiliae* 18, 3 (PG 61:527); St. Augustine, *Serm.* 227 (PL 38:1100); *Serm. Denis* 6, 30, in *Miscellanea Agostiniana* 1 (Rome: Vatican Polyglot Press, 1930), 30–31, and many other references in W. Rötzer, *Des heiligen Augustinus Schriften als liturgiegeschichtliche Quelle* (Munich: Hueber, 1930), 118–20.

80. St. Justin, *Apologia I* 67, 5: "Then we all stand and pray"; 65, 1-2: "We offer intense (*eutonōs*) prayers in common for (*hyper*) ourselves, the newly baptized person, and all others everywhere, that we who have received true teaching may be worthy of being good stewards by our works, and keepers of the commandments, and may obtain eternal salvation"; Tertullian, *Apologeticum* 39: "Oramus etiam pro imperatoribus, pro ministeriis eorum et potestatibus, pro statu saeculi, pro rerum quiete, pro mora finis" (ed. J. Waltzing, Bude collection, p. 82); *De anima* 9, cited above in n. 53, p. 144.

simi, Deum Patrem omnipotentem. . . ." In like manner, the usual General Intercessions (prayer of the faithful) begin with an invitation that is formulated by the celebrant. The same pattern is followed before every rite that is to some extent out of the ordinary, such as the blessings of candles, ashes, and palms, while the bishop addresses more extended exhortations to the people who take part in ordinations or the consecration of a virgin or the dedication of a church. The Our Father of the Mass is also preceded by an exhortation to the faithful: *"Praeceptis salutaribus. . . ."* In most instances, however, the invitation to prayer is reduced to a single Latin word: *"Oremus."* The Gallican liturgy had an exhortation of the celebrant before every priestly prayer; one of these, more expansive than the others, was almost a catechesis on the feast of the day (*Praefatio missae*).[81]

In the East, however, it is the deacon who invites the people to pray and directs them with his "proclamations," as can be seen long ago in the *Apostolic Constitutions*[82] and today in most of the Eastern Churches. The deacon is even more fully the leader of the people's prayer when he directs the litany and formulates the series of intentions.

The Visigothic liturgy had both exhortations by the celebrant (the *missa*,[83] the exhortation before the Our Father, sometimes one before the Creed, and so on) and exhortations by the deacon in the Eastern manner.[84]

II. SILENT PRAYER

BIBLIOGRAPHY

> I. Cecchetti, *"Tibi silentium laus,"* in *Miscellanea liturgica in honorem L. Cuniberti Mohlberg* 2 (Rome: Edizioni liturgiche, 1949), 521–70.
> D. Sartore, "Il silenzio come parte dell'azione liturgica," in *Mysterion. Miscellanea liturgica . . . Salvatore Marsili* (Turin-Leumann: ElleDiCi, 1981), 289–305.

---

81. For example, *Missale Gothicum*, ed. L. C. Mohlberg (REDMF 5), nos. 13, 25, 37, etc.

82. Funk 1:478–86, 488–92, 514–16, 518, 546. — In 410 the Synod of Mar Isaac at Seleucia (near Ctesiphon) speaks several times of the "proclamations" of the deacons from their *bēma* (ambo): can. 13 and 15; texts in J. B. Chabot, *Synodicon orientale* (Paris: Imprimerie nationale, 1902), 265–68. Is a reference to them to be seen earlier in can. 2 of the Council of Ancyra in 314: *kērussein*? — For modern practice see S. Salaville and G. Nowack, *Le rôle du diacre dans la liturgie orientale* (Archives de l'Orient chrétien 3; Athens: Institut français d'études byzantines, 1962).

83. M. Ramos, *Oratio admonitionis. Contribución al estudio de la antigua misa española* (Biblioteca teológica Granadina 8; Granada: Facultad de teología, 1964).

84. For example, *Liber ordinum*, ed. M. Férotin (Paris: Didot, 1904), 83, 145, 182, 217–23, to cite only those formulas that the rubrics of this book explicitly attribute to the deacon. See also J. Pinell, "Una exhortación diaconal en el antiguo rito hispanico, la *supplicatio*," *Analecta sacra Tarraconensia* 26 (1964) 3–25.

After listing the ways in which the faithful participate actively, the liturgical Constitution of 1963 adds: "And at the proper times all should observe a reverent silence."[85] The Roman liturgy has traditionally provided for a period of silence especially after the invitation to prayer; the new liturgical books frequently repeat the recommendation. It is in silence that the unanimity of the assembly is brought into harmony with the incommunicable originality of personal prayer; the invitation to silence is an invitation to mental prayer. Silence provides an opportunity for meditating on the Word of God; it also has its place in the Office where, in continuity with the practice of the early monks of Egypt, each psalm is followed by a period of meditation.[86]

Silence is also an expression of wonder, adoration, and a true sense of God, because language is powerless to express the perfections of the Lord. Here is what the Liturgy of St. James says: "Let all mortal flesh fall silent and remain in fear and trembling; let no earthly thought rule it, for, behold, the King of kings and Lord of lords, Christ our God, is coming to be sacrificed."[87]

III. LITANIC PRAYER

BIBLIOGRAPHY

H. Leclercq, "Litanie," *DACL* 9 (1930) 1540–51.

A. Baumstark, *Comparative Liturgy*, 3rd ed. trans. F. L. Cross (Westminster, Md.: Newman, 1958), 74–80.

P. de Clerck, La *"prière universelle"* dans les liturgies latines anciennes, témoignages patristiques et textes liturgiques (LQF 62; Münster: Aschendorff, 1977). The book provides all the texts and a complete bibliography.

There is a form of prayer by the people that is easier than silence; it is the litany. Its earliest manifestation is the diaconal liturgy that goes back perhaps to the prayer of the synagogues; at the very least it seems to have originated in Syria and, in any case, was already in use at Antioch in the time of St. John Chrysostom.[88] It still occupies a large (perhaps excessive) place in the Eastern rites, where the deacon enunciates a series of intentions for prayer and the people assent to each with the imploring acclamation *"Kyrie eleison."*

---

85. *VSC* 30 (*DOL* 1 no. 30); see *GIRM* 23 (= *EDIL* 1418 = *DOL* 208 no. 1413).

86. *GILH* 201–3 (= *EDIL* 2454–56 = *DOL* 426 nos. 3631–33).

87. Brightman 41.

88. St. John Chrysostom, passages collected in Brightman 478; also *In 2 Cor. homiliae* 18, 3; Egeria, *Itinerarium* 24, 5–6 (SC 296:240–41; J. Wilkinson, *Egeria's Travels* [see n. 25, p. 138], 124); *Constitutiones Apostolorum* VIII, 6, 4 and 8, 6 (Funk 1:479–487).

The West imitated these Eastern litanies in various ways. The Milanese liturgy has such a litany on the Sundays of Lent; the Spanish liturgy also provided for it, and formularies are to be found in various of its old liturgical books. The Rule of St. Benedict prescribed it at the end of the principal Hours of the Office. Scholars disagree on whether it replaced the *Orationes sollemnes* at Rome in the time of Pope Gelasius (492–96). In any case, litanic prayer survived in the Romano-Frankish liturgy in two forms: the *capitella de psalmis*, which were intercessory prayers made up of verses from psalms and placed at the end of Lauds and Vespers (the "ferial prayers"),[89] and the litany of the saints.

In its third section, the litany of the saints,[90] the origin of which is still obscure to us, imitates the style and intentions of the ancient diaconal litanies (the first two sections contain the invocations of the saints and a list of the mysteries of Christ). This litany provided stimulus to prayer during the Roman processions of the people, and it retains its place in the great consecratory actions of the liturgy: Christian initiation during the Easter Vigil, ordinations, consecration of virgins, dedication of churches.

The liturgical reform initiated by Vatican II has restored the General Intercessions to their rightful place in most liturgical actions: in the Mass, under the form of a diaconal litany in which the people respond with a refrain; and in Lauds and Vespers of the Liturgy of the Hours, usually in the form of *capitella*.

IV. THE OUR FATHER

BIBLIOGRAPHY

J. A. Jungmann, *Gewordene Liturgie* (Innsbruck: Rauch, 1941), 137–72.
N. M. Denis Boulet, "Le Notre Père dans la liturgie," *LMD* no. 85 (1966) 69–91.

The Lord's Prayer, which had so important a place in the baptismal catechesis and spiritual treatises of antiquity, was the private prayer *par excellence* of the faithful (the *Didache* urges them to say it three times a day). Since, however, the Our Father was not given to the unbaptized, the liturgy could use it publicly only when catechumens were absent, that is, during the Eucharist; this historical fact perhaps explains why the Our Father is said in a low voice in some rites. It is *par excellence* the prayer of preparation for communion and has been the preferred way of ending the Hours of the Office.

---

89. P. de Clerck, *La "prière universelle" dans les liturgies latines anciennes, témoignages patristiques et textes liturgiques* (LQF 62; Münster: Aschendorff, 1971), 269–75.
90. *Ibid.*, 275–81.

In the Eastern rites it is one of the people's songs (at least in theory, since unfortunately choirs or ministers have often replaced the people); the same was true in Gaul.[91] The other Latin liturgies turned it into a prayer of the priest, while allowing the people to intervene either by saying the final petition, "but deliver us from evil," or by an "Amen" after each petition (this was the practice in the Mozarabic liturgy). Since 1964 the Roman liturgy has adopted the Eastern tradition and given the people the joy of singing the Our Father at Mass;[92] in 1971 the Roman liturgy also turned the Our Father into one of the high points of morning and evening prayer.[93]

§5. The Prayer of the Celebrant

BIBLIOGRAPHY

J. A. Jungmann, *Liturgical Worship* (New York: Pustet, 1941), 125–41.
B. Botte, "La prière du célébrant," *LMD* no. 29 (1949) 133–41.

A distinction can be made among the prayers of the celebrant between those that express his personal devotion, and are thus in a sense private prayers, and those in which he truly acts as president of the assembly and exercises his mediatorial role. The distinction is easy to make in the present Roman liturgy, but has been made more difficult in the Eastern rites by the fact that today even the presidential prayers are said in a low voice (*mystikōs*) and are drowned out by diaconal litanies or the singing of the choir. A further point to be made is that some of the words spoken by the priest are not prayers but actions: indicative formulas, blessings, exorcisms.

We may note at the outset that the principal activities of the celebrant are usually preceded in all the liturgies by a greeting addressed to the people; St. Augustine and St. John Chrysostom already bear witness to this as a traditional practice. The formulas for this greeting are biblical good wishes from the New or even the Old Testament: "Peace be with you," "Peace to all,"[94] "The Lord be with you,"[95] "The grace of the Lord

---

91. Gregory of Tours, *De virtutibus s. Martini* 2, 30, ed. Arndt-Krusch (MGH), 620.

92. SCR. Instruction *Inter oecumenici* (September 26, 1964), 48g (= *EDIL* 246 = *DOL* 23 no. 340g); the Instruction of September 3, 1958, had allowed the faithful to say the Our Father only at Low Masses; see *GIRM* 56a (= *EDIL* 1451 = *DOL* 208 no. 1446a).

93. *GILH* 194–96 (= *EDIL* 2447–49 = *DOL* 426 nos. 3624–26).

94. In the Roman rite *Pax vobis* is the greeting used by bishops; it is the wish uttered by the risen Christ in John 20:19, 26; *Eirēnē pasi* occurs frequently during the Byzantine liturgy.

95. Ruth 2:4; 2 Thess 3:16.

Jesus Christ and the love of God and the fellowship of the Holy Spirit be with you."[96] The response of the congregation, "And with your spirit," is also biblical (see 2 Tim 4:22).

I. THE MAJOR PRIESTLY PRAYERS

Two forms of priestly prayer stand out by reason of their solemnity, their function, and their style: one is the consecratory prayers, of which the Eucharistic Prayer is the model, and the other is the "collects," which as such are typically Latin but which have counterparts in the other rites.

1. *Consecratory prayers*

Pride of place belongs here, of course, to the thanksgiving of the Mass, that is, the "eucharist" (*prex, anaphora, contestatio, illatio, immolatio*), even though at times it has been said almost entirely in a low voice. In the Roman liturgy, however, the same literary genre has been used in the prayers for the consecration of bishops, presbyters, deacons, virgins, abbots and abbesses, baptismal water, chrism, churches, and altars, as well as in the prayer for the reconciliation of penitents and in the nuptial blessing. Furthermore, the Middle Ages made all these formularies begin with the preliminary dialogue and opening words *"Vere dignum . . ."* of the Eucharistic Preface.

In the beginning these prayers were improvisations on set themes, but they were subsequently the first prayers to be given a fixed written form in both East and West, and this at a time when they could profit from the literary genius of the great fourth-century bishops. Their liturgical importance is highlighted by the invitations and dialogue with the people that precede them, by their general style, and, above all, by their spiritual power: they are the sacramental words for the Eucharist and Orders, while the consecration of the chrism is indispensable for the sign of confirmation, and the consecration of the baptismal water, though not required for the validity, does express the symbolism of the sacrament and prepare the recipient for it. Others of these prayers are the high points of the Church's great sacramentals. The consecratory prayers include contemplation of the divine perfections, a proclamation of the economy of salvation, and a call for the sanctifying action of the Holy Spirit.

---

96. 2 Cor 13:13. This greeting, introduced into the Roman Order of Mass in 1969, is the greeting that, with a few variants, is spoken by the celebrant in the Eastern rites (except for the Copts) before the Eucharistic anaphora.

2. *The "collects"*

BIBLIOGRAPHY

B. Capelle, "Collecta," *RBén* 42 (1930) 197–204 (= *Travaux liturgiques* 2:192-99).

The other important form of priestly prayer did not establish itself immediately. It does not occur in the liturgy that St. Augustine celebrated at Hippo, but it is already to be found in the *Apostolic Constitution*; at Rome, its earliest formularies may date from the time of St. Leo.[97] The literary forms of this prayer differed widely in East and West. It was the prayer spoken by the celebrant after the people had prayed; thus it concluded either a diaconal litany or a time of silent prayer. When the prayer had been a silent one, the faithful had already formulated their praise and petitions in their hearts, with a variety known to God alone; the purpose of the celebrant's prayer was to gather up these supplications in a single bundle, to give them public expression, and to reduce them to unity; whence the names *collectio* and *collecta*. In the Roman tradition, this type of prayer is composed in a style marked by a brevity that is stripped of any and all lyricism, and by a rich conciseness that makes translation into other languages difficult; the same is not true of formularies with identical functions in the other liturgies, even the other Latin liturgies.

3. *Characteristics of the great priestly prayers*

Whether as "eucharist" or as "collect," the prayer of the priest is the high point of the celebration; even when the prayer is not sacramental, it "in-forms," as it were, the other elements of worship and makes a real liturgy of them. It expresses the mediation that the priest, whether bishop or presbyter, exercises *in persona Christi* between God and his people. This is why at these moments nothing and no one should be allowed to keep the celebrant's voice from being heard: the faithful are standing in attentive silence and making the prayer their own both by their silent attention and by the "Amen" they say at its end.

This also explains why all individualistic elements and all emotion are eliminated from the formulation of this prayer; it is meant to be collective and universal.[98] The celebrant utters his prayer so as to be heard by all the participants; it is solemnly declaimed and not really sung, since

---

97. Except for the solemn prayers of Good Friday, which were the Roman form of the general intercessions, perhaps from as early as the fourth century; see A. Baumstark, *Comparative Liturgy* (see n. 24, p. 137), 78–79.

98. See R. Guardini, *The Spirit of the Liturgy*, trans. A. Lane (London: Sheed & Ward, 1930), 1–36, 51–69; Jungmann, *Liturgical Worship* (see n. 3, p. 132), 125ff.

the ornamentation of song would distract from the words. Nor should it employ the devices of poetry. It is prose written in elevated and dignified language; only the prose rhythm of the *cursus* is to be found in a good many Roman priestly prayers.[99]

The content of these prayers is the most important of the liturgical *loci theologici*. The reason is that they interpret the shared faith of the assembly; some of them are even sacramental. They harmoniously combine adoration and petition. Above all, perhaps even more than the doxologies, they give the liturgy its special character as worship of the Trinity.

All of the ancient Roman formularies and most of the Eastern formularies carefully follow the same strict plan that was approved by the Third Council of Carthage in 397: *"Ut nemo in precibus vel Patrem pro Filio vel Filium pro Patre nominet; et cum altari adsistitur semper ad Patrem dirigatur oratio"* ("Let no one in praying replace the Father's name by the Son's or the Son's by the Father's, and prayer at the altar is always to be addressed to the Father").[100] The priestly prayers are addressed to the Father, to whom the entire liturgy is directed. The order of the Trinitarian processions is scrupulously observed, even when certain moments in the liturgy might suggest another approach as better (for example, at the mention of the Holy Spirit in the epiclesis of the Mass). In obedience to the command he has given us, we always pray through Christ, and mention of the divine mediator usually serves as a conclusion and final doxology in the priestly prayers.[101] However, in reaction against Arianism, some ancient liturgies (the Spanish, for example) sometimes addressed priestly prayers to Christ himself; the Middle Ages accepted this practice and it was kept in some orations of the Roman Missal.[102]

---

99. L. Laurand, "Le cursus dans le Sacramentaire Léonien," *QL* 4 (1914) 215–18; further developed in L. Laurand, *Manuel des études grecques et latines*, 2nd. ed. by A. Lauras, vol. 4 (Paris: Picard, 1949), 270–96: "Ce qu'on sait et ce qu'on ignore du cursus"; L. Laurand, *Etude sur le style des discours de Cicéron, avec une esquisse de l'histoire du cursus* 3 (Paris: Belles Lettres, 1940³), 353–61.

100. C. Munier, *Concilia Africae* (CCL 149), 333. — See J. Lebreton, "La prière dans l'Eglise primitive," *RechSR* 14 (1924) 7–13, 20–32; B. Neunheuser, "Cum altari adsistitur, semper ad Patrem dirigatur oratio," *Augustinum. Miscellanea Trape* (1985), 102ff.

101. This is one of the subjects that received the most attention from the very beginning of the liturgical movement: L. Beauduin, *Mélanges liturgiques* (Louvain: Mont César, 1954), 44–73 (= *QL* 3 [1912–13] 201–9, 271–80; 4 [1913–14] 350–61; G. Lefebvre, *Catholic Liturgy: Its Fundamental Principles*, trans. by a Benedictine of Stanbrook (New York: Benziger, 1924), 17–36; J. Jungmann, *Die Stellung Christi im liturgischen Gebet* (LQF 19–20; Münster: Aschendorff, 1925), with English trans. by A. Peeler from the 2nd German ed. of 1962, *The Place of Christ in Liturgical Prayer* (London: Chapman, 1965); C. Vagaggini, *Theological Dimensions of the Liturgy*, trans. L. J. Doyle and W. A. Jurgens (Collegeville: The Liturgical Press, 1976), 191–246.

102. All this information is gathered in Jungmann, *The Place of Christ . . .* (n. 101 above); see also Lebreton, *art. cit.* (n. 100 above), 97–133.

II. OTHER PRIESTLY FORMULAS

I shall give only a brief list of the other types of priestly formulas, because these will be explained in the study of the rites of which they are respectively a part.

1. *Indicative formulas*

Indicative priestly formulas occur both in the sacraments and in some sacramentals. At the end of the fourth century the baptismal formula at Antioch was in the indicative form: "N. is baptized in the name of the Father and of the Son and of the Holy Spirit."[103] Earlier still, according to the *Apostolic Tradition* of Hippolytus, anointings at Rome were accompanied by an indicative formula: *"Ungueo te oleo sancto in nomine Iesu Christi."*[104] The consecration of baptismal water would also have passages in the indicative mood, although in these the celebrant addresses no longer a person but the water itself: *"Unde benedico te creatura aquae,"* a procedure that would also be followed in the consecration of altars and elsewhere.

2. *Blessings*

The celebrant often exercises his priestly role in the form of *blessings*. Blessings of things usually take the form of prayers, which present all the characteristic traits described above. Blessings of persons usually take the form rather of a wish, both in the Mass and in the Office, and whether the recipient is the entire assembly or a minister who is about to carry out his function; but they can also be in the form of prayers, as in the Roman *Oratio super populum*. The Visogothic and Gallican Mass had a tripartite solemn blessing that was continued during the Middle Ages and has been restored in the new Roman Missal.[105]

3. *Exorcisms*

Some blessings of things used to be preceded by an exorcism of them; the ancient prebaptismal liturgy gave large scope to exorcisms of persons. An exorcism is an adjuration addressed to Satan by authority that the Church has received from Christ for this purpose. It is a liturgical manifestation both of the hold that the demon has had even on things and places as a result of human sin, and of the victorious struggle carried

---

103. A. Wenger, in St. John Chrysostom, *Huit catéchèses baptismales* (SC 50; Paris: Cerf, 1957), 96–97, gives references.

104. Hippolytus, *Traditio apostolica*, ed. Botte (LQF 39), 50; see 53.

105. See *The Church at Prayer* II, pp. 116 and 219.

on by Christ and continued by the Church in order that everything may return to God.[106]

4. *Private prayers*

At certain moments in the liturgy, and especially during the Mass, the celebrant engages in private prayer. This differs from his properly priestly prayers in its style, its location, and the fact that it is said in a low voice to accompany actions that originally did not suppose any formula.[107] In the East, these secondary prayers can even take the form of a dialogue among the concelebrants or between the celebrants and the deacons.

§6. Problems Connected with Expression in Liturgical Prayer

Among the problems raised by expression in liturgical prayer in the various cultures or civilizations that the Church has encountered throughout the world and down the centuries, only two will be mentioned here. They are singled out because of the importance that the Church itself gives them and because of the discipline created for them: the problem of languages and the problem of music.

I. LANGUAGES IN THE LITURGY

1. *The question of languages in the early Church (first to sixth century)*

BIBLIOGRAPHY

G. Bardy, *La question des languages dans l'Eglise ancienne* (Etudes de théologie historique; Paris: Beauchesne, 1948).

C. Mohrmann, "Les origines de la latinité chrétienne à Rome," *Vigiliae christianae* 3 (1949) 67–106, 163–83.

B. Botte, L. Leloir, and C. van Puyvelde, "Orientales (versions)," *DBS* 6 (Paris: Letouzey, 1960) 807–84.

A. G. Martimort, "Essai historique sur les traductions liturgiques," *LMD* no. 86 (1966) 75–105.

P. Borella, "La lingua volgare nella liturgia," *Ambrosius* 44 (1968) 71–94, 137–68, 237–66 (an important study presented to the liturgical commission that was preparing for Vatican II).

B. Botte, "Les traductions liturgiques de l'Ecriture," in *La parole dans la liturgie,* [XIIIe] Semaine liturgique de l'Institut Saint-Serge [1966] (LO 48; Paris: Cerf, 1970), 81–106.

---

106. E. Bartsch, *Die Sachbeschwörungen der romischen Liturgie. Eine liturgietheologische Studie* (LQF 46; Münster: Aschendorff, 1967).

107. See *The Church at Prayer* II, pp. 130–31.

The Jews already had to face the problem of language, because when they returned from exile they no longer spoke Hebrew but Aramaic, another Semitic tongue. They continued to recite the prayers of their rituals in Hebrew, although they had difficulty understanding them; on the other hand, when the Bible was read in the synagogues of Palestine, the Hebrew text was followed, verse by verse, with an Aramaic translation; these oral translations were eventually put in writing, thus giving rise to the targums.[108] The Jews who lived dispersed throughout the Hellenistic world did not hesitate to translate the Sacred Scriptures into Greek; a number of successive versions were produced, among them the Septuagint, which was to be the most widely used and have the longest life. The task of adapting Semitic idiom to make it intelligible to the Greek mind was a difficult one, but the effort marked a decisive transition: "The Bible emerged from the land of its birth and came in contact for the first time with human beings who did not owe their entire education and formation to it."[109]

The New Testament people of God were even more keenly aware, and from the very beginning, of the language problem. The Church of Christ sought to bring together men and women "from every tribe and tongue and people and nation" (Rev 5:9-10); its desire was that "every tongue confess that Jesus Christ is Lord" (Phil 2:11). On Pentecost day its initial appearance on the scene found men and women "from every nation under heaven" listening as the apostles told them in their own tongues of the mighty works of God (Acts 2:5-11).

In the first community in Jerusalem, Aramaic-speaking and Greek-speaking believers had to live together, and the situation was not without its difficulties (Acts 6:1). At the practical level, from the very beginning the Church celebrated its liturgy in Greek in the large cities of the East. All of the baptized, however, were meant to participate in the assembly and so the Church gradually found itself obliged to provide for the needs of non-Greek-speaking Christians. It did so initially with the help of translators who intervened orally in the course of the ceremonies,[110] and then by giving the celebration a more completely polyglot character: thus in the Church of Jerusalem[111] and the monasteries of Syria[112] the readings and songs were repeated in several languages.

---

108. R. Le Déaut, *Liturgie juive et Nouveau Testament. Le témoignage des versions araméennes* (Rome: Istituto Pontificio Biblico, 1965); *idem, Introduction à la littérature targumique (ibid.,* 1966).

109. J. Coste, "La première expérience de traduction biblique," *LMD* no. 53 (1958) 56–88.

110. M. J. Lagrange, "L'origine de la version syro-palestinienne des évangiles," *Revue biblique* 34 (1925) 481–504.

111. Egeria, *Itinerarium* 47, 3–5 (SC 296:314–15; Wilkinson 146); St. Jerome, *Ep.* 109, 29, ed. J. Labourt, 5 (Paris: Belles Lettres, 1955), 198–99, describing the burial of St. Paula.

112. O. Hendricks, "Les premiers monastères internationaux syriens," *OC* 3 (1958) 165–84.

Translations into the Semitic languages were not difficult, because the Scriptures provided a basis, and because the peoples who spoke these languages already had a literature. But as the gospel made its way outside the large cities and then beyond the empire, a major concern of bishops was to have the Bible translated into languages that hitherto had no written form and no literature; these translations played an important role in bringing such languages to a stage of maturity. The work seems to have begun in Egypt with translations into the Coptic dialects; next came translations into Armenian, Ge'ez (the language of ancient Ethiopia), and Georgian.

The Church of Africa was the first important Latin-speaking Church. It disappeared with the collapse of "Romania" in these regions, for the native peoples had been only superficially assimilated;[113] there was no other Western parallel to the fate of this Church.

The Church of Rome continued to be Greek-speaking until the third century; its liturgy was perhaps definitively Latinized only in the course of the fourth century.[114]

The languages spoken in Gaul and Spain before the Roman conquest left hardly any trace behind. So, too, the barbarians who invaded the Western empire were very quickly Latinized; this was true of the Goths as well, although in Constantinople at the beginning of the fifth century they used to celebrate the liturgy in their own language.[115]

2. Liturgical languages from the seventh to the sixteenth century

The missionary expansion of the Church beyond the frontiers of the old Roman Empire would lead to solutions of the liturgical language problem that differed according to region and to the Church responsible for the missionary effort in that region. Thus the Church that existed beyond the Euphrates and used the Syriac language exclusively—a Church cut off from unity by the Nestorian heresy—experienced an extraordinary missionary flowering that produced lasting results in India and reached into Tibet, China, and beyond. The movement did not, however, create native episcopates in these various countries, so that the liturgy was every-

---

113. C. Courtois, *Les Vandales et l'Afrique* (Paris: Ed. Arts et métiers graphiques, 1955), 126–30; other references in my article, "Essai historique sur les traductions liturgiques," *LMD* no. 86 (1966) 87, n. 22.

114. T. Klauser, "Der Übergang der römischen Kirche von der griechischen zur lateinischen Liturgiesprache," in *Miscellanea Mercati* 1 (ST 121; Vatican City, 1946) 467–82.

115. On Easter 399 St. John Chrysostom marked the beginning of use by the Goths of the church he had assigned to them: *Homilia* 8 (PG 63:499–510); see especially col. 501 (the readings and sermon were in the Gothic language).

where celebrated in Syriac, although the readings and sometimes the songs were translated.[116]

The Byzantine Church, on the contrary, accepted the languages of the countries to which it brought Christianity, and especially the Slavic languages. In our own time the Byzantine rite is the one most ready to allow translation into the modern languages. The Melkites of Syria and Egypt adopted not only Greek but, in the tenth century, Arabic as well; Arabic has also found a place, to some extent, in the liturgy of the Syrians, the Copts, and the Maronites.

In the West, Latin was to remain for centuries the only language indicative of education. It is to be noted, however, that Southern Italy was still within the Greek sphere of influence and that even at Rome, when Greek-speaking Christians once again became very numerous in the seventh century, both Latin and Greek were used in the readings of the liturgy and the rites of the catechumenate, while songs in Greek mingled with songs in Latin. The Papal Mass has preserved the memory of that period right down to the twentieth century in the form of a twofold reading of the epistle and the gospel. In Ireland, where Roman civilization exerted little influence, the native language persisted and developed, but it acquired no real place in the liturgy proper.

The first occasion on which the question of translating the Latin liturgy was explicitly raised was when Sts. Cyril and Methodius were evangelizing Moravia; the objections leveled against their efforts attempted to give theological justification for the *de facto* use of Latin.[117] Nonetheless, even today there are Churches of the Roman rite that celebrate the liturgy in a Slavic translation,[118] while throughout the Middle Ages there were missionaries who compiled liturgical books in the various languages of the Near East and Asia.

3. *Discipline of the Latin Church from the sixteenth to the twentieth century*

It was chiefly in the sixteenth century that the national languages of Western Europe reached their full development and were no longer simply popular dialects as they had been in the Middle Ages. Because the Protestants drew upon an unacceptable theology when they claimed the right to use these languages in the liturgy, the Council of Trent found it-

---

116. J. Dauvillier, "Les provinces chaldéennes de l'extérieur au moyen âge," in *Mélanges offerts au R. P. Ferdinand Cavallera* (Toulouse: Institut catholique, 1948), 260–316.

117. P. Duthilleul, *L'évangélisation des Slaves: Cyrille et Methode* (Bibliothèque de théologie; Tournai: Desclée, 1963).

118. C. Segvić, "Le origini del rito slavo-latino in Dalmazia e Croazia," *EL* 54 (1940) 38–65; S. Smrzik, *The Glagolitic or Roman Slavonic Liturgy* (Cleveland: Slovac Institute, 1959).

self obliged to face the problem in chapter 8 and canon 9 of its twenty-second session.[119] The Council's main concern was to separate the language question from any and all doctrinal considerations and to treat it as strictly a disciplinary matter.

The Council did not think it expedient, however, to accept the vernaculars into the liturgy. The Counter-Reformation afterwards rejected them without qualification, not only at the level of discipline, where the Roman Congregations refused to allow any flexibility even in the missions,[120] but also at the level of principle, where it repeated the same impassioned arguments throughout the eighteenth and nineteenth centuries.

By the mid-twentieth century the pastoral problems caused by the dechristianization of the masses and World War II led to a reconsideration of the discipline of the Latin Church in regard to the language of the liturgy. In the pontificate of Pius XII the Apostolic See was already quite liberal in granting the requests of national episcopates for the use of bilingual rituals in which some formulas were translated,[121] for the repetition of the readings in the vernacular after they had first been proclaimed in Latin, and, finally, for the practice of "the sung Mass with congregational songs in the vernacular."[122]

4. Since the Second Vatican Council

BIBLIOGRAPHY

LMD no. 86 (1966): *Les traductions liturgiques (Congrès international, Rome, 1965)* (especially the articles by Mgr. L. Nagae Satoshi and X. Seumois).

G. Venturi, "Fenomeni e problemi linguistici della traduzione liturgica al passagio da una cultura all'altra," *EL* 92 (1978) 5–75.

J. Gilbert, "Le lingue nella liturgia dopo il Concilio Vaticano II," *Notitiae* 17 (1979) 387–520.

_____, "Evoluzione della problematica relativa alla traduzione liturgica," in *Mysterion. Miscellanea liturgica . . . S. Marsili* (Turin-Leumann: ElleDiCi, 1981), 307–27.

On December 5 and 6, 1962, after lengthy and sometimes impassioned debate, the Council adopted the principle that "the use of the mother

---

119. DS 1749 and 1759; H. Schmidt, *Liturgie et langue vulgaire. Le problème de la langue liturgique chez les premiers Réformateurs et au Concile de Trente* (Analecta Gregoriana 53; Rome: Pontificia Universita Gregoriana, 1950).

120. S. Chen Bao Shin, *Historia tentaminum missionariorum Societatis Iesu pro liturgia sinica in saeculo XVII* (Rome: Collegium de Propaganda Fide, 1951). — F. Bontinck, *La lutte autour de la liturgie chinoise aux XVIIᵉ et XVIIIᵉ siècles* (Louvain: Nauwelaerts, 1962); J. Guennou, "Monseigneur Pallu et la liturgie chinoise," *RHE* 61 (1966) 820–36.

121. P. Card. Gerlier, "Les rituels bilingues . . .," *LMD* nos. 47–48 (1956) 83–97.

122. See my article in *LMD* no. 44 (1955) 161–63. — On the whole question see H. Schmidt, *Introductio in liturgiam occidentalem* (Rome: Herder, 1960), 209–27.

tongue, whether in the Mass or other parts of the liturgy, frequently may be of great advantage to the people."[123] In the following year the Council voted to apply this principle to the Mass, the ritual, and the Office.[124] At the same time, however, it insisted strongly that "particular law remaining in force, the use of the Latin language is to be preserved in the Latin rite";[125] it required that steps be taken "enabling the faithful to say or to sing together in Latin those parts of the Ordinary of the Mass belonging to them"[126] and that in the celebration of the Office "in accordance with the centuries-old tradition of the Latin rite, clerics are to retain the Latin language."[127] Within this framework and the limits it set, the episcopal conferences were empowered to take the steps they judged opportune and to approve translations, but "the enactments of the competent authority are to be approved, that is, confirmed by the Holy See."[128]

Even when it established limits, the Council itself anticipated the possibility of broadening them.[129] At the urgent request of the episcopal conferences, Pope Paul VI first allowed the Preface of the Mass to be said in the vernacular,[130] and then the entire Canon and the prayers of ordination.[131] Finally, on June 14, 1971, the Congregation for Divine Worship sent notice that the episcopal conferences could allow the use of the vernacular in all the texts of the Mass, even when no congregation was present; each Ordinary could give the same permission for the choral or private celebration of the Liturgy of the Hours.[132]

The decision of the Council and the subsequent extensions of it in favor of the vernacular in the liturgy were required by an awareness of the pastoral needs of our age and of the problems raised by the evangelization of Africa and Asia. They also laid a great responsibility on the episcopal conferences and committed them to vast labor, not only because the mass of texts to be translated is so large but also because of the many problems that must be resolved in the work of translation. As a result, the Apostolic See has frequently intervened to define the conditions that

---

123. The words became part of *VSC* 36, §2 (*DOL* 1 no. 36).

124. *VSC* 54, 63a, 76, 78, 101.

125. *VSC* 36, §1 (*DOL* 1 no. 36).

126. *VSC* 54 (*DOL* 1 no. 54).

127. *VSC* 101 (*DOL* 1 no. 101).

128. *VSC* 36, §3 (*DOL* 1 no. 36).

129. *VSC* 54; see 40.

130. Letter *Ho l'onore* of the Cardinal Secretary of State (April 27, 1965) (= *EDIL* 395 = *DOL* 110 no. 766).

131. Permission given by Paul VI on January 31, 1967; confirmed in SCR, Instruction *Tres abhinc annos* (May 4, 1967), no. 28 (= *EDIL* 837 = *DOL* 39 no. 474).

132. SCR, Notification *Instructione de Constitutione* (June 14, 1971), no. 4: *AAS* 63 (1971) 714 (= *EDIL* 2579 = *DOL* 216 no. 1773); see *GIRM*, Introduction 12 (= *EDIL* 1392 = *DOL* 208 no. 1387).

must be met in translations of the Bible, the adaptation required in dealing with the Roman repertory of prayers, and the areas—especially hymns
and some chants—in which a creative effort is legitimate.[133] Special precau-
tions must be taken to ensure exact fidelity in sacramental formulas,[134]
and, as far as possible, the same translation must be used in all countries
speaking the same language.[135] Finally, care must be taken to provide
celebrations in Latin for multilingual communities and for communities
that desire them.[136]

II. LITURGICAL MUSIC

Vatican II devoted chapter 6 of its Constitution on the Liturgy to the
subject of sacred music. This was the first time that an ecumenical council had dealt with the subject; for this reason it should not come as a surprise that the Council was hardly able to disengage itself from the categories
used in the documents of the Apostolic See, from the Motu Proprio *Tra
le sollecitudini* of St. Pius X (November 22, 1903) to the Encyclical *Musicae sacrae* of Pius XII (December 25, 1955) and the Instruction *De musica
sacra* (September 3, 1958). Historical study of the various forms taken
by the Christian musical tradition and the problems raised by liturgical
song in the vernaculars have, here again, made it necessary later on to
develop a broader vision.

---

133. Letter *Dans sa récente allocution* of Cardinal Lercaro to the Presidents of the Episcopal Conferences (June 21, 1967) (= *EDIL* 974–82 = *DOL* 41 nos. 477–86); Communication *Aussitôt après* of A. Bugnini to the Presidents of the Episcopal Conferences (August
10, 1967) (= *EDIL* 983–88 = *DOL* 118 nos. 820–25); Consilium, Instruction *Comme le prévoit*
(January 25, 1969) (= *EDIL* 1200–42 = *DOL* 123 nos. 838–80); SCDW, Declaration *Plures
liturgicae* (September 15, 1969) (= *EDIL* 1963–65 = *DOL* 125 nos. 884–87); SCDW, Instruction *Constitutione apostolica* (October 20, 1969), nos. 2–5, 11–12, 16 (= *EDIL* 1973–76,
1982–83, 1987 = *DOL* 209 nos. 1734–37, 1743–44, 1749); SCDW, Instruction *Liturgicae
instaurationes* (September 5, 1970), nos. 3 and 11 (= *EDIL* 2176, 2184 = *DOL* 52 nos. 514–21
and 529).

134. SCDW, Circular Letter *Dum toto terrarum* to the Presidents of the Episcopal Conferences (October 25, 1973): *AAS* 66 (1974) 98–99 (= *EDIL* 3110–14 = *DOL* 130 nos. 904–8).

135. Letter *Consilium ad exsequendum* of Cardinal Lercaro (October 14, 1964) (= *EDIL*
298 = *DOL* 108 no. 764); SCR, Instruction *Musicam sacram* (May 5, 1967), no. 58 (= *EDIL*
790 = *DOL* 508 no. 4179); Letter *Dans sa récent allocution* of Cardinal Lercaro (June 21,
1967) (= *EDIL* 981 = *DOL* 41, no. 485); SCDW, Instruction *Constitutione apostolica* (October 20, 1969), no. 4 (= *EDIL* 1975 = *DOL* 209 no. 1736); SCDW, Letter *Tandis que cette
Congrégation* (February 25, 1970) (= *EDIL* 2050–55 = *DOL* 138 no. 933).

136. Letter *L'heureux développement* of Cardinal Lercaro (January 25, 1966) (= *EDIL*
574–75 = *DOL* 32 nos. 424–25); SCR. Instruction *Musicam sacram* (May 5, 1967), no. 48
(= *EDIL* 780 = *DOL* 508 no. 4169).

1. *The main historical forms of liturgical music*

BIBLIOGRAPHY

P. Huot-Pleuroux, *Histoire de la musique religieuse* (Paris: Presses universitaires de France, 1957).

S. Corbin, *L'Eglise à la conquête de sa musique* (Paris: Gallimard, 1960).

F. J. Basurco, *El canto cristiano en la tradición primitiva* (Christus pastor 17; Madrid: Maroba, 1966).

Die Musik in Geschichte und Gegenwart. Enzyklopädie der Musik, ed. F. Blume (16 vols.; Kassel: Bärenreiter, 1949–74) (many articles on liturgical music by B. Stäblein, H. Hucke, B. Baroffio).

U. Bomm and W. Heckenback, "Gregorianischer Gesang," *ALW* 1 (1950) 397–443; 4 (1955) 184–222; 6 (1959) 256–90; 7 (1962) 470–511; 9 (1965) 232–77; 14 (1972) 283–328; 20–21 (1979) 281–347; 23 (1981) 377–433. (Despite their title these bulletins are not limited to Gregorian chant or even to Western chant.)

a) "Among the oldest and most outstanding monuments of sacred music the liturgical chants of the different Eastern rites hold a highly important place. Some of the melodies of these chants, modified in accordance with the character of the Latin liturgy, had a great influence on the composition of the musical works of the Western Church itself."[137] Knowledge of Eastern Church music has been greatly facilitated in our time by publication of ancient melodies and by scientific historical studies.[138]

b) We know hardly anything about the music of the old liturgy of Gaul, which disappeared before the discovery of written musical notation; there may, it seems, be some relics of that older music in the Frankish repertory and the repertory of the British Isles.[139]

c) For the Spanish liturgy, in addition to the modern Mozarabic tradition, a magnificent tenth-century monument has survived: the Antipho-

---

137. Pius XII, Encyclical *Musicae sacrae* (December 25, 1955), no. 25: *AAS* 48 (1956) 17–18 (trans. Megivern no. 492). — See E. Wellesz, *Eastern Elements in Western Chant* (Monumenta musicae byzantinae, Subsidia 2, 1; Oxford: Oxford University Press, 1947).

138. For a general introduction to the music of the Eastern rites see E. Wellesz, *Aufgaben und Probleme auf dem Gebiete der byzantinischen und orientalischen Kirchenmusik* (LQF 18; Münster: Aschendorff, 1923). — On Byzantine music see, above all, E. Wellesz, *A History of Byzantine Music and Hymnography* (Oxford: Clarendon, 1961²), and the great collection, *Monumenta musicae byzantinae* (Copenhagen: Ejnar Minksgaard), which was begun in 1935. — On the music of the Eastern rites see the many works of H. Husmann in *OCA* and *OCP* as well as in various journals (e.g., see the bibliographies in *ALW* 20–21 (1979), nos. 903–9; 23 (1981), nos. 258–62).

139. A. Gastoué, *Le chant gallican* (Grenoble: Librairie Saint-Grégoire, 1939), which is a collection of articles published in the *Revue du chant grégorien* from 41 (1937) to 43 (1939). — The fragments (of an antiphonary for the Office) that G. Morin published in *RBén* 22 (1905) 329–56, are late and from the islands, according to the very reliable judgment of A. Wilmart in *DACL* 6:1091.

nary of León, as well as various fragments displaying a musical notation that has not yet been fully deciphered.[140]

d) "Old Roman" chant, that is, the chant that characterized the basilical liturgy down to the thirteenth century, has been the object of noteworthy studies and editions in recent decades, although some aspects of its history have given rise to bitter controversies.[141]

e) The traditional chant of the Ambrosian Church, now restored in accordance with the ancient manuscripts by Dom Gregorio Sunyol, has been preserved down to our own day. Studies of it stress its kinship with Gregorian chant.[142]

f) "Gregorian" chant spread throughout the Latin West during the Carolingian liturgical reform, which attributed it to St. Gregory the Great.[143] Thanks to the paleographical labors of the Abbey of Solesmes,[144]

---

140. The *Antifonario visigótico mozárabe de la Catedral de León* was published in the series Monumenta Hispanae sacra, vols. 5/2 (facsimile edition; Madrid-Barcelona, 1953) and 5/1 (edition of text with notes and indexes by L. Brou and J. Vives; *ibid.*, 1959). — On chant in the Spanish liturgy: *Archivos Leoneses* 8 (1954) (entire volume is on the León Antiphonary); G. Prado, "Estado actual de los estudios sobre la música mozárabe," in *Estudios sobre la liturgia mozárabe* (Toledo: Disputación provincial, 1965), 90–106; D. M. Randel, *An Index to the Chant of the Mozarabic Rite* (Princeton Studies on Music 6; Princeton: Princeton University Press, 1973); *Liturgia y música mozárabes (I° Congreso internacional de estudios mozárabes 1975)* (Toledo: Instituto de estudios visigótico-mozárabes de San Eugenio, 1978).

141. B. Stäblein, *Die Gesänge des altrömischen Graduale (Vat. Lat. 5319)* (Monumenta monodica medii aevi 2; Kassel: Bärenreiter, 1970). — On Old Roman chant: M. Huglo, "Le chant vieux-romain, liste des manuscrits et témoins indirects," *SE* 6 (1954) 96–123; S. van Dijk, "The Urban and Papal Rites in seventh and eighth century Rome," *SE* 12 (1961) 411–86. — Bibliography of B. Stäblein's writings by B. Baroffio in *Rivista liturgica* 65 (1978) 394ff.

142. The fundamental work is still that of M. Huglo, L. Agustoni, E. Cardine, and E. Moneta-Caglio, *Fonti e paleografia del canto ambrosiano* (Archivio ambrosiano 7; Milan, 1956), with complements in E. Moneta-Caglio, "Manoscritti di canto ambrosiano rinvenuti nell'ultimo ventennio," *Ambrosius* 25 (1976) 27–36.

143. See R. van Doren, *Etude sur l'influence musicale de l'Abbaye de Saint-Gall* (Recueil de travaux . . ., 2nd ser., 6; Louvain, 1925); H. Hucke, "Die Einführung des gregorianischen Gesang in Frankreich," *Römische Quartalschrift* 49 (1954) 173–87; J. Smits van Waesberghe, "L'état actuel des recherches scientifiques dans le domaine du chant grégorien," in *Actes du IIIe Congrès international de musique sacrée, Paris 1957* (Paris: Editions du Congrès, 1959), 206–17; B. Stäblein, "Die Entstehung des gregorianischen Chorals," *Musikforschung* (Kassel) 27 (1974) 5–17.

144. The most important inventory of manuscripts, but only for the chants of the Mass, is the one published by the monks of Solesmes, *Le graduel romain. Edition critique. II. Les sources* (Solesmes, 1957). See also P. Jeffrey, "The Oldest Sources of the Graduale: A Preliminary Checklist of Mss. Copied Before About 900 A.D.," *Journal of Musicology* (1983) 316–21. A number of mss. have been published at Solesmes in the *Paléographie musicale* beginning in 1889 (19 vols. in the first series, 2 in the second, initially by Desclée in Tournai, then

its melodies have been restored and published in modern editions, while it has also been given its rightful place by Popes St. Pius X, Pius XI, and Pius XII. The Roman Church urges its use in liturgies celebrated in Latin, because it facilitates participation by the faithful, because its melodies help to understand the text, and because of its unobtrusiveness, serenity, and universality.[145]

g) The end of the Middle Ages and the Renaissance produced a figured music of such high quality that it could be used in the liturgy. It provided the liturgy in fact with many masterpieces, thanks especially to the genius of the so-called Roman School and in particular of Pierluigi da Palestrina († 1594).

2. Present-day problems of liturgical music

BIBLIOGRAPHY

Le chant liturgique après Vatican II (Semaine d'études internationales, Fribourg 1965) (Kinnor 6; Paris: Editions Fleurus, 1965).

LMD no. 108 (1971): La musique dans la liturgie (in particular, the articles of H. Hucke, E. Costa, G. Stefani).

J. Overath and J. Kuckertz, Musica indigena. Einheimische Musik und ihre mögliche Verwendung in Liturgie und Verkündigung, Musiktheologisches Symposium Rom . . . 1975 (Rome: CIMS, 1976).

LMD no. 131 (1977): Musique d'Eglise, pratiques et idéologies.

J. Aldazábal, "El canto en la nueva liturgia," Phase 22 (1981) 399–421 (with a bibliography).

The reform that flowed from Vatican II has profoundly disrupted relations between sacred music and Catholic worship. The greater participation of the people in the celebration and the general shift to use of the vernacular have called in question settled habits, traditional musical repertories, and the role of professional or amateur musicians, choirs, and organists. Meanwhile, the still clearly marked boundary between sacred music and secular music (or liturgical music and music without qualification) has been demolished by the liturgical reform and by contemporary practice.[146]

---

by Peter Lang in Berne); R. J. Hesbert, *Antiphonale missarum sextuplex* (Brussels: Vromant, 1935); *idem, Monumenta musicae sacrae* (5 vols.; Mâcon: Protat; then Saint-Wandrille; then Paris: Nouvelles Editions Latines, 1952–81); *idem, Corpus antiphonalium officii* (5 vols.; REDMF 7–8, 10–12; Rome: Herder, 1963–79). — See W. Apel, *Gregorian Chant* (London: Burns & Oates, 1958).

145. Pius X, Motu Proprio *Tra le sollecitudini* (November 22, 1903); Pius XI, Constitution *Divini cultus* (December 20, 1928); Pius XII, Encyclical *Musicae sacrae* (December 25, 1955); SCR, Instruction *De musica sacra* (September 3, 1958). Text of all these documents in A. Bugnini (n. 50, p. 144) 1 (1953), 15–16, 62–65; 2 (1959), 29–30, 36, 74, 77. — VSC 116.

146. LMD no. 108 (1971) 3 (Editorial). — Same view in J. Aldazábal, "El canto en la nueva liturgia," *Phase* 22 (1981) 399–401.

As a result, there has been an intense creative effort that makes new demands, which in the past seemed impossible to reconcile and which, to say the least, will be fully satisfied only after a lengthy period of trial and error and a selection brought about by the passage of time. The subordination of the music to the nature and rhythm of the celebration, the subordination of the melody to the text, and congregational participation[147] must all be achieved without sacrificing quality.

In any event, there will always be a place, however limited, for the traditional repertory that bears witness to the prayer of many different generations of Christians. There will be a place in particular for Gregorian chant in Latin, for this alone makes it possible for an international assembly to participate comfortably.

Finally, there is a keener awareness today of the fact that in countries with non-European civilizations, the exercise of a creativity reflecting the special genius of these countries is part of the work of implanting the Church.[148]

---

147. See *VSC* 112–14.

148. *VSC* 119 (*DOL* 1 no. 119): "In certain parts of the world, especially mission lands, people have their own musical traditions and these play a great part in their religious and social life. Thus . . . due importance is to be attached to their music and a suitable place given to it, not only in forming their attitude toward religion, but also in adapting worship to their native genius." — Earlier, and in greater detail, in Pius XII, Encyclical *Musicae sacrae*, no. 3: *AAS* 48 (1956) 22–23.

Chapter IV

Liturgical Signs

GENERAL BIBLIOGRAPHY

R. Guardini, *Sacred Signs*, trans. G. C. H. Pollen (London: Sheed & Ward, 1937); trans. G. Branham (St. Louis: Pio Decimo Press, 1956).

A. Baumstark, *Comparative Liturgy*, 3rd ed. by B. Botte, trans. F. L. Cross (Westminster, Md.: Newman, 1958), 130–51.

L. Bouyer, *Rite and Man: Natural Sacredness and Christian Liturgy*, trans. M. J. Costelloe (Notre Dame: University of Notre Dame Press, 1963).

E. J. Lengeling, "Wort und Bild als Elemente der Liturgie," in W. Heinen, *Bild, Wort, Symbol in der Theologie* (Würzburg: Echter Verlag, 1969), 177–206.

Centro di azione liturgica, *Il segno nella liturgia* (Liturgica, nuova ser. 9; Padua: Ed. Messagero, 1970): articles by S. Marsili, S. Cavalletti, E. Zaramella, A. Nocent, P. Scilligo.

R. Coffy and R. Varro, *L'Eglise signe du salut au milieu des hommes* (Paris: Le Centurion, 1972): papers read to the Plenary Assembly of the French Episcopate at Lourdes in 1971.

Symbolisme et théologie (Studia Anselmiana 64, Sacramentum 1; Rome: Herder, 1974).

L. M. Chauvet, *Du symbolique au symbole. Essai sur les sacrements* (Rites et symboles 9; Paris: Cerf, 1969).

B. Kleinheyer, *Heil erfahren in Zeichen. Dreissig Kapitel über Zeichen im Gottesdienst* (Munich: Don Bosco Verlag, 1980).

E. J. Lengeling, "Wort, Bild, Symbol in der Liturgie," *Liturgisches Jahrbuch* 30 (1980) 230–42.

C. Rocchetta, *I sacramenti della fede. Saggio di teologia biblica sui sacramenti quali "meraviglia della salvezza" nel tempo della Chiesa* (Nuovi saggi teologici 19; Bologna: Ed. Dehoniane, 1982).

From the very beginning of the liturgical movement, and especially after the publication of Guardini's well-known book, *Sacred Signs*, historians and theologians have stressed the important role of signs in the liturgy. Let me note straightway that modern anthropologists prefer the word "symbol," because it calls attention to the inherent evocative power

173

of the signifying reality as opposed to the conventional and arbitrary meaning conveyed by the word "sign."[1] We must bear in mind, however, that the central core of all liturgical symbolism is to be found in the Christian sacraments and that classical theology defines these as "signs" that effect what they signify (*significando causant*). For this reason it seems appropriate in the present context to retain the traditional word "sign."

To begin with, liturgical signs form a language that prolongs the words of the liturgy or lends them a greater intensity: the evocative power of signs makes it easier to understand the message, and on the other hand it gives more powerful expression to interior feelings and attitudes. But the liturgy is not simply speech, or dialogue between God and his people; it is also action, covenant; God acts and the people commit themselves to him. His action and his gifts take form in signs and essentially in the sacraments; the commitment of the people to God is sealed by gestures and rites and not simply by words. Or, more accurately, word and action together form a single sign; they are, in the terminology of the Scholastics, form and matter.

Theologians, from the Fathers of the Church down to the Second Vatican Council, have showed that the seven sacraments are prolonged in and, as it were, made to radiate throughout the rest of Christian worship by other signs (sacramentals, *sacramentalia*), which the Church gradually learned to distinguish from the sacraments. They also teach that the sacraments have their basis and ground in the essential sacrament, the incarnation of the Word, for the humanity of Christ is the sign of his invisibly present divinity (a point that is better expressed by the Greek word *mystērion* than by the Latin *sacramentum*). In addition, they rightly assert that the Church itself is a sacrament, manifestation, and presence of salvation.[2]

Thus the entire liturgy is made up of signs: the assembly is a sign, as we saw earlier; so is the bishop or priest who presides over the celebration and the deacons who carry out their ministry in it.[3] Time with its recurring rhythms—day, week, year—is likewise a sign.[4] The sacraments

---

1. F. Isambert, *Rite et efficacité symbolique. Essai d'anthropologie religieuse* (Rites et symboles 8; Paris: Cerf, 1979), 160–65; but Isambert relativizes the distinction.

2. Vatican II, Dogmatic Constitution *Lumen gentium* 1: "Since the Church, in Christ, is in the nature of sacrament—sign and instrument . . ." (Flannery 350); no. 9: "God has gathered together and established . . . the Church, that it may be for each and everyone the visible sacrament of this saving unity" (Flannery 360); no. 48: "He [Christ] . . . set up his Body which is the Church as the universal sacrament of salvation" (Flannery 407). — See R. Coffy, "Eglise sacrement," in R. Coffy and R. Varro, *Eglise signe de salut au milieu des hommes* (Paris: Le Centurion, 1972), 11–72; see also Section III, Chapter II, p. 253ff.

3. See above, Chapter II, p. 113ff.

4. See *The Church at Prayer* IV.

and principal sacramentals, which are at the heart of the liturgy, will be studied in detail in another volume of this series.[5]

It must be acknowledged, however, that the presence and understanding of liturgical signs have been subjected to a radical challenge in our age. The challenge has been issued at times in the name of a "spiritual" religion that will have nothing to do with ritualism, at times, in the name of a spontaneity that is supposedly incompatible with the regimentation inherent in signs. There is also an individualistic reaction against involvement in communities, and the tendency characteristic of our secularized societies and technological mentalities.[6]

But the challenge has also been motivated by fidelity to the very tradition of the Church and has aimed at pruning away the superfluous elements that the past added to the liturgical signs, as well as the artificial explanations it attached to them. This explains the instructions given by Vatican II:

> In this reform both texts and rites should be so drawn up that they express more clearly the holy things they signify.[7]
>
> The rites should be marked by a noble simplicity; they should be short, clear, and unencumbered by useless repetitions; they should be within the people's powers of comprehension and as a rule not require much explanation.[8]
>
> With the passage of time . . . certain features have crept into the rites of the sacraments and sacramentals that have made their nature and purpose less clear to the people of today; hence some changes have become necessary as adaptations to the needs of our own times. For this reason the Council decrees what follows concerning the revision of these rites.[9]

Finally, the adaptation of the liturgy to peoples whose cultures are non-European has made it necessary to ask what meaning certain signs will have for these cultures.

The reform promoted by Vatican II and the needs of adaptation thus call for a more thorough study of the laws of liturgical symbolism; in this we will be helped by contributions from the modern human sciences.

---

5. See *The Church at Prayer* III.

6. E. J. Lengeling, "Wort, Bild und Symbol in der Liturgie," *Liturgisches Jahrbuch* 30 (1980) 234–35.

7. *VSC* 21 (*DOL* 1 no. 21).

8. *VSC* 34 (*DOL* 1 no. 34).

9. *VSC* 62 (*DOL* 1 no. 62).

§1. Laws of Liturgical Symbolism

BIBLIOGRAPHY

I. H. Dalmais, "Transparence des signes, opacité des choses," *LMD* no. 81 (1965) 20–32.

A. Vergote, "Regard du psychologue sur le symbolisme liturgique," *LMD* no. 91 (1967) 129–51.

H. Reifenberg, "Neue Schwerpunkte der Liturgie. Die Bedeutung des optischen Elementes im Gottesdienst," *AL* 12 (1970) 7–33.

R. Scherer, "Philosophische Gedanken zur Symbolverständnis," *ibid.*, 34–53.

R. Bornert, "Die Symbolgestalt der byzantinischen Liturgie," *ibid.*, 54–68.

J. Hennig, "Wandlungen der Zeichenhaften in der römischen Messliturgie," *ibid.*, 285–301.

A. Vergote, "La réalisation symbolique dans l'expression cultuelle," *LMD* no. 111 (1972) 110–31.

LMD no. 114 (1973): *Sémiologie et liturgie*, especially the article of M. Amalados, "Sémiologie et sacrements" (7–35).

P. Hernandez, "Estructura semiológica de la liturgia," *Salmanticenses* 22 (1975) 457–97.

F. Isambert, *Rite et efficacité symbolique. Essai d'anthropologie sociologique* (Rites et symboles 8; Paris: Cerf, 1979).

According to the analysis of F. Isambert, a symbol has three aspects: "As signifier it has a meaning and can be grasped by the mind; as a perceptible object it is part of the material universe; and to the extent that the connection between these first two aspects is the result of a consensus, the symbol is a social fact."[10] It is therefore not possible to prescind from the institutional nature of symbolic actions; and when the actions in question are the signs of Christian worship that are prescribed by custom or by the liturgical books, their meaning is to an even greater extent expressed or suggested by the words that may accompany the signs, or even by the history of the rite. The scientific study of a sign's origins can help to recover its meaning, especially since with the passage of time the sign may have been distorted and impoverished or, on the contrary, rendered more complex. In any case, liturgical signs are not arbitrary or conventional.

Liturgical signs have in some instances been taken over from civic life or the surrounding culture, which was already using them as signs. Thus one of Franz Dölger's interests was the comparison of liturgical rites and the practices of the civic life in antiquity or even the practices of the pagan religions.[11] The feudal age, Byzantine ceremonial, and the ceremonial

---

10. Isambert (n. 1), 85; see 172.

11. Especially in the six volumes of his *Antike und Christentum* (Münster: Aschendorff, 1929–50).

of the Renaissance courts also left their mark on the Christian liturgies. But these borrowings, though perhaps valid for a given period, are shot through with ambiguity, because they may jeopardize the evangelical originality of the Church; in addition, they cannot be permanent or universal.

It is easier to account for the choice of signs by their natural aptitude for conveying a liturgical meaning: "It cannot be denied that certain sensible phenomena, especially if cosmic in scale, have an affinity with aspects of the human condition; all things are not able to symbolize anything and everything, and some representations have a privileged capacity for serving as symbols."[12] This aptitude is confirmed by history, sociology, and depth psychology. It is necessary to decode the language which God has written in creation and in things[13] and which he has even inscribed in the innermost recesses of the human soul. This language is grasped all the more easily when the signs are elementary, primitive, and unadorned; this is true even (perhaps above all) for our industrial civilizations and technological mentalities. Nonetheless, even at this level cultural interpretation plays a role: in our part of the world, the color of mourning is black, in the Far East it is white.

As a matter of fact, the majority of liturgical signs are biblical, and the understanding of them is provided by the Sacred Scriptures, which formed and fed the Christian imagination.[14] It is as biblical signs that the sacramental signs signify the grace they contain: the water of baptism is not simply water that washes; the Eucharist is not just any meal but a meal with a historical dimension, being a memorial of the Last Supper; anointing with chrism can be understood only when seen as the act by which kings and priests were consecrated in the Old Testament. When we perform the gestures of prayer and the other actions of the liturgy, we are repeating the gestures and actions of those who have gone before

---

12. Isambert 164.

13. See O. Casel, *The Mystery of Christian Worship, and Other Writings*, ed. B. Neunheuser (Westminster, Md.: Newman, 1962), 87: "The Christian knows . . . that nature groans under sin, along with man; it longs for redemption, which will come to it when it comes to the children of God. But he also knows that nature is a work of God's; because it is, he can love it, see in it the print of God's passing. Yet he stands over it; nature is tool and image of the spiritual. The liturgy, therefore, from the very beginning, from the time when the Lord made bread and wine the elements of the mass, has given nature its part to play. The church was not afraid to take over natural symbols which the heathen had used in their worship and, by putting them in their proper place, to give them their true value. By doing so she has made them holy, just as through the sacraments and sacred gestures, she has made the body holy; in fact the church has given to nature the first fruits of glory, the gifts of the children of God."

14. *VSC* 24 (*DOL* 1 no. 24): "It is from the Scriptures that actions and signs derive their meaning."

us in the faith, back as far as Abraham. The liturgy repeats images that signify for us, as a result of the Bible, the history of salvation.

The transparency of liturgical signs can be reduced by defective use. They are in danger of being eroded by human routine and inattention. Liturgical gestures must be done so as to be seen and understood, but without theatricality; they must remain hieratic and free of sentimentalism; the individual withdraws into the background and lets the action be that of the Church and Christ. In using material things there is too often a tendency to be overly sparing; the result is to impoverish the sign and strip it of its symbolism: a washing that is done with only a few drops of water, an anointing that consists simply in contact with a damp finger, an incensation in which the smoke is hardly visible and the perfume is not smelled, and so on.

Finally, the meaning of rites has often been no less obscured by allegorical commentaries whose authors were forgetful or ignorant of the real origin of the signs and looked instead either for artificial connections with biblical texts that were given fanciful interpretations, or for edifying lessons. This type of interpretation was already to be seen at times in St. Ambrose and would be developed by Theodore of Mopsuestia and then by the Byzantine commentators.[15] The Carolingian period inflicted it on the entire Latin Middle Ages, and there was a resurgence of it in the nineteenth century.[16]

§2. Postures, Gestures, Actions

BIBLIOGRAPHY

L. Gougaud, *Devotional and Ascetical Practices in the Middle Ages*, trans. author and G. C. Bateman (London: Burns, Oates & Washbourne, 1927).

H. Lubienska de Lenval, *The Whole Man at Worship: The Actions of Man Before God*, trans. R. Attwater (New York: Desclée, 1961).

M. Righetti, *Manuale de storia liturgica* 1 (Milan: Ancora, 1964³) 362–415.

Gestes et paroles dans les diverses familles liturgiques. Conférences Saint-Serge, XXIVᵉ Semaine d'études liturgiques . . . 1977 (Bibliotheca EL, Subsidia 14; Rome: Edizioni liturgiche, 1978).

R. Suntrup, *Die Bedeutung der liturgischen Gebärden und Bewegungen in lateinischen und deutschen Auslegungen des 9. bis 13. Jahrhunderts* (Münsterische Mittelalter Schriften; Munich: Fink, 1978).

---

15. R. Bornert, *Les commentaires byzantins de la divine liturgie du VIIᵉ au XVᵉ siècle* (Archives de l'Orient chrétien 9; Paris: Institut français d'études byzantines, 1966).

16. I note that Claude de Vert († 1708) fell into the opposite error when in his *Explication simple, littérale et historique des cérémonies de l'Eglise* (4 vols.; 1706–13) he systematically dismissed the symbolic intention in which the signs originated, and turned these into utilitarian gestures that became symbolic only when they ceased to be useful.

I. THE LITURGY AND THE HUMAN BODY

The liturgy is a source of surprise and even confusion for those whose whole mentality is idealistic: far from being pure mental prayer, the liturgy is expressed orally and takes shape in bodily postures and gestures; these moreover are not left to the spontaneous invention of the individual but are determined by constant laws. The reason for this characteristic of the liturgy is that revelation teaches us not to separate body and soul but to recognize the unity of the human composite as God created it and is now saving it. Dom Capelle remarks:

> The material and the spiritual are not juxtaposed in the human person but are made one, and the union is not a binding of two distinct entities but the intrinsic correlation of two components of one and the same being; the union is in the proper sense a unity, and a substantial unity at that. This is why a purely spiritual worship would not only be inhuman and have to be rejected, but is even impossible.[17]

The body, which is destined for a glorious resurrection, has in the present life already become a temple of the Holy Spirit through baptism; it is fed by the Eucharist, and Tertullian made the point as early as the beginning of the second century that the sacraments are performed on the body in order to sanctify the soul.[18] Furthermore, there is no real thought or feeling that is not spontaneously embodied in a posture or gesture; conversely, a posture, gesture, or action involve the whole person to such an extent that it expresses, intensifies, or even gives rise to an interior attitude; on this point modern psychology and pedagogy provide striking confirmation of theological tradition. Finally, these signs are required by the communal nature of liturgy: unanimity of hearts finds expression at least as much in bodily postures as in singing, or at least is expressed more easily by means of them.[19] Moreover, the language of words, especially the words of the celebrant, is made more intelligible by gestures. Christ used gestures to perform miracles that he could have worked simply by

---

17. B. Capelle, *Travaux liturgiques de doctrine et d'histoire* 1 (Louvain: Mont César, 1955), 40. — See R. Guardini, *The Spirit of the Liturgy*, trans. A. Lane (London: Sheed & Ward, 1930), 85–106.

18. Tertullian, *De resurrectione mortuorum* 8, 3 (CCL 2:931).

19. *VSC* 30 (*DOL* 1 no. 30): "To promote active participation, the people should be encouraged to take part by means of acclamations, responses, psalmody, antiphons, and songs, as well as by actions, gestures, and bearing"; *GIRM* 20 (*DOL* 208 no. 1410): "The uniformity in standing, kneeling, or sitting to be observed by all taking part is a sign of the community and the unity of the assembly; it both expresses and fosters the spiritual attitude of those taking part"; *GIRM* 62 (*DOL* 208 no. 1452): "There is a beautiful expression of this unity when the faithful maintain uniformity in their actions and in standing, sitting, or kneeling." — See M. Jousse, *L'anthropologie du geste* (Paris: Ed. Resma, 1969).

words; thus he could have healed the man born blind without using saliva and mud.

II. LITURGICAL POSTURES

It has traditionally been the task of deacons[20] to tell the congregation what postures it should adopt; they do so by means of "exhortations" or "proclamations," a good number of which are still familiar to us: *Flectamus genua . . . Levate, Humiliate capita vestra Deo, Procedamus in pace, Ite missa est* in the Roman books, *Humiliate vos ad benedictionem* in the medieval books of the Churches of France, *Offerte vobis pacem* in the Ambrosian rite, *orthoi, proschōmen, stōmen kalōs, stōmen meta phobou* of the Byzantines, and so on.

If there is no deacon, the priest himself or another minister tells the congregation of the appropriate posture. It must be always kept in mind that the purpose is to ensure the existence of interior attitudes and give expression to them; this is why it is especially important to explain to the faithful why they should stand at certain moments, or sit down, or kneel; they will thus discover in these postures the various, complementary aspects of Christian prayer.

1. *Standing*

This position is the proper one for the minister who serves at the altar and in particular for the sacrificing priest, as St. John Chrysostom observes[21] and as the Israelite tradition indicates (Sir 50:13).

Standing is also the primary liturgical posture of the faithful. In its natural and obvious meaning, standing is a sign of respect: people stand up in the presence of one whom they wish to honor. This is why the assembly should stand for the entrance and departure of the celebrant; they also rise in response to his greeting. They stand during the proclamation of the gospel, just as the Israelites stood to listen to the Lord who was speaking to them (Exod 20:21; 38:10; Neh 8:5; Ezek 2:1; Dan 10:11).

But standing was also the usual posture for Jewish prayer,[22] and it is

---

20. *GIRM* 21 (*DOL* 208 no. 1411): "For the sake of unformity in movement and posture, the people should follow the directions given during the celebration by the deacon, the priest, or another minister." — See *GIRM* 61 (*DOL* 208 no. 1451): "At Mass he [the deacon] has his own functions: he . . . sometimes gives directions regarding the assembly's moving, standing, kneeling, or sitting."

21. St. John Chrysostom, *In Epist. ad Hebraeos homiliae* 18, 1 (PG 63:135–36).

22. Mark 11:25; Luke 18:13; see Gen 19:27; 1 Sam 1:26; 1 Kgs 3:15. — See H. Cazelles in *Gestes et paroles dans les diverses familles liturgiques* (Bibliotheca EL, Subsidia 14; Rome: Edizioni liturgiche, 1978), 91.

likewise the characteristic position for Christian prayer, as is clear from the paintings in the catacombs, the sculptures on early sarcophaguses, and the works of the first ecclesiastical writers. It is why the faithful still stand up when uniting themselves to the solemn prayers of the celebrant.

Standing is the characteristic paschal posture: that is why ancient Christian discipline and the discipline of the East even today prohibit kneeling on Sundays and during the fifty days after Easter.[23] The reason is that by his passage Christ freed us from sin and death; we are no longer slaves and no longer act as persons who are ashamed; in God's presence we remain most respectful indeed, but we are also confident, because we share in the dignity of being his children: "The practice of not kneeling on the Lord's Day is a symbol of the resurrection by which, thanks to Christ, we have been delivered from sin and from the death which he put to death."[24]

Standing is also the proper posture of those who await the blessed parousia: in the presence of the Son of God only they remain standing who have nothing to fear from his justice (Mal 3:2); the Hebrews in Egypt probably stood as they ate the Passover in haste, always ready to set out (Exod 12:11); finally, the elect in heaven stand as they give thanks (Rev 7:9; 15:2). This eschatological meaning completes and controls the others; as St. Basil observes: On the first day of the week we stand for prayer "not only because, being risen with Christ and obliged to seek the things that are above, we call to mind . . . on the day devoted to the resurrection the favor bestowed on us, but also because this day is to be seen as in a way an image of the world to come.[25]

2. *Kneeling*

The importance of prayer offered while standing should not lead us to ignore the place of prayer on one's knees in the Christian tradition. Paschal joy alternates with penance; prayer on one's knees is specifically penitential, characteristic of days of fasting, a sign of mourning, humility, and repentance. According to St. Basil, to kneel "is to show by our action that sin has cast us to the ground."[26]

---

23. St. Justin, *Apologia I* 67, 5 (ed. Pautigny, 142–43); Tertullian, *De oratione* 23 (CCL 1:271–72); *De corona* 3, 4 (CCL 2:1043); St. Cyprian, *De dominica oratione* 31 (ed. Hartel; CSEL 3/1:289); Council of Nicaea, can. 20 (ed. Bruns, 20); St. Basil, *Traité du Saint Esprit* 27 (ed. B. Pruche; SC 17:236–38); St. Benedict, *Regula monachorum* 19; etc.

24. St. Irenaeus, Fragment 7 of a treatise on Easter, ed. W. Harvey (Cambridge, 1857; reprinted 1949), 2:478; PG 6:1364–65.

25. St. Basil, *Traité de Saint Esprit* 27 (SC 17:236–37). — On standing for prayer see P. Borella, "La preghiera in piedi nei tempi festivi," *Ambrosius* 52 (1976) 233–42.

26. St. Basil, *ibid.* (SC 17:238). — See St. Justin, *Dialogus cum Tryphone* 90, 5, ed. G. Archambault 1 (Textes et documents 11; Paris: Picard, 1909), 84–85; Tertullian, *De ora-*

But kneeling is not exclusively a sign of penance. It is also the posture for private prayer: one kneels in order to meditate silently on a reading, as the monks of Egypt used to do. St. Stephen knelt before his martyrdom (Acts 7:60), and we find the same posture being adopted for prayer in very ordinary moments by St. Peter (Acts 9:40), St. Paul (Acts 20:36), and the Christians who accompanied Paul when he was getting ready to leave (Acts 21:5); Paul himself tells us that "I bow my knees before the Father" (Eph 3:14).[27]

At a relatively recent period Western piety introduced periods of prayer on one's knees when adoring the Eucharist and receiving Communion. In this second instance, the posture did not allow the faithful to come to Communion in procession, and it is hardly compatible with the reception of Communion in the hand.[28]

3. Sitting

Sitting is the position taken by a teacher who instructs and a leader who presides. This is why the bishop has a chair or *cathedra* from which he presides or speaks. His priests sit around him on benches.

But the congregation is also asked to sit during certain parts of the celebration. In antiquity, houses of worship had no chairs for the faithful, but some bishops had them sit on the floor for the readings and the sermon, although other bishops refused this accommodation. But the faithful were already accustomed to sitting in the apostolic communities (Acts 20:9; 1 Cor 14:30). Sitting is, in fact, the posture proper not only to teachers but also to listeners: the child Jesus sat among the teachers (Luke 2:46); Mary sat at the Lord's feet as she listened to his words (Luke 10:39). That is why the faithful generally sit for all the readings (except the gospel), the meditative chants, and the sermon.

---

tione 23, 4 (CCL 1:272): "Ieiuniis autem et stationibus nulla oratio sine genu et reliquo humilitatis more celebranda est" ("During the periods of fasting and on the station days no prayer should be offered except on the knees and with every other sign of a humble spirit," trans. E. J. Daly in Tertullian, *Disciplinary, Moral and Ascetical Works* [New York: Fathers of the Church Inc., 1959], 182).

27. See the references given in A. George, *Etudes sur l'oeuvre de Luc* (Paris: Gabalda, 1978), 421, n. 5.

28. On kneeling prayer in the history of the Latin liturgy see P. Borella, "La preghiera in ginocchio," *Ambrosius* 52 (1976) 37–48, 403–17; B. Neunheuser, "Les gestes de la prière à genoux et la génuflexion dans les Eglises de rite romain," in *Gestes et paroles . . .* (see n. 22, p. 180), 153–66. — For the East see E. Bertaut, "Génuflexions et métanies," *Dictionnaire de spiritualité* 6 (Paris: Beauchesne, 1967), 213–26.

The faithful may also sit during the period of meditative silence, which it is good to allow them after communion.[29]

4. *Bowing*

The exhortation to bow the head precedes the solemn form of blessing at Mass: *Inclinate vos ad benedictionem* ("Bow your heads and pray for God's blessing"). The Masses for the weekdays of Lent in the old Missal had a prayer *Super populum*, which the deacon announced with the words, *Humiliate capita vestra Deo* ("Bow your heads to God"); the prayers themselves sometimes referred to this posture. But a genuflection was often substituted for a bow, as when, for example, the faithful knelt or genuflected for the celebrant's blessing. The monastic liturgy has by and large kept moments of prayer during which the monks remain in a deep bow. Finally, the Order of Mass provides that the celebrant bow while saying certain private prayers of petition; so, too, a deep bow is used in greeting the altar or the bishop.[30]

5. *Prostration*

In the present Roman liturgy prostration is rather rare; it is now prescribed only for those who are to receive a definitive consecration from the bishop: ordinands, virgins, abbots and abbesses, and who prostrate themselves while the litany of the saints is sung over them. The Romantic period gave prostration melodramatic meanings that were always alien to the liturgy and are to be rejected. It is enough to recall that, in the Bible, prostration is a frequently used posture for prayer (Gen 17:3; Deut 9:18; Neh 8:6; Tob 12:16; Jdt 9:1; 10:1-2; 2 Mac 10:4; Mark 17:6; Matt 26:39; Rev 4:10; etc.). It was used more frequently in the early and medieval liturgy, where all the sacred ministers would prostrate themselves,[31] even the entire assembly. The posture was one of solemn petition.

6. *Walking in procession*

In addition to extraordinary processions connected with moments in the liturgical year or with special circumstances in the life of the Church,[32]

---

29. *GIRM* 21 and 121 (= *EDIL* 1416, 1516 = *DOL* 208 nos. 1411 and 1511). In the second of the two passages the words *omnibus sedentibus* ("all may sit . . .") are omitted in the 1975 edition.

30. *GIRM* 84, 98, and 234 (= *EDIL* 1479, 1493, 1629 = *DOL* 208 nos. 1474, 1488, 1624).

31. According to some Frankish *ordines* it was customary for the celebrant and his ministers to venerate the altar at the beginning of Mass: *OR* XV, 15; *OR* XVII, 25 (Andrieu, *OR* 3:99, 178, 179); there is an echo of this at the beginning of the liturgical action on Good Friday.

32. Processions will be discussed in *The Church at Prayer* III.

ordinary celebrations involve movements and shifts of location that are processional acts: the entrance procession of the celebrant and ministers; the gospel procession; the bringing of the offerings; the procession of the faithful for communion. "While the songs proper to these movements are being sung, they should be carried out becomingly in keeping with the norms prescribed for each."[33]

7. Facing the east

Prayer said facing east was very important in the early liturgy outside of Rome.[34] It determined the "orientation" of churches and, to some extent, the position of the celebrant at the altar, whenever it was thought that he, like the faithful, should face the east.[35] The eastward position was a Christian substitute for the Jewish practice of praying while facing toward Jerusalem. The Roman Church did not pay any heed to it in building its basilicas; it seems even to have found the whole notion suspect as a survival of paganism among the faithful,[36] and it is likely that those rubrics of the *Ordines Romani* that prescribe it were additions made in Frankish territory.[37] The practice has today fallen into disuse.

III. LITURGICAL GESTURES

Some of the gestures used in the liturgy are purely utilitarian, for example, the washing of hands after certain actions. Others serve as natural accompaniments to words being spoken and underscore the meaning of these; for example, the gesture of pointing to the bread and wine during the Roman Eucharistic Prayers or the Eastern anaphoras. There are also

---

33. *GIRM* 22 (*DOL* 208 no. 1412).

34. Tertullian, *Ad nationes* I, 13, 1–5, and *Apologeticum* 16, 9–10 (CCL 1:32 and 116); Origen, *De oratione* 32 (PG 11:556–57); *Didascalia Apostolorum* 12 (ed. R. H. Connolly 119–20); St. Basil, *Traité du Saint Esprit* (SC 17:233, 236). — On the expression "Conversi ad Dominum," with which a number of St. Augustine's sermons end, see P. de Clerck, *La "prière universelle" dans les liturgies latines anciennes* (LQF 62; Münster: Aschendorff, 1977), 50–56.

35. F. Dölger, *Sol salutis . . .* (LQF 16–17; Münster: Aschendorff, 1920), 98–108, 115–93, 245–58; C. Vogel, "Versus ad Orientem," *Studi medievali* (Spoleto), 3rd ser., 1/2 (1960), 447–69 (= *LMD* no. 70, pp. 67–99); idem, "Sol aequinoctialis. Problèmes et technique de l'orientation dans le culte chrétien," *RevSR* 36 (1962) 175–211; idem, "L'orientation vers l'Est du célébrant et des fidèles pendant la célébration eucharistique," *OS* 9 (1964) 3–37; O. Nussbaum, *Der Standort des Liturgen am christlichen Altar vor dem Jahre 1000. Eine archäologische und liturgiegeschichtliche Untersuchung* (2 vols.; Theophaneia 18; Bonn: Hanstein, 1965); M. Metzger, "La place des liturges à l'autel," *RevSR* 45 (1971) 113–45.

36. St. Leo, *In Nativitate Domini sermones* 7, 4–5, ed. J. Leclercq and R. Dolle (SC 22bis; Paris: Cerf, 1964²), 156–61.

37. See Andrieu, *OR* 2:7.

gestures of respect or veneration for persons and things, and these gestures can at times be taken from the customs of the surrounding society; for example, the action of hiding the hands under a vestment or scarf while carrying a revered object is taken over from the court ceremonial of the Late Byzantine Empire;[38] the joining of hands is the gesture of a vassal rendering homage to his lord.[39] All these gestures have to a greater or lesser extent continued in existence through liturgical history, depending on the degree to which the reason for them is more or less profound and natural.

Other gestures are specifically Christian creations; for example, the sign of the cross. Some gestures are still richer in meaning because they are biblical and at times were used even by Christ himself. Some are sacramental (e.g., the laying on of hands), but are not restricted to the sacraments. The kiss of peace is undoubtedly already a liturgical gesture in the apostolic writings. Breathing upon someone is usually a gesture of exorcism, but it can also be used in communicating a sanctifying power. Most of these gestures will be studied in the context of the various liturgical actions of which they are a part. Four gestures, however, call for mention here.

1. *The sign of the cross*

As early as the beginning of the third century in Africa and at Rome, the making of a sign of the cross on the forehead during the rites of initiation seems already to be a traditional way of showing that the person belonged to Christ and to be regarded as a kind of invisible seal; Christians also made the sign of the cross on themselves rather frequently.[40] It was then extended to the various senses and became an exorcistic gesture.[41] Another form of the sign of the cross is the gesture of blessing, made either with all the fingers extended and joined or with some fingers extended and the others closed; the manner varied according to the practice of different Churches and different periods, and was also influenced by allegorical considerations; Easterners have often become accustomed to giving a blessing while holding a cross. Finally, the large sign of the cross (forehead to breast to shoulders) that is familiar to modern believers seems of relatively late origin; at times it has come to be associated mechani-

---

38. M. Righetti, *Manuale di storia liturgica* 1 (Milan: Ancora, 1964³), 403-4.

39. "But," says J. B. Molin in J. Gelineau, *Dans vos assemblées* 1 (Paris: Desclée, 1971), 240, "this gesture is also found in the Far East as a help to recollection and finding God within oneself."

40. Hippolytus, *Traditio apostolica* 21 and 42 (ed. Botte, LQF 39, pp. 54-55, 98-99); Tertullian, *De resurrectione mortuorum* 8 (CCL 2:931); idem, *De corona* 3, 4 (CCL 2:1043); etc. — See B. Botte, "Un passage difficile de la Tradition apostolique sur le signe de la croix," *RTAM* 27 (1960) 5-19.

41. Hippolytus, *Traditio apostolica* 20 (Botte 44-45).

cally with wrongly interpreted formulas (*Benedictus qui venit . . ., omni benedictione . . ., in nomine Domini . . .*).[42] It has long been a gesture associated with the beginning or end of the gospel reading; that is why it is always made at the beginning of canticles taken from the gospels. Finally, in the current Missal it has become a public gesture that marks the beginning of the liturgy of the Mass.

2. *Striking the breast*

This is a gesture of repentance and humility, as in the case of the tax collector of the parable (Luke 18:13) or of the witnesses of the crucifixion (Luke 23:45).[43]

3. *Lifting the eyes to heaven*

This gesture, which is attributed to Jesus in the Roman Canon (even in the oldest form of the text as found in St. Ambrose[44]), is repeated by the celebrant when he uses this Eucharistic Prayer at Mass. None of the four New Testament accounts of the Last Supper mention such a gesture, but the gospels do speak of Jesus acting thus at the first multiplication of the loaves (Matt 14:19; Mark 6:41; Luke 9:16), at the beginning of his proclamation of the beatitudes (Luke 6:20), during the prayer that precedes the raising of Lazarus (John 11:41), and at the beginning of the high-priestly prayer (John 17:1). The rubrics in the Missal of St. Pius V prescribed this action for the priest at various points in the Mass; but it had been used by the faithful generally in the early centuries.[45]

4. *Elevation and extension of the hands*

The gesture has always been used by the celebrant during the presidential prayers of the Mass and the principal consecratory actions. Far from

---

42. On the sign of the cross see F. J. Dölger, "Beiträge zur Geschichte des Kreuzzeichens," *Jahrbuch für Antike und Christentum* 1 (1958) 5–19; 2 (1959) 15–29; 3 (1960) 5–16; 4 (1961) 5–17; 5 (1962) 5–22; B. Fischer, "Il segno di croce come ricordo e commemorazione del battesimo," in *Rinnovati in Christo e nel Spirito, l'Initiazione cristiana* (Bari: Ecumenica editrice, 1981), 189–211.

43. See the Old Testament gesture of striking oneself on the thigh: Jer 31:19; Ezek 21:17. — St. Augustine, *Serm.* 67, 1 (PL 38:433) complains about the faithful who strike their breasts every time they hear the word *Confiteor* and do not attend to the meaning "I praise," which the verb can have in the Latin Bible.

44. St. Ambrose, *De sacramentis* IV, 21–22 (SC 25bis:114–15); see *Constitutiones Apostolorum* VIII, 12, 36 (Funk 1:508). — See B. Botte, "Et elevatis oculis in caelum. Etude sur les récits liturgiques de la dernière Cène," in *Gestes et paroles . . .* (see n. 22, p. 180), 77ff.

45. Tertullian, *Apologeticum* 30, 4 (CCL 1:141); see *Testamentum Domini* I, 35, ed. I. Rahmani (Mainz: Kirchheim, 1899), 83: "Sursum oculos cordium vestrorum" ("Lift up the eyes of your hearts").

being reserved to him, however, it was a gesture used in prayer by all Christians of the early centuries, as is clear both from the texts and from iconography.[46] In using it, Christians were doubtless taking over a Jewish practice, [47] but they gave it a new meaning. Tertullian writes:

> Not only do we lift up our hands, but we also stretch them out to the Lord, and, modeling ourselves on the passion of Christ (*dominica passione modulantes*), we confess him in prayer. . . . Moreover, when we adore God with modesty and humility, we make our prayers much more acceptable to him, if we do not lift our hands in an exaggerated way, but to a moderate and suitable level, and if we do not lift our faces in an arrogant manner.[48]

There are many other passages that bring out the same point: as Moses by raising and extending his arms ensured the victory of his people (Exod 17:9-14), so Christ saved us by raising and extending his arms on the cross; our prayer imitates his and is associated with his triumphant intercession.

IV. LITURGICAL ACTIONS

The liturgy is not content with simple gestures; it includes actions as well. Strictly speaking, the liturgy in its entirety is an action, but at certain moments it requires either the people or the celebrant alone to perform an action of the material order to which it gives a spiritual meaning: thus the confection of chrism by the bishop is an act of the perfumer's art, as Exodus 30:35 says; in enclosing the relics beneath an altar that he is consecrating, the bishop does a mason's work; the agape of the early Christians was a real family meal that was solemnized by prayer and at which the bishop presided; the liturgy for a funeral includes all the tasks associated with burial. The charitable collections taken for the support of the brothers and sisters are a true part of the celebration, as is already attested by St. Paul and St. Justin.

---

46. The texts are reproduced with a commentary in the fine article of V. Saxer, " 'Il étendit les mains à l'heure de sa Passion.' Le thème de l'orant(e) dans la littérature chrétienne des IIe et IIIe siècles," *Augustinianum* 20 (1980) 335–65; A great many pictorial images are reproduced in J. Wilpert, *Die Malereien der Katakomben Roms* (2 vols.; Freiburg: Herder, 1903) = *Le pitture delle catacombe romane* (2 vols.; Rome: Desclée, 1903). — See also W. Rordorf, "Les gestes accompagnant la prière d'après Tertullien, *De oratione* 11, 30 et Origène, *Peri euchēs* 31, 32," in *Gestes et paroles* . . . (n. 22, p. 180), 191–203.

47. Exod 17:9-12; Ps 28:2; 63:4; 134:2; 141:2; Isa 1:15; Lam 3:41.

48. Tertullian, *De oratione* 14 and 17 (CCL 1:265–66); trans. based on French trans. by Saxer (n. 46, above), 337.

§3. Liturgical Vestments and Insignia

BIBLIOGRAPHY

J. Braun, *Die liturgische Gewandung im Occident und Orient* (Freiburg: Herder, 1907).

P. Batiffol, "Le costume liturgique romain," in his *Etudes de liturgie et d'archéologie chrétienne* (Paris: Gabalda and Picard, 1919), 30–83.

L. Duchesne, *Les origines du culte chrétien. Etude sur la liturgie latine avant Charlemagne* (Paris: Thorin, 1889; Paris: E. de Boccard, 1920⁵), 399–419. ET: *Christian Worship: Its Origin and Evolution*, trans. M. L. McClure (London: SPCK, 1920), 379–98.

M. Righetti, *Manuale di storia liturgica* 1 (Milan: Ancora, 1964³), 584–642.

Andrieu, *OR, passim* but especially 2:234-35, 310-22; 4:129-84.

P. Salmon, *Etude sur les insignes du pontife dans le rit romain* (Rome: officium libri catholici, 1955).

I. GARB OF THE FAITHFUL IN THE ASSEMBLY

While instructing the Corinthians about their liturgical assemblies, St. Paul recalls one of the traditions he had passed on to them, namely, that men are not to pray with "head covered," while women are not to pray or prophesy with "head unveiled"; the latter must keep their heads covered. He justifies these prohibitions with arguments that the exegetes have still not fully explained. He concludes, however, by saying that "if any one is disposed to be contentious, we recognize no other practice, nor do the churches of God" (1 Cor 11:2, 4-5, 16). Was this the Jewish custom of his day, or was it a Hellenistic custom?[49] In any case, the tradition was maintained until the twentieth century and was even ratified in the 1917 Code of Canon Law (can. 1262, §2); it has now fallen into disuse.

From the third century on, the veil was in a special way the sign of virgins consecrated to the Lord; by the fourth century the liturgical action that established them in this state was known as the *velatio* or "veiling."[50]

Finally, there is one occasion on which the faithful wear a distinctive liturgical dress: their initiation. After their baptism they are given a white garment, the precise form of which is left to custom; adult neophytes are to wear it at their confirmation and during the Mass that follows directly on their baptism; formerly they did not lay it aside until Easter Saturday, that is, a week after their baptism.[51]

---

49. E. B. Allo, *Saint Paul. Première Epître aux Corinthiens* (Etudes bibliques; Paris: Gabalda, 1935), 253–68; J. Huby, *Saint Paul. Première Epître aux Corinthiens* (Verbum salutis 13; Paris: Beauchesne, 1946), 240–54; C. Spicq, *Epîtres aux Corinthiens*, in L. Pirot and A. Clamer, *La Sainte Bible* 11/2 (Paris: Letouzey, 1948), 244–48.

50. See *The Church at Prayer* III, Chapter 7: "The Consecration of Virgins."

51. See *The Church at Prayer* III, Chapter 1: "Christian Initiation."

II. VESTMENTS AND INSIGNIA OF CELEBRANTS
   AND MINISTERS

1. *In the early centuries*

It seems that in the very early centuries those who exercised the various degrees of sacred orders or the various ministerial functions did not wear any distinctive insignia or vestments for the liturgical celebration. They were distinguished only by the place (*topos*) they occupied in the assembly[52] and, of course, by the role they played.

Soon, however, garb was required that was distinct from everyday dress, although in the beginning it differed only by its purpose and the beauty of the materials. Thus, toward the end of the fourth century, Theodore of Mopsuestia finds the following statement in the book that he is citing for the rite of initiation: "The bishop, wearing vestments of light and shining linen. . . ." He offers this comment: "The bishop does not wear his usual clothing nor does he wear his ordinary outer garment; a vestment of fine, bright linen envelops him."[53] He also describes the garb of the deacons at Mass: "They wear a vestment that befits the [invisible] reality, for their outer garb is more sublime than they are: over their left shoulder they throw the *orarion*, which hangs at equal length in front and behind."[54] The *orarion* is also attested as an insignia of the deacon in the so-called canons of Laodicea.[55] St. Ambrose supposes that catechumens can easily identify the bishop, his priests, and his deacons; does this mean that at Milan too they were distinguished by their dress?[56]

---

52. St. Clement of Rome, *Epist. ad Corinthios* 40, 5, ed. A. Jaubert (SC 167; Paris: Cerf, 1971), 166–67. — In the period of the *OR* the physical *place* occupied in the assembly was so characteristic of an order received that in the description of the ritual of ordination specific reference is made to the newly ordained person taking the place that would henceforth be his: "dum vero consecratus fuerit [diaconus], dat osculum episcopo et sacerdotibus et stat ad dexteram episcoporum"; "et stat [presbyter] in ordine presbyterii"; "et tunc iubet eum [episcopum] domnus apostolicus super omnes episcopos sedere" (*OR* XXXIV, nos. 10, 12, 42). — It is not possible to interpret Origen as alluding to the liturgical vestments of the Christian priest when he comments on the passages of Leviticus that describe the priestly vestments of the old covenant: *In Leviticum homiliae* 4, 6, and the whole of 6; ed. M. Borret (SC 286; Paris: Cerf 1981), 180–85 and 268–97.

53. Theodore of Mopsuestia, *Homiliae catecheticae* 13, ed. R. Tonneau and R. Devreesse (ST 145; Vatican City, 1949), 369, 395–96; see *Homilia* 14 (*ibid.*, 431).

54. *Homilia* 15 (*ibid.*, 463).

55. Canons 22–23 forbid the use of the *ōrarion* by the lower clergy: H. T. Bruns, *Canones apostolorum et conciliorum* 1 (Berlin: Reimer, 1839), 76. — In the West the word *orarium* had a variety of meanings: Andrieu, *OR* 2:235, 312; *OR* 4:134–37; see P. Batiffol, "Le costume liturgique romain," in his *Etudes de liturgie et d'archéologie chrétienne* (Paris: Gabalda et Picard, 1919), 79–83.

56. St. Ambrose, *De sacramentis* I, 4, 6 (SC 25bis:62, 64); VI, 16 (*ibid.*, 82).

Once the texts[57] and especially iconography provide us with sufficiently concrete documentation for Western usage, we find that the bishop's garb is that which citizens of quality wore in functions of civic life: the *tunica*, a long robe of white linen; over this the *paenula*, a woolen outer garment that was very roomy and covered the arms;[58] over the *tunica* and under the *paenula* he wore the *dalmatica*, a shorter, ornate garment that was a mark of honor and probably corresponded to the *colobus* of senators.[59] By the end of the fourth century the *dalmatica* had also become the distinctive garment of Roman deacons;[60] later on, the popes would allow deacons of other Churches the privilege of wearing it.[61]

Another papal insignia, found from the end of the fifth century on, is the *pallium*, a long scarf of white wool that is worn around the shoulders, with one end hanging in front, the other in back. This was initially a distinction granted by the emperors to their court; later on the wearing of it would also be a privilege granted by the pope to certain bishops as a sign of the jurisdiction he granted them over other bishops.[62] In the East, however, mosaics and frescoes always show bishops wearing this same scarf (*ōmophorion*) over the same roomy cloak (*phelōnion*), although there is no trace of it having been granted to them by the Apostolic See; on the contrary, it is probable that the custom came to Rome from the East. In pictorial representations of both East and West bishops wear ornate sandals (*compagi*).[63]

2. From the Ordines Romani *(eighth century) to the* Caeremoniale episcoporum *(1600)*

a) *Description and origin.* Ordo Romanus I, which was compiled at the beginning of the eighth century, describes the vestments and insignia

---

57. Most of the texts usually cited (e.g., by Batiffol [n. 55], 30–34) do not refer to the liturgical celebration; this is the case in particular with the letter of Pope Celestine I, *Ad episcopos per Viennensem et Narbonensem provincias* (Jaffé-Wattenbach, *Regesta* . . . no. 369; PL 50:431).

58. Batiffol 35–47; L. Duchesne, *Christian Worship: Its Origin and Evolution*, trans. M. L. McClure (London: SPCK, 1903), 379–81; M. Righetti (n. 38, p. 185), 587–90.

59. The *dalmatica* is already mentioned in the Passion of St. Cyprian, *Cypriani acta proconsularia* 5 (CSEL 3:cxiii): "Cum se dalmatica exspoliavisset et diaconibus tradidisset, in linea stetit."

60. Ambrosiaster, *Quaestiones Veteris et Novi Testamenti* 46, ed. A. Souter (CSEL 50; 1908), 87 (= PL 35:2246).

61. Pope Symmachus (498–514) to the deacons of Arles, *Vita Sancti Caesarii* 1, 42, in *S. Caesarii opera*, ed. G. Morin, 2 (Maredsous, 1942), 313; St. Gregory the Great in 599 to the archdeacon of Gap, *Registrum* IX, 219, ed. Ewald-Hartmann (MGH, *Epist.*), 2:211.

62. Duchesne 384–90; Batiffol 57–71; P. Salmon, *Etude sur les insignes du pontife dans le rit romain* (Rome: Officium libri catholici, 1955), 21–23.

63. Duchesne 395; Salmon 21–23.

that we have already seen; the *paenula*, however, is henceforth called the *planeta*.[64] Two further pieces of clothing are added, probably from monastic usage: the *anagolaium* or cowl and the *cingulum*,[65] and for the pope a new insignia, the *mappula*, which consuls used to signal the opening of public games.[66]

The stole was unknown in Rome, but in Spain and Gaul it was the only distinctive mark of a deacon, as the *ōrarion* was in the East; priests also wore it, but in a different manner.[67] The fusion of the Roman liturgy with the Gallican liturgy in the Carolingian period brought the addition of the stole to the vestments worn at Rome and extended the wearing of the maniple to priests;[68] furthermore, Franco-Germanic usage, which, via its pontifical, exercised such a great influence on the later Roman liturgy, modified the terminology used for vestments and introduced a new item of clothing, the *cappa* or cope, which replaced the chasuble in many ceremonies.[69]

The crozier and ring, which were already being used in seventh-century Spain, were imported from there into Gaul, and thence into Germany; from here they were finally introduced into the Roman books; the crozier, however, was never accepted into the papal liturgy.[70] The miter followed

---

64. The *planeta*, a dark-colored, rainproof outer garment, was worn by all ministers in the time of *OR* I, but they removed it during ceremonies: this was the origin of the *chasuble pliée* (the chasuble with the sides cut away and hanging front and back) that was in use down to our own day. But according to the same *OR* I, the pope, other bishops, and priests also wore a *planeta* which they did not remove and which had been given to them at their ordination as significative of their rank: *OR* XXXIV, nos. 11 and 27; the *planeta* was therefore no longer an outer garment but a symbol of dignity. — See Batiffol 40–42; Duchesne 380–81; Andrieu, *OR* 4:132–34.

65. *OR* I, no. 34 (Andrieu, *OR* 2:78). — In fact, *OR* I, no. 34 also speaks of a *linea dalmatica*, which was distinct both from the *linea* and from the *maior dalmatica*. — The *anagolaium* would be known in Germanic lands as the *humerale* and later as the *amictus*. — On all this see Batiffol 51–53.

66. The *mappula* is thus the origin of the maniple. See *OR* I, nos. 37–38; Batiffol 55. — A very extensive documentation on the *mappula* of the Roman consuls is to be found in the consular diptychs; a list and some reproductions of these are given by H. Leclercq in *DACL* 4:1094–1145. — The *pallea linostina* of *LP* 1:225 is also regarded as an ancestor of the maniple; see *ibid.*, 171 and 189.

67. Duchesne 390–91; Andrieu, *OR* 4:129–31. — See M. Marinone, "Un'antica testimonianza iconografica sull'uso della stola diaconale in Occidente," *EL* 90 (1976) 88–99.

68. *OR* VI, no. 11; VIII, no. 1ff.; see Andrieu, *OR* 2:235, 312; 4:130–39. — See Duchesne 383–84.

69. In the beginning, *casula* was synonymous with *cappa*; later on, it became a synonym of *planeta*: see Andrieu, *OR* 4:149–53; see also *OR* X, nos. 2–8, and Righetti 607–11; Salmon 45–46.

70. On the ring: Salmon 24, 36, 39, 41; on the cross: *ibid.*, 24, 36–39, 43–45, 71; P. Salmon, "Aux origines de la crosse des évêques," in *Mélanges en honneur de Mgr Michel Andrieu* (Strasbourg: Palais universitaire, 1956), 373–83. — On the episcopal insignia in

the opposite route: it appeared first, under the name of *phrygium*, as a nonliturgical headdress of the popes in the ninth and tenth centuries;[71] at the end of the twelfth century it was introduced into the rite of episcopal ordination in the Roman Pontifical[72] and then acquired different forms until the three types of miter now in use came to be listed in the rubrics of the fifteenth century. Finally, the stockings, gloves, double tunicle, and a vestment to be worn under the alb (the *camicia*, ancestor of the rochet) all seem to be of Frankish origin.[73]

From the twelfth century on, the specifically liturgical vestments were for practical purposes those which would be prescribed in the *Caeremoniale episcoporum*. Any further development was limited to form: the vestments acquired the name *paramenta*, "adornments," and were weighted down with embroidery, gold trim, precious stones, and descriptive or allegorical designs; they lost their flexibility and roominess, to the point of becoming unrecognizable.[74]

b) *Blessing of the liturgical vestments and insignia.* It is not certain that a false decretal of Pope Stephen I[75] can be used to prove that the practice of blessing liturgical vestments was already widespread from the midninth century on. In any case, the first formulary appeared at that time in the ritual for the dedication of churches (which had long since included blessings for various objects used in worship),[76] and the texts of the blessing would subsequently be developed either in that context or in the ritual for ordinations.[77] The formulas did not vary much over the centuries: from

---

their entirety: T. Klauser, *Der Ursprung der bischöflichen Insignien und Ehrenrechte* (Krefeld: Scherpe, 1948²).

71. Andrieu, *OR* 4:169–84; Salmon, *Etude sur les insignes . . .*, 27–28, 40–46, 72; B. Sirch, *Der Ursprung der bischöflichen Mitra und päpstlichen Tiara* (Kirchengeschichtliche Quellen und Studien 8; St. Ottilien: Eos Verlag, 1975).

72. Pontifical of Apamea; Andrieu, *PR* 1:151–52.

73. On the stockings see Andrieu, *OR* 2:311–12. — The double tunicle is perhaps already to be seen in *OR* I, no. 34; it is certainly in *OR* VIII, nos. 1 and 4. — The *camicia* is in *OR* VIII; see the commentary of Andrieu, *OR* 2:312–14. — The gloves: Righetti 611–12; Salmon 36, 39, 68, 72. — The pectoral cross appears for the first time in the Pontifical of William Durandus (Salmon 68–72). — For completeness I note the existence of the *rationale*, an episcopal ornament introduced in the Middle Ages but not retained later on (Salmon 41, 44–45); see K. Hanselmann, *Das Rationale der Bischöfe* (Paderborn, 1975).

74. See Righetti 590–605.

75. This became part of the *Decretum* of Gratian, *De consecrat.*, dist. 1, c. 42 (ed. Friedberg, col. 1305).

76. Sacramentary of Saint-Amand, Paris, Bibl. Nat., ms. lat. 2290: J. Deshusses, *Le sacramentaire grégorien* 3 (Spicilegium Friburgense 28;1 Fribourg: Editions universitaires, 1982), no. 4135; also in Florence, Bibl. Medicea Laurenziana, ms. *Edili* 121, from the end of the ninth or the beginning of the tenth century (Deshusses, *ibid.*).

77. It is as part of the ritual of dedication that they were incorporated in the *PRG* XL, 79–82 (= Vogel and Elze 1:152–54) or in the *Pontificale Lanaletense*, ed. Doble (HBS 74),

the Romano-German Pontifical they passed into the twelfth-century Roman Pontifical[78] or were taken over by William Durandus.[79] The entire set is found quite unchanged, except for abridgment, in the Roman Pontifical of the Tridentine reform and the Roman Ritual of 1925.[80] Finally, the rite of episcopal consecration included formulas for the blessing of the crozier, the ring, the miter, and the gloves.[81]

c) *Medieval allegorizations.* The Middle Ages saw numerous attempts to explain the allegorical meaning of the liturgical vestments and insignia.[82] In particular, similarities with the liturgy in Leviticus were rather frequently invoked. These explanations were quite artificial, but, since St. Paul himself did not spurn the method,[83] it is not surprising that the liturgy should have kept echoes of it in the three categories of formulary commonly used until 1967: the words that the bishop spoke in clothing the newly ordained,[84] the prayers that bishop and priest respectively used in vesting for Mass,[85] and the blessings in the Pontifical.

3. *Current discipline*

The liturgical movement of the twentieth century sought, first of all, to give the vestments of celebrants and ministers a form that was both closer to the original and more artistic. But some simplification was also needed, and Vatican II expressed a desire for it.[86] It was effected in stages by the Instruction *Pontificalis ritus* of June 21, 1968[87] and the *General Instruction of the Roman Liturgy.*[88] Here is what the *General Instruction* has to say:

---

p. 15, or in Reims 340. They are in the ritual for ordinations in the so-called Pontifical of Egbert, ed. W. Greenwell (Surtees Society 27; 1853), 16–17.

78. Andrieu, *PR* 1:201; see *PR* 2:451–52.

79. Andrieu, *PR* 3:520–21.

80. PR, Part 2; RR of 1952, tit. 9, c. 1–2.

81. See *The Church at Prayer* III. — The PR of 1968 has a blessing, with a single prayer, of the ring, crozier, and miter, which may be used *tempore opportuno* but apart from the ceremony of ordination.

82. Salmon 9, 15, 19.

83. When he describes the Christian's equipment for battle: Eph 5:11-17.

84. See *The Church at Prayer* III.

85. The two sets of prayers were in the MR from 1570 to 1969, after the *Praeparatio ad missam* (there was even a third set, *quando pontifex celebrat private*, but it took all the prayers from the first two sets). The missals of the Middle Ages contained many and varied formularies: Martene, M 468–73.

86. VSC 128.

87. *AAS* 60 (1968) 406–12 (= *EDIL* 1099–1138 = *DOL* 550 nos. 4457–96); commentary by F. Dell'Oro in *Rivista liturgica* 56 (1969) 118–43. The prescriptions of this Instruction are found in the new *Caeremoniale episcoporum,* nos. 56–64.

88. The *General Instruction* underwent five revisions after its first edition of April 6, 1969, in order to reflect the advance of the liturgical reform as a whole (see the details in *EDIL*, pp. 465–69 and in *DOL*, p. 465, at asterisk in notes). The articles on vestments are

298. The vestment common to ministers of every rank is the alb (*alba*), tied at the waist with a cincture (*cingulo*), unless it is made to fit without a cincture. An amice (*amictus*) should be put on first if the alb does not completely cover the street clothing at the neck. A surplice (*superpelliceum*) may not be substituted for the alb when the chasuble or dalmatic is to be worn or when a stole is used instead of the chasuble or dalmatic.

299. Unless otherwise indicated, the chasuble (*planeta seu casula*), worn over the alb and stole, is the vestment proper to the priest celebrant at Mass and other rites immediately connected with Mass.

300. The dalmatic, worn over the alb and stole, is the vestment proper to the deacon.

301. Ministers below the order of deacon may wear the alb or other vestment that is lawfully approved in each region.

302. The priest wears the stole around his neck and hanging down in front. The deacon wears it over his left shoulder and drawn across the chest to the right side, where it is fastened.

303. The cope (*pluviale seu cappa pluvialis*) is worn by the priest in processions and other services, in keeping with the rubrics proper to each rite.

A bishop always wears his ring as a sign of his bond with the Church, the spouse of Christ. When he celebrates a liturgical action, he wears the same vestments as a priest. It is appropriate, however, that for ordinations and solemn rites he follow the traditional practice of wearing a dalmatic under the chasuble. Finally, at moments indicated in the rubrics, he puts on the miter and supports himself with the crozier or pastoral staff (*baculus*). The pectoral cross, which may be worn even over street clothing, is the most recent of the episcopal insignia.[89] The *pallium* is bestowed by the pope on metropolitan archbishops, and on them alone,[90] as a sign of their jurisdiction over the bishops of their province. Since the Middle Ages abbots and certain prelates not of episcopal rank have had the privilege of using various episcopal insignia; Pope Paul VI, implementing a directive of the Council, considerably limited this privilege.[91]

---

numbered 297-310 (= *EDIL* 1692-1705 = *DOL* 208 nos. 1687-1700, according to the 1974 text; variants in previous editions are indicated in the notes).

89. The pectoral cross appeared for the first time in the Pontifical of William Durandus; Salmon 68-72.

90. Paul VI, Motu Proprio *Inter eximia episcopalis* (May 11, 1978): *AAS* 70 (1978) 441-42 (= *DOL* 554 nos. 4542-43).

91. *VSC* 130. — Paul VI, Motu Proprio *Pontificalia insignia* (June 21, 1968): *AAS* 60 (1968) 374-77 (= *EDIL* 1089-98 = *DOL* 549 nos. 4447-56). — See F. Dell'Oro in *Rivista liturgica* 56 (1969) 101-18; on the history of these privileges, see, in addition to Salmon's book, J. Heckel, *Mitra und Stab der wirklichen Prälaten ohne bischöflichen Character* (Kirchenrechtliche Abhandlungen 104; Stuttgart: Enke, 1928).

The choral vesture that cardinals, bishops, lesser prelates, and canons are to wear when not celebrating or concelebrating is regulated by the Instruction of the Secretariat of State, March 31, 1967,[92] and the Circular Letter of the Congregation for the Clergy, October 30, 1970.[93]

III. MEANING OF THE LITURGICAL VESTMENTS

"In the Church, the Body of Christ, not all members have the same function. This diversity of ministries is shown outwardly in worship by the diversity of vestments. These should therefore symbolize the function proper to each ministry. But at the same time the vestments should also contribute to the beauty of the rite."[94] It is true, of course, that the Catholic faith teaches us to see in bishop, priest, and deacon an invisible and inalienable resemblance to Christ; but it is also natural that in the exercise of their role—in the fullest sense of the word: *In persona Christi*—they should wear a garb that reminds others and themselves of what they are and what ought to be made manifest in them. In addition, the full-length white robe called the alb signifies a withdrawal from the bustle of life and from utilitarian tasks; above all, however, it recalls the royal and priestly vestment worn in the heavenly liturgy by the Lord of glory and by the angels and the elect.[95]

IV. LITURGICAL COLORS

The Eastern Churches for the most part attach no importance to the color of the liturgical vestments. The Western Churches, however, have thought that the use of different colors helps "to give effective, outward expression to the specific character of the mysteries of the faith being celebrated and, in the course of the year, to a sense of progress in the Christian life."[96] The number of colors and the norms for their use were left rather vague in local practice, and it was only in about the twelfth

---

92. *AAS* 61 (1969) 334–30 (= *EDIL* 1333–61 = *DOL* 551 nos. 4497–4532).

93. *AAS* 63 (1971) 314–15 (= *EDIL* 2190–95 = *DOL* 552 nos. 4533–37). — On canonical dress in ancient times see A. Gréa, *La sainte Liturgie* (Paris: Bonne Presse, 1909), 79–119.

94. *GIRM* 297 (*DOL* 208 no. 1687).

95. The importance of liturgical vestments is acknowledged even by Protestants who do not recognize a ministerial priesthood; see R. Paquier, *Traité de liturgique* (Neuchâtel: Delachaux et Niestlé, 1954), 120–29, and especially 122: "It is natural that a man who officiates at the Church's worship should be garbed in a manner that befits the task assigned to him and gives visible expression to what he is doing; . . . he who performs a cultic function is not acting in a private capacity but as a minister of the Church."

96. *GIRM* 307 (*DOL* 208 no. 1697). — See Paquier (n. 95 above), 127–29.

century that serious attention began to be given to the subject;[97] it was usual, however, for dark vestments to be worn in outdoor processions. White was the only color suggested by biblical symbolism, for it was the color of the clothing of Christ in his transfiguration, of the angels in their appearances, and of the redeemed in the Apocalypse.[98]

The Roman rite finally settled upon six colors: white, red, green, violet, black, and rose. The use of all these is continued in the *General Instruction of the Roman Missal*,[99] but with some flexibility; in particular, the use of black is now optional in Masses for the deceased and may be replaced by violet. In addition, episcopal conferences can decide upon and propose to the Apostolic See adaptations that better meet the needs and mentalities of the various peoples.[100]

§4. Material Elements

BIBLIOGRAPHY

F. Cabrol, *Le livre de la prière antique* (Paris: H. Oudin, 1900), 333–63.

R. Guardini, *Sacred Signs*, trans. G. Branham (St. Louis: Pio Decimo Press, 1956), 41–64.

O. Casel, *The Mystery of Christian Worship, and Other Writings*, ed. B. Neunheuser (Westminster, Md.: Newman, 1962), 87–88.

I. H. Dalmais, *Introduction to the Liturgy*, trans. R. Capel (Baltimore: Helicon, 1961), 119–24.

C. Vagaggini, *Theological Dimensions of the Liturgy*, trans. L. J. Doyle and W. A. Jurgens (Collegeville: The Liturgical Press, 1976), 43–69.

This section will not deal with the objects that the Church blesses in order to sanctify the regular use of them by Christians in their secular (that is, noncultic) life[101] but solely with the things the Church uses in the liturgy.

The actions of Jacob, Moses, and the prophets, as well as the laws governing Aaronic worship, had accustomed the Hebrews to regard certain material elements as symbols of relations between God and his people and as means of expression in the liturgy. There were, for example, the stones set up to commemorate encounters with God (Gen 28:18) or to receive the victims of sacrifice (Exod 20:23; Deut 27:5-7; 1 Mac 4:44-47);

---

97. See Righetti 613–15 and especially J. Braun, *Die liturgische Gewandung im Occident und Orient* (Freiburg: Herder, 1907), 728–60.

98. E. B. Allo, *L'Apocalypse* (Etudes bibliques; Paris: Gabalda, 1921²), 48–50.

99. The detailed regulations are in *GIRM* 308–10 (= *EDIL* 1703–5 = *DOL* 208 nos. 1698–1700).

100. *GIRM* 308, last paragraph (= *EDIL* 1703 = *DOL* 208 no. 1698).

101. These blessings will be discussed in *The Church at Prayer* III.

the oil poured out (Gen 28:18) or used in anointing kings and priests; the incense whose smoke suggested the ascent of acceptable prayer to God (Ps 141:2); the water of ritual purifications; the ashes or dust thrown upon the head as a sign of penitential grief;[102] the bunch of hyssop used in rites of purification;[103] the salt "of the covenant with your God" that purified the offering of first fruits (Lev 2:13; Num 18:19; see Mark 9:49) or made water wholesome to drink (2 Kgs 2:20).

Christ, too, made certain material elements serve as symbols of the new covenant, but the symbols in this case are efficacious: bread, wine, water, oil, perfume are sacramental signs. The Church, imitating the Lord's institutional activity, uses things to extend the sacramental signs, as it were, or to prolong them; thus it uses water, oil, perfume, and bread in other rites. In addition, it uses things in the liturgy in order, as it were, to give material embodiment to images of the Old and New Testament, thus turning them into pedagogical actions: new fire, light, stone, ashes, the milk and honey typical of the Promised Land,[104] and so on. Sometimes it has taken over Old Testament usages, as, for example, incense (though the heavenly visions of the Apocalypse encouraged it here) or the sprinklings of the altar in the Gallican ritual of dedication.[105] At times, finally, the biblical tradition cannot completely explain a symbolism, and we must allow for a legitimate borrowing from pagan practices.[106]

Most of the rites in which these various material elements are used will be studied in their proper place. It will be enough here to say something about light, incense, and holy water because these are used so widely in the liturgy.

---

102. For the act of throwing dust or ashes on one's head as a sign of sadness and grief see 2 Sam 13:19; Jdt 4:15; 9:1; Esth 4:1; 14:2 (Vg); Lam 2:10; Dan 9:3; 1 Mac 3:47; 4:39. — Also found is the gesture of lying on ashes (Esth 4:3; Jonah 3:6), which would subsequently be imitated by Christians and play a part in some medieval rituals for Extreme Unction.

103. Hyssop is an aromatic plant whose dense and hairy leaves make it suitable for sprinkling; thus in Exod 12:22 (see Heb 9:19) the Israelites are to use a bunch of hyssop for applying the blood of the lamb to the doorposts and lintels at the time when the Lord is to pass by; in Lev 14:4 hyssop is probably used for the seven sprinklings of a leper who is to be purified; in Num 19:18; the hyssop is expressly used in sprinkling purifying water in a case of legal uncleanness; on the basis of this last rite Psalm 51:7 expresses a desire for an interior cleansing that will be God's work. As late as the Pontifical of 1961, hyssop was prescribed in the ritual purification of the church, altar, and clocks that are to be dedicated; its use was already attested in *OR* XLII, no. 29, XLI, no. 12, and *Ge* 3, 76.

104. On the drinking of milk and honey see *The Church at Prayer* III, Chapter I.

105. Exod 29:12; lev 8:11-15; see A. Chavasse, *Le Sacramentaire gélasien* (Tournai: Desclée, 1958), 41.

106. See O. Casel (see n. 13, p. 177), 87: "The church was not afraid to take over natural symbols which the heathen had used in their worship and, by putting them in their proper place, to give them their true value."

1. Light

BIBLIOGRAPHY

F. Dölger, *Sol salutis. Gebet und Gesang im christlichen Altertum* (LQF 4-5; Münster: Aschendorff, 1925²).

_____, "Lumen Christi . . .," in his *Antike und Christentum* 5 (Münster: Aschendorff, 1936), 1-43.

Light provides the liturgy with a number of symbolisms. The light of the sun plays an important role, of course, since to anyone familiar with the Bible the rising and setting of the sun recall Christ as the Sun of justice; with the aid of this symbolism the Church was able effectively to counter the infatuation with the cult of the sun at the beginning of the fourth century.

Here, however, mention must be made above all of the part played by lights, lamps, candelabra, and candles. In the Old Testament, a flame fed by virgin oil burned constantly in the tent and before the Lord (Exod 27:20; Lev 24:2-4; 1 Sam 3:3) on a seven-branched golden lampstand (Exod 25:31-40); so, too, St. John in the Apocalypse saw "seven torches of fire" burning before him who sits on the throne (Rev 4:5) and seven golden lampstands surrounding the Son of Man (Rev 1:12-13). Lights, which had been used in the synagogues and at Jewish domestic liturgies, are also attested in the early Christian assemblies (Acts 20:8), where they certainly served as more than a utilitarian source of illumination. As early as the third century the action of lighting the lamps at nightfall inspired some magnificent Christian prayers[107] that were subsequently used and more fully developed in the service known as the *lucernarium*; the Easter candle doubtless had its origin in the *lucernarium*. Lights are at once a sign of joy, a reminder of a holy presence, and a symbol of the prayer to which they bear witness or to which they invite; they appeared around the tombs of the martyrs, then in the basilicas, then before altars and icons, and, at a much later date, before the Blessed Sacrament.

The Church of Jerusalem created another expressive gesture of the Easter liturgy: the *Lumen Christi*. The baptismal lamp or candle also has an obvious and important symbolism. On the other hand, the use of torches and candles at burials is perhaps the continuation of a Roman custom to which Christians gave a new meaning. So, too, the carrying of candles in the procession on February 2 acquired a permanent importance only because it provided an illustration of the Canticle of Simeon with its phrase *"lumen ad revelationem gentium"* ("a light of revelation to the Gentiles").

---

107. Hippolytus, *Traditio apostolica* 25 (Botte, LQF 39, pp. 64-65); the *Phōs hilaron* certainly dates from the third century (see *The Church at Prayer* IV, 169.)

Light-carrying ministers also served as an escort of honor; the custom was inspired by Roman protocol[108] but it was likewise so natural that it deserved to be retained. The honor was given first to bishops, who in the ceremonial of *Ordo Romanus* I were preceded by seven *cereostata*, a practice maintained at Rome and Lyons; because these candlesticks were set down near the altar after the arrival of the cortege, they became the adornment of any altar at which the local bishop celebrated a solemn Mass. The two candlesticks now carried by acolytes are a reduced form of the ancient practice. The same honor is given to the gospel, which is carried in procession with a similar cortege.

2. *Incense*

BIBLIOGRAPHY

C. Atchley, *A History of the Use of Incense in Divine Worship* (Alcuin Club Collections 13; London: Longmans, 1909).

E. Fehrenbach, "Encens," *DACL* 5 (1922) 2–21.

A. M. Forcadell, "El incienso en la liturgia cristiana," *Liturgia* (Silos) 10 (1955) 219–25.

As I noted above, incense was used in Jewish ritual as a very expressive symbol of prayer (Ps 141:2); before the Holy of Holies in the temple there was an altar of gold on which aromatic incense was burned as a sacrifice of praise each morning and evening.[109] In the heavenly temple of the Apocalypse the same rite continues, with angels as its ministers, but the vision is purely symbolic: it is the prayers of the saints that are in fact being offered (Rev 8:3-5). Let me digress for a moment to observe that the thurible in this passage (*libanōton, thuribulum*) is not what we today call a censer; it is rather a receptacle for carrying live coals from one altar to another. Another vision in the Apocalypse (5:8) shows us the twenty-four elders each holding a bowl of incense that is being consumed (*thymiamata*); the symbolism is the same.

Despite these biblical models, the Western Church waited a long time before allowing incense to be burned in the liturgy,[110] perhaps because the gesture had an idolatrous meaning in the surrounding pagan world. The East doubtless did not have the same unpleasant memories; in any case, by the end of the fourth century perfume burners were brought into

---

108. P. Batiffol, *Etudes de liturgie et d'archéologie chrétienne* (see n. 55, p. 189), 209–13.

109. Exod 30:1-10, 34-38; 37:25-29; Num 4:11; 1 Kgs 6:20-21; Luke 1:8-11.

110. Tertullian, *Apologeticum* 30, 6 (ed. J. Waltzing, p. 71); St. Augustine, *Enarrationes in psalm.* 49, 21 (CCL 38:591). — The texts of St. Ambrose that are proposed as witnesses to the use of incense in the liturgy (*In Lucam* 1, 1; *Liber de Joseph patriarca* 3, 17) are, it seems to me, being misinterpreted.

the Church of the Holy Sepulcher at Jerusalem during the Sunday vigil, at the moment when the gospel of the resurrection was about to be read;[111] incensations in the proper sense are attested by Pseudo-Dionysius for the Syrian areas, where they would subsequently play such a major part.[112]

At Rome, incense and perfume burners were used extensively in the funeral liturgy, wherein the practice had been traditionally allowed. Subsequently, stationary perfume burners on stands were permitted in the basilicas, both to purify the air and to honor the place itself,[113] or they were suspended by chains before relics and icons. Finally, in the authentically Roman *Ordines* of the seventh and eighth centuries the honorary cortege accompanying the pope and the gospel included not only the seven *cereostata* but a *thymiamaterium* carried by a subdeacon: here again the vessel was a simple burner on which aromatic incense was burned; the practice was probably borrowed from imperial protocol.[114] In *Ordo V*, that is, in the Rhineland of the mid-tenth century, the word *thymiamaterium* was replaced by *thuribulum*, which had already been used in the Gelasian Sacramentary and reflected Gallican terminology.[115] At the Offertory of the Mass the same *Ordo* included a rite for the offering of incense that is already attested by Amalarius as a Frankish practice and that was doubtless inspired by the no less Gallican ritual of dedication.[116]

3. Holy Water

BIBLIOGRAPHY

A. Franz, *Die kirchlichen Benediktionen im Mittelalter* 1 (Freiburg: Herder, 1909), 43–220.
M. Righetti, *Manuale di storia liturgica* 4 (Milan: Ancora, 1959²), 525–32.

In its origin and in its most common use in antiquity and down to our own time, holy water was purificatory water, such as had been used in the pagan religions; it was to be sprinkled in sacred places, but only after being sanctified by a prayer that the Church said to exorcise and purify the water itself; the formularies, which are chiefly Gallican and

---

111. Egeria, *Itinerarium* 24, 10 (SC 296:244–45; Wilkinson 125).
112. Pseudo-Dionysius, *Hierarchia ecclesiastica* 3, 2 and 4, 2 (PG 3:425 and 473); French trans. by M. de Gandillac (Paris: Aubier, 1943), 264 and 282.
113. *LP* 1:174, 177, 183, 233, etc.
114. Andrieu, *OR* 2:80 (= *OR* I, no. 41); 2:82 (no. 46); 2:88 (nos. 59 and 61); etc.
115. *Ibid.* 2:195.
116. *Ibid.* 2:218; Amalarius, *Liber officialis*, Prooemium 21, ed. J. M. Hanssens, *Amalarii opera liturgica* 2 (ST 139; Vatican City, 1948), 18; see references for *Turibulum* and *Tus* in the index in 3:479.

Visigothic in origin, make this intention clear.[117] From at least the sixth century on,[118] salt was mixed with the water, perhaps in imitation of the gesture of Elisha (2 Kgs 2:20-22); still other ingredients were added in the medieval ritual of dedication. The water was meant in every case to be sprinkled in places: homes, houses of worship, fields. Even the Sunday Asperges seems originally to have been a purification of places figuring in the rule of monks.[119] The practice is still followed in the ceremony of dedication and in many blessings.

It was natural, however, that another, more specifically Christian symbolism should be attached to rites using water and that holy water should become a reminder of the paschal mystery and baptism. This is the meaning the Sunday Asperges eventually acquired,[120] and it is why the Missal of 1970 revised the formulary for the Asperges and proposed that it might replace the penitential act.[121] The presence of a holy water font at the doors of churches likewise invites the faithful to sign themselves with holy water as a similar reminder. During the Easter Vigil, in churches and chapels that do not have a baptismal font, holy water is used at the community's renewal of baptismal promises. Finally, the funeral ritual includes the use of holy water at the final farewell, as a reminder that "through baptism the person was marked for eternal life."[122]

§5. Sacred Places

According to canon 1205 of the 1983 Code, "sacred places are those which have been designated for divine worship or for the burial of the faithful through a dedication or blessing which the liturgical books prescribe for this purpose."[123] It is to be observed that this definition repeats

---

117. For the history of the formularies for the blessing of water see especially A. Chavasse, *Le sacramentaire gélasien* (see n. 105, p. 197), 50-56; — see *Gell* 2815-16 (*Benedictio aquae et salis ad spargendum in domum*) and 3011-21 (*Benedictio aquae et salis*).

118. *LP* 1:54 and 127, in the notice on Pope Alexander: "Hic constituit aquam sparsionis cum sale benedici in habitaculis hominum."

119. *Gell* 2859-77; Berlin, Sacr. Phillipps 1667, nos. 1873-95; Supplement of Benedict of Aniane to the Hadrianum, nos. 1473-80.

120. Texts cited by Righetti 4:531.

121. *MR*, ed. of 1970, pp. 889-92; ed. of 1975, pp. 917-20; English ed. of 1974, pp. 892-93; ed. of 1985, pp. 896-97.

122. *RR*, *Ordo exsequiarum*, ed. typica (Vatican Polyglot Press, 1960), Praenotanda 10: "Aspersio qua recolitur inscriptio per baptismum in vitam aeternam"; English translation, "Rite of Funerals," in *The Rites of the Catholic Church* 1 (New York: Pueblo, 1976), 645ff., with revised translation of the Introduction in *DOL* 416 no. 3373ff. (citation from no. 3382).

123. *The Code of Canon Law. A Text and Commentary*, ed. J. A. Coriden, T. J. Green, and D. E. Heintschel (New York: Paulist, 1985), 846 (henceforth: *Code*, with number of canon and with page reference in parentheses for quotations).

the one found in the Code of 1917 (canon 1154), except for one word: the new liturgical books reserve the term "consecration" for persons and use the word "dedication," traditional in antiquity, when speaking of places and altars. It is a fact, of course, that in early practice places and objects were consecrated by their very use, and no need was felt of a special rite; but, as we shall see further on, such a rite has profound catechetical value for the Christian people.

I. THE CHURCH

BIBLIOGRAPHY

A. Raes, *Introductio in liturgiam orientalem* (Rome: Pontificio Istituto Orientale, 1947), 30–40: "De divisione interna ecclesiae ut loci cultus liturgici" (with a bibliography).

_____, "La liturgie eucharistique en Orient, son cadre architectural," *QL* 43 (1962) 101–14 (= *LMD* no. 70 [1962] 49–66).

M. Righetti, *Manuale di storia liturgica* 1 (Milan: Ancora, 1964), 416–85.

J. Gelineau, "Les lieux de l'assemblée célébrante," *LMD* no. 88 (1966) 64–82.

LMD no. 136 (1978): *Des lieux pour célébrer* (Congrès d'art sacré, Avignon, September 1978), especially the papers of P. Jounel, "L'assemblée chrétienne et les lieux du rassemblement humain au cours du premier millénaire" (13–37), and P. M. Gy, "Espace et célébration comme question théologique" (39–46).

Phase 19 (1979), fasc. 111: *Las casas de la Iglesia*.

Codex iuris canonici auctoritate Ioannis Pauli pp. II promulgatus, 1983, canons. 1214–34. English translation in: *The Code of Canon Law. A Text and Commentary*, ed. J. A. Coriden, T. J. Green, and D. E. Heintschel (New York: Paulist Press, 1985).

GIRM 253–80.

Buildings intended for Christian worship differ greatly in their conception not only from pagan temples but from the Jewish temple as well. The temple in Jerusalem was the dwelling of the Lord, as the Tent of Meeting had been in the nomadic period of Israel's history; in addition, it sheltered the Ark whereon God manifested himself between the cherubim, and at its dedication by Solomon it was filled with the Cloud that was the sign of the Lord's glorious presence.[124] Under the new covenant, however, the temple is no longer made by human hands, for the sacred humanity of Jesus is henceforth the temple of God.[125] Christians, being

---

124. 1 Kgs 8:10-13; etc. — See Y. Congar, *The Mystery of the Temple*, trans. R. F. Trevett (Westminster, Md.: Newman, 1962), 3–79; X. Léon-Dufour, "Cloud," in *idem* (ed.), *Dictionary of Biblical Theology*, 2nd, revised and enlarged ed., trans. under the direction of P. J. Cahill, with trans. of new material by E. M. Stewart (New York: Seabury, 1973), 83–85; F. Amiot, "Temple," *ibid.*, 594–97.

125. John 2:19; Congar (see n. 124, above) 112–50. — See PR, *Ordo dedicationis ecclesiae et altaris* (Vatican Polyglot Press, 1977), ch. 2, *Praenotanda* 1.

identified with Christ by baptism, are also temples of the Holy Spirit; in every believer who loves Christ the Trinity makes its dwelling,[126] but the Church as a whole is likewise a temple made of living stones and the dwelling place of God.[127]

If Christians make use of, or build for themselves, structures of stone or brick, these are not temples. They are simply houses in which the assembly can gather for prayer: *domus ecclesiae, oikoi ekklēsias.*[128]

Later on, the Byzantines would give the name *Kyriakon* to such places. Monks for their part would have in their monastery a "place of prayer," an *oratorium.*[129]

Modern Church law distinguishes between a "church" and an "oratory"; what differentiates them is the community for which each is respectively intended: "The term church signifies a sacred building intended for divine worship to which the faithful have a right of access for divine worship, especially its public exercise," while an oratory is intended for a limited group, even if in fact all have access to it.[130]

The purpose of the building determines its entire architecture;[131] changes made in the liturgy and variations in its form will profoundly alter the plan and arrangement of the church. The styles that can be distinguished in churches are not simply convenient archaeological classifications; they express spiritual conceptions that differ according to country and to period. It is therefore necessary to learn to appreciate all of them, or else we will be ignorant of the legitimacy of these conceptions and the great riches they contain;[132] the folk of the classical period who rejected the art of the Middle Ages were no more justified than the people at the end of the nineteenth century who felt alienated from Baroque art. As a matter of fact, Baroque churches represented an important effort at liturgical restoration that had resulted from the Counter-Reformation; the church buildings of the fourteenth and fifteenth centuries, on the contrary, reflected a decadent liturgy that was full of superfluities, distorted by allegorical commentary, and forgetful of the presence of the people.

---

126. Rom 8:9-11; 1 Cor 3:16-17; 6:19-20; 2 Cor 6:16; — Congar (see n. 124, p. 202) 151-57. The theme occurs often in the preaching of St. Augustine.

127. Eph 2:19-22; 1 Pet 2:5; — Congar 157-235.

128. C. Mohrmann, "Les dénominations de l'église en tant qu'édifice en grec et en latin au cours des premiers siècles chrétiens," *RevSR* 36 (1962) 155-74; reprinted in her *Etudes sur le latin des chrétiens* 4 (Rome: Edizioni di storia e letteratura, 1977), 211-30.

129. *Praeceptum* (Augustinian) 2, 2: "In oratorio nemo aliquid agat nisi ad quod est factum, unde et nomen accepit," ed. L. Verheijen, *La règle de saint Augustin* 1 (Paris: Etudes augustiniennes, 1967), 420; St. Benedict, *Regula monachorum* 52: "Oratorium hoc sit quod dicitur, nec ibi quicquam aliud geratur aut condatur."

130. *Code,* can. 1214, 1223.

131. *VSC* 124 and 128.

132. *VSC* 122-23. — See *GIRM* 254, 256; *Code* can. 1216, 1234.

Of all the churches Christianity has known, those of antiquity seem to have been the best adapted to the celebration of the liturgy. They were so organized that the assembly was clearly differentiated into its constituent parts: the altar separated the people from the clergy; the faithful, gathered together in a homogeneous space, had to be able to see and hear from any point in it; this was accomplished by having either a rectangular hall or a plan in which everything radiated from a center or had three rooms, with two forming a transept and with the altar at the point where the three met. The altar was a focal point for all eyes and a true center of the building; sometimes this centrality was emphasized by a ciborium or, later on, by various architectural devices (cupola, lantern, etc.). But the altar was not the only center of the celebration; other very important centers were the chair from which the bishop presided before the Eucharist proper or in ceremonies apart from the Eucharist, and the ambos or rostra[133] from which the lectors read the biblical texts and the deacons uttered their proclamations.

In the churches of the West the bishop's chair was placed at the center of a rather shallow apse and on a higher level than the altar so that he could see the entire assembly in front of him and could be heard by all.[134] Ambos, placed at each side, enabled the readers to tower over the audience and, like the bishop, to be heard by all; the ambo for the gospel was higher and more ornate. At each side of the bishop's chair there was a semicircular bench for the priests; the deacons and other ministers stood.

The churches of the East sometimes provided an original solution to the various problems of arrangement that were posed by houses of worship. Among the Nestorians, for example, there were two distinct rostra (*bēmata*), one for the altar and the celebration of the Eucharist, the other, in the middle of the faithful in the nave, for the bishop's chair, the readers, and, more generally, for the Liturgy of the Word; after the latter had been completed, the celebrant and ministers went in procession from this rostrum to the other.[135]

The Western arrangement, with the bishop's chair and priests' bench in an apse behind the altar, was maintained until the fourteenth century, even where—outside Italy—the celebrant turned his back to the people during the Eucharist proper. As the result of various influences the celebrant and bishop abandoned the apse for movable chairs that were

---

133. A. Raes, *Introductio in liturgiam orientalem* (Rome: Pontificio Istituto Orientale, 1947), 32–33, 37; St. Cyprian, *Epist.* 38 and 39, ed. L. Bayard, 1:96 and 99.

134. Texts of St. Augustine on this point are collected in W. Rötzer, *Des heiligen Augustinus Schriften als liturgiegeschichtliche Quelle* (Munich: Max Hueber, 1930), 79–80.

135. Raes (see n. 133 above) 32; J. Dauvillier, "L'ambon ou bēma dans les textes de l'Eglise chaldéenne et de l'Eglise syrienne au moyen âge," *Cahiers archéologiques* 6 (1952) 11–30.

set to the side and from which they no longer presided over the assembly.[136] The altar, meanwhile, was placed close to the wall of the apse; over it were put pictorial or sculptural decorations that were set increasingly higher and became increasingly more complex. The presence of a numerous clergy, monks, canons, or Mendicants, who sat in stalls and formed a choir, meant that the people were moved ever farther away; at the same time, the altar was, for various reasons, placed behind walls or roodscreens or iconostases.[137] Being cut off in this way from the main altar, the faithful came to prefer the secondary altars and chapels that multiplied through the church building, especially from the fourteenth century on.[138]

Houses of worship have traditionally been decorated so as to provide a festal setting for the assembly and the celebration: hangings, lights, and precious materials have always been used for this purpose.[139] Pictorial decoration in the form of frescoes, mosaics, sculptures, and stained-glass windows contribute to this festive atmosphere; in addition, they function as a kind of prolongation of the liturgical signs, with an emphasis especially on the heavenly and eschatological aspect of the liturgy. This is why iconographic themes cannot be left to chance; in the East they are often predetermined in great detail, but in any case they must be in harmony with the celebration and not distract those present.

The recent liturgical reform urges a return to tradition in the construction and layout of churches: "The general plan of the sacred edifice should be such that in some way it conveys the image of the gathered assembly. It should also allow the participants to take the place most appropriate to them and assist all to carry out their individual functions properly."[140]

The faithful are to be assigned a place that will facilitate their active participation. In his *Apostolic Tradition* Hippolytus required that men and women form separate groups in the assembly; the requirement was linked to the kiss of peace.[141] The same practice seems to have been generally followed in the various Churches and has left its mark in some regions down to our own day, though at times only in certain settings such as graveyards.[142] The new Code has not kept it.

---

136. On this evolution see Andrieu, *OR* 2:144–45; M. Durliat, in *LMD* no. 70 (1962) 100–104.

137. In the East: Raes 36–39. — In various Eastern usages veils are also drawn at certain moments to hide the altar (Raes 35, 38–39).

138. Consequently, in Notre Dame of Paris and in other churches the side chapels are a later addition. — Texts of antiquity calling for but a single altar: M. Righetti, *Manuale di storia liturgica* 1 (Milan: Ancora, 1964³), 504–6.

139. Egeria, *Itinerarium* 25, 8, (SC 296:252–53; Wilkinson 127). — *LP* 1: CXLI–CLIV.

140. *GIRM* 257 (*DOL* 208 no. 1647).

141. *Traditio apostolica* 18, ed. Botte (LQF 39), pp. 40–41.

142. The 1917 Code of Canon Law, can. 1262, §1, still regarded the practice as desirable.

It is appropriate that the sanctuary or place for the priests be set off from the place of the faithful and be large enough to allow the effortless celebration of the liturgy. The sanctuary must contain not only the altar, the true center of the church (I shall speak of it in a moment), but also the celebrant's chair, which is to be so located as to make clear the function of him who presides over the assembly and directs its prayer.

The dignity of the Word of God requires in principle the presence of a stationary ambo (and not simply of a movable lectern) that will make it easier to proclaim the Word, and to which the faithful will spontaneously direct their attention.[143]

Whatever the layout of the building, the choir is to be stationed in such a way as to make clear both its special function and the fact that it is part of the assembly of the faithful.[144]

Finally, it is strongly recommended that the place of Eucharistic reservation be "in a chapel suited to the faithful's private adoration and prayer" or, at the very least, "in a part of the church that is worthy and properly adorned."[145] Provision should also be made either in the church or alongside it for a baptistery and a place for administering the sacrament of penance.

The conditions of modern life underscore the part that the place of worship should have in the lives of the faithful outside the time of its communal use. In our day the faithful have greater difficulty in achieving prayerful recollection and a sense of God's presence; they should have available a place that will provide silence and the needed spiritual atmosphere.[146]

Places and objects intended for use in worship must be beautiful; this is not possible, however, unless they are perfectly adapted to their purpose. This is why the Church has frequently set down rules that *sacred art* must follow.[147] Sacred art is not an autonomous kind of art but, however noble it may be, is only a servant of divine worship; it can only be a reflection or expression of faith; it must share the pastoral concern of the Church, which carefully sees to it that there be nothing to disturb or irritate the sensibilities of the simple. At the same time, it uses all available technical resources and expresses liturgical values in the language of

---

143. *GIRM* 258, 271–72.

144. *GIRM* 274.

145. *GIRM* 276 (*DOL* 208 no. 1666). — On reservation of the Eucharist see *The Church at Prayer* II, pp. 245–49.

146. *Code* (1983), can. 937. — Even Protestants today stress this role of the building used for worship, even though they do not admit an abiding Real Presence of Christ in the Eucharist outside the time of celebration; see Paquier (see n. 95, p. 195) 47.

147. See *VSC* 122–29 and *Code,* can. 1216. The bishop exercises his responsibility in this area through his diocesan commission for sacred art; see *VSC* 46.

its age and its culture; the Church warns against the anachronisms of the archaeologizing mind and against the introduction of Western art forms into countries that have a civilization of their own. Sacred art requires both sincerity and the avoidance of individualism; sometimes it will express itself chiefly in forms marked by grandeur, sometimes it will be radiant amid poverty.

II. THE ALTAR

BIBLIOGRAPHY

J. Braun, *Der christliche Altar in seiner geschichtlichen Entwicklung* (2 vols.; Munich: G. Koch, 1924).

M. Righetti, *Manuale di storia liturgica* 1 (Milan: Ancora, 1964³) 490–553.

H. Iñiguez, *El altar cristiano de los origenes a Carlomagno* 1 (Historia de la Iglesia 19; Pamplona: Ed. Universidad de Navarra, 1978).

Pontificale Romanum. Ordo dedicationis ecclesiae et altaris, editio typica (Vatican Polyglot Press, 1977), ch. 4: "Ordo dedicationis altaris. Praenotanda," pp. 82–85. The Rite is translated in *The Rites of the Catholic Church* 2 (New York: Pueblo, 1980), 250–73, but with a new translation of the Introduction in *DOL* 546 nos. 4398–4427.

The Code of Canon Law, canons 1235–39.

The altar is the most venerable spot in the church, and the consecration of the altar is the principle action in the rite for the dedication of churches.

The altar is first of all a table (*mensa, trapeza*): a dining table at which the priest, who represents Christ the Lord, does what the Lord himself did on Holy Thursday and ordered his disciples to do in their turn in remembrance of him. The first Christian altars were portable wooden tables; this was still the case as late as the mid-fourth century in the Vatican Basilica erected by Constantine.

It was soon thought more fitting, however, that the table be fixed in its place and, in the Latin Church, that it be made of stone, so that all might understand the table to be also an altar and the Eucharist also a sacrifice. The Fathers, of course, had never ceased reminding the faithful that "Christ was the victim, priest, and altar of his own sacrifice" and that "his members and disciples are also spiritual altars on which the sacrifice of a holy life is offered to God."[148] But the celebration of the Eucharist on a stone altar turns the latter into an image of Christ[149] according to a twofold symbolism. First there is the theme of the stone as such:

---

148. PR, *Ordo dedicationis altaris, Praenotanda* 1–2 (trans. in *DOL* 547 nos. 4398–99), and the texts cited there.

149. *Ibid.*, no. 4. — See O. Rousseau, "Le Christ et l'autel," *LMD* no. 29 (1952) 32–39.

the rock from which Moses caused water to flow, "and the Rock was Christ" (1 Cor 10:14), and the foundation stone or cornerstone of the building.[150] Then there is the theme of the stone altar, a theme initiated in Genesis (Gen 28:18) and developed on the basis of Deuteronomic legislation for the offering of holocausts.[151]

In order better to show that the material altar is an image of Christ, who is the sole true altar of the new law, a dedication is performed, in the course of which the altar is anointed with chrism, as Psalm 45 is sung: *"Unxit te Deus, Deus tuus, oleo laetitiae prae consortibus tuis"* ("God, your God, has anointed you with the oil of gladness above your fellows"); incense is burned on the altar table, and lights are placed around it.[152]

The builders of the Roman cemeterial basilicas of the fourth to the sixth century often[153] sought, even if it meant overcoming very great difficulties, to link the body of the martyr with the altar on which the Eucharistic sacrifice was to be celebrated. The connection may have been suggested by the Apocalypse: "I saw under the altar the souls of those who had been slain for the word of God and for the witness they had borne" (Rev 6:9). When the Eucharist is celebrated over the tombs of the martyrs, it is made clear above all that "the sacrifice of the members has its source in the sacrifice of the Head."[154]

Fidelity to this tradition and these rich symbols[155] requires that even today churches have a fixed, immovable altar, the table of which is of natural stone,[156] and that this altar be solemnly dedicated. It is dedicated to God alone, since the Eucharistic sacrifice is offered to him alone; altars may be erected in honor of the saints, but no statue or icon or relic of these saints is to be placed on the altar. In the Roman tradition, on the other hand, it is desirable that relics of the martyrs or other saints be placed beneath the altar, provided they are large enough to be seen as human remains.[157]

In new churches there is to be but one altar, signifying that we have but one Savior and one Eucharist. But there is an advantage in having, in addition, a small chapel, separated from the main body of the church,

---

150. Ps 118:22; Isa 28:16; Acts 4:11; Matt 21:42; 1 Cor 3:14; Eph 2:20; 1 Pet 2:4-7; — P. Lamarche, "Stone," in *Dictionary of Biblical Theology* (see n. 124, p. 202), 582–83.

151. Deut 27:5-7; 1 Mac 4:44-47; see Exod 20:25; — D. Sesboüé, "Altar," in *Dictionary of Biblical Theology* (see n. 124, p. 202), 12–13.

152. *Ordo dedicationis altaris* 22.

153. But not always: the fourth-century basilicas of St. Agnes and St. Lawrence were not yet built over the tomb, but were connected with it by stairs.

154. *Ordo dedicationis ecclesiae* 5 (*DOL* 547 no. 4402).

155. See pp. 216ff.

156. Unless the episcopal conference judges otherwise: *Ordo dedicationis altaris* 9.

157. *Ibid.*, 11.

for weekday Masses and individual visits of the faithful. Contrary to the custom that prevailed at the end of the Middle Ages and during the classical period, the altar is to be separated from the wall of the church, so that the celebrant can easily circle it and celebrate facing the people.[158]

For the celebration of Mass in oratories or even outside places of worship it became customary in the course of the Middle Ages to use portable altars, which might be of high artistic quality or be simply stones containing relics; these altars were consecrated in a rite closely resembling that followed in the consecration of fixed altars. The present discipline of the Church is much more flexible: it is no longer required that a portable altar be of stone; and instead of being dedicated it may be simply blessed.[159] Furthermore, outside of churches and oratories, a celebrant may use an ordinary table, provided it is suitable and that a cloth and a corporal are used.[160]

The respect due to the altar is shown in various ways in the liturgy.[161] Celebrants kiss it at their arrival and at the end of Mass. The table is covered with a cloth and surrounded by candelabra (as the various liturgical actions require) as a sign of reverence and festiveness.[162] A cross, visible to the entire assembly, is placed on or near the altar.

III. THE BAPTISTERY

BIBLIOGRAPHY

L. de Bruyne, "La décoration des baptistères paléochrétiens," in *Miscellanea liturgica in honorem L. C. Mohlberg* 1 (Rome: Edizioni liturgiche, 1948), 189–220.

Actes du Ve Congrès international d'archéologie chrétienne (Aix-en-Provence, 1954) (Studi di antichità cristiana 22; Vatican City, 1957), with numerous studies of baptisteries. Especially recommended in the article of A. Grabar (187ff.).

A. Khatchatrian, *Les baptistères paléochrétiens: Plans, notices, bibliographies* (Ecole pratique des Hautes Etudes . . ., Collection chrétienne et byzantine; Paris: Klincksieck, 1962).

M. Righetti, *Manuale di storia liturgica* 1 (Milan: Ancora, 1964³), 475–80.

Buildings constructed and laid out for use exclusively as baptisteries made their appearance as early as the third century; their decoration was

---

158. *Ibid.*, 7–8; see *GIRM* 262.

159. *Ordo benedictionis altaris, Praenotanda.* — When Easterners celebrate outside a church, they use, not a portable altar, but an *antimension*, a piece of decorated cloth that contains relics and has been blessed by the patriarch.

160. *GIRM* 260, 265; *Code,* can. 932, §2.

161. See L. Gougaud, *Devotional and Ascetical Practices in the Middle Ages,* trans. author and G. C. Bateman (London: Burns, Oates & Washbourne, 1927), 51–65.

162. *GIRM* 269. — The candelabra are reminiscent of Rev 1:12-13.

based on the same biblical typology of Christian initiation that was already being transmitted by Tertullian and Hippolytus. The practice of baptism by immersion required a pool, the piping in of water, and often a heating system as well; the baptistery had to be distinct from the building used for worship and, since the rite of initiation was reserved to the bishop, there was only one baptistery in each city.

In their architecture, which was inspired by the halls for the baths, the baptisteries followed a centralized plan; allegorical considerations suggested an octagonal form.[163] The veneration felt for baptisteries can be seen in the marvelous artistic flowering they stimulated (in Italy down into the Renaissance) and in liturgical rites: in Rome, in particular, a procession of neophytes went on pilgrimage to the baptistery every evening of Easter week.[164]

As adult baptisms became increasingly rare, and especially once the practice of immersion disappeared, baptisteries were reduced in size and came to be placed inside the parish churches, close to the entrance. Canonical legislation spoke no longer of baptisteries but simply of the "baptismal font" (*baptismalis fons*).[165] The desire for community participation often led to the celebration of baptisms not in the baptistery proper but in the sanctuary of the church; the disadvantage of this was that it deprived Christians of the possibility of venerating the place where they had been baptized. The new ritual of 1969 permits this practice to continue,[166] but at the same time it revives the traditional ideal by defining the baptistery as follows:

> The baptistery is the area where the baptismal font flows or has been placed. It should be reserved for the sacrament of baptism and should be a place worthy for Christians to be reborn in water and the Holy Spirit. It may be situated in a chapel either inside or outside the church or in some part of the church easily seen by the faithful; it should be large enough to accommodate a good number of people. After the Easter season, the Easter candle should be given a place of honor in the baptistery.[167]

---

163. F. Dölger, "Zur Symbolik des altchristlichen Taufhauses," *Antike und Christentum* 4 (1934) 153–87; A. Quacquarelli, *L'ogdoade patristica e suoi riflessi nella liturgia e nei monumenti* (Quaderni di "Vetera christianorum" 7; Bari: Adriatica Editrice, 1973).

164. P. Jounel, "Les Vêpres de Pâques," *LMD* no. 49 (1957) 96–111.

165. *Code* (1983), can. 858, §1.

166. RR. *Ordo baptismi parvulorum*, editio typica (Vatican Polyglot Press, 1969), *De initiatione christiana, Praenotanda generalia* 26. The rite is translated in *The Rites of the Catholic Church* 1 (New York: Pueblo, 1976), 3–339; revised translation of the General Introduction in *DOL* 294 nos. 2250–84; the reference here is to no. 2275.

167. *Praenotanda* 25 (*DOL* 294 no. 2274). The new book *De benedictionibus* published in 1984 contains an *ordo* for the blessing of a new baptistery (cap. 25, pp. 321–38). There was already one in *PRG* 52–53 (1:190–92) and in the Pontifical of William Durandus (Andrieu, *PR* 3:533); its essentials came from *Ge* I, 94: *Orationes et preces in dedicatione fontis* (ed. Mohlberg, nos. 730–36).

IV. THE CEMETERY

Although Christians did not from the very beginning have cemeteries of their own and although they took over everything in the funeral customs of their cities that was not incompatible with their faith and their hope, it is easy to distinguish the presence of Christians in the ancient burial grounds, less from the fact that they practiced only inhumation than from the inscriptions and iconography. By the beginning of the third century the Roman community already owned its own cemeteries; only the underground parts survived, however, and in addition their original form was subverted after the Peace of Constantine by the desire of Christians to be buried near the martyrs. In the Middle Ages many people sought the honor of being buried inside the churches, while the other graves clustered around the outside. A cemetery was a place where the bodies of all the brothers and sisters waited for the resurrection; it had to proclaim this expectation and avoid grandiloquence, vanity, luxury, and, much more, any trace of paganism.

Despite the problems created by modern urban growth, the Church still desires that wherever possible it continue to have cemeteries of its own or at least areas in the city's cemeteries that are reserved for the burial of the faithful and have been blessed. When even this is not possible, each grave is blessed individually at the time of the funeral.[168]

§6. Objects Set Aside for Cultic Use

I shall not list in detail all the objects intended for cultic use on which the lesser arts have been lavished in the course of the ages and on which the Church may have bestowed a blessing or even a consecration. The ritual containing these blessings seems to have been compiled originally in Gaul, with the blessings being grouped together after the formularies for the dedication of churches; it is found in the *Missale Gothicum* and the Old Gelasian, then filled out and propagated by the eighth-century Gelasians and finally by the Romano-German Pontifical.[169] I have already

---

168. *Code* (1983), can. 1240. — A formulary for this blessing is already found in *PRG* 54 (1:192–93); it was taken over into the *PR* as early as the end of the eleventh century; the Pontifical of Apamea (Andrieu, *PR* 1:286–88) has a very rich formulary upon which William Durandus drew at the end of the thirteenth century (Andrieu, *PR* 3:500–10). The Pontifical of Clement VII retained only an abridged version of it. The present rite is in *De benedictionibus* (1984), cap. 35, pp. 425–32.

169. A. Chavasse, *Le sacramentaire gélasien* (see no. 105, p. 197), 40–45; *Missale Francorum*, ed. Mohlberg (REDMF 2), nos. 60–68; *Ge* 695–702; *Gell* 2429–50; *PRG* XL, 74–118 and LI (1:150–73 and 185–90).

spoken of the vestments and shall concern myself here only with the sacred vessels, with crosses and icons, and with bells.

I. THE SACRED VESSELS

BIBLIOGRAPHY

F. Eygun, "Les vases sacrés," in R. Aigrain (ed.), *Liturgia* (Paris: Bloud et Gay, 1935), 261–304.

M. Righetti, *Manuale di storia liturgica* 1 (Milan: Ancora, 1964³) 584–615.

GIRM 289–96.

"Among the requisites for the celebration of Mass, the sacred vessels hold a place of honor, especially the chalice and paten, which are used in presenting, consecrating, and receiving the bread and wine."[170]

The cup (*potērion, calix*) is mentioned explicitly in the four accounts of the Last Supper, and also in the words of Jesus according to 1 Corinthians 11:25 and Luke 22:20; it was a biblical sign of both the passion of Christ and the exercise of God's justice in rewarding and punishing.[171] The cup at the Last Supper was a single cup from which all the guests were supposed to drink according to the ritual of the Passover meal; beginning with the letters of St. Paul (1 Cor 10:16) this single cup becomes the symbol of ecclesial unity, the grace of which it contains. This is why the ancient liturgies had to solve the problem of the communion of all the faithful under the species of wine while retaining the principle that there is to be but one chalice on the altar.[172]

The first chalices were of glass; they may have been painted or gilded by way of decoration. By the time of St. Augustine, however, they were being made of precious metals; this would henceforth be the rule, except in times of persecution or penury.[173] Nowadays it is enough that they "be made from materials that are solid and that in the particular region are regarded as noble. The conference of bishops will be the judge in this matter. But preference is to be given to materials that do not break easily or

---

170. *GIRM* 289 (*DOL* 208 no. 1679).

171. The cup of the passion: Matt 20:22; Mark 10:38 and 42; Matt 26:39, 42; Mark 14:36; Luke 22:42; John 18:11. — The cup of divine reward: Ps 16:5; 23:5. — The cup of divine punishment: Isa 51:17 (and the references in *The Jerusalem Bible*, p. 1227, note *j* of the 1966 ed., or p. 1271, note *h* of the 1985 ed.); Ps 11:6 (and references in *The Jerusalem Bible*, p. 795, note *d* in the 1966 ed., p. 825 note *d* in the 1985 ed.) Ps 75:8.

172. M. Andrieu, *Immixtio et consecratio* (Paris: Picard, 1924), 5–19.

173. St. Augustine, *Enarrationes in psalm.* 113, serm. 2, 5–6 (CCL 40:1645; PL 37:1484); St. Jerome, *Ep.* 125, *Ad Rusticum monachum* (regarding St. Exuperius of Toulouse), ed. J. Labourt 7 (Paris: Les Belles Lettres, 1961), 133. — See *LP* 3:195 for the various references to the word *calix*.

become unusable."[174] The cup should be made of a material that does not absorb liquids; if it is made of a metal that can rust, it should be gilded.

"Vessels that serve as receptacles for the eucharistic bread, such as a paten, ciborium, pyx, monstrance, etc., may be made of other materials that are prized in the region, for example, ebony or other hard woods, as long as they are suited to sacred use."[175]

Medieval legislation, which was in force down to our time, required that the chalice and paten be consecrated by the bishop with an anointing of sacred chrism. Many of the formulas for this consecration were of Gallican origin; others appeared for the first time in the Romano-German Pontifical.[176] The Pontifical of 1977 replaced the consecration with a simple blessing which any priest may give but which is marked by a certain solemnity and is normally given during Mass, at the Offertory; all this shows an intention of reserving the chalice and paten for use exclusively in the Eucharist, thus making them "sacred vessels."[177]

II. CROSSES AND ICONS

In modern practice, a cross is to be placed on or near the altar so that it can be easily seen by the assembly.[178] Initially, in the twelfth century, the processional cross was placed opposite the altar by a subdeacon when the cortege arrived;[179] later on, a small cross was placed on the altar or, preferably, a very large one was suspended from the triumphal arch.

According to the ancient tradition of the Church[180] images of the Lord, the Blessed Virgin, and the saints may be legitimately venerated by the faithful. They play no part in the Latin liturgy, however; only a blessing of them is provided, and they are not to be overly numerous or to distract attention from the celebration itself.[181]

---

174. *GIRM* 290 (*DOL* 208 no. 1680). Other prescriptions on the material and shape of the sacred vessels: *GIRM* 291, 294–95.

175. *GIRM* 292 (*DOL* 208 no. 1682).

176. *Missale Francorum* (ed. Mohlberg), nos. 62–65; *Ge* 696–99; *PRG* XL, 88–95 (1:155–56).

177. PR, *Ordo dedicationis ecclesiae et altaris*, editio typica (Vatican Polyglot Press, 1977), ch. 7: *Ordo benedictionis calicis et patenae. Praenotanda* 1 (*DOL* 547 no. 4442).

178. *GIRM* 270.

179. Canon Benedict, *Liber politicus* 29, ed. Fabre-Duchesne 2:148: "Subdiaconus regionarius more solito portat crucem ad altare." — A rite for the solemn blessing of a cross appears for the first time in the eighth-century Gelasians (*Gell* 2447–50); it is subsequently expanded in the medieval pontificals.

180. Second Council of Nicaea (787) (DS 600–3, 605); Council of Trent, Session 25 (DS 1823); *VSC* 111, 125.

181. *GIRM* 278.

Among the Byzantines, on the other hand, icons are required in the place of worship, and certain liturgical acts must be performed before them. They differ from the images of the West not only by reason of this close connection with the liturgy but also by reason of the artistic choices that they embody and the spiritual attitude of the faithful toward them. "Hieratic postures and gestures" and "a more or less determined refusal to show the malleability of bodies and objects" keep those contemplating these images from being distracted from thoughts of heavenly things; "these images bear the impress of Jesus' divine nature and of holiness." Eastern Christians justify the veneration they give to icons on the grounds that these have present in them "a bit of the energy or grace proper" to the personages represented.[182]

III. BELLS

BIBLIOGRAPHY

H. Leclercq, "Cloche, clochette," *DACL* 3 (1914), 1954–77.

M. Righetti, *Manuale di storia liturgica* 1 (Milan: Ancora, 1964³), 481–85.

In the early centuries more or less primitive means were used to summon the faithful for the liturgy; some Eastern churches have continued to use the wooden *simandron* or the *sidêroun*, which are hanging objects that are struck with a mallet. The use of bells (*signum, nola, clocca, campana*) spread toward the end of the fifth or beginning of the sixth century. The Middle Ages assigned them the further function of urging the absent faithful to unite themselves in prayer with the liturgy then being celebrated (this is why bells are rung during the celebration, in the course of the Eucharistic Prayer) as well as of stimulating the faithful to moments of private prayer (ringing of the *Ave Maria* or Angelus).

The eighth-century Gelasian Sacramentaries were the first to include an *Ordo ad signum ecclesiae benedicendum*[183] in the ceremony for the dedication of a church. The *Ordo* was perhaps Gallican in origin and remained essentially unchanged until the 1961 edition of the Roman Pontifical. The rite was a consecration, since it required the use of holy chrism.[184] A dis-

---

182. A. Grabar, *Les voies de la création en iconographie chrétienne, antiquité et moyen âge* (Coll. Idées et recherches; Paris: Flammarion, 1979), 138–39; see P. Evdokimov, *L'art de l'icône, théologie et beauté* (Paris: Desclée De Brouwer, 1970); I. H. Dalmais, "Icônes et liturgie, en marge de quelques ouvrages récents," *LMD* no. 142 (1980) 97–105.

183. *Gell* 2440–46; *Sacramentaire Gélasien d'Angoulême*, ed. P. Cagin (Angoulême: Société historique et archéologique de la Charente, 1919), pp. 143–45.

184. No one knows why William Durandus substituted the oil of catechumens for sacred chrism (Andrieu, *PR* 3:535), still less why the oil of the sick was substituted for it in the Roman Pontifical of 1596.

torted popular view of it turned the consecration into a "baptism"; the rite did in fact include a washing of the bell and anointings, and then perfume-burners were placed beneath it; these various actions were accompanied by the singing of psalms and prayers. The prayers show that the bell was regarded as more than simply a means of bringing the faithful together; it was looked upon as a sacramental, to which the prayer of the Church gave power to dispel demons and bad weather. The reform of 1984 has reduced the inauguration of bells to a solemn blessing that is given in the *Liber benedictionum*, chapter XXX, and not in the Pontifical.

§7. The Dedication of Churches

by P. Jounel

BIBLIOGRAPHY

a) Well-known witnesses from antiquity:

Ambrose of Milan, *Epistola 22 Dominae Sorori* (PL 16:119–26); French translation in *LMD* no. 70 (1962) 141–45.

Eusebius of Caesarea, *Historia ecclesiastica* X, 3–4. French trans. by G. Bardy, 3 (SC 55; Paris: Cerf, 1958), 80–104; English translation by G. A. Williamson, *The History of the Church from Christ to Constantine* (Baltimore: Penguin, 1965), 382–401.

Egeria, *Itinerarium* 48–49 (SC 296:316–19; Wilkinson 146–47).

Gregory of Tours, *In gloria confessorum* 20, ed. B. Krusch (MGH, *Script. rerum Meroving.* I, 2; 1885, reprinted 1959), 309–10; French translation in *LMD* no. 70 (1962) 146–48.

b) Historical studies:

Andrieu, *OR* 4:311–413. This book gives all the references to the euchological texts in the Roman and Frankish sacramentaries.

C. Vogel and R. Elze, *PRG* 2:82–180.

S. Benz, "Zur Geschichte der römischen Kirchweihe nach den Texten des 7. bis 9. Jahrhunderts," in *Enkainia. Gesammelte Arbeiten zum achthundertjährigen Weihegedächtnis der Abteikirche Maria Laach* (Düsseldorf: Patmosverlag, 1956), 62–109.

A. Chavasse, *Le sacramentaire gélasien* (Paris: Desclée, 1958), 36–56.

R. Coquin, "L'oraison *Singulare illud propitiatorium* de la Dédicace," *LMD* no. 78 (1964) 161–75.

A.G. Martimort, "Le rituel de la consécration des églises," *LMD* no. 63 (1960) 86–95.

c) The dedication in the Eastern rites:

R. Coquin, "La consécration des églises dans le rite copte, ses relations avec les rites syrien et byzantin," *OS* 9 (1964) 149–87.

S. Salaville, *Cérémonial de la consécration d'une église selon le rite byzantin* (Vatican City, 1937). Translation of the Codex Barberini in *LMD* no. 70 (1962) 135–40.

d) The present rite (1977):

Ordo dedicationis ecclesiae et altaris, editio typica (Vatican Polyglot Press, 1977).

Rite of Dedication of a Church and an Altar, in *The Rites of the Catholic Church* 2 (New York: Pueblo, 1980), 185–293. Revised translation of the various Introductions in *DOL* 547 nos. 4361–4446.

J. Evenou, "Le nouveau rituel de la dédicace (1977)," *LMD* no. 134 (1978) 85–105.

The dedication of a church is first of all a feast of the people of God who will be called to gather there each Sunday for the celebration of the Eucharist. The very first dedications of Christian basilicas, soon after the Peace of Constantine, were already occasions of great joy, as Eusebius, historian of the early Church, tells us: "And together, the people of every age, male and female alike, with all their powers of mind, rejoicing in heart and soul, gave glory through prayers and thanksgiving to the Author of their happiness, God Himself."[185]

The reason why the feast of a dedication awoke such echoes in civic life was that it was rooted in popular tradition. The pagan world was familiar with the dedication of temples, altars, theaters, and cities. The Old Testament, too, had experience of the dedication of memorial stones (Gen 28:18), altars (Num 7:10-11, 84, 88), and houses (Deut 20:5), and, above all, the successive dedications of the temple: the first, celebrated by Solomon (2 Kgs 8:1-66), and the second in the time of Ezra (Ezra 6:15-18). Every year the Jewish people also celebrated the feast of Hanukkah, which was the anniversary of the purification of the temple and the dedication of the new altar of holocausts by Judas Maccabeus (1 Mac 4:36-59). When the Church of the Middle Ages would set about enriching the symbolism in its liturgy of dedication, it would not fail to draw on this broad biblical background.

I. THE ANCIENT RITUAL FOR A DEDICATION

The ancient ritual for the dedication of a church consisted originally in the celebration of the Eucharist; to this was soon added the deposition of relics of the martyrs beneath the altar.

1. *Celebration of the Eucharist*

Despite the grandiloquence of Eusebius' description of the rites of dedication for the first churches, it is possible to surmise that in the first part of the fourth century the dedication comprised nothing but a celebration of the Eucharist. On this occasion an extensive liturgy of the word, which included "the hearing of words given us by God," "the singing of psalms," and a number of homilies by the bishops present, was followed by "the

---

185. Eusebius of Caesarea, *Historia ecclesiastica* X, 3; ET: *The History of the Church from Christ to Constantine,* trans. G. A. Williamson (Baltimore: Penguin, 1865), 383.

accomplishment of divine and mystical liturgies," "ineffable symbols of the Savior's passion."[186] Fifty years later, St. John Chrysostom would say: "The marvelous thing about an altar is that though by its nature it is nothing but a stone, it is sanctified by receiving upon it the body of Christ."[187]

Once the custom of placing relics of the martyrs beneath the altar became widespread, it was for a long time seen as a felicitous addition but not as obligatory. In his letter of 578 to Bishop Profuturus of Braga, Pope Vigilius still distinguishes between churches in which relics are to be deposed and others which are consecrated simply by the celebration of Mass.[188] The celebration of the Eucharist is enough to dedicate a church, and no other rite can replace it: "*Omnes basilicae cum missa semper debent consecrari.*"[189]

2. The deposition of relics of the martyrs

The Church very quickly saw the connection between the sacrifice of Christ and that of his witnesses, the martyrs. The Apocalypse had already made it clear: "I saw under the altar the souls of those who had been slain for the word of God and for the witness they had borne" (Rev 6:9). The placing of relics of the martyrs beneath the altar is simply a ritual expression of awareness of what martyrdom means. The practice made its appearance as early as the middle of the fourth century. In 386 St. Ambrose told his sister Marcella how he placed the relics of the martyrs Gervase and Protase, which he had just discovered, in the basilica where he himself hoped to be buried some day.[190] Before placing the martyrs' bodies beneath the altar he had celebrated a vigil of prayer with a large throng of the faithful.

Not all bishops had the good fortune to discover the tombs of martyrs, as Ambrose did, just as they were about to dedicate a church. Most of them, however, wanted to place some relic of a martyr in their new place of worship. The result was that beginning in the sixth century the custom spread of using figurative relics known as *sanctuaria* or *brandea*, such as linen that had been touched to a holy tomb. But at this same period it was already a universal custom—except at Rome, which opposed it— to divide up the bones of martyrs. For, according to an ancient liturgical formula, "where a relic is venerated, the entire body is regarded as rest-

---

186. Eusebius, *ibid*. [translated here from the French. — Tr.].

187. St. John Chrysostom, *In II Cor. homiliae* 20, 3 (PG 61:540).

188. Vigilius, *Ep.* 1, 4 (PL 69:18).

189. Decretal attributed at times to Pope Evaristus, at times to Pope Hyginus; text in Gratian, *Decretum* III, *De consecr.*, Dist. 1, c. 3 (ed. A. Friedberg, col. 1294).

190. St. Ambrose, *Ep.* 22 (PL 16:119-26).

ing."[191] The rite for the translation and deposition of relics remained one of the most popular in the liturgy of dedication.

3. *Purification of a pagan temple that had been transformed into a church*

When a pagan temple (the Roman Pantheon, for example) was to be consecrated to the service of the true God, it was first sprinkled with water that had been exorcised. We find St. Gregory prescribing this rite to Bishop Augustine, whom he had sent to bring the gospel to England.[192] Pope Vigilius is a witness to the same practice.

II. THE CELEBRATION OF THE RITE OF DEDICATION IN THE HIGH MIDDLE AGES

The ancient liturgy of dedication had been marked by great reserve; soon, however, the rite underwent extensive development, both in Gaul and in the East. From the twelfth century on, Rome was to incorporate these new elements into its original tradition, and the celebration of a dedication would become the most elaborate rite in the Western liturgy.

1. *The Gallo-Frankish liturgy of dedication*

In Gaul the deposition of relics of the martyrs was preceded by a consecration of the altar, a rite filled with symbolism and reminiscences of the Bible. Just as believers become temples of God by receiving in succession the sacraments of baptism, confirmation, and the Eucharist, so it seemed fitting that an altar should be washed with water and anointed with holy chrism before being decked out for the celebration of the Lord's Supper. Behind the symbolism of Christian initiation, moreover, there loomed the symbolism provided by the dedications of the old law (Gen 23:18; Exod 29:12; 40:27; Lev 8:10-11) and the evocation of the heavenly liturgy (Rev 8:4; 21:14). Thus in the earliest Gallic ritual (first half of the eighth century) the bishop begins by blessing a mixture of water and wine with which he sprinkles first the building and then the altar. He goes on to speak a prayer of blessing over the altar and to anoint the altar five times with chrism and the walls several times as well. Finally, he blesses the linens and sacred vessels. When the altar has been adorned and the lamps lit, the relics are brought in by a large procession of the faithful and placed beneath the altar. The bishop then celebrates Mass.[193]

---

191. *Ge* 805.

192. St. Gregory the Great, *Regist.* XI, *Ep.* 56, ed. Ewald-Hartmann, MGH, *Epist.* 2 (Berlin, 1891), 331.

193. *Sacramentaire d'Angoulême* (ed. P. Cagin), no. 2020.

Frankish *Ordo* XLI, from the middle of the eighth century, adds numerous rites: the bishop knocks on the door before entering; inside, he traces the alphabet on the floor, adds salt and ashes to the mixture of water and wine, and multiplies the sprinklings and anointings, while a priest continually circles the altar and incenses it. The entire ceremony is accompanied by almost continuous psalmody, which provides a mystagogical commentary on it.[194]

2. *The Byzantine liturgy of dedication*

The earliest witness to the Byzantine liturgy of dedication is likewise from the eighth century; but some of the practices it describes, such as the anointing of the altar, are already attested at Byzantium in the sixth century and in Syria as early as the mid-fourth century.[195]

The celebration of the dedication took two days. On the first, the patriarch purified the altar with baptismal water and consecrated it with *myron* (holy chrism); he then spread a cloth on the table and incensed it, and the sanctuary, at length; meanwhile a bishop anointed all the columns in the church with chrism. The prayer of dedication concluded the entire set of rites, which were performed in the presence only of the clergy. On the second day the people were called together to take part in a vigil near the relics of the martyrs and in their festive translation to the church whose *encaenia* were being celebrated. The patriarch then placed the relics in their tomb and celebrated the Eucharist, the "divine liturgy," over them.

3. *The Roman liturgy of dedication*

In the eighth century, the Roman *Ordo* of dedication (*Ordo* XLII) was still faithful to local tradition, as its title shows: *Ordo quomodo in sancta romana ecclesia reliquiae conduntur*,[196] but it had already undergone foreign influences, both Frankish and Eastern.

The bishop went to the church where the relics had been placed and there sang a first litany. He then put the relics on a paten (this is an indication of how small they were) and handed it to a priest; the procession then made its way to the church that was to be consecrated. The bishop entered the building alone, except for a few ministers. There he blessed the water, poured chrism into it, and made the cement with which the tomb for the relics would be sealed. He then "baptized the altar" with the blessed water, and went back outside, where a second litany was chanted. The procession then entered the church to the accompaniment of a third

---

194. *OR* LXI (Andrieu, *OR* 4:337–47).

195. Ms. Vatic. Barberini grec 336, pp. 294–316; French. trans. in *LMD* no. 70 (1962) 135–40.

196. Andrieu, *OR* 4:397.

litany. The bishop placed the relics on the altar, anointed the corners of the tomb with chrism, and put the relics into it along with three fragments of the Eucharistic Body of Christ and three grains of incense. After sealing the cover in place, he anointed the top of it with chrism and likewise anointed the four corners of the altar table. Finally, he spread a cloth on the altar and sprinkled the entire church, using a sprig of hyssop. When these rites had been completed, the celebration of Mass began.

III. MAGNIFICENCE OF THE DEDICATION FROM THE ELEVENTH TO THE TWENTIETH CENTURY

Ordo XLII represented a fusion of the Roman and Frankish traditions, the latter being itself wholly permeated by Eastern influence. The ensuing centuries added nothing substantial but did bring the development of each rite and the multiplication of purificatory sprinklings, anointings, and incensations, as well as of the accompanying antiphons and psalms; in the end, the dedication became the lengthiest rite in the Roman liturgy. The Pontifical of the Twelfth Century, which remained in use down to the twentieth century, required no less than half a day to perform the full rite.

1. *The dedication in the Romano-German Pontifical of the tenth century*

The Romano-German Pontifical of the mid-tenth century has two ceremonials for the dedication of a church. The first[197] combines *Ordo* XLI and *Ordo* XLII, the text of which it copies to the letter, while adding only two orations. The second ritual[198] expands the preceding by adding a number of texts. Here are the main lines of this ritual.

The clergy and people gather at the place where the relics of the martyrs rest. A first litany is sung here, and the bishop blesses water mixed with salt. The procession with the relics then sets out for the church to be dedicated. The doors of the latter are shut; inside, twelve lighted candles have been placed around the perimeter. When the bishop reaches the main door he strikes it with his staff, saying *"Tollite portas,"* but the door remains shut. The bishop then walks around the building while sprinkling it; twice again he repeats his gesture at the main door and circles the building. When the door finally opens at his order, *"Aperi,"* the clergy and people remain outside with the relics and sing a second litany.

The bishop enters with two or three ministers. He first writes the Latin

197. *PRG* 1:82-89.
198. *PRG* 1:124-73.

and Greek alphabets on the floor with the tip of his staff.[199] He then again blesses water into which he has placed salt, ashes, and wine.[200] With this water he traces signs of the cross at the center and four corners of the altar table; he then walks around the interior of the church three times while sprinkling it, and finally he sprinkles the middle of the building. He next reads the prayer—in the form of a preface—for the consecration of a church. After preparing and blessing the cement that will seal the tomb for the relics, he begins the rites of anointing: he twice anoints the center and four corners of the altar table with the oil of catechumens, and then incenses the table. After the second series of anointings and incensations he pours the oil over the entire altar table. He then begins a new series of anointings, this time with sacred chrism, while a priest continually circles and incenses the altar. The bishop then goes to the walls of the church and performs twelve anointings with chrism on them. After returning to the altar and offering incense again, he sings the preface of consecration of an altar, and then blesses the vessels, cloths, and sacred vestments.

The bishop now leaves the church and joins the faithful who have remained gathered outside around the relics. The procession enters the church for the deposition of the relics. The bishop performs this rite while shielded by a veil from the eyes of the faithful. He anoints the four corners of the tomb with sacred chrism before placing the relics in it, along with three particles of the Eucharistic Body of Christ and three grains of incense. When the relics have been placed in the confession, the bishop anoints the cover on the inside, seals it in place, and anoints the outside; he then anoints the four corners of the altar table once again. After a deacon has "clothed" the altar, the bishop offers incense one last time and withdraws to the sacristy, while the church is being adorned and the lamps lit. When everything is ready he makes his solemn entrance into the sanctuary as the singers intone the Introit of the Mass. It is to be noted that each of the rites described is accompanied by psalms, antiphons, and prayers that describe its mystical meaning.

The rites here briefly described underwent no shortening from the middle of the tenth century on. They became part of the liturgy of Rome in the following century; thereafter there were only a few changes in the sequence of the rites and, in the thirteenth century, some additions. It is clear that in the Middle Ages the Roman liturgy of dedication became a

---

199. According to H. Thurston, "The Alphabet and the Consecration of Churches," *Month*, 1910, pp. 621–31, the writing of the alphabet in the form of a St. Andrew's cross is simply a development of the apocalyptic symbol in Rev 1:8; both this and chrism are symbols of Christ. The rite, according to Thurston, is of Irish origin.

200. The use of wine here is perhaps an adaptation of Byzantine practice.

dramatic play, and indeed a play that often had no audience, since the people witnessed only parts of it. Nonetheless the accumulation of signs (water, oil, incense, the torches around the reliquary) yielded a sacral vision of God's dwelling among us. The house of God's people is first of all God's own house.

2. *The dedication according to the* Roman Pontifical *(1595)*

The Roman Pontifical of 1595 reproduced, almost without change, the pontifical composed by William Durandus, bishop of Mende, at the end of the thirteenth century. It is to William, therefore, that the final adjustments in the Roman liturgy of dedication are to be attributed.[201]

The celebration begins at the place where the relics have been stored. While the bishop dons the sacred vestments, the seven penitential psalms are sung. He then goes in procession—but without the relics—to the church that is to be consecrated. He performs the threefold purification of the outside and then enters with some clerics and singers. The *Veni Creator* is sung, and the bishop performs the rites for taking possession of the church (the two alphabets) and purifying it, after which a first prayer of dedication is said. These rites being completed, the bishop and clergy return to the place where the relics have been stored.

The procession for the translation of the relics is then formed, with the people joining it. After halting at the threshold of the church, where the bishop delivers an exhortation, the entire assembly enters. The bishop now proceeds to the deposition of the relics, the incensation, and the anointing of the altar and walls. Then, when the altar has been clothed, Mass is celebrated. The rite contains only a few new texts, among them the *Dirigatur* that accompanies the incensation. Several of these new texts are of Iberian origin.[202]

From some manuscripts of the Pontifical of the Roman Curia William Durandus took an *Ordo* for the consecration of an altar when there is no dedication of a church; this he considerably enriched.[203] It has remained in use down to the present.

3. *The simplification of 1961*

The time is past when a whole congregation has leisure for a lengthy liturgical celebration; moreover, the repetition of the same gestures wearies the attention more than it feeds prayer. Thus a simplification of the *Ordo*

---

201. Andrieu, *PR* 3 (Pontifical of William Durandus), pp. 455–78.

202. Among others the formula *Sanctificare*, the antiphon *Unxit te Deus*, and the response *Induit te*. See *Liber ordinum*, ed. M. Férotin, cols. 29–30 and 21, and *Antifonario de Léon*, ed. L. Brou and J. Vives, p. 443.

203. Andrieu, *PR* 3:478–98.

of dedication had long been desired when Pope Pius XII decided to introduce it. The new *Ordo* was promulgated by John XXIII in 1961.[204] Its authors decided not to choose between keeping or suppressing the rites combined in the medieval *Ordo* but were content simply to eliminate repetitions and limit the extent of the symbolic gestures, sometimes to the detriment of the symbol itself. The loss can be felt in the elimination of the pouring of chrism over the entire altar table; here reason prevailed over poetry. But at least the simplified *Ordo* emphasized the importance of the Mass, which "is part of the consecratory rite," although it did not venture to oblige the bishop to celebrate the Mass himself.

IV. THE NEW ROMAN RITE OF DEDICATION (1977)

The *Ordo dedicationis ecclesiae et altaris*, which Pope Paul VI promulgated in 1977,[205] implements certain principles that should be brought out before we analyze the rites themselves.[206]

1. *The guiding principles of the new Ordo*

The first aim was to give the celebration of the Eucharist the leading role it should have in the dedication of a church; according to tradition it is, after all, "the most important and the one necessary rite" (*Introduction* 15). It is for this reason that the rites of anointing, offering of incense, and lighting of the altar are placed between the Liturgy of the Word and the Liturgy of the Eucharist, both parts of the Mass being essential parts of the dedication. At the beginning of the Liturgy of the Word the bishop solemnly inaugurates the proclamation of the Word in this new building by showing the Lectionary to the people before handing it to the reader. As for the celebration of the Eucharist, it is this that truly turns the altar into the table of the Lord.

The translation of the relics has been restored to its full dignity, even while leaving it optional (in keeping, once again, with ancient usage). This whole ceremony is very rich in meaning when it is possible to bury sizable and authentic relics of a martyr or saint beneath the altar, but it lacks grandeur when the relics are minuscule or inauthentic.

---

204. The publication was in fact a revision of the entire second book of the Roman Pontifical: *Pontificale Romanum, pars secunda emendata* (Vatican Polyglot Press, 1961). Text and explanation in P. Jounel, *Dédicace d'une église* (Paris: Desclée, 1962).

205. *Ordo dedicationis ecclesiae et altaris*, editio typica (Vatican Polyglot Press, 1977). Translation in *The Rites of the Catholic Church* 2 (New York: Pueblo, 1980), 185–293. Revised translation of the Introductions in *DOL* 547 nos. 4361–4445.

206. For a review of the preparatory work on the new rite, along with a discussion of the rite itself, see J. Evenou, "Le nouveau Rituel de la dédicace," *LMD* no. 134 (1978) 85–105.

The symbolic rites of dedication call for the same kind of authenticity. The compilers of the new rite rejected the piling up of signs and the repetition of the same gestures, but wanted to restore full significance to the symbols of water, perfumed oil, incense, and light. The words accompanying these gestures show their relation to the mystery of the Church.

2. *The makeup of the celebration*

The dedication of a church requires the participation of the entire Christian community that will be called to gather there each Sunday from now on. It is therefore preferably to be celebrated on the Lord's Day. The bishop presides, accompanied by the priests who have charge of this community; they concelebrate with him.

When conditions permit, the celebration begins with a procession that starts from outside the church; the procession may include the translation of the relics. At the door of the church the craftsmen who built it make a symbolic transfer of it to the bishop, who in turn entrusts it to the priest in charge and to the faithful. Then all enter the church to the singing of Psalm 24. The bishop takes his place at the presidential chair; there he blesses the water and with it sprinkles the people, the walls, and finally the altar; meanwhile the *Vidi aquam* or a baptismal song is sung. The *Gloria in excelsis* and the collect bring the introductory rites to a close.

a) *The Liturgy of the Word.* When the bishop has said, "May the Word of God always be heard in this place" and has given the Lectionary to the reader, the latter proclaims the first reading, which tells of the "first Liturgy of the Word" that Ezra celebrated in Jerusalem after the return from exile (Neh 8:1-4a, 5-6, 8-10). For the second reading and the gospel, a choice can be made from a large number of pericopes, for example, the passages of St. Paul on the Church being built on Christ as cornerstone (Eph 2:19-22) or his statement, "God's temple is holy, and that temple is you" (1 Cor 3:17) or the description of the Jerusalem that comes down from heaven (Rev 21:1-5a, 9b-14); for the gospel, the declaration of Jesus to Peter, "You are Peter" (Matt 16:13-19) or the Johannine passage on the body of Christ as temple of new covenant (John 2:13-22).

b) *The special rites of dedication.* After the homily and the profession of faith the litanies of the saints are sung, and then, if there is to be a deposition of relics, the bishop places them in the tomb, and a mason seals the aperture. The antiphon *Sub altare Dei* or *Corpora sanctorum* is sung with Psalm 15. The bishop then says the prayer of dedication, which is inspired by the Ambrosian preface for a dedication, and expounds the theology of the mystery of the Church, of which the church building is a sign; it also calls to mind all the benefits human beings will come seeking in the house of God. This prayer is in fact a doublet of the Eucharistic

Preface which, in the initial draft of the rite of dedication, made the Eucharistic Prayer the only prayer by which the building is consecrated and at the same time the sacrament of Christ's Body and Blood is confected. In the Eucharistic Preface we still read: "With hearts full of joy we consecrate to your glory this work of our hands, this house of prayer."

When the prayer of dedication ends, the bishop pours sacred chrism at the center and the four corners of the altar table; he can use this oil to anoint the entire surface as a sign of superabundance, saying, "We now anoint this altar and this building. May God in his power make them holy, visible signs of the mystery of Christ and his Church." He then anoints the walls either twelve or four times while Psalm 84 is sung; if he wishes, he may be assisted in this rite by priests. The incensing of the altar and church follows. A brazier with incense is placed on the altar, or else a heap of incense mixed with wax, which the bishop lights: "As this building is filled with fragrance, so may your Church fill the world with the fragrance of Christ." While the bishop is incensing the altar, priests go around the church incensing the people and the building. Psalm 138 is sung meanwhile. Finally, the altar is clothed and the candles are lit; the bishop, carrying a lighted candle, says: "Light of Christ, shine forth in the Church and bring all nations to the fullness of truth." Many candles are then lit throughout the building, to the singing of the Canticle of Tobias (Vg. 13:10, 13-14ab, 14c-15, 17) or a song in honor of Christ, the Light of the world.

c) *The Eucharistic liturgy.* All the preceding rites have for their purpose to prepare the altar to become the Lord's table. The concelebration of the Eucharist under the presidency of the bishop now replaces signs with the reality of the sacrament. To be noted is the important formulary used in the Preface. It calls to mind in succession "the whole world," which "is your temple, shaped to resound with your name"; the body of Christ that was born of the Virgin Mary and is a holy temple, "the dwelling place of your godhead in all its fullness;" and the Church that is founded on the apostles, enlivened by the Spirit, and ceaselessly built up in love.

After the assembly has shared the Body and Blood of the Lord, a chapel may be inaugurated in which the Eucharist will be reserved; this is done by carrying the remaining hosts there in a procession identical with that of Holy Thursday.

The *Ordo* for a dedication also includes a *Rite for the Dedication of a Church Already in General Use for Sacred Celebrations*. This can be used if the altar has not yet been dedicated and if the building has undergone some important change. All of the introductory rites are omitted or adapted to the situation. The *Rite for the Dedication of an Altar* is almost identical with the one that has already been described, but the readings and the prayer of dedication are proper to it.

Section III

THEOLOGY OF
THE LITURGICAL CELEBRATION

I. H. Dalmais

Introduction

As an analysis of the term shows, the liturgy is an operation or action (*ergon*); it is not first and foremost a discourse (*logos*). This is doubtless the primary reason why theology, as understood for centuries now in the West, has been only very secondarily interested in the liturgy. The lack of interest has been all the greater because the liturgy takes symbol as its preferred mode of expression; it belongs to the world of poetic thought, which yields a product, rather than of conceptual or notional thought, which has for its first concern to fit its object into a framework of precise definition and then to develop its understanding of the object through reasoning and argumentation. At least this describes the procedure of Scholastic theology, which has usually been regarded since the thirteenth century as the most perfect form for a theology aiming at scientific status. This has been the situation in the West at any rate; in the Christian cultures of the East, on the other hand, and especially in the Byzantine tradition, the liturgy has never ceased to be regarded as the most perfect expression of theology, the latter being understood as discourse concerned with what God has chosen to make known of his being and his plan of salvation (the "economy") for his creation. This is what is meant by the often repeated words of Russian theologian Cyprien Kern: "The [architectural] choir of the Church is the chair of theology."

In fact, it is really only the last few decades that have brought the beginnings of a properly theological reflection on the data supplied by the liturgy. The magisterium has set its approval on the main lines of this reflection, especially in the Encyclical *Mediator Dei* of Pius XII (1947) and above all in the Constitution *Sacrosanctum Concilium* of the Second Vatican Council (December 4, 1963). The emphasis here is on the actualization, throughout the entire time of the Church (and through the mediation of the Church, which is structured by its ministries), of the saving action of Christ, especially as this finds expression in the paschal mystery of his passion and glorification.[1] The Council therefore says, in words that have the appearance of a definition:

> Rightly then, the liturgy is considered as an exercise of the priestly office of Jesus Christ. In the liturgy, by means of signs perceptible to the senses, human sanctification is signified and brought about in ways proper to each of these signs; in the liturgy the whole public worship is performed by the Mystical Body of Jesus Christ, that is, by the Head and his members.[2]

There is thus complete unity between the two movements recognizable in every cultic manifestation: the movement of human beings toward God in order to offer him their prayer of adoration and thanksgiving, and the movement of God to human beings, who look to him for the answer to their prayers. The Christian liturgy truly embodies this "wonderful exchange" (*admirabile commercium*); it is, "under the veil of sensible, efficacious signs, the point of encounter, in Christ, of God who sanctifies the Church and the Church who responds by rendering her worship to God."[3]

We must take note, however, of the reserve Christian tradition has shown in adopting the cultic vocabulary of the cultures in which it has been implanted. In Greek, the word *leitourgia*, though given cultic overtones by the Septuagint, belonged first and foremost to the vocabulary of civic life; when used more narrowly for the Eucharist, it was usually accompanied by the adjective "divine" (*theia*). The most usual Latin equivalent was *ministerium* or *officium*; these two words, and more rarely *servitium*, were for a long time the favored words for designating what we have recently come to speak of as "the liturgy."[4] With varied nuances, to which little attention seems to have been paid, all of these words were fairly accurate translations of the Hebrew *avodah*, which had come to be used for all work, but especially manual work. We can see from this what a wealth of meaning is contained in the designation *Opus Dei*, which is used for the liturgy in the Rule of Western monks. The liturgy is, above all else, a work, and indeed *the* work *par excellence*: the one that manifests and brings to fulfillment God's saving action among and through human beings. It is the surest actualization of the *Magnalia Dei*.[5]

---

1. *VSC* 5.

2. *VSC* 7 (*DOL* 1 no. 7).

3. C. Vagaggini, *Theological Dimensions of the Liturgy*, trans. L. J. Doyle and W. A. Jurgens (Collegeville: The Liturgical Press, 1976), 28.

4. On these various terms see E. J. Lengeling, "Liturgie. I. Terminologisches," in H. Fries (ed.), *Handbuch theologischer Grundbegriffe* 2 (Munich: Kösel, 1963), 75–78; French trans. in *Encyclopédie de la foi* 2 (Paris: Cerf, 1965), 480–84.

5. J. Daniélou, *The Lord of History. Reflections on the Inner Meaning of History*, trans. N. Abercrombie (Chicago: Regnery, 1958), 149–67.

It seems, then, that a theology of the liturgical celebration can develop along two lines: that of the action itself, which is in the form of a "celebration," and that of its content and specifically Christian character, namely, the actualization of the "mystery of salvation," especially insofar as this is embodied in the paschal mystery of Christ.

First, however, there is need of locating the Christian liturgy from the viewpoint of cultic activities, for since the time of L. Muratori and especially of F. A. Zaccaria it has often been presented as *Dei cultus Ecclesiae auctoritate constitutus*;[6] this formulation was kept, made more detailed, and given official status in the Code of Canon Law of 1917.[7] I referred above to the reluctance of the early Church to accept this vocabulary, which puts the emphasis too onesidedly on human activity. In its origin the word *cultus* had to do with "cultivating," "taking care,"[8] and was thus ill-suited to bringing out the sacramental character of the Christian liturgy, in which the initiative always belongs to God, who establishes a people for himself, calls it, and gathers it together so that he may enter into communion with it. It is regrettable that the word "rite" has acquired too narrow a meaning and reflects only imperfectly what its etymology would suggest. It owes its properly religious value to the fact that it emphasizes the importance of fidelity to traditional observances that have for their purpose to express in a symbolic way the very order of the universe as willed by God and to ensure its continuance. The kind of relation that was established in the covenants of the Old Testament and has been perfectly fulfilled in Christ opens up vistas that any theology of the Christian liturgy must be careful to keep in mind when it uses a cultic vocabulary.

---

6. Lengeling 80 (French 486).

7. Canon 1256: "Cult is public if it is given in the name of the Church, by persons lawfully deputed, and by means of actions which by the Church's decree are to be offered only to God, the saints, and the blessed; otherwise it is private." The *Code* of 1983, canon 834, repeats the definition of the liturgy that is given in *VSC* 7 and then adds: "This worship takes place when it is carried out in the name of the Church by persons lawfully deputed and through acts approved by the authority of the Church" (p. 597).

8. Cicero, *De natura deorum* II, 18.

Chapter I

The Liturgy as a Celebration

§1. The Liturgical Fact

I. THE LITURGY AS SOCIAL ACT

Whatever the reasons that led to the universal use of the word "liturgy,"[1] the choice seems especially appropriate as a name for the complex of actions often called "cultic." As used originally in the Greek cities, "liturgy" could mean any "public service," but especially services that were costly and were accepted as done in the name of the city because they were linked to its most vital interests. In a culture permeated by religious values (as most of the traditional cultures were), "liturgy" thus understood was predicated first and foremost of actions expressing the city's relations to the world of divine powers on which it acknowledged itself to be dependent. "Liturgy" referred, therefore, not to cultic actions of individuals or private groups but only to those of the organized community, that is, the entire people, who realized that they shared a single destiny and a collective memory. In other words, liturgy belonged to what has sometimes been called a "perfect [or: complete] society." This is why the name can and even ought to be reserved (as it is in official documents) for the exercise of a worship that is public in the fullest sense, that is, a worship actually offered in the name of the community, which acknowledges it as its own.

This situation should make us more aware of the risks involved when the collective psyche is brought into play. In such situations the sense of human companionship reaches a depth rarely achieved elsewhere, for here community can become communion, that is, it can reach a level of in-

---

1. See Introductory chapter, pp. 7-9.

timacy and exchange in which the dialoguing "I" and "thou" become a "we" that is one in heart and mind. At this point there is a great danger that communion may be replaced by a social monolithism or an affective and even sensual rapture, both of which are equally destructive of the inalienable values of the person. It would be presumptuous to think that Christian liturgy is completely free of this danger, but it is doubtless more able than others to overcome it when it remains true to its own nature.

The history of religions—and I am not speaking only of Christianity— displays a doubtless unavoidable tension between the socially organized expression of spiritual values and the call to interiorization and silence that these same values bring with them to an intense degree. These are irreducible components of a genuinely human attitude, and every liturgy must respect them. This is why "liturgy" cannot be viewed solely in terms of "ceremonies." It must be the vehicle of values, it must convey meaning; this implies diversification of the liturgy according to cultural milieu as well as fidelity in expressing the foundational actions that have been handed down in the tradition.

It is through and in gestures that human beings interact with their fellows, and it is through and in gestures that they express their relations with a world that the senses cannot directly grasp. It follows that liturgy, as a complete expression of the involvement of all dimensions of the human being, must be chiefly gestural; it must make discriminating use of the various human gestures in order to bring out their deepest meaning and ritualize them so that once purified of any infrahuman elements still remaining in their secular use, they may become the sensible signs of spiritual realities. This is why all liturgy prefers to use the most basic—one might almost say the most biological—gestures, those in which human beings reveal the deepest needs of their nature and disclose the innermost dynamic of their calling. The first and foremost of these basic gestures is the communal meal. Is it possible to think of a more appropriate sign of the communion attainable by a human group and of the communion that can unite it to the invisible powers, than eating together of one and the same food in which the divinity is somehow also given a share? The same can be said of the bath, the first act by which a newborn child is welcomed into the human community, the lifegiving immersion in which human beings intuitively realize, long before they can reflectively know it, the extent to which all life on our earth has its origin in the womb of the waters. The fact that all Christian liturgies have accepted these two actions as coming from Christ and actualizing his saving work gives these liturgies roots that strike deep into the soil of humanity.

II. THE LITURGY AS SYMBOLIC ACTION

BIBLIOGRAPHY

See the bibliography for Section II, Chapter IV, §1, p. 176.

The gestures that the liturgy ritualizes derive their value less from what they are than from what they suggest. Into the field of the visible and sensible they bring realities or values that in themselves are alien to that field. In other words, the liturgy, being the action of a community that draws upon all its available means of expression, constantly makes use of the symbolic character of these means, be they gestures or words. It can be said that in a sense the liturgy functions as play. In play human beings look beyond the immediate, utilitarian purposes of their actions and pass to a level at which actions that in everyday life are simply means acquire a coherence of their own and yield a meaning that delights not only their authors but those who identify with the game as they watch and listen.[2]

The twofold danger of play is that the departure from the conditions of everyday existence that play makes possible may turn into an escape or into a form of self-absorption. The liturgy avoids these two dangers to the extent that it clearly expresses its reference to situations that completely transcend the present limits of the human condition. The gestures and words of the liturgy carry a meaning and an energy that become present and operative each time that the liturgical action is repeated. There is in fact no liturgy that does not more or less explicitly claim to effect what it signifies. This is precisely what distinguishes liturgical action from every other kind of representation. But for that very reason the liturgy is also always in danger of degenerating into magic if it loses sight of its reference to a transcendent reality that human action by itself cannot apprehend. The properly liturgical value of a rite or text is a function of the echoes that the celebration as a whole is able to awaken in the assembly; in other words, it depends on a recognition of the symbolic meaning of the gestures or words.

The reason is that symbol cannot be reduced to sign, as people too often tend to think. An object, word, or gesture is a symbol only to the extent that it can be immediately understood as vehicle of a meaning that is greater than its own reality or, more accurately, as being something more and other than it appears to be. It is this material density, this concrete value attached to a thing, that gives symbols their realism and en-

---

2. J. Huizinga, *Homo ludens. A Study of the Play-Element in Culture*, trans. R. F. C. Hull (London: Routledge and Kegan Paul, 1949).

sures their validity; they also become more capable of conveying the realities of a spiritual world that extends beyond them and transcends them. It is therefore important to preserve the material density of the elements used in the liturgy: baptism is a washing or, better, an immersion in lifegiving water; in an anointing the oil ought to penetrate what it touches; the Eucharistic meal implies that the participants eat real bread and that, unless there is some serious obstacle, they drink from the cup.

In addition, symbols are multivalent because the sensible reality used is necessarily deficient in relation to the transcendent reality it symbolizes; in many instances there is even ambiguity. Reason finds satisfaction only in clear and distinct ideas; symbolic thinking, on the other hand, is captivated by the constant fluidity of the themes it evokes. Words alone make it possible to bring into focus the meaning intended, but without eliminating the multivalence proper to symbols, for then symbol would be reduced to allegory; an intuitive, comprehensive grasp of meaning would be replaced by an analysis that makes use only of the processes of logical thought. In the course of its history the Christian liturgy has only too often been the victim of this misunderstanding. Far from bringing simplification or the discard of practices whose meaning is no longer grasped, allegorization most often leads to complication and a concentration on secondary details that multiply and proliferate like suckers and end up choking the essential elements that are the vehicles of the richest symbolic values. But it can also happen, at times, that a symbolism initially not perceived can in this way become coherent and recognizable.

III. THE LITURGY AS SACRAL ACTION

R. Otto, *The Idea of the Holy*, trans. J. W. Harvey (London: Oxford University Press, 1923).

R. Caillois, *Man and the Sacred*, trans. M. Barash (New York: Free Press, 1959).

A. G. Martimort, "Le sens du sacré," *LMD* no. 25 (1951) 47–74.

M. Eliade, *The Sacred and the Profane. The Nature of Religion*, trans. W. R. Trask (New York: Harcourt, Brace, 1959).

A. Guillermou, "Du sacré au profane, variations sémantiques sur quatre thèmes: célébration, cérémonie, rite, culte," *LMD* no. 106 (1971) 79–100.

E. Castelli (ed.), *Le sacré, études et recherches. Actes du colloque organisé par le Centre international d'études humanistes et par l'Institut philosophique de Rome, 4–9 janvier 1974* (Paris: Aubier, 1974).

Because of its Christian use (which is based on the Septuagint translation of the Bible), the word liturgy now has inescapable religious and sacral overtones. It has become a specifically cultic term and retains this cast even when it is used for activities in which any religious reference is deliberately excluded.

"Sacred" is one of those words that all and sundry think they understand, but whose content, when an attempt is made to pin it down, proves to be multiform and may even vanish like mist. According to the classic analysis of R. Otto, the sacred is initially experienced as an attitude compounded of fright and attraction (*horrendum et fascinosum*). It is an ambiguous attitude in that it can be aroused by very different causes and that it tells us nothing in advance about the nature and objective value of these causes. As a result, it is open to very serious aberrations and very dangerous deviations; recourse to drugs, hypnosis, and all kinds of pseudoecstasies has been and continues to be all too common. The sacred therefore requires rectification; it is a basically subjective attitude that arises spontaneously in the human depths prior to any intervention of reason or will.

The "religious," on the contrary, requires human beings to exercise their higher powers in recognition of their dependence on realities that transcend them. Acknowledgment of an objectively transcendent being and its unlimited moral perfection implies a new characteristic of the object, namely, *holiness*. This value was gradually made known through biblical revelation; it emerges with special clarity in Isaiah's inaugural vision of God (Isa 6). But it is only the full revelation of the mystery of divine holiness in the person of Christ that enables us to recognize its ultimate effects in human behavior.

At the start, the revelation of divine holiness came through a manifestation of power in a cultic context. It began in the dazzling vision of the burning bush on Horeb and reached its climax in the theophany at Sinai. The sense of the sacred that it elicited was such that death seemed inevitable. At the same time, however, the community found itself turned into a "holy people," empowered now to deal with the holy God and transcend the limitations of secular existence. In this first covenantal liturgy we can see the essential characteristics every liturgy must have if it is not to betray its mission. When Isaiah once again experiences that inaugural theophany, but this time in the explicitly liturgical setting of the sanctuary, he discovers its real meaning: the God to whom all worship in the temple is directed and who is to be the dynamic source of the whole life of the "holy people" is not only an all-powerful being who manifests himself in an explosion of the most fearsome energies of the cosmos; he is also a being of utterly spotless purity and perfection and one who jealously demands uprightness. He requires that the community which is his offer him the total gift of itself, one that excludes any and all self-seeking. The liturgy cannot be reduced to a meticulous observance of rites and a respect for cultic prohibitions; it must have its origin in purified hearts that are completely given to God. Here we have the basis for the personalist requirements of a sacrality that does not betray the vocation proper to human beings.

These requirements were to be made known fully when Christ came and replaced the symbolic presence of God (*Shekinah*) in the secrecy of the Holy of Holies with his actual presence in the incarnation of the divine in one who is fully human. At that moment, Christ began the true spiritual worship that consisted in the offering of his own body, which is the new and definitive temple in which the holy God dwells in all his fullness. Christ seemed to be abolishing the sacred by removing the hitherto uncrossable boundary separating creatures—which are profane in themselves—from a divine Beyond. In fact, however, he was bringing the sacred to fulfillment; he was setting human beings free to follow their call to a sacrality consisting of the holiness that alone can provide a solid basis for the dignity of the person. This is why Christians, to the extent that they live in accordance with their dignity as members of the ecclesial body of Christ, must in every act and aspect of their lives offer in Christ the spiritual sacrifice which was foretold by the prophets (Mal 1:11) and to which the Fathers of the Church constantly refer[3] in keeping with the directives of St. Paul (Rom 12:1). Within Christianity a liturgical celebration properly understood can only be the ritualized expression of this spiritual worship in its ecclesial manifestation. All this represents a real revolution of outlook in comparison with normal religious behavior.

It is a revolution because human beings and human groups cannot find in themselves, and express by means completely their own, the final word about their being and destiny. Would it be possible for them to project themselves, hypostasize themselves, in an ideal "I" which they could then worship and in which they would learn to transform themselves by contemplating and imitating it? Any such attempt could only be idolatrous, the idol in this case being the ghostly counterpart that human beings set up for themselves; this counterpart is most often nothing but their own "shadow side" and therefore deserves the anathemas that echo throughout the biblical tradition. The risk of this kind of idolatrous religion is always present, given the concrete condition of human beings, for this is characterized by a self-sufficient turning in on the self that the Christian tradition has always interpreted as the manifestation of a refusal to be open to transcendence.

The danger is especially marked in our time as a result of a deliberate and at times brutal confrontation between, on the one hand, purely human liturgies of the state or of social groups claiming to be the predestined com-

---

3. M. Jourjon, *Les sacrements de la liberté chrétienne selon l'Eglise ancienne* (Rites et symboles 12; Paris: Cerf, 1981), chapter 1.

munity of the future and, on the other, religious liturgies that find their justification in a living communion with God and in the consciousness of being the expression of a community whose destiny transcends the limitations of history. This opposition is new in the brutal forms that we see it taking in so many places. It could not have come about if two millennia of Christianity had not slowly brought to light the repercussions of the distinction between two levels of reality: the human level with its coherent secular dimensions, and the level proper to the holiness of a personal God who is clearly untouched by all the ambiguities inherent in the "sacred," but who also, without losing anything of his transcendence, calls the human race to share his very own life. In this light we are better able to appreciate the multivalence and ambiguities of "natural" liturgies, as well as the confusions in which they have always been to a greater or lesser extent involved and of which even Christian cult has not managed to remain free in every case.

IV. THE LITURGICAL ASSEMBLY AS CELEBRATION AND FEAST

BIBLIOGRAPHY

F. Isambert, "Fête," *Encyclopaedia universalis* 6 (1970) 1046–51.
_____, *Le sens du sacré. Fête et religion populaire* (Coll. Le sens commun; Paris: Editions de Minuit, 1982).

The word "celebration" has increasingly come to be seen as the most suitable description of the liturgical action. The development has not been an arbitrary one, for the word has surprisingly rich overtones in the Latin religious language in which it originated. We can see there

a combination of three factors or circumstances, one or other of which, however, may be lacking in exceptional cases. The point of departure or occasion for a celebration is usually an important or sensational event (*festivitas, solemnitas*). The event, whether present or commemorated, then leads to the calling of an assembly, a more or less large and solemn gathering (*conventus, coetus, frequentia*). This, finally, leads to the festal action (*actio, effectio*), which is the third constitutive element in a typical celebration. As a rule, the action is communal, comprising the combined activities of many or even of an entire populace and involving the life of society, the family, or the state in one or other manner. Sometimes this action is the reason for the assembly, but in every case it constitutes the celebration in the strict sense. For to celebrate is primarily to do something in common and in a solemn religious way. This rather complex idea of celebration originates in Latin conceptions but the reality is found among all ancient peoples, Jews as well as Greeks (though the technical language may be missing at times).[4] Everywhere, moreover, in pagan and above all in Jewish thought, the religious element is always an almost inseparable part of all real celebrations, however secular these may appear to be. . . . In Christianity, with its essentially religious and even eschatological outlook, a celebration is always cultic.[5]

The same remarks apply to the *feast*, which was originally inseparable from a celebration. The word itself suggests a break in the continuity of everyday life. As a result, it has quite natural ties with the idea of the sacred, for the attitude conveyed by the word "sacred" attests that a Beyond has broken into the ordinary life of the human race and into its secular universe, though the Beyond is marked by an ambiguity that will be removed only through the revelation of Holiness. This revelation alone, therefore, will make it possible for the feast to become fully what it strives to be. For if the ordinary passage of time is suspended, the purpose is not to give way to chaos and to open the door to every kind of excess. The reason is rather that a Presence has shown itself to human beings. This manifestation calls for their response and also makes the response possible, because it is a gift and a favor. It is in the idea and reality of the festive celebration that the liturgy finds its authentic meaning.

§2. The Liturgy as Act of the Church

The specific nature of Christian cult depends on that of the assembly that practices it. The Church of Christ sees itself as the people of God in its messianic fulfillment, as a manifestation on earth of the mystery of God the Savior (1 Tim 3:16), and as a community participating in the definitive covenant by which it has pleased God to bind himself to a people he has freely chosen to benefit from the economy of salvation and bear witness to it among the nations.[6] The Church's liturgy has for its function, then, not only to offer God the worship due to him but also to make this mystery of salvation (the characteristics of which remain to be determined) present and active among human beings.

I. THE LITURGY OF THE PEOPLE OF THE COVENANT

"Now therefore, if you will obey my voice and keep my covenant, you will be my own possession among all peoples; for all the earth is mine, and you shall be to me a kingdom of priests and a holy nation" (Exod

---

4. The Greek word was *heortē*; the corresponding Latin words were *feria* and *festus*.

5. J. Hild, "Notion et structure classique d'une célébration," *LMD* no. 20 (1949) 114–15, 116.

6. See Vatican II, Dogmatic Constitution *Lumen gentium*, chapter 2.

19:5-6). This formula with its Deuteronomic overtones is acknowledged to be the charter establishing the people of the covenant. They were a people with all of the sociological complications and even sluggishness that the word "people" implies, all the historical determinisms, all the contingencies in necessary structures. But they were also a people whose specific and proper function was to exercise a priestly office of mediation between God and humankind. As a result, the life and history of the people (at least as understood by the redactors of the Priestly tradition and especially by the Chronicler) was centered on the sanctuary, which contained primarily the Ark of the Testimony (Exod 26:33; 40:21), later called "Ark of the Covenant" in Deuteronomy (10:8; 31:9, 26). As visible expression of the covenant, the sanctuary was the place where God and people met. There was a serious danger that the people would narrow their vision to this material setting and the rites performed there. Only with and through Christ would they fully grasp the true character of a spiritualization that had begun to emerge in outline in the prophets.

When Jesus announces that "the hour is coming, and now is, when the true worshipers will worship the Father in spirit and truth" (John 4:23) and when he declares, speaking of the "temple of his body" (so the Gospel of John interprets him): "Destroy this temple, and in three days I will raise it up" (John 2:23), he establishes the setting for a new and definitive covenant. The First Letter of Peter transposes the charter of the Mosaic assembly (*Qahal*) and proclaims: "You are a chosen race, a royal priesthood,[7] a holy nation, God's own people, that you may declare the wonderful deeds of him who called you out of darkness into his marvelous light" (1 Pet 2:9). This conception of the people of God will be normative for the Church and especially for its liturgy. For, as Vatican II puts it, while the liturgy is not the sole activity of the Church, it is nonetheless

> the summit toward which the activity of the Church is directed; at the same time it is the fount from which all the Church's power flows. For the aim and object of all apostolic works is that all who are made children of God by faith and baptism should come together to praise God in the midst of the Church, to take part in the sacrifice, and to eat the Lord's Supper.[8]

The new situation begun by the passage of Jesus, who was thereby established as Christ and Lord, transformed the priestly character of the covenanted people. Communities that put their faith in him realized from the very beginning that they were living in the "time of the Messiah"; the characteristic traits of this new age gradually emerged into clarity on the

---

7. Or, as the *Traduction oecuménique de la Bible* has it: "a priestly community of the king."

8. VSC 10 (*DOL* 1 no. 10).

basis of various traditions. One of the most important, which is hardly suggested in the Old Testament texts, is the priestly function as a constitutive part of Christian messianism. This element received its definitive explanation in the Letter to the Hebrews, to which the tradition has referred ever since. The supreme priestly act, namely, the offering of the perfect sacrifice by which the human race, now reconciled to God, can be presented to him as an acceptable oblation and can receive in return his blessing in its fullness, was accomplished perfectly, once and for all (*ephapax*), by Christ, who declared as he entered this world: "Sacrifice and offerings thou hast not desired, but a body thou hast prepared for me; in burnt offerings and sin offerings thou hast taken no pleasure. Then I said, 'Lo, I have come to do thy will, O God,' as it is written of me in the roll of the book" (Ps 39:7-9 according to the LXX). The Letter continues: This is why "by that will we have been sanctified through the offering of the body of Jesus Christ once for all" (Heb 10:5-10).

Unlike other religions, then, the Christian religion does not renew or repeat an original "foundational action," but renders present to all times and places the efficacy of an action performed once for all by him who is forever the sole priest (*sacerdos*) of his Church. It is as envoys and deputies appointed to an apostolic ministry that some members of the Church are delegated by Christ, through a special charism of his Spirit, to perform the liturgical actions in the bosom of the ecclesial community and thereby act as visible representatives of the Lord and sovereign Priest (*sacerdos*) of this Church (*in persona Christi*).[9] But the community in its entirety is also priestly because it has its life from the same Spirit; it is the Body of Christ, that is, the living active expression of his presence among human beings.[10]

It follows from all this that the liturgy has a twofold function in the Church: to *constitute* the Church and to *express* the Church. The first is the work chiefly of the sacramental liturgy; the second, that of the liturgy of praise, which follows the rhythms of time. The Eucharistic liturgy is *par excellence* the *sacrament* of the ecclesial mystery: "a sign and instrument, that is, of communion with God and of unity among all men."[11] In liturgical action human beings exercise fully the power given to them through baptism, namely, to be active members of a community in which the reign of God is proclaimed and begun. Consequently, the Christian liturgy has no place for passive spectators.[12] As soon as the liturgical func-

---

9. On this point see B. D. Marliangeas, *Clés pour une théologie des ministères: In persona Christi, in persona Ecclesiae* (Théologie historique 51; Paris: Beauchesne, 1978).

10. See *Lumen gentium* 10.

11. *Ibid.*, 1 (Flannery 350).

12. See *VSC* 11, 14, etc.

tion begins, all who take part in it are in the official service of God as persons who have been regenerated in the innermost depths of their being and have been led as by a new act of creation into the divine world of which they are now citizens.

II. ACTIONS THAT CONSTITUTE THE CHURCH

It is by means of its liturgical celebrations and especially its sacramental rites in the strict sense that the Church gives its children birth into the faith, feeds them, and strengthens them throughout the course of their earthly pilgrimage. In normal circumstances, faith is inseparable from the sacraments of faith. The history of the various liturgies shows us how the Church has applied itself to bringing out by meaningful rites the various angles from which the life of faith can be viewed with its stages that are analogous to, but not necessarily tied up with, the stages of natural life.

The first rite that inevitably comes to mind is the complex whole consisting of baptismal initiation and its consolidation by the "seal of the Holy Spirit." Yet it is most certainly in the Eucharistic celebration, the center and summit of all Christian liturgy, that this function of the liturgy is exercised most fully. The Eucharistic liturgy is the efficacious sign of the reality, both divine and human, that makes up the Church. For, through communion in the Body and Blood of the Lord who makes them part of his redemptive sacrifice, distinct individuals—separated and even opposed by all the seeds of division that they carry within themselves by reason of their sinful condition, but washed in the redemptive bath of baptism and brought into the kingdom that the Lord inaugurated in his resurrection—become a single being, a multiform but cohesive and solidly articulated organism. In this organism a single vital sap, a single flow of life from him who is at once head and fullness (or fulfillment), a single lifegiving breath (the Spirit) that works differently in the different members, make it possible for the whole to grow harmoniously, through the ministry of all, to the full stature of the perfect Human Being—a climax reached on the day where there will no longer be aught but a single Christ presenting himself to the Father at the term of a passage now completely accomplished.

We might follow throughout the sacramental organism these signs that directly or indirectly constitute the ecclesial body: the restoration of members through reconciliation, the transmission of hierarchic powers and the perpetuation of the apostolic tradition in the sacrament of orders, and finally marriage, which elevates to the level of the concerns proper to the kingdom the command God gave at the outset regarding the complementarity and fruitfulness of the sexes, and which thereby turns human love into a sign of the divine agape. The anointing of the sick fits Christians spiritually for the special state of illness; it indicates the new function assigned them in the Church and makes them privileged witnesses of the mystery of redemption. But because the state of illness is abnormal, the sacrament is also a sign of messianic restoration, which may possibly be anticipated in bodily healing.

We might even go beyond the seven sacraments (in the strict sense of "sacrament") and study all the other Christian rites from the viewpoint of the construction of the Church. None of them is completely without a part in this building up of the body. The various "mysteries" that the Church, universal or local, has thought it ought to add to the seven sacraments would not deserve the name "liturgical" if they did not play some part in the great and ultimate "mystery": the carrying out of God's eternal plan to gather everything together in Christ.

III. ACTIONS THAT EXPRESS THE CHURCH

Nonetheless, most of these second-rank actions provide primarily a set of very profound and rich insights into that inner reality, not directly perceptible in itself, by which the Church carries out God's plan of salvation in the world. This function of the Church's actions is a consequence of the incarnation and its economy, which the Creator freely chose. Because the Church itself is a parable and sacrament of the kingdom, its liturgy expresses, in the form of mystery, the ultimate realities of this kingdom. And the expressiveness is not something accidental and added on; it is rather the shining out of the divine-human being that is the Church. By the sole fact that it exists, and according to the modalities of this existence, the Church expresses what it is and what it accomplishes.[13]

But what the Church is and does is too complex a reality to be adequately expressed in a particular rite that bears the stamp of a particular culture.[14] It is not possible to exaggerate the necessity of invoking all the liturgical creations of East and West if we are to have an accurate idea of what the Church, with the self-consciousness it has developed up to now, intends to express in its liturgy. A characteristic emphasized in one liturgical rite may appear only in veiled form elsewhere. Would it be noticed in this broad "elsewhere" if it had not taken clear shape in some particular place?

Furthermore, this comparison or, better, this synoptic view alone makes it possible to distinguish between essential constants and secondary developments that are the result of the particular needs and tastes

---

13. See *VSC* 2 and Eph 4:11-16.
14. See *VSC* 37-38.

of a given community. The former, however defective or clumsy the form they take, are expressions of a reality whose two aspects must be firmly asserted: the divine side, which is immutable and perfect, and the human, which changes and depends on the varied conditions in which the Church must live its life. Quite often, moreover, a sign that is inadequate, clumsy, or affected, may draw our attention to an aspect of the Church that is veiled in the major liturgies with their classic lines and balanced masses. Thus an insufficiently attentive eye may quite often fail to see in the very sober Roman liturgy one or other nuance that is nonetheless lightly penciled in.

At moments when the various Churches face new situations and new cultures and are led to revise the expression of their liturgies, special care is needed to ensure that the revised liturgy will manifest in the best possible measure both fidelity to apostolic tradition and to the heritage received from the ancient Churches and, at the same time, the essential traits of each particular culture and the nuances of these that emerge most clearly at the present time.

IV. THE DOUBLE MOVEMENT OF THE LITURGY: GLORIFICATION OF GOD AND SANCTIFICATION OF THE HUMAN RACE

BIBLIOGRAPHY

J. M. Hanssens, "De natura liturgiae ad mentem sancti Thomae," *Periodica de re morali canonica liturgica* 24 (1935) 127*–35*.

O. Lottin, *Morale fondamentale* (Tournai: Desclée, 1954) 350–63 and 434–35, with bibliography on 363 and 435.

J. Lecuyer, "Réflexions sur la théologie du culte selon saint Thomas," *Revue thomiste* 55 (1955) 339–62.

C. Vagaggini, *Theological Dimensions of the Liturgy*, trans. L. J. Doyle and W. A. Jurgens (Collegeville: The Liturgical Press, 1976), 124–56.

As we think of the liturgy, our attention is drawn first to the movement toward God in prayer of adoration and praise; this prayer, after all, plays so great a part in the liturgy that each time the faithful participate in it they are called upon anew to be converted, to detach themselves from earthly things, and to give themselves to contemplation. The liturgy is thus an outstanding school for the service of the Lord; it refines our sense of God.[15]

---

15. See *VSC* 2, 57, 33, 59. — This point is particularly stressed by R. Guardini, *The Spirit of the Liturgy*, trans. A. Lane (London: Sheed & Ward, 1930), 130ff.

The various Christian liturgies have always made preferential use of the heritage of the biblical psalms and canticles, either repeating these in their original form or deriving food from them for new compositions, prayers, or songs. The Christian liturgy has inherited from the Old Testament the contemplation of the divine perfections and the practice of thanking God for his "wonderful deeds" in creation and in his merciful interventions in behalf of his people. The consciousness of sin and spiritual wretchedness only accentuates this sense of a God who loves, pities, and heals. Now that Christ has revealed the inner secrets of the divine life to us, doxologies (often from Paul) have a Trinitarian form. The celebrant's prayers, which are normally addressed to the Father, always rely on the mediation of Jesus, the Son of God, and mention the Holy Spirit. In the Jewish tradition, most often at least, those who pray "bless God" (*eulogia*), but the Christian liturgy prefers thanksgiving (*eucharistia*), which is a cry of gratitude for the redemptive work of Christ and at the same time adoration of the eternal plan of the God who has called us and anticipated us with an unmerited love.[16] By the very fact of coming together, the liturgical assembly is a manifestation—an epiphany—of salvation in Christ. It expresses this chiefly in the Eucharistic celebration, which is both a "sacrifice of praise" and an efficacious memorial of the redemptive act.[17]

All this shows clearly the transformation that the idea of "cult" has undergone, and the degree to which it is of itself inadequate as a description of the Christian liturgy. Classical moral theology often discussed the liturgy in the framework of Aristotelian ethics and in the light of the Latin moralists, especially Cicero. In that context cult was seen as all the ways in which human beings try to express the relations they ought to have with God. Cult was regarded as proceeding from a permanent disposition called "religion," but at the same time it comprised distinct and specific actions aimed at manifesting the disposition and having it alone as their object.[18] Two closely connected attitudes could be distinguished in cult: the "honor" given to God in recognition of his excellence, and "submission" (*obsequium, servitus*).[19]

Revelation did not simply rectify and purify the demands cult made of human beings; it inaugurated a completely new order. First of all, God has spoken in the language of human beings and the unknowable has made

---

16. On this whole subject see L. Beauduin, "Essai de manuel fondamental de liturgie," chapter 1: "Le terme du culte: La Sainte Trinité," in his *Mélanges liturgiques* 1 (Louvain: Mont César, 1954), 45–73.

17. J. Juglar, *Le sacrifice de louange* (LO 15; Paris: Cerf, 1953).

18. St. Thomas repeatedly uses the verb *exhibere* with reference to acts of cult; e.g., *Summa theologiae* II-II, 81, 7; 83, 3; 84, 1 and 2

19. A. G. Martimort, "Le sens du sacré," *LMD* no. 25 (1941) 48–49 and the references given there.

itself known. Then, too, he has manifested his glory in numerous interventions. Finally, the coming of Christ has caused the light of God's glory to shine before the eyes of our mind (*"per incarnati Verbi mysterium nova mentis nostrae oculis lux tuae claritatis infulsit"*[20]). For the Christian, then, cult and the virtue of religion are inseparable from faith and charity; the liturgy expresses the dialogue between God and his people, and the proclamation of God's word has an important and original place in it that is without analogue elsewhere. In giving ritual form to the sacrificial offering Christ made of himself to the Father for the salvation of human beings, the Christian liturgy aims not only to offer a cult to God but also to bestow the grace of God on human beings. Because the liturgy effects what it signifies, all of its actions have, in a way, a sacramental character.

Admittedly, the sacramentality takes various forms, and the efficacy is not always the same in degree. The Letter to the Hebrews tells us that "the word of God is living and active, sharper than any two-edged sword, piercing to the division of soul and spirit, of joints and marrow, and discerning the thoughts and intentions of the heart" (Heb 4:12). Therefore, while the Word of God is not a sacrament in the strict sense, its proclamation in the liturgy has a special and unmatched authority and power.[21] Moreover, it is the power exerted by this Word in the saving actions of Christ that founds the efficacy of the Church's sacramental actions, whether the celebrant refers to the actions of Christ in a petition that asks, with the certainty of being heard, for the intervention of the Spirit whom Christ sent upon his Church to sanctify it and do a new work of creation in it (*epiclesis*) or whether he declares *in persona Christi* that the intervention is now taking place. In every case it is the priesthood of Christ, exercised in the liturgy, that ensures the unity of the double movement of glorification of God and sanctification of humanity; sanctification, moreover, is in the final analysis completely related to the earthly accomplishment of the heavenly liturgy in which God is all in all.[22]

The Church that is a pilgrim on earth cannot forget that it is a citizen of heaven. What the pattern of the tabernacle shown on the mountain (Exod 25:9) was for Moses, the Letter to the Hebrews and the Apocalypse are for the Church. For, even though the Church is a sacrament of the kingdom of God and has received the first fruits of the kingdom through the sending of the Spirit on Pentecost, it remains nonetheless in the realm of figures as long as it exists on earth: "Now we see in a mirror dimly" (1 Cor 13:12); we are "called children of God, and so we are . . . . it

---

20. Roman Preface for Christmas (*Gr* 38), in which H. Ashworth sees the hand of St. Gregory.

21. A. Card. Bea, "Valeur pastorale de la parole de Dieu," *LMD* no. 48 (1956), 138.

22. *VSC* 8 and 48.

does not yet appear what we shall be" (1 John 3:1-2); "Your life is hid with Christ in God. When Christ who is our life appears, then you also will appear with him in glory" (Col 3:3-4). This singular interplay of earth and heaven is characteristic of the Christian liturgy. There are not two liturgies, any more than there are two Churches. Rather, as the same Church is a pilgrim on earth and triumphant in heaven, so the same liturgy is celebrated here below in figurative rites and without figures "beyond the veil" in the heavenly sanctuary.

The first generations of Christians had an exceptional awareness of the unity of earthly Church and heavenly Church. By his victorious ascension Christ had broken through the boundaries of creation; he had triumphed over time and taken human nature with him into the heavenly sanctuary where Israel had accustomed itself to seeing myriads of angels performing their service around Adonai. Henceforth, those on earth would not simply imitate what was done perfectly on "the mountain of God," in heavenly Zion; they would actually take part in that solemn liturgy.[23] The spirit of the Letter to the Hebrews and the Apocalypse enlivens the early Eucharistic Prayers of all the Christian rites and permeates their ceremonial. Anyone taking part in the Sunday liturgy of the Byzantine rite, for example, receives an almost physical impression of the eschatological character of the liturgy when the doors of the sanctuary open for the procession with the gospel or with the holy gifts. The choir meanwhile stresses the point that these processions are not simply symbolic imitations but real participations in the heavenly liturgy; thus the procession with the gospel is followed by the *Trisagion*, that is, the song Isaiah heard the seraphim singing during the great theophany that marked the beginning of his prophetic ministry (Isa 6). During the procession with the holy gifts the choir announces, in an endless melody whose repeated and interwoven arabesques seem free of the conditions of time: "Let us, as mysterious icon of the cherubim, sing the Thrice Holy to the lifegiving Trinity; let us leave aside all earthly concerns and receive the King of the universe who is invisibly escorted by the angelic hosts. Alleluia." The Roman rite is more restrained but no less realistic about the supraterrestrial character of the liturgy. The Canon, or traditional Eucharistic Prayer of the Roman liturgy, asks that the Church's offering be carried to the heavenly altar by the hand of God's angel.[24]

---

23. On this point see E. Peterson, *The Angels and the Liturgy*, trans. R. Walls (New York: Herder and Herder, 1964).

24. For the correct interpretation of this text see B. Botte, "L'ange du sacrifice," in *Cours et conférences des Semaines liturgiques* 7 (Louvain: Mont César, 1929), 209–21; *idem*, "L'ange du sacrifice et l'epiclèse de la messe romaine au moyen âge," *RTAM* 1 (1929) 285–308.

§3. The Ministerial Exercise of the Priesthood of Christ

I. A SINGLE PRIEST: PRESENCE OF CHRIST IN THE LITURGY

BIBLIOGRAPHY

Actus Congressus internationalis de theologia Concilii Vaticani II, Romae diebus 26 septembris—1 Octobris 1966 (Vatican Polyglot Press, 1968), 272–338: *Thema IV. De praesentia Domini in communitate cultus* (papers of L. Ciappi, B. Duda, J. A. Jungmann, A. G. Martimort, B. Neunheuser, K. Rahner).

G. Cingolani, *L'assemblea e la sua partecipazione al sacrificio eucaristico* (Rome, 1970), 47–59.

A. Cuva, *La presenza di Cristo nella liturgia* (Rome: Edizioni liturgiche, 1973).

E. J. Lengeling, "Zur Aktualpräsenz Christi in der Liturgie," in *Mens concordet voci. Pour Mgr Martimort* (Paris: Desclée, 1983), 518–31.

In the ecclesial economy of the new covenant there is but a single priest, Christ himself. Since the liturgy is an expression of the priestly character of this economy, it is necessarily a privileged place of Christ's presence to his Church: a directly active presence in strictly sacramental celebrations, an indirectly active presence in the signs that the Church, led by his Spirit and instructed by his Word, sets before the faithful. Classical theology expresses the first kind of presence in the formula *ex opere operato*, the second in the formula *ex opere operantis Ecclesiae*. The meaning is that in the first case the saving power of Christ is exercised, provided only that the will of those participating in the celebration place no positive obstacle and that the forms recognized by the Church are observed, according to the degree of importance assigned to them. In the second case it is the faith and love of the Church that directly ensure the efficacy of the celebration.

The liturgical constitution of Vatican II lays heavy emphasis on the various ways in which Christ manifests his presence in liturgical celebrations.[25] In the celebration of the Eucharist he goes so far as to completely strip the bread and wine of their natural mode of existence in order to make of them his own Body and Blood, which are present under the "species" or "appearances" of these elements. In baptism and confirmation he gives water and oil the power to lead the recipient into the paschal mystery of rebirth and the full exercise of new life according to the Spirit. In the other sacramental rites, this power (*virtus*) of Christ is exercised through various signs: gestures that have their meaning made clear by accompanying words and that can vary from liturgy to liturgy or even in the historical development of a particular liturgy.

---

25. *VSC* 7.

The reading of the Scriptures brings the assembly another mode of Christ's presence. In ensuring this presence the gospel evidently plays an unparalleled part, which the whole of Christian tradition puts on a level comparable to the Eucharistic Presence. This explains the exceptional signs of respect shown to the Book of the Gospels: lights, incenses, kisses. But since all the texts of the Old and New Testaments are a privileged expression of the Word of God, in them, too, Christ, the subsistent Word in whom all the Scriptures have their fulfillment, makes himself heard and known in some degree.[26]

II. MINISTERS OF CHRIST: *IN PERSONA CHRISTI*

BIBLIOGRAPHY

B. D. Marliangeas, *Clés pour une théologie du ministère: In persona Christi, In persona Ecclesiae* (Théologie historique 51; Paris: Beauchesne, 1978).
A. G. Martimort, "In persona Christi," in *Mens concordet voci* (Paris: Desclée, 1983), 330–37.

In appointing his apostles Christ acquired for himself "authorized representatives," *locum tenentes* who are associated in a special way with his own apostolic mission, not simply as participants, along with the rest of the ecclesial body, in his kingly and prophetic priesthood, but as "stewards of the mysteries of God" (1 Cor 4:1)—ministers of the Spirit's gifts for the building up of the ecclesial body. In their liturgical functions more than in their other ministerial actions these representatives are called to act *in persona Christi*. In strictly sacramental actions their role even becomes a purely instrumental one, though it must be kept in mind that the instrument in this case is a person whose freely elicited intention is indispensable for the validity of the sacramental act.[27] In addition, all ministers, whether ordained or appointed for a particular occasion, participate collegially in the normal performance of the sacramental act; their participation depends on the various functions entrusted to them and is exercised ultimately under the authority of the bishop whose collaborators they are.

III. THE CHURCH, BODY OF CHRIST

As the ecclesial body of Christ the liturgical assembly in its entirety is also a sign of his presence. For while all Christians, by reason of their

---

26. A. G. Martimort, "Praesens adest in verbo suo . . .," in *Actus Congressus internationalis de theologia Concilii Vaticani II, Romae diebus 26 septembris—1 octobris 1966* (Vatican Polyglot Press, 1968), 300–15.

27. St. Thomas, *Summa theologiae* III, 64, 8, and n. 108 of A. M. Roguet in his edition of this section of the *Summa: Les sacrements* (Paris: Revue des jeunes, 1945), 247.

baptism, which makes them members of this ecclesial body, participate in the threefold ministry that Scripture recognizes Christ as having, they do not do so as isolated individuals. Since Pentecost, the Spirit who anointed Jesus to be priest, prophet, and king dwells within the Church in his fullness; he gives his gifts to each member according to the function assigned that member in the ecclesial organism as a whole; Christ, as head of the Church, distributes these functions by communicating his powers to those whom he has appointed as his apostles and to the successors they in turn chose for themselves. But the same Spirit dynamizes the entire body to make of it, in St. Augustine's fine phrase, "a single Christ loving the Father." This is why, for example, the body in its psalmody and prayer can apply to itself expressions that in their strict meaning belong to Christ alone. Furthermore, just as it is in liturgical celebrations that ordained ministers most perfectly represent the Christ who structures, teaches, and sanctifies his Church, so too the mystery of the Church as body of Christ can be most clearly seen in these same celebrations, in which the Church anticipates by means of signs, and in the sacramental mode, the community of life that is promised in its fullness at the Parousia.[28]

The liturgy is thus inseparably an act of Christ and an act of the Church. From Christ it receives all of its power to bring the mystery of salvation to fulfillment. But, apart from the clearly defined cases to which classical theology has reserved the name "sacraments," that is, actions in which this power is exercised directly through rites performed by competent ministers, the Church as Spouse of Christ exercises sovereign authority in organizing its liturgy and ensuring its effectiveness; in all this the Church is moved by the Spirit whom it has received as its dowry and as the first fruits of its inheritance. Liturgical texts, and still less the indispensable ritual directives accompanying them, do not by themselves constitute the liturgy. They are simply means of carrying out the liturgy when they are applied to the purpose for which they were instituted, namely, the communication of the mystery of salvation. If we look otherwise upon texts and rubrics, we are likely to fall into a ritualism of a magical kind that is incompatible with a genuinely religious outlook.

---

28. VSC 7–8.

Chapter II

The Liturgy as Celebration of the Mystery of Salvation

BIBLIOGRAPHY

O. Casel, "Art und Sinn der ältesten christichen Osterfeier," *JLW* 14 (1934) 1–78. French trans. by J. C. Didier: *La fête de Pâques dans l'Eglise des Pères* (LO 37; Paris: Cerf, 1963). Other works of Casel are listed below in the bibliography on p. 266.

J. Daniélou, *The Bible and the Liturgy* (Notre Dame: University of Notre Dame Press, 1956).

LMD no. 30 (1952): *L'économie du salut et le cycle liturgique.*

L. Bouyer, *Liturgical Piety* (Notre Dame: University of Notre Dame Press, 1955).

P. Wegenaer, *Heilsgegenwart. Das Heilswerk Christi und die "virtus divina" in den Sakramenten* (LQF 33; Münster: Aschendorff, 1958).

The Liturgy and the Word of God (Collegeville: The Liturgical Press, 1959).

C. Vagaggini, *Theological Dimensions of the Liturgy*, trans. L. J. Doyle and W. A. Jurgens (Collegeville: The Liturgical Press, 1976), 3–123.

L'économie du salut dans la liturgie. Conférences Saint-Serge, XVIIᵉ Semaine d'études liturgiques 1970 (Bibliotheca EL, Subsidia 25; Rome: Edizioni liturgiche, 1982).

S. Marsili, "La liturgia, momento storico della salvezza," in *Anàmnesis* 1 (Turin: Marietti, 1974), 47–136.

C. Rocchetta, *I sacramenti della fede. Saggio di teologia biblica sui sacramenti quali "meraviglia della salvezza" nel tempo della Chiesa* (Nuovi saggi teologici 19; Bologna: Edizioni Dehoniane, 1982).

Ever since the fourth century the principal liturgical functions, and especially those marking the stages of Christian initiation with the Eucharistic memorial as the climax, have been described in the Greek-speaking Churches as *mystēria*, in the Syriac-speaking Churches as *raze*, and in the Latin Churches either as *mysteria* (a transliteration of the Greek word) or as *sacramenta* (which became the accepted translation of the Greek *mystēria*). Unfortunately, the original overtones of these words faded away in the course of times; in the languages that arose from Latin, for example, "sacrament" generally comes to be reserved for the seven rites whose privileged place came to be seen as a result of doctrinal reflection. When the Fathers of Vatican II on several occasions spoke of the Church as the universal "sacrament" of salvation, they contributed greatly to a recovery of the original richness of the term,[1] although they did not explicitly bring out the liturgical repercussions of this broadened meaning.

§1. Mystery in the Biblical and Christian Tradition

1. *The term "mystery" among the ancients*

The word *raz*, an Aramaic transliteration of an originally Iranian term, appeared first in apocalyptic texts; in the beginning it was used especially to describe the deliberations of the supreme council of the Achemenid empire (Dan 2:17-18, 27-30), and already had eschatological overtones. The Greek translations of the Bible and writings that have come down to us only in Greek use *mystērion* in the same sense; the Septuagint never uses *mystērion* to translate the Hebrew *sod* (secret).

The reason for this abstention was that the Greek word was charged with religious overtones. As early as the classical period (Herodotus, the tragedians, Plato) it was used in the plural as a name for private cults into which individuals were inducted by way of rites of *initiation* that they were obliged to keep completely secret. Unlike the official cults, these private cults claimed to ensure the salvation of their practitioners by giving them a participation in the cosmic cycles of death and rebirth; this they received through communion with a divinity who, after being hidden from view for a time in the kingdom of death, had escaped his fate as though by a new birth (regeneration). After being transposed into the perspectives proper to Platonic philosophy, this interpretation was to have an unanticipated future in Hellenistic culture and especially in Neoplatonism, for philosophy was transformed into a "mystagogy" that, in some circles at least, gave an ever larger place to "theurgic" rites.

2. *"Mystery" in St. Paul*

The evolution just sketched would eventually give rise to long-lasting reservations against a revival of the word *mystērion* as a designation of Christian rites. But the development was not yet discernible at the time when St. Paul, following the lead of apocalyptic texts, did a great deal to acclimate *mystērion* in the Christian communities. The single use of the word in the Synoptic tradition (Matt 13:11; Mark 4:11; Luke 8:10)

---

1. Vatican II, Dogmatic Constitution *Lumen gentium* 1; 9; 48. — Texts given above in n. 2, p. 174.

is likewise in the apocalyptic line, as is the use made of it in the Johannine Apocalypse (1:20; 10:7; 17:5, 7).

It is nonetheless possible to see in Paul's writings the influence of various meanings that the word had in the Greek world. In the Letters to the Colossians and Ephesians in particular, a development can be discerned that would have a decisive impact on Christian usage. For, while the word as used in Paul remains essentially rooted in the soil of the apocalypses, it also conveys a clear awareness (already to be found in the Synoptic tradition) that the "mystery of the kingdom" or of the "divine lordship" is henceforth manifested in Jesus, who has been established and proclaimed as "Christ" (see 1 Cor 1:23; 2:1, 7; Rom 16:25-26). Therefore it is in and through the preaching of Jesus Christ, and of him crucified, that the "mystery" is presently being manifested, for it was on the cross that the radical antithesis between the mysterious and previously hidden Wisdom of God and the supposed wisdom of this world was clearly shown. The Letters to the Ephesians and Colossians bring out the consequences of all this for the concrete life of the ecclesial community, while at the same time emphasizing the eschatology that is now being brought to fulfillment.

3. In the Fathers

Paul's teaching on the mystery was continued throughout the patristic period, though not without reservations as far as its terminology was concerned. It is worth noting, for example, that Tertullian rejects the Latin transposition, *mysterium*, though this had long been in use, and prefers the term *sacramentum*, so rich in overtones in its Roman usage; it is with this as his starting point that he lays the foundations of Latin sacramental theology.[2] But the multivalence of the word "mystery" is more clearly felt in Greek.[3] Thus, when Ignatius of Antioch speaks of observance of the "Lord's Day" (Sunday) replacing observance of the Sabbath because Sunday is the day "on which our life was raised up through him and his death," he adds: "It is through this mystery that we received the faith, and it is because of it that we persevere in order to be acknowledged as disciples of Jesus Christ, our only Master."[4]

---

2. See the chapter on Tertullian, by E. de Backer, in J. de Ghellinck, *Pour l'histoire du mot "sacramentum"* 1. *Les Anténicéens* (Spicilegium Sacrum Lovaniense 3; Louvain: Spicilegium, 1924), 59–152.

3. For the use of the word *mystērion* in the Fathers see K. Prümm, *ZKT* 61 (1937) 391–425 (Origen); 63 (1939) 207–25 (Hippolytus), 350–59 (Athanasius); J. C. M. Fruytier, *Het woord "musterion" in de Catechesen van Cyrillus van Jeruzalem* (Nijmegen, 1950); G. Fittkau, *Der Begriff des Mysteriums bei Johannes Chrysostomus* (Bonn: Hanstein, 1953). — See the review of these last two works by J. Daniélou, *RechSR* 42 (1954) 602–10.

4. *Magnes.* 9, 1 (SC 10:102–5).

The celebration of the new Passover, the "memorial" of the death and resurrection of Christ, was at a very early date seen and proclaimed as the supreme "mystery" of the Christian faith. In his *Dialogue with Trypho* St. Justin often refers to it, because "the mystery of the lamb" in the Mosaic Passover "was a prefiguration of Christ,"[5] but it is Melito of Sardis who first uses the phrase, "mystery of the Pasch."[6] Not until Eusebius of Caesarea, however, is the vocabulary of "mystery" explicitly adopted in speaking of "the memorial of the great sacrifice of Christ, according to the mysteries he has passed on to us," "for David already alluded [Ps 39:3-9 LXX] to the *mystery* of the new covenant of Christ that is today celebrated openly among all peoples."[7] And, even more explicitly: "First our Savior and Lord himself offered sacrifice, and now all the priests of all nations who derive their priesthood from him do likewise, when in accordance with the canons of the Church they enact *the mysteries of his body and blood* under the symbols of bread and wine."[8]

There is reason to think that from the middle of the fourth century on this liturgical use of *mystērion* was generally accepted, both for baptism and, even more definitely, for the Eucharist. The preferred form was the plural *mystēria*, which even became a technical name for the Eucharistic celebration, especially in areas that followed the Syrian tradition. The same was true of the Aramaic *raze* in the Syriac-speaking Churches. We may even think that the use of this word in apocalyptic texts, from the Book of Daniel on, helped not a little in promoting the cultic use of *mystērion* among Christians.

It would take longer to overcome Latin reluctance to use this terminology. The plural *mysteria*, in particular, would long have for Christians the technical sense it had acquired centuries earlier in Latin usage, which reserved it for "mystery cults" of Greek or Eastern origin. Nonetheless, beginning in the second half of the fourth century *mysterium* (singular or plural) would increasingly be used as a synonym for *sacramentum*. The most that can be said, according to C. Mohrmann, is that by reason of the different origins of the two words and the nuances each had in Latin use, *mysterium* was preferred when the emphasis was on the spiritual realities hidden beneath the letter of the Scriptures, while *sacramentum* was preferred for the actions by which Christians were initiated into those real-

---

5. St. Justin, *Dialogus cum Tryphone* 40, ed. G. Archambault 1 (Textes et documents 8; Paris: Picard, 1909), 178; see 24,44, 68, 78,85,138 (pp. 108, 196, 330; and vol. 2 [Textes et documents 11], 20, 60, 74).

6. Melito of Sardis, *Sur la Pâque* 11 and 15, ed. O. Perler (SC 12; Paris: Cerf, 1966), 64 and 68.

7. Eusebius, *Demonstratio evangelica* I, 10 (PG 22:92).

8. *Ibid.*, V, 3 (PG 22:368).

ities (there was still a reluctance to call these actions *mysteria*).[9] But this distinction soon lost its force, both in St. Augustine[10] and in St. Leo.[11] Only in the Scholastic period would *sacramentum* definitively acquire the technical meaning it has kept down to our own time.

4. *Sacrament, sign, symbol, mystery*

These hesitations and restricted uses of words were a drag on the development of a theology of liturgy that could do justice to the many and complex realities such a theology must take into account. In fact, as I pointed out earlier, down to our own time classical Western theology focused almost exclusively on the limited sphere of sacramental functions in the narrow sense. Once we give "sacrament" its older and broader meaning, we realize that in the Church, the "universal sacrament of salvation," everything is somehow sacramental, that is, everything is the vehicle of a meaning and an efficacy belonging to a different order from the realities of direct experience, and that this is so because the Church of Christ is a sign and anticipation of the "mysteries of the kingdom."

Beyond a doubt, we must make use of other tools of thought than the one hitherto usually employed. Western sacramental theology has given preference to the idea of sign. St. Augustine first sketched this idea in a very specific context, and Peter Lombard then made use of it in his *Sentences*; the thirteenth-century masters and especially St. Thomas Aquinas were the ones who developed it fully. The substitution of it for the idea of "sacrament as mystery," which had been introduced by Isidore of Seville, was not however without its difficulties.[12] The primary need, of course, was to safeguard the realism and efficacy of the Christian sacraments. But the careful distinctions that the twelfth century made in showing how this efficacy was the mark of the "seven sacraments" as compared with all the other rites of the Church required that the seven be set apart from the body of "mysteries." On the other hand, the idea of "mystery" seemed too rich and too imprecise to serve as the kind of investigative tool increasingly needed for the development of an argumentative theology that used Scholastic methods based on Aristotelian logic. The passage "from symbol to dialectic," to which a scholar called our attention

---

9. C. Mohrmann, "*Sacramentum* dans les plus anciens textes chrétiens," in her *Etudes sur le latin des chrétiens* 1 (Storia e letteratura 65; Rome: Edizioni di storia e letteratura, 1958), 233–44.

10. See *Ep. 55 ad Januarium* 1 CSEL 33:170; *Serm.* 190, *In die Natali* 7 (PL 38:1007).

11. See J. Gaillard, "La théologie des mystères," *Revue thomiste* 57 (1957) 44–52.

12. On all this see A. M. Roguet, "Notes doctrinales thomistes," in his edition of *Somme théologique: Les sacrements* (Edition de la Revue des Jeunes; Paris: Desclée, 1945), 255–62.

some time back,[13] was doubtless to a large extent inevitable and necessary. The idea of sign, with the distinctions and nuances that St. Thomas,
final link in a long chain of development, provided in his *Summa theologiae*, gave an intelligent and balanced explanation of one of the most important parts of the Christian liturgy; had this understanding and balance
been maintained in the following centuries, the extreme reactions of the
Reformers might have been avoided.

On the other hand, the idea of sign, whatever the adaptations made
of it, did not allow the development of a theology, even of the seven sacraments, that takes all their aspects into account and, above all, that properly
situates them within the liturgical rites as a whole. The special status of
the seven, with the emphasis on their role as means of salvation, did bring
out their direct relation to Christ in his work of salvation and especially
in his passion; but, by the same token, the emphasis was on the effect
of the sacraments and therefore on their causality. Theologians attempting to determine the manner of this causality would find themselves moving
in the same world as canonists desirous of determining the conditions that
must be met to ensure sacramental efficacy. Everything connected with
the external forms in which the sacramental action takes place became
secondary. Theologians as such could ignore them, since these externals
did not seem to have any intelligibility in themselves. A more penetrating
study of "sign" that brought out its relation to the mind and distinguished
between natural and conventional signs only emphasized the distance—a
distance already implicit, in fact, in Augustinian intellectualism, which
had become the channel for views originating in the "mystagogy" of the
writings of Pseudo-Dionysius and closer to Proclus than to Plotinus. The
result was that two radically different kinds of intelligibility crisscrossed:
that of "mystery" and that of "sacrament."

The West had gained the ability to use strictly defined ideas and carefully elaborated analogies; it had failed to work out a theology of the
liturgy that would safeguard the realism of cultic action, not only in the
principal rites (directly ordained by Christ himself for communicating his
saving grace to human beings) but in all the developments that took place
in the local Churches in the course of time. Theological reflection yields
a single whole; the predominant role that the Latin Middle Ages gave to
the redemptive passion and the element of vicarious satisfaction undoubtedly did not respect the full balance of the divine plan of salvation in sufficient measure to ensure a right understanding of its cultic expression. The
end result was a twofold theology of the Christian rites: a *sacramental
theology* based on a "descent," that is, the communication to human be-

---

13. H. de Lubac, *Corpus mysticum* (Théologie 3; Paris: Aubier, 1944), 255–84: "Du
symbole à la dialectique."

ings of a salvation worked directly by God, and a *liturgical theology* based on an "ascent," which would restore to the Church's rites their value as external and social manifestations of the virtue of religion, that is, as cultic acts in the narrow sense of the term (I have already pointed out how inadequate "cultic act" is as a reflection of the true nature of Christian liturgy). This dichotomy clearly led to an impasse or aporia, since it is the liturgy in its entirety, from the principal sacraments to the least rite, that expresses the encounter of sinful but redeemed humanity with God who saves it in Christ and whose Spirit gradually permeates all human religious activities in order to turn them into actions of God's children, the citizens of the heavenly city.

The point I made at the very beginning of this section needs to be repeated over and over: liturgy belongs in the order of "doing" (*ergon*), not of "knowing" (*logos*). Logical thought cannot get very far with it; liturgical actions yield their intelligibility in their performance, and this performance takes place entirely at the level of sensible realities, not as exclusively material but as vehicles of overtones capable of awakening the mind and heart to acceptance of realities belonging to a different order. As the author of the treatise *The Divine Names* observed in continuity with the entire Platonic tradition, the humblest of these sensible realities can serve to express what cannot be defined in concepts and ideas.

When we move into this world of thought that is symbolic and "poetic" (i.e., productive of a work), "mystery" comes into play.[14] The location of mystery at the center of a theology of liturgy in place of the technically developed idea of sacrament supposes that we have moved from a "logical" to a "phenomenological" approach. In other words, it supposes that instead of trying to explain divine realities by means of analogies from the created world, we confine ourselves to a description of the manifestations of the divine in the universe that is accessible to us. For "mystery" implies "revelation" (*apocalypsis*). Things will bring echoes of the divine only to ears already open to hear God speaking in the Scriptures as these are understood in the ecclesial community. Only then will the two traditions about "mystery"—the one transmitted by St. Paul in continuity with the apocalypses, and the one inherited from Hellenism—turn out to converge in Christ who is the "mystery" in the fullest sense because he is the very revelation of God in the humanity of Jesus. But by this very fact the "mystery" is also closely linked to time.

§2. The Christian Liturgy and the "Time of Salvation"

It is widely acknowledged that the role played by "time" is one of the

---

14. On all this the reader may profitably consult J. Maritain, "Sign and Symbol," in his *Ransoming the Time*, trans. H. L. Binsse (New York: Scribner's, 1946), 217-54.

most notable characteristics, or perhaps even *the* specific characteristic, of biblical revelation. O. Cullmann did not hesitate to write: "The specifically 'Christian kernel,' as we derive it from all the Primitive Christian sources, really stands or falls with the redemptive history."[15] This means that "revelation" (*apocalypsis*), as understood in Christianity, takes place through events. Adopting a perspective suggested by the gospel tradition, the Fathers of the Church, St. Irenaeus chief among them, endeavored to show that in his earthly existence Christ "recapitulates" this history of salvation and discloses the mystery it contains.

In the Israelite mind time is linear and has three main phases: time before creation, the duration of this world between creation and the "Day of the Lord," and the last times that follow that Day ("last times" is a vague expression that seems to vary in meaning from author to author). In any case, time as a whole contains only two events that alter its nature: creation and the Day of the Lord. The time between these two, that is, historical time, is punctuated by divine manifestations (theophanies) and numerous covenants (Noah, Abraham, Moses), but it is nonetheless a homogeneous whole.

Christ broke this continuity, however, for the kingdom is now at hand and "is among you," and yet the course of historical events goes on. The resurrection whereby Jesus was established as Christ and Lord is now the decisive event, being the outcome of all that went before and the explanation of all that will follow.

But it is not only the order within time and the meaning of history that have been changed. Even more radical than the replacement of the prince of this world by the Lord is the ontological transformation that brings humanity and with it the whole of creation from the time of development and evolution into the time of recapitulation, that is, a time of involution. Properly speaking, this change affects the time of the Church or, more accurately, it constitutes this time. Cosmic time continues on its course, seemingly unchanged; historical time is given a new direction, but the nature of the events that mark its course is in no way altered. Nevertheless, a new time makes its appearance: a time of plenitude or fulfillment; it represents the realization of a new and final phase in the divine plan of salvation.

This new time is the time of the Church, the time of the "recapitulation" of all creation in the total Christ.[16] After a short transitional period of fifty days following upon the resurrection, the time of the Church be-

15. O. Cullmann, *Christ and Time*, trans. F. V. Filson (rev. ed.; Philadelphia: Westminster, 1964), 29.

16. I. H. Dalmais, "Le temps de l'Eglise," in *L'Eglise et les Eglises* (Chevetogne, 1954), 87–103.

gins with the bestowal of the Spirit on Pentecost. To give it its true name, this time is the time of the Spirit who brings about the new creation and will eventually put an end to the unfolding of historical duration. In itself this "messianic time" is hidden; it is a time of "mystery" that will end in the "revelation" (*apocalypsis*) of the unveiled presence (*parousia*) of the Lord who has been directing the entire course of messianic time through his Spirit. Prior to that revelation even the Spirit himself is given only as a first fruits (Rom 8:23) or a pledge (2 Cor 1:22), for while the kingdom is already present it is not yet manifested.

But this "first gift" of the Spirit[17] is enough to make the time of the Church radically new. The Spirit who had rested upon the prophets only temporarily and in anticipation of what was to come is now given in close connection with the death and glorification of Christ (John 7:39); he causes the Church to exist by giving a single soul to the body made up of redeemed human beings, those who "have washed their robes and made them white in the blood of the Lamb" (Rev 7:14) and have passed with him from darkness into the kingdom of light. But the Spirit is also the "other Paraclete" who is just as really and personally present in the world, even though in a hidden way, as the Son was in the time of his incarnation. He manifests himself in his gifts; as such he is the Church's dowry as well as the pledge of the kingdom. This is why every Christian liturgy has at its heart an "epiclesis" or earnest plea that the Spirit may descend upon the ecclesial assembly and make known there the mysteries of the kingdom.

The paradoxical extension of time between two dialectically related moments will be eliminated only at the parousia when Christ "delivers the kingdom to God the Father . . . . that God may be everything to every one" (1 Cor 15:24, 28). Meanwhile, it constitutes the mystery of the time of the Church, during which the Lord is at once present and absent: so intimately present that he acts directly in the sacraments, which are instrumental prolongations of the action of his sacred humanity,[18] and yet also absent, for he is seated at the right hand of the Father, whence he shall come again to judge the living and the dead. The time of the Church is therefore *eschatological time*, because no radical innovation is still to come, since the work of creation and revelation is complete; but it is also *historical time*, during which the whole work of creation is progressively recapitulated and revelation is continually remembered.

The specific character of the "new cult" as established in the first Christian communities is to be seen in its purpose: the building up of the body of Christ to its full human stature. That is why the early Church focused its worship entirely on the celebration of the "Lord's Supper," in which

---

17. Fourth Eucharistic Prayer of the Roman Missal of 1970.
18. St. Thomas, *Summa theologiae* III, 62, 5.

Christ is present in the midst of his followers. On the one hand, this celebration recalls the meal that Jesus took with his disciples on the eve of his death, as well as the further meals that he took with them during the Easter season after his resurrection. On the other hand, it foretells and anticipates the eschatological fulfillment that Judaism had often presented in the form of a messianic banquet. In this way, each celebration of the Lord's Supper in early Christianity proclaimed that the mystery of salvation was completely fulfilled in Christ.

§3. Celebration of the Paschal Mystery

I. THE PASCHAL MYSTERY

The liturgical expression of the mystery of salvation is thus to be explained by the new content that "paschal mystery" acquired in Christ. As the Constitution *Sacrosanctum Concilium* says:

> As Christ was sent by the Father, he himself also sent the apostles, filled with the Holy Spirit. Their mission was, first, by preaching the Gospel to every creature, to proclaim that by his death and resurrection Christ has freed us from Satan's grip and brought us into the Father's kingdom. But the work they preached they were also to bring into effect through the sacrifice and the sacraments, the center of the whole liturgical life. . . . From that time onward the Church has never failed to come together to celebrate the paschal mystery: reading those things "which were in all the Scriptures concerning him" (Lk 24:27); celebrating the eucharist, in which "the victory and triumph of the Lord are again made present" [Trent, Session 22]; and at the same time giving thanks "to God for his inexpressible gift" (2 Cor 9—15) in Christ Jesus, "in praise of his glory" (Eph 1:12), through the power of the Holy Spirit.[19]

The origins of this paschal celebration go back to the initial establishment of God's people at the Exodus and the covenant on Sinai. Whatever its original meaning and its connections with the festivals of springtime,[20] the Mosaic Passover was enriched, even before Christ's coming, with a whole set of symbolic and spiritual themes. On the basis of the "Poem of the Four Nights," which is found in the Palestinian Targum, R. Le Déaut has brought out some of the most characteristic elements of this Passover theology in ancient Judaism.[21] At a very early stage the celebration of Pass-

---

19. VSC 6 (*DOL* 1 no. 6).

20. H. Haag, "Pâque," *DBS* 6 (1960) 1120–49.

21. R. Le Déaut, *La nuit pascale. Essai sur la signification de la Pâque juive à partir du Targum de l'Exode 12, 42* (Analecta biblica 22; Rome: Pontificio Istituto Biblico, 1963); *idem*, French translation of the *Poem of the Four Nights* in *Targum du Pentateuque* 2 (SC 256; Paris: Cerf, 1979), 96–98.

over was connected with the salvific experience of deliverance and with the covenant that gave that deliverance its meaning. The attention paid by the prophets to the "Day of the Lord" undoubtedly contributed in large measure to making the Passover celebration both a recall of the work of creation as being also the beginning of God's plan of salvation (Isa 42:5-6; 44:24-26) and a foreshadowing of its eschatological fulfillment, thus suggesting a messianic hope. This hope acquired a clearer form, in a soteriological perspective, due to the very early linking of the covenant at Horeb with the Abrahamic covenant but also, and more specifically, with the immolation of Isaac (the *Aqedah*); this last was recalled by the immolation of the Passover lamb, which could take place only in the temple at Jerusalem, whose location was identified with the Moriah of Genesis 22:2. Inspired by New Testament allusions to them, the entire patristic tradition would repeat and develop this set of interconnected themes.

Two lines of thought are recognizable in the patristic development.[22] One, which pairs *pascha* and *passio*, emphasizes the full and definitive accomplishment of the saving plan through the passion and resurrection of Christ, in which we then participate through the sacraments of baptism and the Eucharistic banquet (1 Cor 5:7). The other, which makes use rather of the pair *pascha-transitus* and becomes increasingly prominent from Origen on, emphasizes what is still left for us to do. In this second approach, the sacraments, which in the successive stages of Christian life actualize both the prefigurations found in the Mosaic Passover and their fulfillments in the passion and resurrection of Christ, occupy the foreground in the Easter celebration and its mystagogical interpretation. This approach is solidly rooted in passages of Paul (especially Rom 6:3-5; 1 Cor 5:7; 11:26); it was to be applied especially in the interpretation of the complex of rites involved in baptismal initiation, both during the ceremony itself and in the mystagogical catecheses, several collections of which have come down to us.[23]

The best synthesis of the various motifs that made their appearance— usually in scattered fashion—during the patristic period is given us by St. Augustine. He endeavors, especially in his Letter to Januarius, to bring out the unique and specifically sacramental character that the paschal celebration has by its nature. In his view, it differs radically in this respect from the feast of Christmas, which simply commemorates an event. He explains:

---

22. R. Cantalamessa, *La Pâque dans l'Eglise ancienne* (Traditio christiana 4; Bern: Peter Lang, 1980), xiii–xxxii.

23. Most of these are conveniently brought together in A. Hamman, *L'initiation chré-tienne* (Lettres chrétiennes 7; Paris: Grasset, 1963; reprinted, Paris: Desclée De Brouwer, 1980); English trans.: *Baptism: Ancient Liturgies and Patristic Texts*, ed. A. Hamman, Eng. ed. T. Halton (Staten Island, N.Y.: Alba House, 1967).

There is a *sacramentum* in a celebration when a past event is so commemorated that something to be devoutly received is also seen to be signified. Thus in celebrating Easter we not only remember the past event—the death and resurrection of Christ—but at the same time we omit nothing that is attested about it in order to bring out its meaning as *sacramentum*.[24]

Augustine is the last witness to this interpretation of sacrament as "mystery." When St. Leo echoes him and uses his very words, he does so with reference to the reading of the gospel: the hearing of the gospel (he says) will, if interiorized, permeate us with the mystery of what happened in the past. Thus, as M. B. de Soos explains it, "the sacred mysteries (other than the Pasch) win for us helps to sanctification that differ according to the mystery in question; the paschal celebration offers us all these helps at once, and more abundantly than in the rest of the year."[25] The perception of what is specific and unique in the paschal mystery has here been replaced by a spirituality of interiorization. In a liturgical year that sets out to celebrate the "myster*ies*,"[26] that is, the most characteristic saving actions of Christ's life (from his birth to his ascension, which leads to the sending of the Spirit), the sense of *the* all-embracing "mystery" as contemplated in its fullness weakens to the vanishing point. That, at least, is what usually happened in the West, even though the Roman liturgy, if we include the developments it incorporated from the Carolingian period on, continued to give primacy to a properly "mystery" approach that was also echoed in a good number of monastic spiritual writers.

In the East, and especially in the Byzantine tradition, several themes—victory over the powers of darkness and death, the liberation of the old Adam by the "new Adam," the dawn still shot through with shadows, the renewed creation that will be fully revealed at the parousia—were orchestrated with ever-increasing fervor in poetic compositions that provide the framework of the liturgical offices and in iconography. The emphasis in the latter, and especially in Russian iconography, is on the cosmic repercussions of the mystery of salvation, which is celebrated as an anticipation of the eschatological kingdom that is already at hand, thanks to the power of the Spirit who is invoked in the *epicleses*. Since Vatican II, and in keeping with intentions emphatically expressed during the Council, the renewal of the Roman liturgy has once more put the paschal mystery, understood in its traditional fullness, at the heart of the liturgical actions and celebrations. Care must still be taken, however, that

---

24. *Ep.* 55 *ad Januarium* 1–2 (CSEL: 33:170).

25. M. B. de Soos, *Le mystère liturgique d'après saint Léon* (LQF 34; Münster: Aschendorff, 1958), 84–85.

26. W. Loeser, "Mystères de la vie du Christ," *Dictionnaire de spiritualité* 10 (1980) 1874–76.

the symbolic expression of the mystery is not obscured by an arid ritual and by mediocre formularies, especially in the lyrical parts of the service.

II. VARYING LITURGICAL EXPRESSION OF THE PASCHAL MYSTERY

The paschal mystery, being the cultic expression of the mystery of salvation as recapitulated in Christ, must bring out the various aspects of the latter as related to the whole range of basic human situations. As Paschasius Radbert wrote: "The birth of Christ and the entire economy of salvation form a single great sacrament, for in this visible human being the divine Majesty invisibly and secretly accomplished what would bring about our consecration and sanctification. This is why the incarnation of God is rightly called a mystery or sacrament."[27]

The liturgical mystery will therefore have to call to mind the manifestation of the incarnate Word from his first appearance on earth to his glorious return in the heavens. In addition, however, since the mystery of salvation covers the entire length and breadth of human history from creation to final consummation, a liturgy that is careful to celebrate the mystery in its fullness will have to represent this entire development ritually. That is the function of the temporal cycle.[28]

Such a liturgy will also have to adapt itself to the various moments and acts involved in human participation in the mystery of salvation. After being born into divine life through baptism, human beings must allow themselves to be molded by the saving acts of Christ until they enter the kingdom of the Father on the day when, as the ancient Latin liturgy of the dead put it, they complete the Exodus from Egypt that began for them sacramentally in baptism. All this is the purpose of the sacramental liturgy.[29]

But while humanity thus enters gradually and, as it were, bit by bit into the kingdom, it also already possesses the pledge of the kingdom and shares in its life. This is why the Eucharistic celebration of the one paschal mystery contains elements that point out its effects at especially significant moments of the life not only of Christ himself but of those also who have allowed themselves to be more perfectly conformed to him by the witness of their life and their death. Thus, in the course of the year the mystery of the Pasch—that is, the "passage of the Lord" by which he delivers his people and the "passage" of this people, in union with Christ,

---

27. Paschasius Radbert, *Liber de Corpore et Sanguine Domini* 3 (PL 120:1275).
28. *VSC* 102–7.
29. *VSC* 59–61.

to intimacy with the Father through the divinizing gift of the Spirit—is reflected in its various aspects.[30]

In order to bring all this out more clearly, the Roman liturgy has established a close connection between the Eucharistic celebration and the Liturgy of the Hours, which expresses and effects the sanctification of time. In a threefold cycle—daily, weekly, and annual—this liturgy shows how the mystery of salvation in Christ permeates the whole of cosmic time. In the annual cycle the history of salvation, as summed up in Christ and organized with him as its center, transforms the symbolism of the vast seasonal rhythms into "mystery." The weekly cycle, regulated by the phases of the moon, which the ancients interpreted as symbol and cause of the mutability of earthly life, transposes the entire order of creation to the level of the mystery of salvation; here the great poem of the Hexaemeron or six days of creation takes on a new meaning, which the various liturgies have taken advantage of, to a greater or lesser extent, by connecting it with the cycle of redemption that is centered on Sunday, the "Lord's Day." The daily cycle, which derives its structure from the rhythms of light and darkness, brings out primarily the symbolic resonances of day and night.

By making this daily cycle the framework for the expression of its contemplation, the Church bears witness to its own paradoxical situation on the boundary between time and eternity. Though still caught up in the distracting concerns of existence in time, the earthly Church—which is both spouse and body of Christ—attunes itself in a measure to the heavenly Church; it takes its place in the choir of the blessed, who with the angels sing continuously: "Holy, holy, holy is the Lord God of the universe; heaven and earth are full of your glory." In doing this, the Church pursues its most essential purpose, which is to ensure the active presence of divine realities under the conditions of our present life—and that is precisely what "mystery" means.

§4. Dom Casel's "Doctrine of the Mysteries" (*Mysterienlehre*)

BIBLIOGRAPHY

O. Casel, *Das christliche Kultmysterium* (2nd ed.; Regensburg: Pustet, 1935 = a collection of separately published articles). — Fourth, expanded edition by B. Neunheuser (*ibid.*, 1960). — English translation: *The Mystery of Christian Worship, and Other Writings* (Westminster, Md.: Newman, 1962).

_____, *Das christliche Festmysterium* (Paderborn: Bonifacius-Druckerei, 1941).

O. Santagada, "Dom Odo Casel. Contributo monografico per una bibliografia generale delle sue opere, degli studi sulla sua dottrina e della sua influenza nella teologia contemporanea," *ALW* 10 (1967) 8–77.

---

30. *VSC* 102–4.

T. Filthaut, *La théologie des mystères. Exposé de la controverse* (Tournai: Desclée, 1954).

E. Schillebeeckx, *De sacramentele Heilseconomie* I (Antwerp: 't Groeit, 1952). In Flemish with French summary.

J. Gaillard, "La théologie des mystères," *Revue thomiste* 57 (1957) 510–51.

E. Schillebeeckx, *Christus sacrament van de godsontmoeting* (Antwerp: 't Groeit, 1959). — English translation: *Christ the Sacrament of the Encounter with God*, trans. P. Barrett, revised M. Schoof and L. Bright (New York: Sheed & Ward, 1963).

The new appreciation of the liturgy as mystery owes a great deal to the thought and labors of Dom Odo Casel (1886–1948). Casel developed his "doctrine of the mysteries" in numerous books, articles, and conferences over a period of about twenty-five years. This doctrine is not, however, necessarily bound up with the personal views of the monk of Maria Laach. The critical discussions to which it gave rise and the biblical and patristic studies that it stimulated have made it possible today to distinguish between what can be regarded as solidly established and what has proved to be more debatable.

I. EXPOSITION OF CASEL'S TEACHING

Casel's formation as a philologist and his own cast of mind made him averse to overly logical presentations. He provided no synthetic view of his teaching as a whole, but the intuitions from which it sprang are brought together and organized especially in the chief work of his mature years: *The Mystery of Christian Worship*. This book yields a good picture of his teaching, especially when it is combined with the complementary passages from later texts that Dom Burkhard Neunheuser, Casel's spiritual heir, added in a posthumous edition.

After explaining that "God's mystery" is first of all God himself who "condescends to his creatures and reveals himself to them" and that "for St. Paul *mystērion* is" secondly "the marvelous revelation of God in Christ . . . . [who] is the mystery in person, because he reveals the invisible godhead in the flesh," Casel goes on to say:

> Thus "mystery" acquires a third sense, which, however, is very closely connected with the first two (which in turn form a unity). Ever since the time when Christ ceased to be visible among us, "what was visible in the Lord has passed over into the mysteries," as St. Leo the Great puts it.[31] We meet his person, his saving deeds, and the action of his grace in the mysteries of worship. As St. Ambrose says, "I find you in your mysteries."[32]

---

31. St. Leo the Great, *Serm.* 61 (74), *De Ascensione Domini II* 2 (SC 74bis:277; PL 54:398).

32. O. Casel, *Das christliche Kultmysterium*, 4th revised and expanded ed. by B. Neunheuser (Regensburg: Pustet, 1960), 22–23; English translation: *The Mystery of Christian*

Therefore

> Christianity in its full and original meaning—the "Gospel of God" or "of
> Christ"—is . . . not a worldview with a religious background nor a reli-
> gious or theological system of doctrine nor a moral code, but a "mystery"
> in the Pauline sense, that is, a revelation of God to human beings through
> theandric acts that are full of life and power, as well as the passage of human
> beings to God that is made possible by this revelation and the gift of grace;
> it is the attainment of the eternal Father by the redeemed Church through
> the sacrifice of total self-giving and through the glory that this produces.[33]

This entrance of the divine mystery on the human scene in the person
of Christ and its permanence in the Church call for a cultic form (*Kultei-
dos*) that is quite different from that of the old covenant. In Casel's view,
this form had been providentially prepared for and suggested in the "mystery cults" of Greco-Roman antiquity. His thought on this point underwent constant refining and nuancing; its final state was set down in texts
from the last years of his life, especially in some conferences of 1947 on
the Letter to the Colossians.[34] In one of these conferences he said:

> The essence of the [Christian] mysteries consists in this, that through
> the visible elements one contemplates spiritual (pneumatic) things and that
> through the audible word the Pneuma himself touches our ears. The same
> principle was at work in the ancient mysteries. . . . That is why the an-
> cient mysteries can help us to a deeper understanding and experience of our
> own celebration of mysteries. . . . The mysteries are an objective action,
> but the initiates experience them in such a way that in faith they see behind
> this action the presence of the divinity.[35]

On the basis of these analogies, which he regarded as inescapable, Casel
thought he could give the following definition of the "mystery of worship" (*Kultmysterium*):

> "Mystery" includes, therefore, the broad concept of ritual "memorial"
> (*anamnēsis, commemoratio*), that is, the ritual performance and rendering
> present of some divine work on which the existence and life of a community
> is based. The sacred action becomes a "mystery" in the full sense when it
> is not concerned merely with this-worldly efforts to maintain the strength
> and life of the worshiping people and to make nature bloom and prosper,
> but when personal union with the worshiped divinity and a blessed sur-

---

Worship (Westminster, Md.: Newman, 1962), 6–8. [Translation of the passages cited here
is from the German. — Tr.] The words of Ambrose are from *Apologia Prophetae David*
12, 58 (PL 14:875).

33. Casel 29 (ET: 12).

34. These texts are among the "other writings" that Neunheuser added in the fourth
German edition. In the English translation the "other writings" are on pp. 97–205.

35. Casel 172 (ET 140–41).

vival of death are at the central objects of religious longing. . . . The goal is *sotēria*, salvation, in perfect communion with the god after death. We may therefore offer this short definition: "A mystery is a sacred cultic action in which a saving deed becomes present in the rite; when the worshiping community performs this rite, it participates in the saving act, and thereby wins salvation."[36]

Casel certainly did not claim that the pagan mysteries exerted a direct influence on Christian worship; on the contrary, he formally rejected this hypothesis, which was undoubtedly popular when he was a young man.[37] He did think, however, that identity of terminology pointed to a basic analogy between the two, not at the level of objects but at the level of modes of expression. Thus he wrote that "the analogy of the ancient mysteries . . . is fundamental for terminology," but he then immediately added: "In its content, though not in its linguistic form, the Christian terminology [for the sacred mysteries] is completely intelligible in the light of Christianity itself."[38]

II. CRITICAL ASSESSMENT

It is doubtless on this point that the "philological" method used by Casel has proved most seriously defective. In a review of the new French edition of *Le mystère du culte* (1964), L. Bouyer could write:

> Dom Casel developed his vision of the soul of early Christianity in a framework that he took over from the comparative history of religions, which was then being fully developed in the great syntheses of W. Bousset and R. Reitzenstein. And, of course, not everything in that framework became outmoded! The basic idea that there is a fundamental structure of the human soul that shines through the most varied rites and myths and, more specifically, that human beings achieve a participation in divine life through mythico-ritual symbols seems to be a permanent gain. No less valuable an acquisition is the vision of life as fundamentally sacred in its fruitfulness as well as in its deaths and rebirths.
>
> On the other hand, the assimilation of the Christian "mystery" to a model already formed in the "mysteries" of Hellenistic paganism does not seem acceptable in the terms in which Casel conceived it, in dependence on the authors just mentioned. It must be said that the assimilation is the result of a mirage: One begins by projecting typically Christian ideas and facts into the data from these religions, then one rejoices to find them there! But that whole process is possible only if one neglects the elementary rules of

---

36. *Ibid.*, 79 (ET: 53–54).
37. *Ibid.*, 53 (ET: 33).
38. *Ibid.*, 34, note 30 (ET: 16, note 2).

strict philological and historical criticism. When Dom Casel thinks he is making a semantic analysis of a word like *mysterium*, he never seems to suspect the first rule of any semantic study, namely, that seemingly related texts cannot be interpreted by separating their key expressions from the divergent lexicographical associations they have in different texts. Thus *mysterium* in the "mystery religions" of Hellenistic paganism, refers directly to an esoteric rite. *Mysterium* in the New Testament, on the other hand, designates the great secret of divine wisdom, namely, God's plan for human history that can be revealed only by his word, which in fact is his definitive Word: Christ and him crucified. Only as a result of a later transfer did *mysterium* as used in Christianity come to designate also the rite through which Christ effectively communicates himself. To neglect or minimize the importance of these facts can only lead to serious confusions.

As a matter of fact, Casel did clearly see the radical difference between the "mystery religions" and the Christian mystery. . . . What prevented him from drawing all the conclusions from this realization was, in addition to an insufficiently critical method, his radical ignorance of the Judaism of the New Testament period. This inevitably led in turn to a failure to appreciate the importance of the Old Testament itself in guiding us to what is new in Christianity. . . . The most extraordinary thing, however, is that Casel's fruitful curiosity made him one of the first to single out the liturgical texts of the Synagogue that are the undeniable ancestors of the Christian and especially the Eucharistic texts.[39]

An even more difficult and controverted question is that of the way in which the mystery of salvation is present in the liturgical mysteries. Dom Casel never stopped insisting that what is present is not simply the effect, that is, the grace bestowed, but the redemptive work itself. He sees this reactualization as necessitated by the fact (which in his view the tradition makes undeniable) that we participate in the mystery of salvation only through a mystical and real participation in the life and death of Christ. This prior participation requires in turn that Christ live and die in the very sacramental action that makes us sharers in him. At times Casel gives the impression of claiming that the reactualization extends even to the historical dimension of the saving action.[40] Elsewhere, however, he firmly repudiates this interpretation.[41]

---

39. *LMD* no. 80 (1964) 242–43.

40. "Mysteriengegenwart," *JLW* 8 (1929) 158, 163, 171, 186; "Glaube, Gnosis und Mysterium," *JLW* 15 (1941) 251–63.

41. "Mysteriengegenwart," *JLW* 8 (1929) 170, 191; "Neue Zeugnisse für das Kultmysterium," *JLW* 13 (1935) 157, 170; "Glaube, Gnosis und Mysterium," *JLW* 15 (1941) 251, 263. In this last article Casel expressed his idea as follows: "The mystery of worship, insofar as it is an image, has . . . power to extract from the historical event the essential of the saving act, which is precisely its abiding meaning for salvation, and to present it and make it present in symbols" (252; cited by T. Filthaut, *La théologie des mystères. Exposé de la controverse* [Tournai: Desclée, 1954], 26).

The patristic basis on which Casel believed he could ground his theology has proved less secure than he thought.[42] On the other hand, students have been able to show that in its essentials his theology is fully consistent with undoubted patristic teaching. He rejoiced to find his thinking reflected in the teaching of the Encyclical *Mediator Dei*, even though this document expressed reserves with regard to certain views on the way in which the mystery is present (*Mysteriengegenwart*).[43] And when the conciliar Constitution *Sacrosanctum Concilium* was published, L. Bouyer did not hesitate to write that

> the heart of the teaching on the liturgy in the conciliar Constitution is also the heart of Dom Casel's teaching. The Constitution's constant citation of the patristic, liturgical, and earlier conciliar texts on which Casel based his interpretation, and its interpretation of these texts on the same lines as Casel show a relation of filiation that will strike all future historians.[44]

III. AFTER DOM CASEL

Some have thought it possible to systematize the insights of Dom Casel using the rigorous methods of speculative theology. G. Söhngen outlined a synthesis in 1946,[45] L. Monden repeated it independently in 1948,[46] and finally E. Schillebeeckx developed it in 1952 in a masterful work that unfortunately was never completed.[47] It takes as its starting point the ongoing actualization of the salvific self-giving that is the essential act of Christ's priesthood. According to the Thomist doctrine of the sacramental character, the ecclesial body of Christ is deputed to make visible—in ways proper to each of the three sacraments of baptism, confirmation, and orders—the exercise of this priestly worship. Therefore, according to the summary of Dom J. Gaillard,

> the one same changeless act of offering that was manifested in the historical acts of our salvation and is still manifested in a different form in the heavenly liturgy now celebrated by the glorified Christ, is also manifested in the litur-

---

42. See J. Gaillard (note 11) 525–29; Filthaut (n. 41 above) 75–80.

43. Gaillard, 520–23.

44. Bouyer, review in *LMD* no. 80 (1964) 242.

45. The principal books of G. Söhngen are *Symbol und Wirklichkeit im Kultmysterium* (Bonn, 1937, 1939²) and especially *Der Wesensaufbau des Mysteriums* (Bonn, 1938). His thought is summarized in his "Le rôle agissant des mystères du Christ dans la liturgie d'après les théologiens contemporains," *QL* 24 (1939) 79–107, and in Filthaut (note 41, p. 270).

46. L. Monden, *Het Misoffer als Mysterie* (Roermond-Masseik: J. J. Romen en Zonen, 1948).

47. E. Schillebeeckx, *De sacramentele Heilseconomie* I (Antwerp: 't Groeit, 1952) (only volume I appeared); see the summary in Gaillard 512–17.

gical mysteries of the earthly Church. This act of offering is the *mystērion* of the saving acts.[48]

The only regret is that this synthesis is too exclusively Christological and does not stress the special role of the Holy Spirit in the actualization of the mystery of salvation.

---

48. Gaillard 541.

Chapter III

The Liturgy and the Deposit of Faith

BIBLIOGRAPHY

K. Federer, *Liturgie und Glaube. Eine theologiegeschichtliche Untersuchung* (Paradosis 4; Freiburg, Switz.: Paulus Verlag, 1950).

B. Capelle, "Autorité de la liturgie chez les Pères," *RTAM* 21 (1954) 5–22.

C. Vagaggini, *Theological Dimensions of the Liturgy*, trans. L. J. Doyle and W. A. Jurgens (Collegeville: The Liturgical Press, 1976), 509–41.

A. Houssiau, "La liturgie, lieu privilégié de la théologie sacramentaire," *QL* 54 (1973) 7–12.

G. Lukken, "La liturgie comme lieu théologique irremplaçable, méthodes d'analyse et de vérification théologiques," *QL* 56 (1975) 97–112.

P. De Clerck, "'Lex orandi lex credendi.' Sens original et avatars historiques d'un adage équivoque," *QL* 59 (1978) 193–212.

—————, "La prière universelle expression de la foi," in *La liturgie expression de la foi*. Conférences Saint-Serge, XXVᵉ Semaine d'études liturgiques . . . 1978 (Bibliotheca EL, Subsidia 16; Rome: Edizioni liturgiche, 1979), 129–46.

A. M. Triacca, "'Fides magistra omnium credentium.' Pédagogie liturgique: pédagogie de la foi, ou par la foi?" in *ibid.*, 265–310.

The liturgy is undeniably one of the sources or, to use the technical term, "places" (*loci*) from which theology can derive the arguments enabling it to develop a systematic and scientific presentation of the Christian faith. But the special character of this *locus* and the conditions under which it must be used depend on the nature of the liturgy itself, and the latter must therefore first be determined. The position to be assigned to this particular *locus* among the *loci theologici* as a whole depends on the very special place of the liturgy in the complex organism of "sacred doctrine," that is, in the communication to human beings, through revelation, of eternal Truth and its plan of salvation in the world.

273

The liturgy is an *action*. Consequently, we cannot treat it as though it were a doctrine and be satisfied to make theological use of the texts alone. In fact, the texts are properly liturgical only to the extent that they have their place within the cultic whole of which they are but one component. The whole includes, in addition, the gestures and melodies that underscore and clarify the theological meaning of the texts. In making theological use of liturgical texts, then, we cannot argue from them as though they were the same in kind as other documents of the tradition. These texts are integral parts of an action, and it is this action, and not simply the texts in it, that must be the subject of study for theologians who wish to base an argument on the liturgy.

But the liturgy is also a *mystery*, that is, a symbolic and efficacious action that renders the mystery of salvation present. This is a second peculiar characteristic of the liturgy that conditions its use for theological purposes. Allowing for differences that would have to be defined, the liturgy is comparable in this respect to the data of the Bible, and especially the gospel, in which doctrinal teaching cannot be separated from the carrying out of the work of salvation. But while the Bible gives priority to the message, the liturgy gives precedence to the accomplishment of the mystery, so that neither texts nor rites have teaching as their primary purpose. Theologians, therefore, have no right to find fault with their vagueness, their use of metaphor, and, for example, their practice of giving Scripture passages a meaning different from the literal sense. An exegesis of the liturgy that does not take into account its poetical character, the importance it gives to verbal correspondences, and its deliberate allusions to details of a rite or a situation, is likely to be misleading. Theologians must put themselves inside the categories proper to cultic and social accomplishment of the mystery of salvation if they are to derive from the liturgical data all the fruits these are capable of providing.

§1. The Liturgy, "Teaching of the Church"

The cited expression was used by Pius XI, who explained his meaning by saying that the liturgy is "the most important organ of the Church in the ordinary exercise of its teaching office."[1] Everyone knows how difficult

---

1. At an audience granted to Dom B. Capelle, abbot of Mont César in Louvain, and reported by the latter in his article, "Le Saint-Siège et le mouvement liturgique," *QL* 21 (1936) 134. — See especially *VSC* 33: "Although the liturgy is above all things the worship of the divine majesty, it likewise contains rich instruction for the faithful. . . . Thus not only when things are read 'that were written for our instruction' (Rom 15:4), but also when the Church prays or sings or acts, the faith of those taking part is nourished and their minds are raised to God, so that they may offer him their worship as intelligent beings . . ." (*DOL* 1 no. 33).

it is to decide what are the expressions of this "ordinary teaching," which by definition requires daily continuity. In trying to determine the ordinary teaching of the Church, students most often look to the common teaching of the Fathers, bishops, and theologians, although strictly speaking only the second of these three groups can authoritatively act as spokesmen for the teaching Church. But how often the study ends in disappointment, since each author queried speaks in function of the needs and culture of a particular setting and time. How, then, is the student to determine the extent to which an author is expressing the common thinking of the Church as distinct from an individual opinion or a reflection of a local tradition? The comparative method can yield only a least common denominator that is indeed enough to show the main lines of the Church's thinking but not enough to define its detail.

A first advantage of the liturgy in this respect is that it is a *collective work*. In it is heard at the very least the voice of a local Church that speaks less to specify its faith than to repeat the word of life to itself and savor it in God's presence. Every liturgy develops on the basis of a common substance that goes back to apostolic times, even if it has been modified by the underlying currents that take shape in a particular Christian community. The formulas and rites that express this substance may be the work of an individual, but if they are to become part of the liturgy they must be accepted by the community as a whole and approved, at least implicitly, by the authority that stands guard over the apostolic tradition. As a result, individual factors and local doctrines become secondary in importance to the properly ecclesial expression of the common faith.

The liturgy is, above all, an *eminently hierarchical work*. In the eyes of theologians a special importance attaches to the authority of those who exercise the pastoral ministry and therefore have the mission of authoritatively preaching the word of truth. The liturgy carries the same weight, but in addition it enjoys the direct support of the Christian community that makes it its own, as well as the authority bestowed by its permanence and its close connection with the accomplishment of the mystery of salvation. The voice heard in the liturgy is not only that of the hierarchy, the "teaching" Church, but also that of the people of God, the entire body with its diversity of ministries; each member collaborates, according to his or her rank, in an activity that involves all the members. This situation, which has no parallel in any other of the organs through which the faith of the Church is expressed and transmitted, once again shows the liturgy to be close in character to the Scriptures, of which it is the living interpreter. The sacred books, though admittedly in an entirely different way because of the direct action of the Spirit who inspired their redactors, are the collective work of the people of God; the liturgy is the ecclesial witness to the fact that sacred history continues to exert its influence in the Church.[2]

I. THE LITURGY AS ONGOING CATECHESIS OF THE CHURCH

The proper function of the liturgy is not to teach but to enable its participants to live out the mystery of salvation. It is therefore the model for all catechesis, since catechesis has for its purpose not simply to pass on correct doctrine, but above all to initiate its recipients into a living faith. The liturgy concentrates on bringing out the fundamental elements of this mystery of salvation, relating them to the paschal mystery, which is the center and as it were the summation of the entire mystery. The Scripture readings and psalmody, which are the basic elements of every Christian liturgy, keep the faithful in direct contact with the purest sources of nourishment for their faith. The arrangement of these readings in the liturgical cycle, and the parallels established between the sacred books, especially those of the Old and New Testaments, help the faithful to understand their deeper meaning in the light of Christ. The songs, prayers, and rites serve as a continuous commentary on the sacred texts.

By leading the faithful to the kind of prayer that suits each situation of Christian life, the liturgy establishes the basis for a dialogue between God and human beings in which each participant sees himself or herself assigned their proper place. The liturgy thus provides material for an entire theology and an entire anthropology, the material being more or less explicitly developed depending on circumstances and traditions. Finally, by reason of its communal character, the liturgy gives an intense experience of ecclesial communion and thus of the communion found in the kingdom of God, the definitive form of which it announces and anticipates in sacramental symbols.

II. LITURGY AND ORTHODOX FAITH

The catechetical value of the liturgy and its ecclesial and active character have led the Church in every period to introduce into its celebrations the themes it considers most important in defending orthodoxy against the threats of heretical deviation and safeguarding the most decisive gains made by the common faith. Whether we look at the development of formularies and rites or the creation of new celebrations, the history of the liturgies, both Eastern and Western, bears witness to this ongoing con-

---

2. J. Daniélou, "The Sacraments and the History of Salvation," in *The Liturgy and the Word of God* (Collegeville: The Liturgical Press, 1959), 21–22.

cern of the Church. At Rome, the traditional formularies retained their great sobriety and did not allow later developments in doctrine or devotion to gain entrance, but these developments were given plenty of room in the creation of new feasts or the addition of new formularies and rites to the ancient heritage. In the East, the important theological developments produced by the Christological and Trinitarian controversies helped greatly in giving the liturgy of the Church of Constantinople—which boasted of being the guardian of orthodoxy—the doctrinal wealth that makes it a catechesis that is always in touch with the people and at the same time focuses on the most essential points of the Christian faith.

§2. The Liturgy as Witness to Tradition

From the early centuries on, the liturgy enjoyed such unchallenged authority that it was often looked upon as a privileged witness to apostolic tradition.[3] An exaggeratedly static conception of tradition was to lead, in this as in other areas, to untenable positions. But despite unfortunate expressions and incautious generalizations, one thing is undeniable: because the liturgy is an institution that is very closely linked to the Church's mission and because it has for its proper purpose to render the mystery of salvation present and active in the Church, it is one of the most reliable expressions of the apostolic tradition that is ever alive in the Church, just as the Mosaic tradition was among the institutions of Israel as these underwent the developments and adaptations required by changing historical situations. The adage *Legem credendi lex statuat supplicandi* had a precise and restricted meaning in the *Indiculus* of Prosper of Aquitaine.[4] But its author was merely summarizing an argument of which St. Augustine, and Tertullian and St. Cyprian before him, had made considerable use. Recourse to the authority of the liturgy has been universal in the Church; in recent times the popes have often appealed to it in the most solemn acts of their supreme teaching office.[5] But the very importance of the liturgy demands that careless appeals not be made to its authority.

I. THE VARIOUS LITURGIES ARE NOT OF EQUAL VALUE

As privileged witness to the belief of a Church, the liturgy's authority

---

3. Testimonies assembled in B. Capelle, "Autorité de la liturgie chez les Pères," *RTAM* 21 (1954) 9–18.

4. K. Federer, *Liturgie und Glaube. Eine theologiegeschichtliche Untersuchung* (Paradosis 4; Freiburg, Switz.: Paulus-Verlag, 1950), 13–16; P. De Clerck, " 'Lex orandi lex credendi': Sens original et avatars historiques d'un adage équivoque," *QL* 59 (1978) 194–206.

5. De Clerck 206–11; see H. Schmidt, "Lex orandi, lex credendi in recentioribus documentis pontificiis," *Periodica* 40 (1951) 5–28.

is simply that of the teacher who approved it. In Latin canon law after the Council of Trent this approbation was reserved to the Apostolic See.[6] But a distinction must be made between the oldest liturgies, which never underwent revision, liturgies whose books have been approved by the Apostolic See, and the Roman liturgy for which this See has direct responsibility.

The lowest degree of theological value belongs to the local liturgies of monasteries and dioceses. Careful inquiry must be made in each case before a theological argument can be based on these liturgies, especially if they are recent compositions and lack a traditional basis; this is the case, for example, with some liturgies of the eighteenth century. The liturgies of the great religious Orders carry more serious guarantees; the fact that they enjoy the consent of communities whose members differ in origin and training means that they express a common spirit even as they help to mold it.

Quite different in value are liturgies that may be called "general," that is, those which have been jointly established over the centuries by various Churches distributed over a wide cultural area, especially if they have been led by an important episcopal see—primatial or patriarchal—around which regional or general councils have met. These liturgies are heirs to traditions that go back to the first centuries of the Church's life, and we may think of them as expressing common thinking in the style best suited to a particular cultural milieu. It is especially interesting, in this context, to trace the transformations that liturgical practices undergo as they pass from one culture to another, especially if the cultures are at different levels; we might think, for example, of the Ethiopian liturgy in relation to the Coptic, of which it is a particular expression, or, from other points of view, of the adaptations that the Roman liturgy underwent in Gallo-Frankish territories, and of its relations with the Milanese and Visigothic liturgies.

Since the Council of Trent, the Roman liturgy, which in time almost completely ousted the other Latin liturgies (and which in the process was enriched by many elements developed outside of it), has been the only living liturgy in the West. It carries a special guarantee in that it expresses the belief of the "Mother and Teacher of Churches" and has developed its organization under the direct oversight of the popes,[7] some of whom personally composed many of its texts. It is therefore an especially important theological source for knowledge and understanding of the Church's living tradition.

---

6. See p. 120.

7. The reader will bear in mind that the organization of the liturgy, like anything that falls under the ordinary power of jurisdiction, does not always commit the pope as supreme and infallible ruler of the universal Church.

II. THE LITURGY IS A COMPLEX ACTION

Theologians must first concentrate on the liturgical action as a whole and interpret each element, text, or rite in terms of the place it occupies in the whole and in the light of its relations with the other parts.[8] If they do so, they will, for example, avoid explaining a sacrament solely by the words that practice makes us to think of as essential. Texts of the magisterium, the Fathers, and the Doctors of the Church that are cited in the liturgy receive from this context a new meaning that must be determined in each case.

Since the liturgy is part of the tradition, it must be interpreted in the light both of history and of a comparative study of the various liturgies. Being hieratic in character, liturgies are naturally conservative; in their present form many components are difficult to explain and must be relocated in the cultural milieu in which they saw the light. Sometimes history is unable to provide the explanation, but the comparative method offers a new tool of research. It will always be useful in getting at the deeper meaning of a liturgical datum as distinct from the outer garment it has received in a particular cultural setting. It must be remembered, however, that the liturgy is a living thing and that theologians must look at it primarily as it is presently organized. The historical and comparative methods are only tools, even if indispensable ones, and must be used in the light specific to theology if the purpose is to do more than construct a history of doctrines or institutions.

It is obvious that liturgical documents, like all others used by theologians, must be interpreted according to their literary or ritual genre. Judgments of this kind are often difficult and require a profound knowledge both of the structure of the various liturgies and of the cultural setting in which they belong. It is relatively easy, of course, to distinguish between readings, which have instruction as their direct purpose; prayers, in which elements of the faith are explicitly recalled as the basis for petitions; and the lyrical parts, the chief purpose of which is to create an atmosphere favorable to contemplation of the mystery. It is much less easy, however, to determine the relative importance and limits of these various components in a liturgical whole, and still less to determine the role of the rites in relation to the words and the precise part played by symbolism and by what belongs to the basic "sacramentalism" of the liturgy.

---

8. We cannot overemphasize the contribution of song, and especially of Gregorian chant, in understanding the meaning that the liturgy gives to particular words, and the emphasis it intends to put on them; see E. Cardine, "Psautiers anciens et chant grégorien," in *Richesses et déficiences des anciens psautiers latines* (Collectanea Biblica Latina 13; Vatican City, 1959), 249–58.

Special attention must be paid to texts from the Scriptures or the Fathers. The liturgy sometimes understands them in a sense very different from their literal sense. It is quite clear that such liturgical interpretations are useless for determining the revealed datum that is transmitted by the sacred books. On the other hand, the Word of God remains alive in the Church, and it is in the liturgy that this life has its highest manifestation.[9] The liturgical interpretation of scriptural passages possesses, therefore, a theological importance of the highest order. As St. Bernard says, when the Church "alters the meaning or place of the words of scripture, the new composition has greater authority than the original; it is perhaps as much more authoritative as truth is greater than figures, light than shadow, mistress than servant."[10] He explains this greater perfection by the excellence of the Church's contemplation, of which the liturgy is the expression. Theologians can therefore appeal to the liturgical uses of Scripture, not as though they themselves were Scripture, that is, the source of the faith, but as privileged witnesses to the faith; they can appeal especially to the harmony that many liturgies try to establish between the pericopes from the two Testaments as they organize their lectionaries.

The same holds for all other cited texts. When they are incorporated into the liturgy, passages from the Fathers and Doctors become expressions of the belief not solely of a pastor or a man eminent for his teaching but of a whole community and even of an entire group of Churches living in widely separated places and times. It is not to be forgotten, however, that the primary role of the liturgy is not to teach but to convey an experience of the mystery of salvation and that consequently it uses modes of expression best adapted to the body of the faithful. "Historical" texts, such as the "legends" of the Breviary, the passions of the martyrs, or the synaxaries, follow quite different laws than history does and reflect quite different concerns. They bear witness only to the wonder felt in the Church at the great works God accomplishes in his saints.

---

9. L. Bouyer, "The Word of God Lives in the Liturgy," in *The Liturgy and the Word of God* (Collegeville: The Liturgical Press, 1959), 51.

10. *In vigiliam Nativitatis sermo 3* 1, in S. Bernard, *Opera*, ed. J. Leclercq and H. Rochais, 4 (Rome: Editiones Cistercienses, 1966), 212.

Index

The following pages list the people, places, and events about which a pertinent statement is made in this book. By no means should this index be considered a complete listing of the scores of people, places, and events recorded in this book.

Secret, 254
Sēdrē, sedro, 33, 34, 41
Sedulius, 148
Seljuk conquest, 39
Semitic culture, 29
Sentences (Peter Lombard), 257
Septuagint (LXX), 92, 230, 236, 242, 254
Serapion, bishop of Thmuis, 26
  Euchologion of, 25, 40
Serbs, 35
Servitum, 230
Servitus, 246
Sharar, 34
Shekinah, 238
Shlimo, 33
Sick, anointing of. *See* Anointing of the sick.
Sign, 257–59
Significando causant, 174
Sign of the cross, 186, 221 (*see also* Liturgical gestures)
Signs, liturgical, 173–224
Silent prayer, 153–54, 158
Sinai
  covenant on, 262
  theophany at, 237
Sinodos (Coptic), 43
Sixtus V, Pope, 68, 120, 121
Slavonic (Slavic) language, 35, 36, 45, 164
Sociology, 18
Sod, 254
Söhngen, G., 271
Solemnitas, 239
Solemnity of St. Joseph, 70
Solesmes, Abbey of, 73, 169
Solitary Mass, 111
Solomon, Odes of, 24, 148
Solomonic Restoration (1271), 42
Soteria, 269
Spanish liturgies, two traditions of, 53, 57 (*see also* Liturgy)
Spielraum (J. Pascher), 128
Spirit (breath), 243, 268 (*pneuma*)
Spirit, sending of at Pentecost, 264
Stabat mater, 61

Staroveries, 38
Stational Masses, 95
Statuere, 125
Stephen I, Pope St., 192
Stephen, St. (martyr), 182
Stercky, Louis, 122
Stōmen kalōs, 180
Stomen meta phobou, 180
Studios, 36
Sub altare Dei, 224
Subdeacons, 107
Suger, Abbot, 58
Summa de ecclesiasticis officiis, 61
Summa theologiae, 258
Sunday, 79, 91, 259
  assembly on, 134, 135, 139
  Mass, 142
  readings on, 135
Sunyol, Dom Gregorio, 169
Symbol (term), 257–59
  three aspects of (Isambert), 176
  vs. sign, 173–74
Symbolic actions, 176
Symbolism, liturgical, 175–78
Symeon of Thessalonica, archbishop, 36
Synagogue, homily inherited from, 139
Synaxaries, 280
Syncretism, 128
Synod
  of Diamper (1599), 31
  of Dwin (506), 39
Synoptic tradition, 254–55
Syria, Frankish principalities in, 32
Syriac language, 29, 31, 32, 165–66, 253, 256
Syrian liturgies. *See* Liturgy.
Syro-Antiochene (Jacobite) rite, 32–33
Syro-Malabar Church, 31
Syro-Mesopotamian tradition, 24, 42

Table of the Word, 76
Teaching of the Apostles, 24, 91
Te decet laus, 150
Te Deum, 49, 148, 150